England Rambler

Historical selections from the London Rambler and other Catholic periodicals

England Rambler

Historical selections from the London Rambler and other Catholic periodicals

ISBN/EAN: 9783337277024

Printed in Europe, USA, Canada, Australia, Japan

Cover: Foto ©Lupo / pixelio.de

More available books at **www.hansebooks.com**

HISTORICAL SELECTIONS

FROM

THE LONDON RAMBLER

AND OTHER CATHOLIC **PERIODICALS**.

ST. LOUIS,
DUGGAN & CO., THIRD STREET.
PRINTED AT THE LA SALLE PRESS, CARONDELET.
1860.

The following papers have been selected for republication on account of their intrinsic value as contributions to Modern History. The idea of collecting them was **suggested by the** *establishment* **of a** *Printing Office in the* La Salle Institute*;—an Asylum wherein orphan* **and other** *destitute* **boys** *are received, and in which* **they are employed, during** *a portion of the* **day,** *in learning trades and other useful occupations. Whatever profit may result from the sale of this volume will be applied to the charitable* **institution from** *which it issues.*

THE CHURCH AND THE PEOPLE.

[From the Rambler.]

For more than eighteen hundred years a society has existed among men, which is without parallel in any other empire, dominion, or institution, from the dawn of creation until now. It has beheld every other society and every other power pass away and perish, while neither death nor decay has touched itself. It has seen so marvellous a change come over the whole human race, that the man of this day seems almost a different species of being from the man of the days of its infancy. So wide is the gulf which divides the distant epochs, that we call one of them "ancient times," and the other "modern times;" and can scarcely realise the actual existence of a state of things such as was in being when this society had its birth. Kingdoms, laws, customs, arts, manufactures, literature, and the very language of man itself, have been swept away by the torrent of ages, and this society alone survives.

Yet, wonderful to tell, this society has never for a single day ceased to maintain a mortal conflict with the powers of the world in which it is placed. Other institutions which long survive the catastrophes around them, maintain their ground by avoiding all share in the struggles of man with man. They live, because they are either harmless or forgotten. But here the law of existence is absolutely reversed. This enduring society never knows one hour's true peace, one hour's repose, one hour's oblivion. It measures its strength with every competitor. It meets every foe on his own terms. It treats every friend with suspicion, and has to watch all his movements, lest he prove a more pernicious enemy than its open adversaries. It is never wearied, as it is never safe from attack. The more fiercely it is opposed, the more rapidly it comes forward; the more frightful the slaughter in its ranks, the more heroic the courage of those who hasten to take the place of

the dead and the **dying.** Again and again the world has counted it destroyed, paralysed, or changed; but behold, it is **at** this very hour as young, as vigorous, as mighty as ever; **and as** eager **for** the contest, as if it had **never** known the **agonies of martyrdom,** or the treachery of **deceitful friends.**

Yet again, and more wonderful still, this society is more perplexed, agitated, and thwarted by its own members, than by the most terrible of its open foes. Infallibly taught from on high in many things, and bound down by a divine law to a rigid obedience in many matters of detail and practice, it is nevertheless made up of millions of souls, not one of whom is safe from sins of the deepest dye, while the vast majority of their number are of a very ordinary degree of goodness, and while, except in the case of its supreme head, not one of them is personally safe from the most fatal errors of judgment and doctrine. Scattered throughout the habitable world, its children have to act for themselves in unnumbered myriads of emergencies, to maintain conflicts with every conceivable species of opponent, and against disadvantages which apparently must inevitably overwhelm them, and in the end must blot them out from among men.

But still that society lives; and at a moment when its chief is an exile from his own home,[a] driven away by as contemptible a band of petty scoundrels as ever dishonoured the worst of ends, it is more united in itself than at almost any other period of its existence, and is girding up its loins for a fresh battle with those powers of the world which it has again and again subdued and destroyed. Never at any previous era in its history has it been so free from all open scandals in its children; never were they more affectionately attached to their highest earthly ruler; never was the attention of wise and thinking men more anxiously directed to its movements, or more confidently expecting from it some great and glorious deeds, to save the world from calamity and woe. Such is the Catholic Church, the stumbling-block of the ungodly, the puzzle of the philosopher, the annoyance of the politician;

[a] Written in 1849.

but the joy, the solace, and the strength of those who believe.

In this state of affairs, it cannot be unprofitable to compare the peculiar nature of the relations of the Church to the world about her, with the positions in which she has been placed in other ages since the day when she ceased to be the Church of one favoured nation, and became the Church of all mankind. For it is one unfailing characteristic of her destiny, that the *form* of her relationship to the world is ever changing, so that her policy is ever new, and her weapons of warfare, which once were all-powerful for victory, must be perpetually changed for others fashioned in a different mould. Herself immutable, she has to wage warfare with a Proteus which knows not stability; and as her adversaries' tactics are not the same for two centuries together, she must adapt herself to their ceaseless variations, and ever smite them with arms like their own.

That the present position of the Church in the world is unparalled in any previous stage of her existence, the dullest eye can see. She has, in fact, herself united with the will of this world, to place herself upon a footing which it never crossed the brain of the wildest dreamer of a few hundred years ago to establish in his own day. Willingly—nay more, eagerly—she plants herself on new ground, and entrenches herself behind fortifications as unlike to her defences of old, as the cannon-proof fortresses of this time are unlike the picturesque and battlemented towers within which our mail-clad fathers fought and conquered. The *idea*, in a word, which now reigns in Europe and America, and which the Church must seek to bend to her own purposes, is radically and irreconcilably in opposition to the ideas of every age through which she has hitherto passed.

The old idea of the Christian world was this : that the Christian religion was to be taken as the basis of all civil society, and that the interests of the secular power were identical with those of the Christian Church. On this principle the Church fought her first battle with Heathenism, under the rulers of Imperial Rome. It was the very principle on which those bloody persecutors martyred the hosts of the faithful. The Pagan magistrate identified Paganism with the well-being of the state; and he smote the Christians with unsparing slaughter, because he looked upon them as foes to his own rights and powers. He either could not, or would not, give credit to their assertions, that while they rendered to their God the undivided homage of their hearts, they were ready to pay an obedience to the civil authority in all things not absolutely forbidden by their faith. It never occurred to him to conceive of our modern theories of government, or to attempt to separate, by a rigid line of demarcation, the spiritual from the temporal power. The Christian therefore became an outcast from the pale of society, an alien from the commonwealth of his fellow-creatures; and when the haughty Roman suffered him to worship his Lord in peace, it was because he deemed him too insignificant to disturb the repose of a people which owned Jove for its god and Cæsar for its emperor.

And thus, when the supreme civil power itself became Christian, it instantly united itself, heart and hand, with the Church of Christ. Never for a moment did the Emperor or Empress, whether orthodox or heretical, imagine it to be a possibility, that the Christian religion should be a thing with which the state, as such, had nought to do. The notion that its duties, as an institution for temporal ends, could be so distinctly separated from the duties which every man owes to his God, as an accountable and immortal soul, never found a place in their theorisings. To assert that the secular arm, when Christian, could trust with undoubting confidence any human being whom the Church condemned, they would have counted a denial of the divine authority of the Church itself. How far a Christian monarch should seek to crush the idolatries of Paganism, was simply a question as to the practicability of the deed. As for taking cognisance of the rights of private judgment, or supposing that because a man was sincere in a false creed, therefore he was to be put upon a level with the orthodox,—such a theory simply never occurred to them. The Arian sovereign upheld Arianism, because he counted Arianism to be true. The Catholic sovereign upheld Catholicism, because he believed Arianism to be a soul-destroying heresy. Whatever a ruler was himself, that he sought by all lawful means in his power to compel his people also to be.

For we must recollect that Christian antiquity knew nothing of the modern notion that *several* creeds can be all equally true. Though they had no printing-presses, and believed the sun to go round the earth, with a thousand similar physical errors, they were yet sufficiently gifted with common sense to consider that black is not white, that two is not one, and that the words, "the Gospel of Jesus Christ," did not mean twenty or thirty different and contradictory gospels. Whether they were Catholic or heretical, they were guiltless of this new absurdity, each one considering that he alone had possession of *that one doctrine* which was revealed by Jesus Christ to his Apostles. Hence, whatever a man believed, that he counted it his duty to propagate by all practicable means. Had he been told that, after all, it was a "matter of opinion" whether our Lord was the eternal Son of God, or no, he would have viewed the person who gave him the information with about the same astonishment as we should regard a man who said it was a "matter of opinion" whether or not the three angles of a triangle are equal to two right angles. The civil governor, therefore, based his government upon a certain system of religious doctrine as being *true*, not as being expedient or permissible. By what means, or to what extent, he sought to propagate this truth, or how far he counted it desirable to identify his government with that of the Church, were all distinct questions of mere expediency. His fundamental principle ever was this, that there is but one true religion, and that the magistrate, believing in this religion, is bound by his duty to God never to cease to act upon this belief, both as a magistrate and as a man.

On this idea the social and political life of Europe was based, amidst all the conflicts and revolutions through which it has passed. Under the Roman emperors, under the barbarians in the middle ages, in the very tumult of the Reformation itself, every state and every individual recognised this principle as incontrovertibly true. The Teutonic conquerors,

Alaric, Theodoric, and Clovis, when they swept away the powers of the emperors, upheld the creed of the vanquished, and adopted its doctrines as the basis of the sovereignties they set up. In the darkest centuries which followed, the rudest civil power paid a sort of homage to the morality of the Gospel, as that before which every human rule ought necessarily to bow. It was the recognition of the indefeasible rights of Christianity which lent so mighty a strength to Church, when in feudal times she mitigated the reckless tyrannies of the powerful, and impressed upon the age of chivalry some semblance of religious purity and truth. And when men's minds were corrupted, and society grew rotten almost to the very core,—when Paganism, learning, luxury, and relaxation of ecclesiastical discipline, combined to call down the judgments of God, and to tempt whole nations to a revolt against the faith itself,—still was the dogma of our own age unknown; and they who were the first to cast off allegiance to Rome, were as zealous as ever in upholding the identity of the interests of the civil power with those of that one creed which they themselves professed to believe as true. Still did the old idea reign in Europe, all through the agonies of that day of conflict. In submission to its dictates, every Protestant kingdom commenced its anti-Catholic operations; and in reliance upon its potent efficacy, the spirit of despotism forged fresh political chains for the subjugated nations of Europe. The recognition of the right of private judgment was an audacious falsehood in the lips of kings; they recognised no rights, either spiritual or temporal, except their own; and the only excuse that could be urged in palliation of their cruel persecutions, was the fact that the universal consent of mankind still regarded Christianity, in some form or other, as the only legitimate foundation of social and political, as well as of private, morality.

By and bye, as time went on, a new idea arose. Two circumstances combined to make men think that if the old idea was true in itself, and was once expedient, yet in modern days its application would be cruel, unjust, and undesirable. Conscientious persons who claimed to separate from the Catholic Church, on the right of their own judgment, soon saw that it was the height of folly and wickedness to deny to others what they claimed for themselves, and that if religious doctrines were matters of opinion only, it was monstrous for any man to rule his fellow-creatures upon his own private opinions, while their opinions were directly opposed to his own. To this source we must look in some measure for the origin of the new idea. Yet this honest conviction would have been powerless to shatter the fabric of Protestant theological despotism, if it had not been aided by that radical revolution in the system of secular government itself, in which England has taken the lead amongst the nations of the world. So long as the supreme authority was lodged in the hands of one man, or one small oligarchy, the principles of religious toleration must have been powerless, and uttered only to be condemned and proscribed. But when a new theory sprang to light, or rather when the principles of Magna Charta were carried out to their legitimate consequences, the monstrous iniquity of the adoption of the old idea by a Protestant government began to break upon the vision of all honest and clear-sighted men. That a government consisting of one man, or of a certain number of men all united in one faith, and that faith the Catholic faith, which they all held to be the *only* true religion given by God for the salvation of sinners,—that such a government should adopt this religion as the foundation of its authority, the guide of its laws, and the very life of its daily operations, was but natural. But that a body of representatives, elected by men of every variety of creed, and representing the opinions of their electors, should dare to select one creed from amidst the host about them, hedge it around with persecuting penal laws, pamper it with the wealth of stolen treasures, persecute those who could not conscientiously admit its truth and excellence, and fashion their decrees in conformity with its peculiar sectarian dictates,—such a system was **too** iniquitously tyrannical, and too absurdly self-contradictory, **to** endure the shock of ages, or to issue in any thing but the reproach of those who maintained it.

And thus the new idea was born, and grew, and strengthened.

In some modification or other, it is now gradually gaining the mastery throughout the civilised world. There is scarcely a state in Europe or America which has not yielded some token of homage or fear to the new-born doctrine, that, either as a matter of duty or expediency, the civil power must separate itself from the spiritual, and affording to all religions an equal protection, pay special obedience to none. We say nothing as to the truth or wisdom of this theory. We do not impugn the system of other days. We do not assert that the modern notion is justly applicable in any one particular instance, or not. We take it simply as a fact, as the great fact of modern times, as a fact which, in the eyes of religious men, is of infinitely greater moment than those countless swarms of novelties which, in the judgment of men of the world, are the distinguishing marks of this age of anxiety and change. And that the ancient relations of Church and State can by any possibility be permanently maintained in a country which unites a representative government with any great variations in the religious opinions of its individual citizens, we hold to be the most visionary of expectations. The dominance of a class, the power of traditional feelings, the continuance of tranquillity and prosperity, may for a while postpone the development of these potent principles, but in the end, wheresoever the people rule and the people are not unanimous in their creed, we shall see connexion between the spiritual and the secular powers assimilated, with more or less exactness, to the stage of things which now prevails in the United States or in France.

What, then, will be true wisdom in us, who are devoted with our whole hearts and souls to the upholding and the propagating the faith of the Catholic Church? Where shall we place our feet, that we may stand firm in the mortal conflict which we must wage, as long as the world shall last? What line of conduct shall we adopt? What modes of thought shall we most sedulously cultivate, that we may be most faithful to our Master's cause, and win souls to his service and his glory? In every age it has been the practice of the Church to adapt her operations to the exigencies of the time, and to meet the world with its own weapons. What, then, shall we do now? What *can* we do? What *must* we do? In one word, we must recognise mankind as *free*. It is the people with whom we have to do, a people individually their own masters, and collectively supreme in the state; both in theory, and more or less in fact, politically free. The Church is cast into the midst of a giant democracy. She has to commend her divine claims to millions and millions of souls, with no more aid from secular authority or traditional associations than the Apostle possessed when he pleaded before Festus, or than a Bishop of the fourth century, when he preached the Gospel to an imperial hearer. The democratic element is triumphing around us; kings and nobles are becoming the servants of the people; the mechanic laughs to scorn the religious convictions of the monarch, because he himself is become an integral portion of the sovereign power; he claims for himself the same rights of thought which are accorded to the mightiest in the land; he maintains that as he rules, so also he will think for himself; and he is prepared to account that to be the one true faith which upholds the civil government which he himself maintains, and in which he has bound up all his dearest earthly interests.

This is our age's interpretation of the words of Holy Scripture, that the powers that are, are ordained of God. Once, a Cæsar reigned alone, and Nero was the power ordained of Heaven. Once, again, an aristocracy ruled, and they were the powers which God bade us obey. Now, all is changed or changing; in some countries already every man of full age is a master in the state; in our own land we are hastening on to the same condition; the toiling millions have become "the higher power;" and if the Church would rule the world once more, if she would tame its unholy passions, if she would place her magic spell upon its tremendous strength, and bid it do her bidding, she must recognise it as what it is in very deed.

The strength of the Church is, in truth, in this fierce democracy. Her deepest strength, indeed, ever lay in the poor and despised, but she gained no little aid from the support of the royal and the noble, when she took good heed against their enticing snares. But now, her old friends are powerless to aid her. They have proved false friends, for the most part. They have given her assistance, hoping that she would sanction their enormities; therefore she is shaking them off and disowning them, not so much because they are themselves mighty no more, as because they have played her false, and sought to convert her friendship into slavery. And every where, where she essays her new part, she triumphs with most signal success. She has the most striking power wherever she least relies upon the secular arm. In the midst of the turbulent storms of revolution and democratic frenzy her soothing voice is heard, and lulls to peace and rest those angry spirits which spurn every human restraint. A few years ago she rode in safety on the waves of a popular revolution in Belgium. In France she gathers strength amid every excess of democratic passion, and rules the heart of the legitimatist, the republican, and the Bonapartist, with equal sway. In England, while the popular power advances with slower, yet most certain step, she is year by year extending her bounds, uniting her members, and beating down the besotted prejudices of days that are past. In Ireland, she has flourished in **never-**fading youth amidst persecutions that have never ceased, reigning in the souls of the poor alone: In the United States, she has won so strange a mastery over a restless and haughty race, that the first of great modern republics promises to become a Catholic nation. Throughout the whole earth, whensoever she has been fairly placed in the midst of *the people*, and has sought to win her way to their hearts by spiritual weapons alone, a glorious success has crowned her efforts, and devoted multitudes have cast themselves in love and veneration at her feet. She has nothing to fear from the increase **of the** power of the people. She has but to recognise **in them the** rights which they possess, and they will serve **her** with an affection and a simplicity of purpose which **few of** her crowned and purpled protectors have ever known.

Little, however, will be our success, **if** we fail to recognise also that freedom of *thought* which is the mark of our day, and is, in some sort, the consequence of its political freedom.

If heresy is to be conquered, and unbelief made to give place to faith, it must be by our admitting to the full that independence of mind to which man is really entitled, and which he will not yield before any conceivable accumulation of those authorities which of yore had such power in the world. Every class, and every people, are becoming daily more and more impressed with a conviction of the worth of intellectual greatness and acquirements, in contrast with the old vulgar worship of wealth and grandeur. From the insane profaneness of those who would deify man's reason, to the humblest teacher of the elements of knowledge to the poor, we are united in treading underfoot the empty, frivolous shows of other days, and in valuing that which is spiritual, moral, and intelligent, above all other things that are good. Gross and sensual, ungoverned and ungovernable, as we still are, to a frightful extent, yet it is undeniable that a homage is now paid to the claims of the intellect which was never rendered by any former age.

Hence it has followed, that those whom the Church summons to her obedience put forth demands which never yet were made, but with which she *must* comply, if she would do her duty faithfully. The whole world of European and American thought defies her to the contest. High and low, the philosopher and the mechanic, cast in her teeth a charge which they dare her to disprove. They have laid aside many of the old arms of Protestantism. They do not meet the claims of Catholicism by asserting that Protestantism alone is true, and therefore Catholicism is false. They are ashamed of the former cry of blood-thirstiness which they were wont to raise against the priesthood and children of Rome. They are meeting us with a pretence often, indeed, urged before, and now sometimes urged in all honesty and candour, though in real ignorance. They say we are behind the age—that we are incompetent to take our place in the republic of thought and reason—that we would reduce man's intelligence to a miserable level of mediocrity and dulness—that we would falsify history—that we dread the discoveries of science—that we shirk biblical criticism—that we would chain down the imagination. They point to the gigantic works of the human intellect which have been produced without the sanction of, or in direct opposition to, Catholicism. In England, more especially, they bid us look back three hundred years and see how the state has thriven under Protestant sway, while ruin and disaster have been the lot of almost every Catholic people. They tell us to look at the vast body of English literature, at its energy, its grace, its honesty, its purity (as they count honesty and purity), and challenge us to make good our claims to be sent by God, by elevating and purifying that reason which God has given to man. They ask, why have Spain, and Portugal, and Italy, and Austria, and South America fallen, while England, and Protestant Germany, and France (ninetenths infidel), and North America, are the ruling powers of the human race?

To the spirit which dictates this defiance, we must, heart and hand, address ourselves, if we would do our duty in our generation, and not be fools and traitors where our fathers were wise men and conquerors. We *know* that this imputation that is cast upon us is false. We know that if ever there was a falsehood, as daring as it is shallow, it is the assertion that obedience to a faith which comes from God is a slavery of that reason which came from the same almighty hand. There is not a Catholic in the land who would not repudiate with indignation the imputation, that his intelligence is less free than that of any race of men upon earth. It is no more slavery to us to believe what we are sure is the word of God, than it is slavery to comprehend and believe the demonstrations of Euclid. Our intellect follows the laws of reason in trusting to an inspired authority as independently as when it is convinced that two and two make four. There is not a syllogism in the whole range of mathematical truth more complete than the great Catholic argument (1), that if God has given us a revelation, and made it our duty to believe the doctrines of that revelation, He must have made the statement of those doctrines intelligible to our understanding, and shewn us what they are; (2), that there is no intelligible statement of those doctrines put forward by any body claiming to be taught by God except that which is put forward by the Catholic Church; and consequently (3), that the decrees of the Catholic Church are *true*. It is no more a slavery to a man's understanding to believe in transubstantiation than to believe that the earth is round. We believe both the one and the other upon testimony; and instead of its being the act of a bondslave to believe in the Real Presence, it is the delight of our intellect, as a free, reasoning agent, to know that this doctrine is true, just as it is our delight to reject the notion that the earth is flat or square. And so also in the whole domain of art, philosophy, science, and literature. They who are themselves Catholics are well aware that they receive from their religion the greatest possible assistance to their natural faculties in every species of human cultivation; that so far from working, as it were, in chains, they are conscious of a living, spiritual freedom, to which every man who is not a conscientious Catholic is a stranger.

Knowing this, then, it will be our truest wisdom to act upon it, not merely by compulsion and unwillingly, but boldly, energetically, and of our own accord. We must come forward as our fathers did six hundred years ago, and be the foremost in the work of intellectual cultivation. We must throw our whole strength upon the busy realms of thought, prepared and expecting to conquer. We must compel men to own that the only true intellectual freedom is to be found in obedience to the Faith, by proving to them, that they who own that Faith have a power to make all truth their own, such as none others can attain to. We must shew no fear, no hesitation, no signs of a wish to take advantage of people's ignorance and slowness of perception. We must lift up our voice, and never cease to say, that as the whole domain of possible knowledge is the lawful possession of man's reason, so he alone is in a state to seize all truth with a firm and enduring grasp, who has attained to a knowledge of those truths which are eternal, and of which the visible world is but the outward manifestation and result. Every reasonable being is aware that we might as well assert that a knowledge of the laws of gravity is a hindrance to a man in building a house, as that a knowledge of spiritual and eternal truths is a hindrance to the study of material and temporal truths. But so long as the Catholic is content to take little part in the moving thought of his day, or protests against the advancement of human knowledge, as though it were something in its very nature in opposition to the truths of revelation—so long will our generation suspect him of some secret design upon the common sense and understanding of his fellow-creatures.

It is scarcely possible to overstate the importance of a sound and well-considered view of this truth in the present posture of Catholic affairs in this kingdom. Notwithstanding a few iniquitous things which yet remain, the Catholic religion is at length practically emancipated in England. There is scarcely a day that passes without shewing, in some way or other, that the attention of the best and the most thoughtful in the country is concentrating upon us. The claims of Protestantism are hourly made less of. The Church of England's day is gone by. She has stood still and the world has passed her, and left her to her complainings. We alone remain to be feared, to be honoured, to be loved. Our own youth are panting for the struggle in the arena of thought. Intelligent, open-hearted, pious, and patriotic, like the horse that chafes and champs the bit before the race begins, the young Catholic laity and clergy are burning to shake off the hindrances which a want of sufficient training has long laid upon the Catholic mind of England, and to seize that place among their countrymen which already almost invites their claim. From within and without we are called upon to cultivate the energies of the mind to the highest possible perfection—to teach men to reason clearly and to judge calmly and vigorously—to purify the taste—to elevate the imagination—to widen the circle of human knowledge, and to lay its foundations deep in that thorough mastery of some few subjects of study, without which the most extensive acquirements are little better than the small-talk of a fashionable drawing-room, or the gossip of a daily newspaper.

Rightly or wrongly, our age has come to estimate every man by what he is in himself. Centuries ago, a man's office or rank gave him a certain real claim to have his opinions and *dicta* respected, because those who held sacred or secular

offices, or stood high in rank, were ordinarily the best educated
and the ablest thinkers in society. But this is so no longer.
A man's chief influence depends upon his personal character
and acquirements, whatever be his administrative functions.
The most unreserved and glad *obedience* is constantly rendered to those administrators of the laws, in their official capacity, for whose personal opinions no one has the smallest
regard. The habits of other times would be mere superstition
in ourselves. It was once right and reasonable for the inferior
to regard those who were his superiors in station, with a universal respect for their words on all subjects whatever. In
those days, scarcely any but the clergy could read or write,
and for ages, any high degree of cultivation was confined to a
favoured few, whether ecclesiastics or laymen. But now the
gifts of knowledge are spread abroad far and wide. There is
many a machanic in the land who is better educated and more
intelligent than many a peer. The distinctions of rank are
almost nominal, and the distinctions of office are confined to a
difference of administrative or functional powers alone. A
claim to infallibility only makes a man laughed at. Even the
Evangelical party in the Established Church are getting
ashamed of turning a favourite preacher into a Pope. While
the Catholic rejoices with never-fading joy in his own possession of an infallible authority in matters of faith, and while
the better classes of Protestants are in their secret souls yearn-
ing for some infallible guide to set them free from the religious doubts which afflict them, at the same time Catholic and
Protestant together are united in attributing infallibility to a
divinely guided authority alone, and in testing the claims of
every other authority among men by its actual qualifications
for respect and deference.

How, then, can we overrate the importance of the highest
practicable cultivation of the natural faculties in ourselves, if
we would command the attention and enlist the sympathies of
our fellow-men? Whether we like it or no, we must take them
on their own ground. We must appeal to the principles which
they already admit. We must present ourselves to them in a
guise which they **will** honour. In China the Catholic priest

is dressed in the fantastic garb of the country, and wears a tail of hair three feet long. In Syria, his beard hangs down to his waist. In England, he is neat **and close** shaven, and is clothed in black. And such must be our wisdom in clothing the mind within. It must be vested after the model of the age in which we live, so far as that model is not positively sinful. The Chinaman admires the flowing robes, the Oriental venerates the beard, and to our eyes there is nothing more correct, more gentlemanlike, or more worthy of respect, than a priest in his proper ecclesiastical dress. And thus, would we bring the power of our religion to bear upon the dense mass of unbelief and heathenism which has overspread the land, we must attack it armed with those weapons before which alone it will yield. We must exhibit to it the spectacle of a vast body of men, each devoted with his whole powers to the faith which is revealed, each animated with one and the same spirit of love, purity, and humility, yet each retaining the personal characteristics of his own mind, each cultivated to the highest point within his power, each independent in thought in all matters which are open to discussion, each vigorous, animated, refined, well informed, and charitable to the defects and errors of all around him.

Such are some few of the facts of this new phase in the world's existence in which we find our lot to be cast. The old landmarks of thought are gone, a deluge has swept over the world; a rapid vegetation is again commencing, rank and baneful, or lovely and lifegiving, according as it is left to its own uncultured vigour, or is tended with wisdom, and breathed upon by the gales of grace from heaven. We are placed in the midst of an innumerable host of men, with power in their hands, with daring freedom in their thoughts; but not without a love for order, and a desire for truth and goodness ; and according as we take them upon their own ground, and be ourselves also wise in our generation, shall we find them our friends or our foes, the servants of Jesus Christ, or rebels against his authority, and the mad destroyers of their own selves. May God grant that we may be *wise as serpents*, as well as simple as doves.

SCHOOLS OF THE BENEDICTINES.

(From the Atlantis, — JOHN H. NEWMAN.)

THE rise and extension of these Schools seems to us as great an event in the history of the Order, as the introduction of the sacerdotal office into the number of its functions. If Pope Gregory took a memorable step in turning monks of his convent into missionary bishops charged with the conversion of England, much more remarkable was the act of Pope Vitalian, in sending the old Greek monk Theodore to the same island, to fill the vacant see of Canterbury. We call it more remarkable, because it introduced an actual tradition into the Benedictine houses, and consecrated a system by authority. It is true that from an early date in the history of monachism, extensive learning had been combined with the profession of a monk. St. Jerome was only too fond of the Cicero and Horace, whom he put aside; and, if out of the whole catalogue of ecclesiastics we had to select a literary Father, the monk Jerome, *per excellence*, would be he. In the next century Claudian Mamercus, of Vienne, employed the leisure which his monastic profession gave him to gain an extensive knowledge of Greek and Latin literature. He collected a library of Greek, Roman, and Christian books, "quam totam monachus", says Sidonius of him, "virente in aevo, secretâ bibit institutione".[a] And in the century after, Cassiodorus, the cotemporary of St. Benedict, is well known for combining sacred and classical studies in his monastery. The tradition, however, of the cloister was up to that time against profane literature, and Theodore reversed it.

This celebrated man made his appearance at the end of the century which the missionary Augustine opened, and just about the time when the whole extent of England had been converted to the Christian faith. He brought with him Greek as well as Latin Classics, and set up schools for both the learn-

[a] Mabillon Annal. Bened. t. I, p. 32.

ed languages in various parts of the country. Henceforth the curriculum of the Seven Sciences is found in the Benedictine schools. From Theodore [a] proceeded Egbert and the school of York; from Egbert came Bede, and the school of Jarrow; from Bede, Alcuin, and the schools of Charlemagne at Paris, Tours, and Lyons. From these came Raban and the school of Fulda; from Raban, Walafrid and the school of Richenau; Lupus and the school of Ferrières. From Lupus, Heiric, Remi, and the school of Rheims; from Remi, Odo of Cluni; from the dependencies of Cluni, the celebrated Gerbert, afterwards Pope Sylvester the Second, and Abbo of Fleury, whom we have already introduced to the reader's notice, though not by name, in the former part of this sketch, as repaying a portion of the debt which the Franks owed to the Anglo-Saxons, by opening the schools of Ramsey Abbey, after the inroad of the Danes.

And now, at length, in addressing ourselves to the question, how such studies can be considered in keeping with the original idea of the monastic state, we think it right to repeat an explanation, which we made at an earlier stage of our discussion, to the effect that we are proposing nothing more than a survey of the venerable order of St. Benedict from without; and we claim leave to do as much as this by the same right by which the humblest among us may freely and without offence gaze on sun, moon, and stars, and form his own private opinion, true or false, of their materials and their motions. And with this proviso, we remind the reader, if we have not sufficiently done so in our present pages, that the one object, immediate as well as ultimate, of Benedictine life, as history presents it to us, was to live in purity and to die in peace. The monk proposed to himself no great or systematic work, beyond that of saving his soul. What he did more than this, was the accident of the hour, spontaneous acts of piety, the sparks of mercy or beneficence, struck off in the heat, as it were, of his solemn religious toil, and done and over almost as soon as they began to be. If to-day he cut down a tree, or relieved the famishing, or visited the sick, or taught the ignorant, or

---

[a] Vid. Daniel, Etudes Classiques, p. 100, etc.; Launoy, de Scholis Opp. t. 4. 1.

transcribed a page of Scripture, this was a good in itself, though nothing was added to it to-morrow. He cared little for knowledge, even theological, or for success, even though it was religious. It is the character of such a man to be contented, resigned, patient, and incurious; to create or originate nothing; to live by tradition. He does not analyze, he marvels; his intellect attempts no comprehension of this multiform world, but on the contrary it is hemmed in, and shut up within it. It recognizes but one cause in nature and in human affairs, and that is the First and Supreme; and why things happen day by day in this way, and not in that, it refers immediately to his will. *a* It loves the country, because it is his work; but " man made the town", and he and his works are evil. This is what may be called the Benedictine idea, then viewed in the abstract; and, as being such, we gave it the title of "poetical", when contrasted with that of other religious orders; and we did so, because we considered we saw in it a congeniality, *mutatis mutandis*, to the spirit of a Poet, who has perhaps greater title of that high name than any one else, as having received a wider homage, and that among nations in time, place, and character, further removed from each other. *b*

Now supposing the historical portrait of the Benedictine to be such as this, and that we were further told that he was concerned with study and with teaching, and then were asked, keeping in mind the notion of his poetry of character, to guess

---

a Quoties videtur contra naturam aliquid evenire, quodammodo non contra naturam e t, quia rerum natura hoc habet eximium, ut à quo est, semper ejus obtemperet jussis. Paschas. p. 155, Opp. ed. 1618.

b This analogy between the monastic institute and Virgil is recognized by Cassiodorus, who, after impressing on his monks, in the first place, the study of Holy Scripture and the Fathers, continues, " However, the most holy Fathers have passed no decree, binding us to repudiate secular literature; for in fact such reading prepares the mind in no slight measure for understanding the sacred writings". Presently, " In some cases indeed, Frigidus obstiterit circum praecordia sanguis ", so as to hinder a man's perfect mastery whether of human or divine divine letters; but even with but a poor measure of knowledge, *he may be able to choose the life which follows in the next verse*, " Rura mihi et rigui placeant in vallibus amnes"; for "*it is even congenial to monks to have the care of a garden, to till the land, and to take interest in a good crop of apples*"—de Inst. div. litt. 28. Here, by the bye, is in fact the same contrast between the "Felix qui" and the "Fortunatus est ille", which is suggested to reader in our former article (*Atlant.*, vol. i. p. 17). Mr. Keble, in a passage of his beautiful Prelections, p. 648, considers Virgil to allude to Lucretius in the " Felix ", while he ascribes to himself the " Fortunatus ".

what books he studied and what sort of pupils he taught, we should without much difficulty conclude, that Scripture would be his literature, and children would be the members of his school.[a] And, **if we were** further asked, what was likely to be the subject-matter of the schooling imparted to these boys, probably we should not be able to make any guess at all; but we surely should not be very much surprised to be told, that the same spirit which led him to prefer the old basilicas for worship instead of any new architecture of his own inventing, and to honour his emperor or king with spontaneous loyalty more than by theological definitions, would also induce him, in the matter of education, to take **up** with the old books and subjects which he found ready to his hand **in the** pagan schools, as far as he could religiously do so, rather than venture on any experiments or system of his own.[b] This, as we have already intimated, was the case. He adopted the Roman curriculum, professed **the** Seven Sciences, began with Grammar, that is, the Latin classics, and, if he sometimes finished with them, it was because his boys left him ere he had time to teach them **more**. His choice of subjects **was his** fit recompense for choosing. He adopted the Latin **writers** from his love of prescription, because he found **them in** possession. But there were in fact no writings, after Scripture, more congenial, from their fresh and natural beauty, **and** their absence of intellectualism, to the monastic temperament. Such were his schoolbooks; and, as "the boy is father of the man", the little monks, who heard them read **or** pored **over them,** when they **grew up,** filled the atmosphere of the monastery with the tasks **and studies with** which they had been imbued in their childhood.

For so it was, strange as it seems to our ideas, these boys were monks[c] — monks as truly as those of **riper** years. About St. Benedict's time the Latin Church innovated upon

---

[a] Mos in Benedictino ordine usatissimus scholas instituere, et pueros cum pietate tum litteris imbuere. Dechery in Lanfranc. Opp. p. 28. Brower. Antiqu. Fuld., pp. 35-38.

[b] On the monastic schools taking up the imperial, vid Guizot Civil. vol. 2, p. 100, etc. Vid. also Ampère, Hist Lit., t. 2, p. 277.

[c] Thomas, Disc. Eccles., t. 1, 821.

the discipline of former centuries, and allowed parents, not only to dedicate their infants to a religious life, but to do so without any power on the part of those infants, when they came to years of reason, to annul the dedication. This discipline continued for five or six centuries, beginning with the stern Spaniards, nor ending till shortly before the pontificate of Innocent the Third. Divines argued in behalf of it from the case of infant baptism, in which the sleeping soul, without being asked, is committed to the most solemn of engagements; from that of Isaac on the Mount, and of Samuel, and from the sanction of the Mosaic Law; and they would be confirmed in their course by the instances of compulsion, not uncommon in the early centuries, when high magistrates or wealthy heads of families were suddenly seized on by the populace or by synods, and against their remonstrances, tonsured, ordained, and consecrated, before they could well take breath and realize to themselves their change of station. Nor must we forget the old Roman law, the spirit of which they had inherited, and which gave to the father the power even of life and death over his refractory offspring.

However, childhood is not the age at which the severity of the law would be felt, which bound a man by his parent's act to the service of the cloister. While these oblates were but children, they were pretty much like other children; they threw a grace over the stern features of monastic asceticism, and peopled the silent haunts of penance with a crowd of bright innocent faces. "Silence was pleased", to use the poet's language, when it was broken by the cheerful, and sometimes, it must be confessed, unruly voices of a set of school-boys. These would sometimes, certainly, be inconveniently loud, especially as St. Benedict did not exclude from his care lay-boys, destined for the world. It was more than the devotion of some good monks could bear; and they preferred some strict Reform, which, among its new provisions, prohibited the presence of these uncongenial associates. But, after all, it was no great evil to place before the eyes of austere manhood and unlovely age a sight so calculated to soften and to cheer. It was not adolescence, with its curiosity, its pride of knowledge and its sensitiveness, with its disputes and emulations, with its exciting prizes and its impetuous breathles efforts, which St. Benedict undertook to teach: he was no professor in a university. His convent was an infant school, a grammar school, and a seminary: it was not an academy. Indeed, **the** higher education in that day scarcely can be said to exist. It was a day of bloodshed and of revolution; before the time of life came, when the university succeeds the school, the student had to choose his profession. He became a clerk or a monk, or he became a soldier.

The fierce northern warriors, who had won for themselves the lands of Christendom with their red hands, rejoiced to commit their innocent offspring to the custody of religion and of peace. Nay, sometimes with the despotic will, of which we have just now spoken, they dedicated them, from or before their birth, to the service of Heaven. They determined, that some at least of their lawless race should be rescued from the contamination of blood and licence, and should be set apart in sacred places **to** pray for their kindred. The little beings,[a] of three or four or five years old, were brought in the arms of those who gave them life, to accept at their bidding the course in which that life was to run. They were brought into the sanctuary, spoke by the mouth of their parents, as at the font, put out their tiny hand for the sacred corporal to be wrapped round it, received the cowl, and took their place as monks in the monastic community. In the first ages of the Benedictine Order, these children were placed on a level with their oldest brethren. They took precedence according to their date of admission, and the gray head gave way to them in choir and refectory, if junior to them in monastic standing. They even voted in the election of abbot, being considered to speak by divine instinct, as the child who cried out, "Ambrose is Bishop".[b] If they showed waywardness in community meetings, inattention at choir, ill behaviour at table, which certainly was not an impos-

---

[a] Calmet. Reg. Bened., t. 2. pp. 2, 4, 116, 278, 335–6, 380, 385. Vid. also Thomassin. Disc. Eccl., t. 1, p. 821, and Magagnotti's Dissert. in Fleury's Disc. Pop. Del.
[b] Calmet, t. 2, p. 324. This early dedication of the monk might tend to suggest or defend the abuse of boy priests. Vid. S. Bernard. de Off. Ep. 7.

sible occurrence, they were corrected by the nods, the words, or the blows of the grave brother who happened to be next them: it was not till an after time, that they had a prefect of their own, except in school hours.

That harm came from this remarkable discipline, is only the suggestion of our modern habits and ideas; that it was not expedient for all times follows from the fact that at a certain date it ceased to be permitted. However, that, in those centuries in which it was in force, its result was good, is seen in the history of those heroic men whom it nurtured, and might have been anticipated from the principle which it embodied. The monastery was intended to be the paternal home, not the mere refuge of the monk: it was an orphanage, not a reformatory; father and mother had abandoned him, and he grew up from infancy in the new family which had adopted him. He was a child of the house; there were stored up all the associations of his wondering boyhood, and there would lie the hopes and interests of his maturer years. He was to seek for sympathy in his brethren, and to give them his own in return. He lived and died in their presence. They prayed for his soul, cherished his memory, were proud of his name, and treasured his works. A pleasing illustration of this brotherly affection meets us in the life of Walafrid Strabo, Abbot of Richenau, whose poems, written by him when a boy of fifteen and eighteen, were preserved by his faithful friends, and thus remain to us at this day. Walafrid is but one out of many, whose names are known in history, dedicated from the earliest years to the cloister. St. Boniface, Apostle of Germany, was a monk at the age of five; St. Bede came to Wiremouth at the age of seven; St. Paul of Verdun is said by an old writer to have left his cradle for the cloister; St. Robert entered it as soon as he was weaned; Pope Paschal the Second was taken to Cluni, Ernof to Bec, the Abbot Suger to St. Denis, from their " most tender infancy".

Infants can but gaze about at what surrounds them, and their learning comes through their eyes. In the instances we have been considering, their minds would receive the passive impressions which were made on them by the scene, and would be moulded by the composed countenances and solemn services which surrounded them. Such was the education of these little ones, till perhaps the age of seven; when, under the title of "pueri",[a] they commenced their formal school-time, and committed to memory their first lesson. That lesson was **the** Psalter—that wonderful manual of prayer and praise, which, from the time when its various portions were first composed down to the last few centuries, has been the most **precious** *viaticum* of the Christian mind in its journey through the wilderness. In early times St. **Basil** speaks of it **as the** the popular devotion in Egypt, Africa, and Syria; and St. Jerome had urged its use upon the Roman ladies whom he directed. All monks were enjoined to know it by heart; the young ecclesiastics learned it by heart; no bishop could be ordained without knowing it by heart; and in the parish schools it was learned by heart. The Psalter, with the Lord's Prayer and Creed, constituted the *sine qua non* condition of discipleship. At home pious mothers, as the Lady Helvidia, whom we have already introduced to the reader, taught their children the Psalter. It was only, then, in observance of a universal law,[b] that the Benedictine children were taught it;—they mastered **it, and** then they passed into the secular schoolroom,—they next were introduced to the study of grammar.[c]

By Grammar, it is hardly necessary to say, was not meant, as now, the mere analysis or rules of language, as denoted by the words etymology, syntax, prosody; but rather it stood for scholarship, **that is,** such an acquaintance with the literature of a **language, as implied** the power of original composition **and the** *vivâ voce* use of it. Thus Cassiodorus defines it to be "skill in speaking elegantly, gained from the best poets and orators"; St. Isidore, "the science of speaking **well**"; and Raban, "the science of interpreting poets and **historians,**

---

[a] Calmet, t. 1, p. 495.   [b] Thomass. Disc., t. 2, p. 280, etc.

[c] The following sketch is **drawn** up from **the works of** the Benedictines, in in Biol. Max. Patr., tt. 14, 15, 17, 18, 21; Mabillon's Acta SS. Bened.; Ceillier's Auteurs, tt. 18–20; Neander's Hist., vol. 6, Bohn; Guizot, Hist. Civil, vol. 2; Bohn; Ampère, Hist. Lit., t. 3; and two recent works of Mgr. Landriot's Ecoles Littéraires, and P. Daniel's Etudes Classiques, to which we are much indebted for many points of detail. Vid. also M. l'Abbé Lalanne's Influence des Pères, and P. Cahour's Etudes Classiques.

and the rule of speaking and writing well". In the monastic school, the language of course was Latin; and in Latin literature first came Virgil; next Lucan and Statius; Terence, Sallust, Cicero; Horace, Persius, Juvenal; and of Christian poets, Prudentius, Sedulius, Juvencus, Aratus. Thus we find that the monks of St. Alban's, near Mayence, had standing lectures in Cicero, Virgil, and other authors. In the school of Paderborne there were lectures in Horace, Virgil, Statius, and Sallust. Theodulf speaks of his juvenile studies in the Christian authors, Sedulius and Paulinus, Aratus, Fortunatus, Juvencus, and Prudentius, and in the classical Virgil and Ovid. Gerbert, afterwards Sylvester the Second, after lecturing his class in logic, brought it back again to Virgil, Statius, Terence, Juvenal, Persius, Horace, and Lucan. A work is extant of St. Hildebert's, supposed to be a school exercise; it is scarcely more than a cento of Cicero, Seneca, Horace, Juvenal, Persius, Terence, and other writers. Horace he must have almost known by heart.

Considering the number of authors which have to be studied in order to possessing a thorough knowledge of the Latin tongue, and the length to which those in particular run which are set down in the above lists, we may reasonably infer, that with the science of Grammar the Benedictine teaching began and ended, excepting of course such religious instruction, as is rather the condition of Christian life than the acquisition of knowledge. At fourteen, when the term of boyhood was complete, [a] the school time commonly ended too, the lay youths left for their secular career, and the monks commenced the studies appropriate to their sacred calling. The more promising youths, however, of the latter class were suffered or directed first to proceed to further secular studies; and, in order to accompany them, we must take some more detailed view of the curriculum, of which Grammar was the introductory study.

This curriculum, [b] derived from the earlier ages of heathen philosophy, was transferred to the use of the Church on the authority of St. Augustine, who in his *de Ordine* consi-

---

[a] Calmet, Reg., t. 1, p. 495.
[b] Brucker Phil., t. 3, p. 594, etc. Appul. Florid. iv. 20.

ders it to be the fitting and sufficient preparation for theological learning. It is hardly necessary to refer to the history of its formation; we are told how Pythagoras prescribed the study of arithmetic, music, and geometry; how Plato and Aristotle insisted on grammar and music, which, with gymnastics, were the substance of Greek education; how Seneca speaks, though not as approving, of grammar, music, geometry, and astronomy, as the matter of education in his own day; and how Philo, in addition to these, has named logic and rhetoric. Augustine, in his enumeration of them, begins with arithmetic and grammar, including under the latter history; then he speaks of logic and rhetoric; then of music, under which comes poetry, as equally addressing the ear; lastly, of geometry and astronomy, which address the eye. The Alexandrians, whom he followed, arranged them differently; viz., grammar, rhetoric, and logic or philosophy,[a] which branched off into the four mathematical sciences of arithmetic, music, geometry, and astronomy. And this order was adopted in Christian education, the first three sciences being called the Trivium, the last four the Quadrivium.

Grammar was taught in all these schools; but for those who wished to proceed further than the studies of their boyhood, seats of higher education had been founded by Charlemagne in the principal cities of his Empire, under the name of public schools,[b] which may be considered the shadow, and even the nucleus of the universities which arose in a subsequent age. Such were the schools of Paris, Tours, Rheims, and Lyons in France; Fulda in Germany; Bologna in Italy. Nor did they confine themselves to the Seven Sciences above mentioned, though it is scarcely to be supposed, that, in any science whatever, except Grammar, they professed to impart more than the elements. Thus we read of St. Bruno of Segni (A.D. 1080), after being grounded in the "litteræ humaniores", as a boy, by the monks of St. Perpetuus near Aste, seeking the rising school of Bologna for the "altiores scien-

---

[a] The Quadrivium was called "philosophy". Ampère, t. 3, p. 267.
[b] Charlemagne's schools taught Grammar, Rhetoric, Leges, Canones, Theology biblical and patristical. Vid. Thomass. Dic. t. 3, p. 271–294; Ampère, Hist., t. 3, p. 267.

tiæ".ᵃ St. Abbo of Fleury (A.D. 990), after mastering, in the monastery of that place, grammar, arithmetic, logic, and music, went to Paris and Rheims for philosophy and astronomy; and afterwards taught himself rhetoric and geometry. Raban (A.D. 822) left the school of Fulda for a while for Alcuin's lectures, and learned Greek of a native of Ephesus. Walafrid (A.D. 840) passed from Richenau to Fulda. St. William (A.D. 980), dedicated by his parents to St. Benedict at St. Michael,s near Vercellæ, proceeded to study at Pavia. Gerbert (A.D. 990), one of the few cultivators of physics, after Fleury an Orleans, went to Spain.ᵇ St. Wolfgang (A.D. 994), after private instruction, went to Richenau. Lupus (A.D. 840), after Ferrières, was sent for a time to Fulda. Fulbert too of Chartres (A.D. 1000), though not a monk, may be mentioned as sending his pupils in like manner to finish their studies at schools of more celebrity than his own.ᶜ

History furnishes us with specimens of the subjects taught in this higher education. We read of Gerbert lecturing in Aristotle's Categories and the Isagogæ of Porphyry; St. Thodore taught the Anglo-Saxon youths Greek and mathematics; Alcuin, all seven sciences at York; and at some German monasteries there were lectures in Greek,ᵈ Hebrew, and Arabic. The monks of St. Benignus at Dijon gave lectures in medicine; the abbey of St. Gall had a school of painting and engraving; the blessed Tubilo of that abbey was mathematician, painter, and musician.ᵉ We read of another monk of the same monastery, who was ever at his carpentry, when he was not at the altar; and of another, who worked in stone. Hence Vitruvius was in repute with them. Another accomplishment was

---

ᵃ Vit. ap. Brun. Opp. ed 1759.   ᵇ Brucker, t. 3, p. 645.
ᶜ Thomass. Disc. t. 2, p. 296--8.
ᵈ Fredegodus of Canterbury (A.D. 960) wrote in Greek. Vid. Cave's Hist. Litt. in nom. In the Life of St. Odo of Canterbury we read that his patron Athelm " Græcâ et Latinâ linguâ magistris edocendum eum tradidit, quarum linguarum plerisque, tunc temporis in gente Anglorum usus erat, à discipulis beatæ memoriæ Theodori archiepiscopi profectas. Factusque est in utraque linguâ valdè gnarus, ita ut posset poemata fingere, continuare prosam, et omnia, quicquid ei anima sederet, luculentissimo sermone proferre". Mabillon Act. Sæc. 5, p. 289.
ᵉ We quoted in our former article a passage from Brower on the arts cultivated at Fulda. For a parallel in the East, vid. the account of the monks of Theodore Studita, vit. p. 29, Sirmond.

that of copying manuscripts, which they did with a perfection unknown to the scholastic age which followed them.^a

These manual arts, far more than the severer sciences, were the true complement of the Benedictine ideal of education, which, after all, was little more than a fair or a sufficient acquaintance with Latin literature. Such is the testimony of the ablest men of the time. "To pass from Grammar to Rhetoric, and then in course to the other liberal sciences", says Lupus, speaking of France, is "fabula tantum".^b "It has ever been the custom in Italy", says Glaber Radulphus, writing of the year 1000, "to neglect all arts but Grammar."^c Grammar, moreover, in the sense in which we have defined it, is no superficial study, nor insignifiant instrument of mental cultivation, and the school-task of the boy became the life-long recreation of the man. Amid the serious duties of their sacred vocation, the monks did not forget the books which had arrested and refined their young imagination. Let us turn to the familiar correspondence of some of these more famous Benedictines, and we shall see what were the pursuits of their leisure, and the indulgences of their relaxation. Alcuin, in his letters to his friends, quotes Virgil again and again; he also quotes Horace, Terence, Pliny, besides frequent allusions to the heathen philosophers. Lupus quotes Horace, Cicero, Suetonius, Virgil, and Martial. Gerbert quotes Virgil, Cicero, Horace, Terence, and Sallust. Petrus Cellensis quotes Horace, Seneca, and Terence. Hildebert quotes Virgil and Cicero, and refers to Diogenes, Epictetus, Crœsus, Themistocles, and other personages of Greek history. Hincmar of Rheims quotes Horace. Paschasius Radbert's favourite authors were Cicero and Terence. Abbo of Fleury was especially familiar with Terence, Sallust, Virgil, and Horace; Peter the Venerable, with Virgil and Horace; Hepidamn of St. Gall took Sallust as a model of style.^d

Nor is their anxiety less to enlarge the range of their classical reading. Lupus asks Abbot Hatto through a friend for leave

---

^a Guizot. Civil., t. 2, p. 236; Hallam, Lit. i., 1, 87.
^b Ep. 1. ^c Muratori Dissert. 43, p. 831.
^d The School of Ouen produced 500 writers in 50 years. Landriot, p. 135. Vid. the curious Letter of Gunzo, Marten., Ampl. Coll. t. 1, p. 294.

to copy Suetonius's Lives of the Cæsars, which is in the monastery of St. Boniface in two small *codices*. He sends to another friend to bring with him the Catilinarian and Jugurthan Wars of Sallust, the Verrines of Cicero, and any other volumes which his friend happens to know either that he has not, or possesses only in faulty copies, bidding him withal beware of the robbers on his journey. Of another friend he asks the loan of Cicero's *de Rhetoricâ*, his own copy of which is incomplete, and of Aulus Gellius. In another letter he asks the Pope for Cicero's *de Oratore*, the Institutions of Quintillian, and the commentary of Donatus upon Terence. In like manner Gerbert tells Abbot Gisilbert, that he has the beginning of the *Ophthalmicus* of the philosopher Demosthenes, and the end of Cicero's *Pro rege Deiotaro;* and he wants to know if he can assist him in completing them for him. He asks a friend at Rome to send him by Count Guido the copies of Suetonius and Aurelius which belong to his archbishop and himself; he requests Constantine, the lecturer (scholasticus) at Fleury, to bring him Cicero's *Verrines* and *de Republicâ*, and he thanks Remigius, a monk of Treves, for having begun to transcribe for him the Achilleid of Statius, though he had been unable to proceed with it for want of a copy. To other friends he speaks of Pliny, Cæsar, and Victorinus. Alcuin's Library contained Pliny, Aristotle, Cicero, Virgil, Statius, and Lucan; and he transcribed Terence with his own hand.

Not only the memory of their own youth, but the necessity of transmitting to the next generation what they had learned in it themselves, kept them loyal to their classical acquirements. They were, in this aspect of their history, not unlike the fellows in our modern English universities, who first learn and then teach. It is impossible, indeed, to overlook their ressemblance generally to the elegant scholar of a day which is now waning, especially at Oxford, such as Lowth or Elmsly, Copleston or Keble, Howley or Parr, who thought little of science or philosophy by the side of the authors of Greece and Rome. Nor is it too much to say, that the Colleges in the English Universities may be considered in matter of fact to be the lineal descendants or heirs of the Benedictine schools of Charlemagne.ᵃ The modern of course has vastly the advantage in the comparison; for he is familiar with Greek, has an exacter criticism and purer taste, and a more refined cultivation of mind. He writes, verse at least, far better than the Benedictine, who had commonly little idea of it; and he has the accumulated aids of centuries in the shape of dictionaries and commentaries.

ST. URSULA AND THE ELEVEN THOUSAND VIRGINS.ᵇ

(From the Rambler.)

THE life of St. Ursula is one that has much interest for the Englishman; she and her companions are said to have been natives of our island, and are supposed to have been connected with royal personages, the proof of whose existence would throw some light on the annals of our country. The author of the present remarkable work, which forms a part of the great Bollandist collection, confesses in the outset the difficulties which surround him. The lives of saints are generally meant for spiritual reading, not for historical criticism; and the pious reader is apt to be disedified rather than encouraged in his devotion, if, instead of a swimming narrative of the wonders of the inner life, or miraculous external manifestations of sanctity, he finds only the truth of details called into question, and the traditionary legend criticised. There are persons who would think it almost a sacrilege to allow themselves to doubt about St. Ursula. But, on the other hand, there are most pious and learned Catholics who have almost resigned the hope

---

ᵃ "If Colleges, with their endowments and local interests .. are necessarily .. of a national character, it follows that the education which they will administer will also be national, and adapted to all ranks and classes of the community. And if so, then again it follows that they will be far more given to *the study of the Arts* than to the learned professions, or to any special class of pursuits at all; and such in matter of fact has ever been the case. They have *inherited* under changed circumstances the position of *the monastic teaching founded by Charlemagne*, and have *continued* its primitive traditions, through, and in spite of, the noble intellectual developments, to which Universities have given occasion". Newman's Office and Work of Universities, p. 340, 1.

ᵇ De S. Ursula et undecim millibus Sociarum, Virginum et Martyrum Coloniæ Agrippinæ. Auc. V. de Buck, Presb. S. J. Brussels, Greuse, 1858.

of reducing her history to any decent degree of probability. Baronius does not hesitate to call it "well-nigh fabulous." Between these two extremes there has been every variety of opinion with regard to all the principal circumstances of the history, the number of her martyred companions, and the epoch of their death.

So little is known of these saints, and that so varying in detail and so uncertain, that their history cannot come under the usual idea of hagiography, but must belong to the critical and historical class of books. And as the first work of a critic is to destroy, so several of F. de Buck's earlier chapters are occupied in destroying the authenticity of the documents from which the common history of St. Ursula is taken. Several of these are *revelations* or visions of certain persons, since canonised or beatified, with which they were favoured on the occasion of the excitement which followed the discovery of the repositories of the relics of the martyrs in the twelfth century. The unknown bones were taken to certain persons famed for their sanctity, who found no difficulty in divining the names and history of the persons to whom they had belonged.

It certainly would be satisfactory if these histories could be proved to agree with genuine historical monuments, especially as those who "revealed" the information are reckoned among the saints. But as this proof was impossible, it only remained for the Bollandist father to show how, without any charge of mendacity or imposture against the person who is supposed to make the revelations, however strongly a divine inspiration may be asserted, such visions are always suspicious, to be trusted with the greatest caution, and, in fact, only fully believed after the event has proved them to be true. The "revelations" about St. Ursula come from two persons. Those of St. Elizabeth of Schönau are proved to be not divine, because, while they do not go beyond the power of mere imagination, they have all the properties of the products of an excited fancy: she had her revelations while in a diseased and feverish state— while she was herself desirous, or expected by others to have them, or was asked to answer a question proposed to her; she saw many things over and over again; she revealed many things, word for word, as she had read them in the Gospels or other histories; while, on the contrary, many were contradictory to one another and to historical truth. Besides all this, St. Elizabeth was too positive, and hardly modest enough in asserting her inspiration, which she could confirm by no miracles or other requisite signs of the supernatural. With regard to the visions of B. Hermann Joseph, the other author of these revelations, F. de Buck, while allowing that he passed nearly the whole of his life in a state of ecstasy, with his mind continually fixed on God and on sacred things, yet maintains that persons in this conditions have complete liberty of imagination and fancy. With Papebroche and Benedict XIV., he distinguishes the substance of their visions from the accidents. The mind may really be fixed on divine things, and may be assisted by God in the contemplation of them; yet the active imagination and fancy may be surrounding the central idea passively impressed on the mind with all kinds of additions, which owe their origin not to God but to the mind itself, and yet are liable to be confused with that which the mind receives from God.

Instances of the same kind take place continually. In our daily meditations we all know that the grace of God and the gift of faith help us to apply our minds to the mysteries we contemplate : yet we each have our own way of representing these mysteries; the imagination of each person, though assisted by God, gives the mystery a different clothing and colour. In other words, we each of us represent these things to ourselves in a different way. Whence this difference? Certainly not from God's assistance; which, though one and invariable, yet leaves the imagination at liberty. The case of ecstatics is the same, only raised to a higher power. While we meditate, we are generally sufficiently alive to external things to know exactly where our fancy begins to transport us beyond the phenomena which actually surround us. But in an ecstasy people see no more of external things than they do in sleep; the external term of the comparison is wanting; and the internal image is the only phenomenon that presents itself, and is therefore necessarily judged to be a true representation of a present reality. In an ecstasy, therefore, persons are much more liable to be deceived than otherwise. In saying this, we do not detract either from the high state of an ecstatic, or from the sanctity of those who give entire credit to all they have imagined in that state. The grace of God was with them in elevating their mind, and in abstracting it entirely from things of earth; but it did not destroy the freedom of the imagination. Though their outward senses were closed, their minds were wakeful, and every inward power was increased in activity. It is for this reason that we must not expect such visions to contain historical truth. Not that God is unable to teach us such truth by means of visions, for He has often done so; many visions of saints, as those of St. Ignatius of Antioch, St. Felicitas, and others, were really fulfilled: we only affirm that when God helps us to fix our minds entirely on the mysteries of our faith, He generally leaves our imaginations free to surround these mysteries with such clothing and colouring as our imagination and fancy are able to produce.

After disposing of these visionary histories, our author conducts us to Geoffrey of Monmouth, whose historical authority is annihilated by comparing his fictions with the real history of the Armorican Britons. From all these sources, however, the author gathers up a small thread of consenting tradition, which he follows till he is able to set the history of St. Ursula on a certain basis. The conduct of this inquiry leads him to give a most interesting account of the invasion of Gaul by Attila and the Huns in the middle of the fifth century, introduced by an essay on the origin and first wanderings of that people, and on their history to the end of the fourth century, in which he sums up all the learning, ancient and modern, that has been expended on that obscure point. He traces with great completeness their incursion into Gaul; on their return from which he proves that they massacred the martyrs of Cologne. There is not very much positive testimony that Cologne was one of the cities destroyed by them; but by a minute analysis of the annals of that town he proves that certain ravages there committed must be attributed to the Huns, of whose wholesale brutality he brings sufficient examples. The last point to be proved was the British origin of the martyrs, which he owns rests on a less sure foundation than the rest of the legend. Yet the most ancient traditions concur in calling them British; and the political state of Britain at that epoch makes their emigration probable; especially when contemporary history contains traces of the presence of Britons at the mouths of the Rhine, where they appear to have acted as missionaries. The received legend of the 11,000 virgins under St. Ursula emigrating together, then making their pilgrimage to Rome, and being butchered on their return at Cologne, is absurd enough; but that there was some such pilgrimage, which served as the foundation of the legend, is proved from a passage of St. Gregory of Tours. Altogether, then, the history of St. Ursula rests on a real foundation; under the disfigured traditions much truth lies hid, which may be brought to light by means of a diligent comparison of the data of the traditions with the data of other historical documents of the era.

The author sums up his history in the following manner. It is a great mistake to suppose that there are no monuments of St. Ursula and the 11,000 virgins more ancient than the eleventh century and the irruption of the Normans. By a comparison of different documents, we can show that a monastic basilica was built in honour of the virgins about the year 500, or at least before the beginning of the seventh century. No more valid testimony than this can be required. Next, there is a sermon for their festival-day, which must have been composed between the years 731 and 834, and by which it appears clearly that at that time the memory of the holy virgins was fresh, not only in Cologne, but in Batavia and Britain. Rather more ancient than this is the office of the virgins which was used at Cologne. Next come a series of archives and deeds relating to the basilica of the "holy virgins," or "the 11,000 holy virgins," as it is indifferently called; the most ancient of these is of the year 852. Lastly come certain martyrologies of the middle of the ninth century. All these monuments are previous to the entrance of the Normans into Cologne in 881.

It is therefore evidently false to assert that all the history of St. Ursula was invented after the departure of the Normans, when the people of Cologne began to recover their peace and quiet. On the contrary, there is a vast series of monuments previous to that time, the earliest of which approaches close to the time of the martyrdom. But the evidence does not rest entirely on written monuments. In the year 1640 the catacomb where the virgins were said to be buried was opened, and every thing was found which could verify the written evidence. The antiquity of the tomb was proved by the coins found in it; its Christian character, by the bodies not having been burned. The bodies had been wrapped up in their garments, as martyrs were ordered to be buried; the arrows and weapons with which they had been killed were found with the bones; on one shelf there were nothing but heads, arms, legs, and other parts of bodies; in the corners, vases full of sand that had been saturated with blood; in fact, most of the proofs of martyrdom which are reckoned valid when found in the catacombs of Rome.

Since, therefore, it would be absurd to doubt of the martyrdom of some persons to whom these monuments belong, it remains to inquire who they were, and who killed them. The traditions, however various in other points, agree in this that the Huns were the murderers; and the different circumstances fully agree with this account. The virgins are said to have died in defence of their chastity, not for any articles of the faith; this corresponds with the accounts we have from different authors of the boundless licentiousness of the Huns. Again, the instruments of their martyrdom were arrows—the especial, almost the national weapon of the Huns.

It only remains, therefore, to investigate the road which the Huns must have taken in their retreat from Gaul in 451. They entered Gaul by Coblenz, in the winter; occupied Metz about March 25, and besieged Orleans till the middle of June. They had taken the city, and were carrying off their booty, when Aetius came on them unawares and routed them. They then retired to Chalons-sur-Marne, whither Aetius pursued them, and fought the famous battle, in which 200,000 human beings are said to have perished. Attila lost his camp, the

Goths lost their king Theodoric, and both sides seem to have dreaded another engagement. Aetius did not follow up his victory, as he thought the Huns a good counterpoise against the Goths and Franks, who otherwise might combine against the Romans. Attila therefore kept quiet for some time, till he saw that he was not attacked; and then fell upon the Vermandois, and took Soissons, Cambray, and Arras, which he entirely destroyed; and afterwards penetrated to Tournay, and then to Tongres, and so into Thuringia, a territory then so called on the left bank of the Rhine—from whence, in order to reach his own country, he must have crossed the river at Cologne. By a comparison of dates, F. de Buck makes out that this passage must have taken place about the middle of October; while, one the other hand, the martyrdom of the holy virgins is placed on the 21st of that month. All these things together lead to the conclusion that these martyrs really suffered at Cologne at the hands of the Huns, on the return of the barbarians from their fatal expedition into Gaul, about Oct. 21, 451.

Who, then, were these "eleven thousand virgins"? The number is authentic, and is found on the oldest monuments: but according to the most ancient traditions, it is not for a moment to be supposed that they were all virgins, but only some of the chief of them, whose martyrdom was more striking; the rest were of both sexes, including priests and fathers and mothers of families, in fact, all the victims of an irruption of barbarians into a great city. They were called martyrs, because the custom of those times was to honour with that title every one who suffered death unjustly with piety and patience. Some of these, and especially some of the virgins, may easily have been British damsels, passing through Cologne on their way to or from Rome, as the tradition relates; others may have been captives brought from the sacked towns of Gaul, and put to death here by the Huns, because the bridge over the Rhine was broken, and Aetius was pressing on behind them, and it would have been difficult to take their captives across.

Our short summary of F. de Buck's goodly folio will suffice to show to what category of books his work belongs. It is no brilliant à-*priori* theory of history, but it is a laborious and minute comparison of a vast quantity of historical monuments, collected with immense patience, and put together with great acumen and good sense. The result is not a work for pious meditation, but a repertory for the historian of the fifth century. The respectful but free way in which untenable traditions are treated is a lesson and a model for other writers; and we cannot withhold the expression of our admiration at the manner in which historical truth is brought to light, at the expense of no matter what prejudices or cherished traditions. Though the work naturally appeals only to the few, those few are persons who require every now and then to be reminded that facts are better than baseless theories or fanciful generalisations.

HOFER AND THE TYROLESE WAR OF INDEPENDENCE.

THE records of war are ordinarily the records of little else besides misery and crime. Even when the amount of abstract injustice is not equal on both sides engaged, there is little to honour or admire in the animating principles of the belligerents; while in the actual conduct of their deadly rivalry there is rarely any thing to be discerned but a contest of passion, bloodthirstiness, and selfishness. For the most part, nations quarrel like children, and fight like devils.

What are popularly termed "religious wars" are no exception to the rule. However holy the professed object of one party involved, the conduct of such wars has been almost always, to a considerable extent, unchristian and detestable. Purity of motive and uprightness and mercy in action have been usually confined to a small handful of individuals. The dominant spirit has been entirely that of this world, even while its watchwords have been most distinctively the language of the Gospel and the Cross.

Here and there, however, the eye of the historian detects a brighter spot in these long dismal annals of darkness and horror. It is possible to point to episodes in the wide history of bloodshedding, when men have fought like Christians, and not like beasts or devils; wielding the sword not only in word, but in reality, "in the name of God;" penetrated with a sense of the awful responsibility they had undertaken, and with emotions of love and mercy beating in their hearts, while their **arms has** been lifted up to strike, and their countenance has shown no trace of fear.

To the Catholic it is consolatory to reflect, that it has been under the influence of the faith that the most striking exhibitions of this really Christian warfare have been displayed to his fellow-creatures. Insulted as we are by the vilest imputations of cruelty, licentiousness, and disregard of all ties of patriotism, it is **a glorious thing to turn** silently and read the histories of wars in which, under the direct sanction of Catholicism, human **nature** has shown itself courageous, enduring, patriotic, and merciful, to an extent altogether unapproached by those who taunt us with every degrading vice. While it is daily dinned into our ears, till we are well-nigh stunned, **that** under the dark influence of Popery the world must necessarily go backwards, and all our powers be paralysed, until, by the sheer repetition of extravagant charges, we begin almost to suspect that **we** are rogues without knowing it, it is soothing **to let** the imagination wander back to countries where Catholicism has been embraced and really acted on, unmolested either by Protestant preacher or liberal statesman; where it has shown its vivifying power over the soul, unaided and unhindered either by royal patronage or aristocratical wealth. While the world is driving on at its own chosen rate of "progress," **it is instructive** to turn and watch the ways of other and humbler races, whose civilisation has not consisted in railways, crystal-palaces, screw-steamers and the penny-post; but in simplicity, hardihood, comparative poverty, and unmitigated "Romanism."

For, after all, "progress" is not necessarily progress to happiness and greatness. There is a knowledge which is more stultifying than ignorance; there is a power which is more degrading than weakness. It is possible to be great, glorious, and heroic, with very simple appliances; and the utmost amount of material civilisation, comfort, and order, is perfectly compatible with a very low degree of excellence in all that is most honourable in man, as man, and in woman, as woman. It is not crabs alone that can " progress " backwards.

Perhaps no spot in Europe is more suggestive of the reminiscences of a noble yet simple civilisation than the mountainous district of the Tyrolese Alps. Bordering upon Switzerland, that country of pretence, hypocrisy, and tyranny, for generations has been found a race where faith and patriotism have dwelt in intimate alliance, and the achievements of labouring mountaineers have rivalled those of the most celebrated soldiers of the world. The traveller, reeking from the hot and artificial life of England or France, on reaching the Tyrol finds himself in a new world of freshness and genial simplicity. He is surrounded by a people among whom education is not only general but universal, for none can marry unless they can read and write; but who, nevertheless, are all Catholics, and, as a race, as universally devout as perhaps any nation has ever been since Christianity has existed. Manly, frank, and vigorous, the Tyrolese unites in a remarkable degree, a devotion to a royal house with a personal independence of mind and capacity for practical action. His wealth is little, but his desires are few; he has the art of mingling pleasure with labour; the vices of civilisation are knonw to him more by report than by experience; he loves the liberties of his country like a rational man, who knows that there can be no liberty without law, and no law without obedience; and in the possession of rare and present advantages, he is content to live on without schemes of change, and to love that which is, all the more dearly because his country has flourished for centuries **under** institutions and with habits almost identical with those which he sees around him still.

If the stranger question him as to the past history of his country, he perceives, nevertheless, that in his open and peaceful mind there yet linger memories of a bloody struggle, when all this **fair** state of tranquillity and labour was for a time crushed beneath the heel of cruelty and a godless lust of dominion. Even among his favourite sculptured images, the works of the hereditary handicraft of his people, and for the most part religious in its aspect, singular figures appear, little known, or altogether unheard of, out of his own country. In innumerable houses appears a warlike innkeeper ; and, stranger still, in modern times, a Capuchin friar sword in hand, the remembrance of whose deeds is cherished by every rank with a fervour of gratitude, in comparison of which the recollections of the heroes of other countries are faint and dim. If there is such a thing **as** lasting national thankfulness, Hofer, the landlord of an inn at Passeyr, and Haspinger, the Capuchin, nicknamed Redbeard, have unquestionably lived in the affections of their fellow-countrymen with a posthumous glory seldom equalled in countries of more artificial cultivation, where the hero of yesterday is usually forgotten in the hero of to-day.

The history of that struggle which was long maintained by Hofer, with the aid of the Capuchin and other subordinates, against the overwhelming power of France and Bavaria, is indeed one of the most extraordinary records of courageous and skilful resistance against irresistible force which modern annals have preserved. Like so many of the miseries of Europe during the last seventy years, it had its origin in the revolution in France. For many centuries the Tyrolese had enjoyed as large an amount of national liberty as was possible under the old political system of Europe. Subjected to the sway of the Austrian house of Hapsburg, the people were nevertheless practically free. In their mountain fastnesses they possessed a constitution in many respects similar to that of the great free cities of Germany in the middle ages. That virtual independ**ence** which the powers of advancing commerce secured to Lubeck, to Freiburg, to Hamburg, to Erfurt, to Cologne, to Ratisbon, and many other centres of peaceful traffic, was confirmed to the simpler Tyrolese by the strength of their mountain passes, and the undaunted vigour, courage, and straightforwardness of their personal character. The imperial dominion, purely monarchical as it was in **name**, was held in check by many local rights and privileges, and still more by the **in**fluence of a moral and physical nobleness, so that the position of a Tyrolese was practically as free and self-legislating as that of the electing and governing classes in representative England at this very hour.

In the earlier period of the "Reformation," when the dominion of Austria in Switzerland was tottering to its foundations, the allegiance of the Tyrol, still stedfast in the ancient faith, was conciliated by a renewed confirmation of its hereditary privileges; and thus externally free, subject to its own taxation alone, and with political power diffused alike through the peasantry and the nobles, the Tyrol remained up to the battle of Austerlitz a free, honoured, prosperous, simple, and Catholic country, amidst the shock of empires and the degradation of all principle which characterised the eighteenth century of European history.

At length the storm burst upon the heads of the mountaineers. Such a race as the Tyrolese was intolerable alike to the military autocracy of Napoleon, and the crafty officialism of such monarchs as Louis XIV. of France and Joseph II. of Austria. Joseph, however, had left the Tyrol but little injured by those pernicious "reforms" through which he had reduced his German subjects to so low a level of religion, morals, and political strength; and the attachment of the Tyrolese to the Austrian monarchy remained ardent and unimpaired. When Austria, however, was prostrated at Austerlitz, and Napoleon, unresisted, set about the re-arrangement of the various territories which formed the old Germanic empire, on no country did the hand of the conqueror fall more heavily than on the Tyrol. The policy of Napoleon at that moment lay in elevating the minor states of Germany to some species of rivalry with the power of Austria, hitherto, save so far as Prussia was concerned, exclusively preponderant. He sought to convert the petty electors into the creatures of France, or rather of himself, by turning their sovereigns into kings and dukes, and by enriching them with spoils torn from their more powerful neighbours. Wurtemberg was made a kingdom, and received the Austrian possessions in Swabia. Baden became a grand-duchy, with the gift of Constance, the Breisgau, and the Ortenau. Bavaria shared the most largely in the booty. Her elector was turned into a king; with the sovereignty (such as it was, when conferred by Napoleon,) of Anspach and Bayreuth, stolen from Prussia, and a considerable slice of the Austrian territories, of which the most important portion was the Tyrol. The creatures of the conqueror and his Bavarian serf-king endeavoured to infuse an anti-German spirit into his subjects; and on the 1st of January 1806 the Bavarian State-Gazette announced the great achievement with the words, "Long live Napoleon, the restorer of the Bavarian kingdom!" while a herd of writers attempted to prove that the Bavarians were not German by ancestry, but originally a Gallic tribe under Gallic sovereigns.

Nowhere was the usurping power of Bavaria more hateful than among the Tyrolese mountains. A hundred years before they had been engaged in a conflict with these same grasping Bavarians, and had successfully resisted their invading troops, who as now were in alliance with the French. In June 1703 the Bavarian elector had entered the Tyrol at the head of 16,000 men; and seizing Innspruck, its capital, had advanced up the country with the view of subduing the people in their fastnesses. The whole country rose in arms, and the German soldiery felt what it was to attack a peasant-patriot in his own home. One of the chief leaders of the people was of no higher rank than that of postmaster; but the Bavarians were almost annihilated. Shot down by the riflemen, crushed by huge masses of rock and timber rolled upon them from the tops of the cliffs, one after another of the various divisions of the invading army gave way and fled. The peasants even fabricated cannon from hollowed fir-trees, sufficiently fire-proof to stand eight or ten discharges. In the end, of the 16,000 who had entered the Tyrol, only 5000 ever regained Bavaria.

A less prosperous issue attended the heroic resistance made in 1806 to the enforcement of the Bavarian usurpation, accompanied as it was by a reckless violation of the engagement by which Maximilian Joseph, the Bavarian sovereign, had bound himself to respect intact the national rights and customs of the Tyrolese people. The act by which he professed to inaugurate his rule over the Tyrol, dated January 14, 1806, promised "not only strongly to uphold the constitution of the country and the well-earned rights and privileges of the people, but also to promote their welfare." This pledge, moreover, was repeated again and again with an obstrusive reiteration, which, to those who knew what Bavaria meant by promoting a nation's welfare, was sufficient to awaken the gravest apprehensions.

In a certain sense amiable and benevolent, Maximilian of Bavaria was a true disciple of the Austrian Joseph II. Nominally Catholic, nominally liberal, and nominally philosophical, the political system adopted and carried out by the "reforming" emperor was in reality and result as anti-Catholic, despotic, and shallow, as any one of those many theories which have been devised for the sudden regeneration of mankind in the cabinets of self-conceited sophists. The Bavarian king lost no time in proving himself an adept in this pernicious school. Every thing the Tyrolese held dear, every thing that constituted their happiness in this life and their hopes for eternity, was attacked under the pretence that it was for their good that national honour, personal liberty, venerated customs, and religious objects of veneration, should be torn from them and trampled under foot by insolent strangers. "Jesuit obscurantism" was, of course, the cant cry with which the new measures were heralded. Vulgar Bavarian official insolence entered into a league with the infidel frivolity of the French philosophism of Voltaire and the Revolution, and hand in hand proceeded to "reform" the Tyrol.

The first blows were naturally aimed at what they called "superstition." The Tyrol abounded with small mountain chapels, whose artistic simplicity was a symbol of the pure, honest, and fervent piety which loved thus to remind itself of the nothingness of time and the goodness of God, wherever the labourer's toils were carried on, or the traveller's steps might take him. Even now, the few that remain of these monuments of humble devotion touch the heart of the non-Catholic visitor, and how much more that of the Catholic, more sweetly than the most magnificent achievements of Christian art in the rich centres of a luxurious population. But to the Bavarian and French illuminati these were hateful objects; and the Tyrolese saw them levelled to the ground with every mark of ridicule and contempt; while images, crucifixes, relics, long held in veneration and associated with the reminiscences of generations of faith, were destroyed, or, what was worse, sold to the Jews.

When religion was thus treated, liberty of course fared no better. In former times, no recruits for the Austrian service were levied by the emperor in the Tyrol, with the exception of those for the rifle-corps; and these enjoyed peculiar privileges of their own, electing their commanders and wearing their national dress. The Bavarians laughed at these rights; and an attempted military conscription served only to kindle the ardour of the mountaineers to a more strenuous determination to seize the first moment for throwing off the usurping yoke. The ancient Tyrolean diet was unceremoniously dissolved, the Bavarians not even thinking it worth while to preserve the semblance of independence; while they showed their contempt for Tyrolean nationality by abolishing the very name of the Tyrol, and calling the country "Southern Bavaria." By way of crowning these injuries with reckless insult, they actually sold by auction the ancient national edifice, or castle, which by a popular legend was held to confer on its possessor the lawful right to the sovereignty of the nation. New and exorbitant taxes were levied, and collected with every display of coarse and insolent brutality, among a people who hitherto had taxed themselves, and that with a gentle hand. Altogether, short of universal pillage, massacre, and confiscation, it would have been difficult for an unpopular government to have done more to exasperate the feelings of a conquered people to the highest pitch of indignation.

Such was the condition of affairs in the Tyrol, when Austria roused herself to an attempt to throw off the dominion of Napoleon. The French emperor was engaged in the Spanish Peninsula: the galling bitterness of the new dominion was felt to be more trying than all the abuses of the old German empire; while Napoleon's conduct towards the Pope, whom he had imprisoned in Rome itself, had roused the indignation of all good Catholics. In the beginning of the year 1809, Austria raised an army of four hundred thousand men, and issued proclamations, calling upon every true-hearted German to strike for the liberties of his country. We need not follow the course of the brief struggle that ensued, when Napoleon, dividing the eastern nations of Germany from the western, led his troops, with but one severe reverse at Aspern, from victory to victory; till the battle of Wagram annihilated the hopes of Austria, and the peace of Vienna saw her stripped of fresh portions of her territory, for the advantage of France, Bavaria, and Russia. It was in the Tyrol alone that for a time the cause of justice and religion seemed about to triumph. Had all Germans been like the brave and Catholic Tyrolese, there would have been no need of Waterloo. The record of their fruitless devotion, and the mournful end of their most distinguished leader, is among the saddest and most truly glorious episodes which adorn the history of Christian patriotism.

Andrew Hofer was at that time forty-two years of age. He was the landlord of an inn at Passeyr, in the Passeyrthal, a valley among the mountains about half-way between Innspruck and Trent, on the right hand of the road as the traveller journeys from the former to the latter town. Some years before the Bavarian usurpation, he had represented his native valley at the national diet, and had strenuously opposed the anti-Catholic measures which Joseph II. had been endeavouring to introduce among the Tyrolese. Later, he had served as captain of a rifle-corps against the French in 1795; and when, in 1805, the transference of the Tyrol to Bavaria took place, the Austrian Archduke John had parted from the patriotic innkeeper with a shake of the hand, and an expression of hope that they would meet again in better times.

Among his countrymen he possessed remarkable popularity. Tolerably well educated, and of that open, cordial, genial disposition which his countrymen dearly loved, he was as powerful in frame as he was pious in heart and upright in life. His make is described as Herculean in breadth; though he stooped in the shoulders, from his early carrying of heavy weights over the mountains. His voice was gentle and agreeable, his countenance handsome, and rendered striking by an immense dark beard, which hung almost to his waist, in accordance with a custom prevailing among the innkeepers of the valleys. Hofer, moreover, is reported to have cherished his beard with peculiar attention, in consequence of a wager of a pair of oxen which he had made with some of his friends. His portrait shows him in the ordinary dress of his class, with a low-crowned broad-brimmed hat, decorated with a black curling feather; a red waistcoat, across which were broad green braces of a peculiar make, supporting black chamois-leather breeches; and over all a loose green coat. His knees were bare, and his mighty legs encased in high boots. On his ample chest reposed his crucifix, a silver medal of St. George, and the gold medal and chain sent him by the emperor. To a stout black belt was attached his sword, literally his broadsword. His spirit was best seen when he was at his prayers; and his broad, honest, manly face shone with that deep and unaffected devotion which was the life-spring of his patriotism, and at once animated and chastened his undaunted courage. He dealt in wine, corn, and horses; his business-intercourse was extensive, and he was known and respected to the extreme Italian frontier of his country.

The moment that Austria believed that the hour was come for a general effort at bursting the intolerable bondage imposed by Napoleon, Hofer was summoned to Vienna, and the plans were laid for a rising among the mountaineers. The town-population was either too much under the control of Bavarian officials, or too lukewarm in its attachment to its religion and its old loyalty, to be taken into the arrangements. How well the peasantry were to be trusted is shown by the fact, that while, on a moderate estimate, not less than 60,000 men were cognisant of what was going on, and participators in the intended revolt, not one betrayed the secret. At Innspruck, the Bavarian commander Kinkel remained quietly with his army, directing his attention solely to the expected advance of an army from Austria, and utterly unconscious of the mine about to be sprung at his feet.

Suddenly the whole country burst into a flame. Unsuspected by their military rulers, many thousand Tyrolese were in arms, organised, commanded by duly-oppointed leaders, and waiting only for the signal agreed on, to meet and attack the Bavarians and the French troops then quartered in the Tyrol. On the **9th** of April the signal was given. Sawdust and little pieces of wood, with red flags fastened to them, were seen by the anxious eyes of the people to be floating down the stream of the Inn. The sky had been dark and gloomy, and favoured the midnight gathering of the peasant-soldiery. By three o'clock the van advanced up the Pusterthal; and in a few hours fires were lighted all over the mountain-heights, and the valleys re-echoed with the clanging of alarm-bells and the booming of distant guns.

Every where the insurgents were greeted with the most enthusiastic demonstration on the part of the peasantry. The village-bells rang as they passed; men, women, and children flocked out to cheer them. The aged and blind were brought out of their cottages to bless them, and pray for their victory: in crowds they gathered around them, shaking their hands, touching their clothes, and even kissing their horses.

The first blow fell upon a body of Bavarian sappers, who had been detached to blow up the bridge of St. Lorenzo, in the Pusterthal, in anticipation of an advance of the Austrian army. The Tyrolese riflemen, from their hiding-places, picked off the Bavarians as they approached to their work, and the entire detachment, amazed and terrified, took to flight. Wredef, their commander, however, speedily came up at the head of two battalions, and the fight began. The Bavarian artillery was quickly captured, and thrown into the river; but being joined by a strong detachment of French, the issue of the day for a time seemed doubtful. A small accession of Austrian horse turned the scale in favour of the mountaineers, and the French and Bavarians fled, suffering immense loss. The unerring rifles of the peasantry shot them down from every side; rocks and timber dashed down the cliffs upon their heads; and the day ended in a decisive victory.

Hofer was not present in person, being engaged with the peasantry of Passeyr, Meran, and Algund, in occupying a road near Sterzing, with the intention of dislodging another body of Bavarians there stationed. On the morning of the 11th the fight began, and the Bavarians for a time defied all Hofer's attempts; though they suffered frightfully from the Tyrolese rifles, the very artillerymen being shot down by the side of their guns. At last a waggon loaded with hay, and driven by a girl, the daughter of a tailor named Camper, advanced towards the Bavarians; behind which the Tyrolese advanced upon the open plain on which the Bavarians were stationed, protected by their artillery against a peasant host armed with pitchforks, spears, and every rude implement they could lay their hands on. The bullets whistled past the heroic girl, as she guided the characteristic screen, and shouted to her countrymen, "On with you! who cares for Bavarian dumplings?" A desperate struggle ensued, and the best officers of the Bavarians were killed, and the whole body either slain or made prisoners.

Meanwhile, a third party of peasantry had been rising in the lower valley of the Inn, whose aim was to seize upon Innspruck, and destroy the Bavarian power at its centre. A wealthy peasant, or farmer, was the leader of his countrymen, by name Joseph Speckbacher,—a man who showed extraordinary energies and heroism during the war now commencing. He was a tall and powerfully-built man, about forty years of age, stooping in his gait, with a serious and even sad countenance; though on the mention of the war, or of the interests of his country, his face gleamed with brightness, and he stood erect with sudden ardour. His father, who was superintendent of the salt-works at Halle, and had fought with distinction against the Bavarians, died when Joseph was but six years old. A few years afterwards his mother also died, and he was sent to school; but could not be taught either to read or write: he was of a wild, roving disposition, and the discipline of a school was intolerable to his untamed spirit. When he was twelve years old, he formed a connection with some others as wild as himself, and roamed about the Bavarian forest country, living a kind of poaching, rascally life, a source of annoyance to all whom he came across, and a disgrace to his name and country. In one of his expeditions, one of his companions was killed before his eyes by a Bavarian soldier; and from that day Speckbacher was struck with a deep sense of the degraded character of the life he had been leading. He instantly reformed, and the whole energies of his character were devoted to the duties of a respectable life. At twenty-seven years old he married a woman of some little property, who persuaded him to learn reading and writing. Thus making up for the deficiencies of his boyhood, he became a person of considerable importance in his native country; and in the war of independence exercised an authority over his fellow-countrymen of the same kind, though inferior in degree, to that possessed by Hofer himself. From every church-tower in the valley the alarm-bells pealed. Throughout the day women and children were employed in distributing in all quarters scraps of paper, on which was written "It is time!" As soon as night arrived, Speckbacher seized upon the city of Hall. Lighting numerous watch-fires on one side of the walls, as if he were about to attack it on that quarter, he himself, in the darkness, went round to the opposite gates, and presented himself as a common passenger for admittance. The *ruse* succeeded; the gates were opened; Speckbacher with his followers rushed in and made prisoners of the garrison, amounting to 400 men.

On the morning of the 11th, the attack on Innspruck began. Each party had made what preparations were possible; the Bavarians placing artillery on the bridges, and taking up the best positions for defence; the Tyrolese blocking up every outlet for escape for the enemy, whom they already regarded as vanquished; blockading the roads leading from the city with barricades of trees, and destroying the bridges over the streams. Early on the morning of the 12th, a body of the peasantry advanced, armed with muskets, and poles with bayonets fastened to the ends, and seized one of the bridges leading to the city. The impetuosity of their charge overwhelmed the Bavarians, many of whom were killed at their guns before they had time to discharge them. Shouting "Vivat Franz! Down with the Bavarians!" they drove the troops before them, striking them down with the butt-ends of their muskets, forcing them headlong into the river, and closely following the remainder to the city-gates, and entering with them.

It was now 9 o'clock in the morning, and the battle became

general. Such of the Bavarians as were stationed on the roofs and at the windows of the houses, were attacked with so fierce a fire, that they threw down their arms in the streets and begged for mercy. In other houses the citizens fought for the peasants, and murderous discharges from the houses and towers were poured upon the soldiery. Dittfurt, the second in command under Kinkel, fought desperately in the streets, encouraging, entreating, and commanding his men; and at length, almost alone, threw himself upon a body of the Tyrolese who were in possession of the house of the commander-in-chief, and pressing him to surrender. He had already received two wounds in his body; a third ball now struck him in the breast; he fell on his knees, while the blood gushed from his mouth. Some peasants came near to make him prisoner, when he raised himself, and called feebly to his men to advance, and not fly like cowards. A fourth ball smote his head, and he dropped insensible. Four days afterwards he died, cursing and blaspheming in wild delirium. He was deservedly abhorred by the peasants, having made himself peculiarly obnoxious by the cruelties he had practised upon them in the discharge of functions sufficiently odious in themselves. He had boasted, that "with his regiment and a couple of squadrons he could disperse the ragged mob." As he lay dying in the guard-house, in the midst of the peasants he had scorned and persecuted, he asked who had been their leader. "No one," they said; "we fought for God, for the emperor, and for our country." "That is strange," said he; "for I saw a leader repeatedly pass me on a white horse." This saying produced a conviction in the minds of the Tyrolese that St. James, the patron of the city of Innspruck, had fought among them.

By 11 o'clock, Innspruck was in the hands of the patriots. The Bavarian cavalry, at the beginning of the day, had done much execution among them; but the Tyrolese, adopting the only feasible plan of fighting with horsemen, had dispersed whenever they charged, keeping up at the same time an irregular but slaughtering fire, which mowed down the soldiers, unable to reach their adversaries. When the infantry surrendered, a panic struck them, and they fled in all directions, heedless of their officers. The Tyrolese, however, stopped their flight; and rushing on them with pitchforks, forced them to dismount, and seized the horses for their own service. A small party at first escaped, and fled from the city; but Speckbacher pursued and made them prisoners. He captured also a picket which had been stationed on one of the bridges, and had taken refuge in a convent. Seizing an immense fir-tree, fifty of the peasants swung it in their arms as a battering-ram, with which they burst open the convent-gates, and carried off the discomfited soldiers.

Thus ended the second day of the war. **It was closed** amidst rejoicings characteristic of the loyalty **of the** Tyrolese peasantry. Innspruck resounded with shouts and acclamations. The imperial eagle was taken down from the tomb of Maximilian, decorated with ribbons, and carried in procession through the streets; it was then fixed in a house, and crowds flocked in to look at it, and kiss it. On a triumphal arch, hastily raised, were placed the portraits of the Emperor and the Archduke John, with lighted candles all around; while every passer-by knelt in respect, and cried "Long live the Emperor!"

Wearied at length with the watching of the previous night, the conflict of the morning, and the rejoicings of the day, the victors fell asleep, many in the city, many in the neighbouring orchards, and sought a brief repose. It was indeed to be brief; for at 3 o'clock on the following morning (the 13th) the alarm-bells again clanged forth from the city-towers and the neighbouring villages. The French were upon them in strength, in company with fresh Bavarian troops. The night was scarcely over, when they had forced their way through the pass where Hofer was stationed, though with severe losses from the peasants' rifles. A lieutenant, with an advanced guard, approached the city-gates, and had scarcely passed the triumphal arch, where the pictures of the emperor and archduke were fixed, when a ball struck him dead from his horse. The gates were instantly barricaded with every available instrument. Casks and waggons blocked up the road-way; the house-doors were closed, and every preparation made for a bloody street-fight. In an incredibly short time the conflict was ended in the city. Two hundred of the assailants lay dead, and the remainder retreated to the main army, which lay on a rising ground in the neighbourhood. The Tyrolese offered the commander terms of capitulation, which were instantly rejected, and the attack began. The impetuosity and fire of the peasantry overwhelmed both French and Bavarians. The slaughter was immense; and by half-past eight o'clock in the forenoon, terms of surrender were actually signed, and the whole body capitulated. The victors returned into Innspruck in triumph, the band of the captives leading the way, and compelled to play in honour of their conquerors. The prisoners amounted to the immense number of 8000 infantry, 1000 cavalry, with two generals, ten staff-officers, and above 100 officers of lower grades.

The greatness of the Tyrolese showed itself most conspicuously in this moment of triumph. Irritated as they had been by usurpation, insult, cruelty, and tyranny, they stayed their hands from every species of retaliation, treating their prisoners with the utmost humanity. One man alone suffered any thing from them, and that rather as a joke than as serious infliction: a tax-gatherer, who had boasted that he would grind down the people till they would gladly eat hay to support their wretched lives, was forced to swallow a quantity of hay for his dinner. Their heroic nobleness met the usual return with which the mercy of Christians is repaid by the savage, unscrupulous, and ungrateful world. A report was industriously spread that the Tyrolese had murdered the prisoners in cold blood; and Napoleon, with his usual lying effrontery, was guilty of the infamy of issuing a proclamation of outlawry against Chastelan, who soon joined the Tyrolese as their military leader, condemning him, if taken prisoner, to be shot within four-and-twenty hours. A year afterwards, when Berthier, one of Napoleon's marshals, was at Vienna, as envoy to the court of Austria, he met Chastelan, and had the hardihood to turn the whole of this piece of villany into a jest.

The peasantry were now masters in their own country, and the Bavarian authority was for the time destroyed. A few skirmishes and struggles took place, but with no decisive result upon the actual condition of either party. By the beginning of May, however, Napoleon was in a position to attack the Tyrolese with forces against which resistance must be in the end hopeless. He sent a considerable body of troops, under Lefebvre, a brutal German of the merciless old military school, who made the people feel in full force the frightful horrors of war. Every leader who fell into his hands he shot like a traitor, and his troops committed every species of outrage upon the unresisting people of the villages. At the pass of Staub, on Ascension-day, many of the Tyrolese had left their post for the purpose of hearing Mass in the church, and those who remained were surprised by Lefebvre's soldiers, and, after a noble struggle, overpowered, and ferociously butchered on the spot. At the town of Schwartz, the most horrible cruelties were perpetrated. The Bavarians, in superior numbers, and after a prolonged conflict with the Tyrolese under Speckbacher, finally possessed themselves of the town, burnt it to the ground, and murdered every one of the inhabitants, hanging hundreds of them to the trees, and nailing their hands to their heads. At the village of Vomp, the Bavarians set fire to the houses to the sound of drums and hautboys, and shot the inhabitants as they attempted to escape from the flames.

Yet not once did these noble mountaineers retaliate. Their honest, hearty souls knew no law but that of the Gospel, and their only mode of venting their feelings lay in a rustic jest. The Bavarians then, as now, were notorious for their fondness for beer and the coarse lumpiness of their persons, and the Tyrolese accordingly nicknamed them "Bavarian hogs;" and when they came within hearing, were in the habit of saluting them with the usual country noises with which pigs were driven along, crying to them "Tschu, tschu, tschu! — Natsch, natsch!" On one occasion, indeed, some one proposed to requite the Bavarian atrocities by sending back the prisoners maimed in one ear, so that they might be recognised if found again fighting against the Tyrolese; but Hofer would not hear of the cruelty for a moment.

Disasters now followed close upon one another: the Austrian officers began to despair, or yielded to cowardice; and Hofer's energies were taxed to the utmost to prevent an entire disorganisation of their forces and the ruin of the revolt. Napoleon's defeat at Aspern, on the 21st and 22d of May, gave new hopes to the Tyrolese patriots. Two days before that date, Innspruck had fallen into the hands of the French and Bavarians; but now the sudden recal of Lefebvre to Germany inspirited the undaunted peasantry, and they gathered together with extraordinary rapidity and resolution. Hofer was ably seconded by a courageous, though somewhat headlong German, Eisenstecken, who had been appointed as his adjutant by the Austrian commander-in-chief. Speckbacher, a giant in strength, with the eye of a mountain-eagle, and unsurpassed in readiness and daring, was also at his side. Above all, the "fighting Capuchin," Father Joachim Haspinger, with a brother-friar, Peter Thalguter, now appeared on the scene, exercising an astonishing influence upon the minds of a race like the Tyrolese, who valued above all things the two qualities of pure devotion and personal courage. The Capuchins entered into the thickest of the fight, and struck down their adversaries with blows from heavy wooden crosses; and being young and athletic men, they did great execution. Hofer addressed the following characteristic proclamation to his fellow-countrymen:

"Dear Brothers of the Upper Innthal!—For God, the Emperor, and our dear native country!

"To-morrow, early in the morning, is fixed for the attack. With the help of our holy Mother, we will seize and destroy the Bavarians; and we confide ourselves to the beloved Jesus. Come to our assistance; but if you fancy yourselves wiser than Divine Providence, we will do without you.

"ANDREW HOFER."

On the 29th of May a struggle took place which once more made the Tyrolese masters in their native country. Speckbacher, with six hundred men, attacked the Bavarians on the bridge of Hall, drove them back, and destroyed the bridge.

The Tyrolese were in possession of the farm of Rainerhof; and thrice the Bavarians renewed the attack upon it, and were thrice repulsed. During this fight at the farm another of those incidents took place which showed the intensity of the feeling which animated the patriotic peasantry. A young woman who lived in the house brought out a small cask of wine to refresh the Tyrolese, and walked up with it on her head to the scene of battle, heedless of the fire of the Bavarians. A ball struck the cask, and she was forced to let it go; but instantly recovering herself, she clapped her thumb on the hole made by the bullet, and called to her fellow-countrymen to come instantly and drink the wine.

The battle lasted through the day; the Capuchin especially distinguishing himself, and showing great military talent. At one moment he was on the point of being run through the body by a Bavarian soldier, when a Tyrolese rifleman saved him by shooting the Bavarian dead on the spot. At night a kind of truce was agreed to, of which the Bavarians took advantage to retire during the night, wrapping their cannon wheels and horses' hoofs in hay, to avoid all noise, and enjoining silence among the troops under pain of death. At Hall Speckbacher attempted, but in vain, to stop their retreat; his own son, a child of ten years old, actually picking up the enemies' balls as they fell around him, and putting them in his hat, till his father had him carried off by force and placed in a spot of safety. A similar feat of hardihood was displayed shortly afterwards by Speckbacher himself. In disguise he entered the fortress of Cuffstein, still in the possession of the Bavarians; paid a visit undetected to the governor, extinguished a lighted grenade with his hat, spoilt the working of the fire-engines, and cut the cables of some vessels that were moored beneath the fortress-walls.

The triumph of the Tyrolese was, however, short. The battle of Wagram once more laid Austria prostrate at Napoleon's feet; and the conqueror compelled the emperor to withdraw all his troops from the Tyrol. The peasantry now began to feel how vast was the difference between their own heroic devotion to the house of Austrian and the mercenary services of German commanders. The moment that Napoleon turned his arms in large force against the Tyrol, the Austrian leaders, Buol and Hormayr, hurried their retreat from the devoted land, issuing a proclamation as they fled recommending the Tyrolese to the care of Lefebvre, the brutal general whom Napoleon had placed at the head of the invading forces. These forces amounted to the large number of between thirty and forty thousand, and were composed of French, Bavarians, and Saxons.

At such a juncture it was impossible but that the courage of the peasantry should falter. Hofer himself never quailed. When Hormayr, the selfish German, who all along had begrudged to the native leaders their natural influence over their countrymen, now hastened away, Hofer said to him, "Well, I will undertake the government; and as long as it is the will of God, I name myself Andrew Hofer, host of the Sand at Passeyr, Count of the Tyrol." Hormayr, who was of the infidel school of modern Germany, and ridiculed alike the faith and the loyalty of the Tyrolese, laughed at language so little known in courts and camps, and went his timorous way. Returning then to his own house, Hofer met Speckbacher, himself infected with a general dismay, flying from the country in a carriage with some Austrian officers. As he passed him, he cried, "Wilt thou also desert thy country?" and sought a brief hiding-place in a cave among the cliffs overhanging his own valleys. There he poured out his soul in prayer; and issuing forth, betook himself to the monastery of the brave Capuchin Haspinger. Haspinger yielded to his ardent entreaties, and a conference of a few patriots was summoned to concert measures for attacking the advancing French. Suddenly they were joined by Speckbacher, whose heart had been smitten by the passing words of Hofer, as he sat by the side of his Austrian companions, and who had left them at the first resting-place, and was now returned to fight once more for the good cause.

The struggle soon began, and again the heroism and military genius of the peasants and their humble leaders triumphed over invading power; and but for the personal triumphs of Napoleon elsewhere, would have been permanently victorious. The history of this last phase in the Tyrolese war is one of the most melancholy of the many mournful episodes which every where attended the terrible career of Napoleon. In the whole course of the French revolutionary wars, and the subsequent conflicts in which Napoleon Bonaparte shook Europe to its foundations, two spots stand out pre-eminent for their loyalty, their piety, their unexpected skill, and the extraordinary success which crowned their arms until subdued by powers utterly overwhelming. And nowhere was the reckless wickedness of the conquerors more signally displayed than in their treatment of the noble leaders who long led their fellow-countrymen to victory. These spots were La Vendée and the Tyrol; both of them places where Catholicism still ruled in the hearts of a united and simple people, and produced fruits of innocence in peace, as conspicuous as were the fruits of heroism and mercy which it produced in time of war.

At first the advancing French were unopposed. Lefebvre entered Innspruck, and with his usual brutality plundered and burnt the villages in his course. The agreement which had been made between the Austrian Emperor and the French had stipulated for an amnesty to all engaged in the former war; but in place of an amnesty, Lefebvre published a list of proscribed names, of which of course Hofer's was the chief. It included also such of the noble and upper classes as had fought with the peasantry. These savage acts set the whole country in flames. The whole of the Tyrol, says the historian Menezl, flew to arms. The young men placed in their hats the bunch of rosemary gathered by the girls of their heart, the more aged a peacock's plume, the symbol of the house of Hapsburg; all carried the rifle, so murderous in their hands. They made cannons of larch-wood, bound with iron rings, which did good service; they raised *abattis*, blew up rocks, piled immense masses of stone on the extreme edges of the precipitous rocks commanding the narrow vales, in order to hurl them on the advancing foe; and so directed the timber-slide in the forest-covered mountains, or those formed of logs, by means of which the timber was run into the valleys, that they might command the most important passes and bridges, and so enable the people to shoot immense trees on the advancing troops with tremendous velocity.

Lefebvre divided his army into four divisions, with which he attacked the heart of the Tyrol simultaneously from as many different points. On the 4th of August a desperate battle took place between one of these *corps d'armée*, consisting chiefly of Saxons, and the Tyrolese, who were under the command of the Capuchin, on the heights above the town of Oberau. The conflict was frightful and bloody. The Tyrolese adopted their usual tactics, and harassed the Saxons with incessant firing, and that never-ending repetition of assault which was so paralysing to regular soldiery of the old German school. The Saxons had got possession of the town of Oberau, and when the fortune of the day turned in the patriots' favour, they stormed the town, and took prisoners the whole of the Saxons, who had not succeeded in cutting their way through the Tyrolese and joining the main division. Nearly a thousand Saxons were left dead on the ground. An immense number were captured; seven hundred of whom contrived to escape from their guards, and were recaptured by the armed women and girls. The courage of the women was indeed one of the most striking proofs, at once of the indomitable spirit of the people and of the universality of the horror of Bavarian rule. And these martial feats were not confined to the female peasantry alone. The Baroness of Sternbach, mounted on horseback and armed with pistols, accompanied the patriots, and shared in the command. In the end, she was seized in her own castle, imprisoned in a house of correction at Munich, and then carried to Strasburg, deprived of her estates, insulted, and threatened with death. Her courage never failed her.

A similar fate to that which the Saxons encountered befel the invading division which marched up the valley of the Inn. In the darkness of the night of the 8th of August, after being repulsed by the Tyrolese, this body of troops, under Burscheidt, retreated as silently as possible over the bridge of

Poutlaz. The infantry passed unheard, with stealthy steps; but when the cavalry followed, the noise of the horses' feet betrayed them to the watchful mountaineers, who were posted on the heights above. Instantly the crash came. Rocks and trees were rolled headlong upon the bridge, overwhelming men and horses together: the darkness adding fresh terrors to the attack, and the fallen bodies blocking up the road to those who were behind. The commander, with a few of his troops, escaped to Innspruck; the rest were all either killed or captured.

The third division met a similar reception in the Pusterthal. Twelve hundred of the invaders lay dead on the field, and their companions retreated in hopelessness. As for the fourth division, it made no attempt to penetrate into the heart of the country.

Other conflicts took place between the mountaineers and the Germans under their principal leaders. The troops commanded by Lefebvre were almost cut to pieces by the peasantry headed by the Capuchin and Speckbacher. The Tyrolese performed prodigies of strength and valour. They dragged the cavalry from their horses, and killed them with their staves; Lefebvre himself scarcely escaped their hands, although he had taken the precaution to dress like a common soldier, to avoid being made the especial mark of the riflemen. One peasant is reported to have actually carried a three-pounder, which he had captured, on his shoulders across the mountains. An old man, above eighty years of age, grappling in deadly struggle with a Saxon soldier, shouted, "In the name of God!" and threw himself with his foe headlong down the precipice on which he had been posted. As elsewhere, the peasantry were not without the help of the nobles; and Count Mohr was especially conspicuous among the people of Vinstchgau. In the midst of all this slaughter and triumph, the Christian spirit of the Tyrolese never failed to soften the horrors of warfare; and they carried their wounded enemies carefully to the neighbouring villages, to be tended and healed.

The 13th of August drove the Bavarians out of the country once more. The Capuchin said Mass for the Tyrolese in the open air, and then led them on to the assault at Isel. Four hundred Bavarians speedily lay dead in heaps, crushed beneath the clubs and stalwart arms of the impetuous mountaineers. At night the enemy fled, and the whole valley of the Inn blazed with the watch-fires of the victors; while Lefebvre kept his own fires burning to deceive the Tyrolese into a belief that he was still encamped close by.

On the 15th, the Festival of the Assumption, Hofer made a kind of triumphal entry into the capital of his native country, now a third time delivered by him from its invaders. It was now that the purity of his patriotism and his religious honesty appeared in their brightest light. Forced by the prostration of the Austrians to assume the position of a military dictator, he used his power solely with a view to the preservation of the constitution of his country, and to the enforcement of the laws of religion and of public order. The disturbances which in the agitation of the times had begun in Innspruck, ceased the moment his authority was felt in exercise. His first work was to order a general thanksgiving to Almighty God for the success of the Tyrolese; and the festival was celebrated throughout the country with the deepest devotion and utmost solemnity. He instituted a search for stolen goods—including those taken from the Bavarians themselves—in every house in Innspruck; and imposed a heavy fine on every one who had secreted property not his own, however inconsiderable in value.

The title he assumed was that of Imperial Commandant of the Tyrol; and the proclamations and edicts which he issued were obeyed with the most scrupulous readiness by the people. He did not set himself, says the historian before quoted, above his equals, and followed his former simple mode of life. The Emperor of Austria sent him a golden chain and three thousand ducats,—the first money received by the Tyrol from Austria; but Hofer's pride was not raised by this mark of favour, and the naïveté of his reply to those who brought the gifts was a subject of ridicule to those who valued court-ceremoniousness above hearty simplicity. "Sirs," said he, "I thank you. I have no news for you to-day. I have, it is true, three couriers on the road, and the Schwantz ought long to have been here; I expect the rascal every hour." He permitted no pillage, and no disorderly conduct; and guarded public morals with such strictness, as to publish an order against the indelicate mode of female dressing which had been imported by the French, of which, he said, "many of his good fellow-soldiers and defenders of their country have complained." The conclusion of this proclamation is too characteristic of the homely honesty of the man to be omitted. "It is hoped," it wound up, "that these women will, by better behaviour, preserve themselves from the punishment of God; and in case of the contrary, must solely blame themselves should they find themselves disagreeable covered with dirt.—Andrew Hofer, chief in command in the Tyrol." It may safely be said that this document stands unique among the proclamations of victorious soldiers.

Another of his proclamations may be given at full length, as showing what sort of man he was; and as standing in striking contrast with the "general orders" and "despatches" which we are accustomed to see from the pens of the generals and statesmen who are strangers to the principles which animated the noble-hearted Tyrolese. Some degree of discontent and ill-feeling had arisen in the southern part of the Tyrol, during the absence of the commandant of that part of the country, and the people had treated the troops with incivility and harshness. This unpatriotic conduct called forth the singular phenomenon of an order from the commander-in-chief; not as is the case in ordinary warfare, enjoining the soldiery to spare the people, but bidding the people treat the soldiery with consideration. Hastening to Botzen, Hofer quieted the irritation by the following:

"BEST-BELOVED SOUTH TYROLEANS,

"It is with great displeasure that I have learnt your ill-treatment of my troops. I publish now, my dear brave countrymen and brothers in arms, this proclamation, that the well-thinking may know how to behave to those who are conducting themselves so ill. From my heart, which beats for you all, I detest robbery and depredations of every sort; I hate contributions and extortions; and be assured that I will not pardon these mean actions.

"It is the duty of every brave defender of his country to watch **over** the honour, and cultivate **the** affection of his neighbour, **that** he may **not incur** the displeasure of the Almighty, who defends us so miraculously. **Dear** brothers in arms, recollect yourselves. Against whom **do** we fight? Against friends or against foes? Against our enemies we have fought **and** conquered, and will still fight against them; but not **against** our brothers, who have been already so much oppressed. Consider that we ought to protect and assist **our** fellow-creatures, who are unable to carry arms. What would the world, the witness of our conduct,—what would our posterity say, were we not to fulfil these **duties**? The glory of the Tyrolese would be lost for **ever.**

"Dear countrymen, the whole world is astonished at our deeds. The name of the Tyrolese is already immortalised; and it is only necessary that we should fulfil our duty towards God and our neighbour, to complete a work so gloriously **begun.**

"**Brave** countrymen and brothers in arms, supplicate the Creator **of** all things, who is alike able to defend or destroy kingdoms at His pleasure, and He will guide you. Who at this moment would wish to disturb our tranquillity? **I summon** all the clergy, and those who are unable to bear arms, to assist and protect my **troops, and** such as are not able to render them **any service, to implore God on** their knees to bless **our endeavours.**

"**I further** acquaint all public bodies, towns, villages, **and my** troops in general, that as so many irregularities have happened in consequence of the conduct of commandants of their **own** choosing, during the absence of Joseph Morandell, whom I had appointed commandant **of the** Southern Tyrol, no proclamations, orders, or arrangements **are** to be attended to, unless issued and signed by him.

"ANDREW HOFER,
Commander-in-Chief of the Tyrol.

" *Bolzen, 4th Sept. 1809.*"

Such was the internal government of the Tyrol, when all was lost through the faithlessness of that court which Hofer and his devoted followers had served so well. History affords few more striking illustrations of the words of king David, "Put not your trust in princes," than the desertion of these heroic peasantry by the "noble" house of Hapsburg, when Napoleon's renewed victories brought about the treaty of Vienna, concluded on the 10th of October. In this compact *the Tyrol was not even mentioned.* The self-sacrificing people were handed over to the tender mercies of bloody and despotic France and revengeful Bavaria, without a word of stipulation in their favour. A heartless manifesto was despatched to them by the Archduke John,—the very man who had been foremost in inciting them to support him and his house, when Austria rose against Napoleon, in which he simply bade them disperse, and offer no longer a useless resistance. He added not a hint of security against the savage vindictiveness of their enemies, not a word of apology for Austria in having thrown overboard her solemn pledges *never* to forsake the Tyrolese.

Vast bodies of French and Germans now entered the Tyrol; but the people, as a nation, could rise no more against them, for their heart was broken. In some parts they fought with the energy of desperation against the invaders, accounting nothing so miserable as submission to such rulers, in whose eyes nothing was held sacred. The inhabitants of the Passeyr and Algund flocked to Hofer, and compelled him to lead them to the last dying struggle. For a brief space the patriots seemed about to conquer. At Meran, they cast from the heights such numbers of the invading soldiery, that it was said that the French fell like autumn-leaves into the town. A division of cavalry which attempted to surround them was actually annihilated. Rusca, who led bands of Italian brigands in the interest of the French, lost 500 dead and 1700 prisoners.

They still retained, however, their love of humour and their Christian mercifulness. A French major who had formerly fired a village in cold blood fell into their hands; but at the interference of the Capuchin his life was spared. At one place, while the French artillery was bombarding their position, the peasants set up a huge barn-door as a mark for the **gunners to aim at**, and at every shot they thrust up a ludicrous stuffed figure by way of joke. All, however, was vain; resistance gradually died away, and the French hanged and shot **the most** distinguished of the patriot leaders to their hearts' content.[a] These courageous men died as they had lived, quailing neither on the field of battle nor at the place of judicial murder.

Hofer, with **his** wife and child, took refuge among the heights of the Tyrolese Alps. **He** was implored by his country**men to fly; but he would never** leave the soil where he had **been born, and of whose people** he had deserved so well. A traitorous priest, one Donay, **in the pay of** France, discovered and betrayed **his** hiding-place; and on the night of the 27th of January **a body** of *three thousand six hundred* French and Italian troops went to seize him in his mountain refuge. The calm dignity with which Hofer surrendered himself could not save him from the brutal insults of the Italians. They tore his beard, pinioned him, and dragged him half-naked and barefoot over the ice and snow down the cliffs into the valley. He was instantly put into a carriage and despatched to Mantua. His death was predetermined by Napoleon; and orders were sent from Milan to shoot him within four-and-twenty hours. Four hours before his death he wrote the following letter to his brother-in-law:

"My beloved **wife is to have Mass said** for my soul at St. Marie's. **She is to have prayers offered** in both parishes, and **is to** let the under-landlord give my friends soup, meat, and **half-a-bottle** of wine each. The money I had with me I have distributed to the poor; as for the rest, settle **my** accounts **with** the people as justly as you can. All in **this** world, fare**well**, till we meet in heaven to praise **God** eternally. Death appears to me so easy, that **my eyes have not** once been wet on account of **it**.

---

[a] During the pillage of the monastery of Seeben by the French, a nun threw herself down a precipice to escape from their hands.

"Written at 5 o'clock in the morning; and at 9 o'clock I set off, with the aid of all the saints, on my journey to God."

On his way to the place of execution he passed the barracks where other Tyrolese prisoners were confined. They crowded round him, fell on their knees, and begged his blessing. He blessed them, and entreated their pardon for any wrong he might have done them; and declared his conviction that in the end the Tyrol would return to the rule of the Emperor Francis. To Manifesti, the priest who attended him to the last, and to whom he made his confession, he gave his money to be distributed among his countrymen, his snuffbox, and his rosaries. Twelve soldiers were drawn up to execute the bloody decree. The drummer in attendance presented a handkerchief to Hofer to bind his eyes, and he was bid to kneel down in the usual way. He declined the handkerchief, and exclaimed with a strong voice, "I have been used to stand upright before my God, and I will stand to deliver up to Him the soul He gave." He then gave the signal to fire; but, whether from the agitation of the soldiers or not, they were obliged to fire thrice before he lay dead. The first volley brought him on his knees, the second stretched him on the ground, a third shot released his soul. It was the 20th of February, 1810, when this horrible murder was perpetrated.

Afterwards, when the Austrian dominion was re-established in the Tyrol and the north of Italy, the Tyrolese brought their hero's body back to his native mountains. A marble monument to his memory stands in a church at Innspruck, and his family were ennobled.

Of his two most distinguished companions, Haspinger the Capuchin soon escaped to Vienna; where also, after extraordinary sufferings and dangers, Speckbacher arrived to taste the proverbial ingratitude of princes. The Bavarians hunted him among the mountains in troops, swearing to cut his skin into boot-straps. At Dux his flight was stopped by snow, and the Bavarians attacked a house where he took refuge. He leapt through the roof and got away, though hurt in so doing. For twenty-seven days he wandered starving and frozen, amongst the forests, now buried in snow. For four days together not a morsel passed his lips. At length he came by chance upon a mountain-hut where his wife and children had hidden themselves. The Bavarians tracked him, and advanced to the capture; he seized a sledge lying by, placed it upon his shoulders, and walked out to meet them as if he were a domestic employed in his ordinary labour, and passed undetected. Then he hid himself in a cave on the Gemshaken, from which the thawing snows of springs, which slide down in masses to the valleys, carried him down one day for a mile and a half; he disengaged himself at last from the snow, but one of his legs was dislocated, and he could not regain his cave. In dreadful agony he crept to a neighbouring hut, where he found two men, who took him to his own home at Rinn, where his wife and children were returned. To his dismay he found the Bavarians in possession, and his only chance of escape lay in being buried in a hole beneath the bed of the cows, where his servant Zoppel daily brought him food. So imminent was the peril of discovery, that even his wife was left uninformed of his presence. For seven weeks he lay hid in this living tomb, till he was sufficiently recruited to cross the mountains, now free from snow. He reached Vienna; but the royal house he had so faithfully served had no smiles for him in his adversity. He bought a little property with the remnant of his possessions; but he was unable to pay the whole of the purchase-money, and he lost all he had. At length he would have been reduced to beggary, had not he actually entered as steward into the service of Hofer's son, who had been better treated by the emperor, and had received an estate at his hands.

When Napoleon finally fell, the Tyrol passed again to Austria, and now remains under its dominion. It is still one of the brightest spots of Christendom; the home of diligence, labour, simplicity, piety, and happiness. The seeds of decay and the elements of revolution are scattered far and wide in almost every other country in Europe; but if there is one people who gives promise of a long-lasting vigorous vitality, to be destroyed only by the overwhelming pressure of external force, it is the race which still cherishes the memory of Andrew Hofer.—*Rambler.*

THE DEATH OF HOFER.

(From the German of Julius Mosen.—By James Clarence Mangan.)

At Mantua long had lain in chains
 The gallant Hofer bound;
  But now his day of doom was come
  At morn the deep roll of the drum
Resounded o'er the soldiered plains.
 O Heaven! with what a deed of dole
 The hundred thousand wrongs were crowned
  Of trodden down Tyrol!

With iron-fettered arms and hands
 The hero moved along
  His heart was calm, his eye was clear—
  Death was for traitor slaves to fear!
He oft araid his mountain bands,
 Where Inn's dark wintry waters roll,
 Had faced it with his battle-song,
  The Sandwirth of Tyrol.

Anon he passed the fortress-wall,
 And heard the wail that broke
  From many a brother thrall within.
  "Farewell!" he cried "Soon may you win
Your liberty! God shield you all!
 Lament not me! I see my goal.
 Lament the land that wears the yoke,
  Your land and mine, Tyrol!"

So through the files of musqueteers
 Undauntedly he passed,
  And stood within the hollow square.
  Well might he glance around him there,
And proudly think on by—gone years!
 Amid such serfs *his* bannerol,
 Thank God! had never braved the blast
  On thy green hills, Tyrol!

They bade him kneel; but he with all
 A patriot's truth replied—
  "I kneel alone to God on high—
  As thus I stand so dare I die,
As oft I fought so let me fall!
 "Farewell!"—his breast a moment swoll
 With agony he strove to hide—
  "My Kaiser and Tyrol!"

No more emotion he betrayed.
 Again he bade farewell
  To Francis and the faithful men
  Who girt his throne. His hands were then
Unbound for prayer, and thus he prayed.—
 "God of the Free, receive my soul!
 And you, slaves, "Fire!" So bravely fell
  Thy foremost man, Tyrol!

MAITLAND ON THE REFORMATION.

(From the Rambler.)

Essays on Subjects connected with the Reformation in England. By the Rev. S. R. Maitland, D.D., F.R.S. F.S.A. London, Rivingtons.

"CLEAR your mind of cant, sir!" said the great philosopher of common sense one day to his *fidus Achates*, or to one of that listening crowd to whom the sage was wont to dispense wisdom in sentences as blunt as pithy. We do not, indeed, remember whether this admirable advice was given by Johnson in reply to one of the ordinary Boswellian platitudes respecting liberty of conscience and religious persecution; but whether it was or not, Dr. Maitland might very appropriately have prefixed it as a motto to the very remarkable volume whose title the reader has just perused. The late librarian of Lambeth is in truth one of the most pertinacious and most successful of the foes to theological *cant* whom our age has had the good fortune to produce. "Pamphlet Maitland," as he is sometimes termed, has written and published above a score of books, letters, and pamphlets, directed solely to the smashing of some of the vulgar fallacies which supply the Protestant world with that ample store of parrot-phrases with which it seeks to pacify the cravings of our time for accurate historical knowledge, and for some real, honest, consistent system of religious belief. And now he has added to our libraries a goodly volume, shewing up the deceits and trickeries of the standard authorities for Protestant historical belief, and winding up with an elaborate defence of the good nature, Christian sincerity, and piety of—"bloody" Bishop Bonner!

Dr. Maitland's *Dark Ages* is known to every well-informed student, and therefore we shall now say nothing of the good service he did to the cause of the Catholic religion by the publication of that curious and interesting book. Notwithstanding the eminently unpopular character of its sentiments, the

Dark Ages has reached a second edition, and it has left no educated person the slightest pretence for repeating the commonplace cant respecting those times which have been truly said to be *dark*, inasmuch as people in general knew nothing whatsoever concerning them. The present volume of Essays on the Reformation will, we fear, hardly find an equal number of readers, partly because the subjects on which it treats are too uniform in character, partly because the book has necessarily a very large number of quotations, and partly because it strikes mercilessly on prejudices still dearer to the minds of Englishmen than even the long-cherished belief in the wickedness, ignorance, and superstition of the middle ages. Persons who are quite ready to be convinced that the mediæval period abounded in men of genius, piety, and learning, and who will revel in Dr. Maitland's stories of manuscripts, libraries, and studious monks, are not yet quite prepared to be told that the "martyrs" under Queen Mary very often richly deserved the fate they got, and that Bonner, Bishop of London, was a good, kind-hearted Christian, much more desirous of saving people's souls than of burning their bodies, and oftentimes an unwilling administrator of the cruel laws of the age in which he lived. Such, however, is the gist of these Essays, though their author is as stout a Protestant as ever, and as zealous a believer in the Church of England as by law established as when he first took orders within her communion. We shall now proceed to give our readers an account of the arguments by which our author establishes his views, and shall then offer a few remarks on the general question of persecution for religious opinions, as applicable both to the age of the English Reformation and to our own and future periods.

It is an historical fact (tolerable or intolerable, according to a person's own ideas,) that nearly 300 persons were put to death in England during the reign of Queen Mary, for some reason or other connected with their religious belief. Dr. Maitland puts the number at 277. Whatever the exact number, however, the fact is certain, that something approaching to 300 men and women—a few of the tender sex being included in the list—were either burned alive, or in some other way deprived of life, for some cause immediately consequent upon the propagation of Protestantism. The common English idea is, that all these persons were martyrs to the Gospel; that is, that they were pious and devoted Christians, whose sole crime it was that they would not worship images, believe in transubstantiation, or uphold the enormities and vices of the Roman Catholic priesthood. The sovereign of the realm is pictured by the imagination as a ravaging wolf among harmless lambs, accompanied and abetted in her murderous attacks by two other wolves—Gardiner, Bishop of Winchester, and Bonner, Bishop of London. The ferocious Queen is supposed to have been a singular example of blood-thirstiness and cruelty, in a country of piety, moderation, and enlightenment; and the two Bishops, her instruments in bloodshedding, to have been two devilish butchers, whose thirst for blood was equal to their devotion to the supremacy of the Pope of Rome, and to what the Anglican liturgy used to term "his detestable enormities."

When, however, we have succeeded in "clearing our minds of cant," we find that this *pictorial* history of the reign of Queen Mary is as nearly as possible a simple, unadulterated falsehood. We find, in the first place, that so far from its having been a result of the faith of the Queen and the Bishops, that many persons were put to death for their religion, this notion of the lawfulness and necessity of what is termed persecution was upheld and acted upon by every man who called himself a Christian, whether Catholic or Protestant, Calvinist or Arminian, Lutheran or Socinian. There was not perhaps a solitary individual in England who maintained that it was **wrong that** *he himself* should persecute, however clamourously **he** asserted that it was contrary to the spirit of the Gospel that he himself *shoud be persecuted*. The modern idea, now so generally maintained in word, though **nowhere** consistently acted upon in deed, that it is wrong to inflict any punishment upon a man because of his religious opinions, was no more known to our forefathers than it was known to them that a man might go from London to Bath in two hours and a half. Every civil government regarded itself, if not exactly a judge in matters of religion, yet at least as authorised to imprison, scourge, banish, and kill any one or more of its subjects who professed a creed which found no favour in the eyes of the ruling power. The difference between one government and another was simply in the degree of the punishment inflicted, and between the nature of the authorities or tribunals whose decrees were accounted decisive as to what constituted the heresies to be chastised by the secular arms. Catholic governments looked to ecclesiastical judgment to decide what was or what was not heresy, and then took upon themselves to imprison, fine, torture, burn, or hang the convicted heretics according to their own good pleasure; while Protestant governments set up courts of inquisition of their own, with powers and objects precisely similar to the tribunals of the Catholic Church, except that they united in one depositary of authority both the right to decide theologically and the power to imprison, fine, torture, burn, and hang their victims at discretion.

To talk, therefore, of its being a peculiar feature of the Catholic Church, that she persecutes those who will not obey, is an absurdity. Every body persecuted, even to blood, 300 years ago; and to this very day every body persecutes, even to disqualifications, fines, and imprisonments. If persecution is wrong and monstrous at all, a double share of the blame is to be charged to Protestants, for this reason, that they do not even profess that they have an infallible guide to direct them, and do not pretend to say that none can be saved but those who agree in their views. The Catholic has some reason on his side when he calls for the temporal punishment of heretics, for he claims the true title of Christian for himself exclusively, and professes to be taught by the never-failing presence of the Spirit of God. But however this be, it is certain that there is no more foundation for the vulgar belief, that persecution is the special characteristic of the Catholic Church, than for the old legend of the phœnix, or for believing, like Lord Monboddo, that the human race once had tails like monkeys.

Further than this, when we examine the real history of the English Reformation, it appears that it is altogether a delusion to suppose that piety and devotion had any thing whatever to do with the "martyrdoms" of a vast number of the persons put to death under Queen Mary. It is mere twaddle and cant to call them "martyrs" at all. They were no more martyrs than Thistlewood was a martyr, or than the Red Republicans who were shot in the streets of Paris a year ago were martyrs. They were seditious scoundrels, who made the Gospel a cloak for treason—the legitimate progenitors of the republican revolutionists who would now set Europe in flames, and overthrow the "monstrous regiment" of kings, nobles, and parliaments, that they themselves may fill the vacant thrones and share the plunder. The Scotch author of *The Monstrous Regiment of Women*, when he flung that precious medley of metaphysics, Bible-texts, blasphemy, vulgarity, and nonsense at the head of the lawful Queen of England, was an apostle of sedition and not of Christianity; he broached theories which upset the foundations of the social system itself; and if he had lived in France in these days of ours, would doubtless have taken his place by the side of Barbès, Raspail, and the other Red Republicans lately convicted by the tribunal of Bourges.

This is Dr. Maitland's deliberate opinion of the character of very many of the leading Protestants, and he considers that they impressed the very same character upon the movement generally. Whatever might have been the sincerity of many individuals among the Protestants, as a body they took the initiative in assaulting Queen Mary and her rights as a sovereign, in a manner which left her no alternative but to put them down by rigour and bloodshed. A large number of the influential writings of the time are classed by Dr. Maitland under the following heads:

"I. Those which have generally a revolutionary tendency—which discuss the subject of government in such a way as to inculcate, not only the doctrine that the people have a right to resist the ruler whenever in their opinion he commands what is wrong, but that they are the source of power, and are answerable to God, not only for their delegation of it to fit persons as rulers, but for the use which they allow to be made of it by those to whom they have delegated it; and from whom upon the misuse of that power they are bound to resume it—these ideas being illustrated, enforced, and familiarised by perpetual repetitions of and allusions to histories respecting rulers deposed and killed by their subjects.

"II. Those which were specially directed against Queen Mary individually, and which were of two kinds. (1.) Those which denied her right to the throne on the general ground of her sex, or on the more particular ground of illegitimacy. (2.) Those which were directed against her personal character, and which, by charging her with cruelty, oppression, &c., were calculated to render her odious.

"III. Those which were directed against foreigners, and in particular against the Spaniards, and the Spanish match; and which, under a profession of patriotism, urged that the people and the country had been, or would be, betrayed and sold into the hands of strangers and foreigners of the basest description, by whom they would be enslaved and oppressed without mercy, unless they rose up and expelled them.

"IV. Those relating to the change in religion—representing it both as a judgment in itself, and as a sin which would bring down further judgments—and generally threatning judgments on the people of the country for rejecting the word of God, and embracing or tolerating idolatry and superstition."

In truth, it was utterly impossible for any government to stand which tolerated the attacks that were made upon Mary by the Puritan party: more especially was her government provoked by that band of cowardly hypocrites who fled the country and are termed the Frankfort exiles, and who from their place of security launched fulminations against the English monarch as coarse and indecent as they were ferocious and profane. Never were writings put forth more utterly alien to the spirit of that Gospel which they professed to uphold. Nowhere in the annals of controversy and politics do we meet with more striking records of what would have been foolhardy madness if it had come from residents in the realm of England, but was mere reckless, braggart ferocity when its authors were safe from the arm they provoked to strike them. These tracts of the exiles were, however, brought over to this country and scattered far and wide among the people, and stimulated the ignorant multitude to excesses which it became impossible for the Government to pass by. Calmly and peaceably as the first months of Mary's reign went on, when once the first opposition to her was put down, the united efforts of the exiled ministers and of the designing courtiers and men in power at home speedily called for the severest measures on the part of the Queen's administration. Politics and religion became mixed up so inextricably that it was impossible to treat them any longer apart, or to view the unconvinced Protestant in any other light than that of a preacher of sedition and revolution. The land swarmed with publications which lashed the populace into frenzy; and though we cannot doubt that their authors generally took good care of themselves, and allowed the blows of the secular arm to fall upon the more unoffending and conscientious, still it must be borne in mind that the laws could make no distinctions between individuals, and that Mary's ministers were compelled to treat the whole Protestant party as one body of men—as bitterly hostile to her throne as to her religion.

Dr. Maitland thus describes the kind of publications from which he deduces a conclusion substantially the same as that we have expressed:

"It has been already stated, that a great object of the books which were written and sent over to this country by the Protestant exiles, was to promote a revolution in the English Government by the dethronement of Queen Mary. The only difficulty in proving this is that which arises from having to make a selection amidst superabundance of evidence. It is true that much which would have increased that difficulty is lost. Many of the worst productions of that period—the worst, not only in a moral and religious point of view, but as being the most prejudicial, passing from hand to hand, or from mouth to mouth, amongst the worst people, and such as were most easily excited to the worst practices—the profane ballad, that regaled the devotees of the ale-house; the seditious broadside, scattered in the streets by unseen hands; the interlude, that amused a simple and untaught audience with blasphemous ribaldry concerning the holiest and most sacred mysteries of religion—these are now seldom to be met with. But for our purpose the loss is the less to be regretted, because they mostly lie open to the objection, that as there probably never was a time when their authorship could be certainly fixed, so it is altogether impossible at this distance of time to attempt any thing of the kind; and, also, that for any thing we can prove, these very abominations may have been forged by the enemies of the Puritans for the express purpose of bringing them into trouble. I lay no stress, therefore, on works of this description, though it may, on some occasions, be worth while, for the sake of illustration, to refer to them. But I will beg the reader to bear in mind, that however obscure our intelligence respecting them may be, these things were in existence, and in active operation, while I quit them to speak, as Doctor (afterwards Archbishop) Parker did to the Lord Keeper Bacon, of certain books, "that went then about London, being printed and spread abroad, and their authors *ministers of good estimation*.... At which, said Parker, *exhorrui cum ista legerem*. Adding, "if such principles be spread into men's heads, as now they be framed, and referred to the judgment of the subject to discuss *what is tyranny*, and to discern whether his prince, his landlord, his master, is a tyrant by his own fancy and collection supposed; what Lord of the Council shall ride quietly-minded in the streets among desperate beasts? what minister shall be sure in his bedchamber? Important questions. I do not know what the Lord Keeper answered."

Another feature in the controversial writings of the Reformation period, which Dr. Maitland brings prominently forward as illustrative of the real spirit of the opposing parties, is the disgusting coarseness, indecency, and violence of many of the Puritan authors. Not only was the style of the Protestant writers such as to provoke to the utmost the forbearance of the Queen and her advisers, but it is so intolerably vile that few readers of the present day have ever had an opportunity of fairly comparing the writings of the Catholics with those of the Protestants of that period. None but those who have gone to the original writers, and studied their productions in unmutilated editions, can form any idea of the grossness of sentiment and language of many of these supposed martyrs to the truth and purity of the Gospel. The modern reader knows the writings of his Protestant ancestors only through expurgated and judiciously selected extracts. The skilful editor draws his pen through all that would shock the feelings of our own more decent time, leaving only a little hyperbolical statement and apparently honest vehemence, which charity readily puts down to a pardonable excess of zeal in men persecuted for the Gopel's sake.

But when the controversial books of the day are perused in their integrity, we are startled to find that we have been cheated into a species of pity or respect for a set of unprincipled men, whose thoughts and words could only now be paralleled in the haunts of the lowest and most shameless of our race. It is impossible to put down the excesses of the Puritan writers to the age in which they lived, and at the same time to give them credit for being themselves Christian men. Their excesses are of a character utterly inconsistent with the first elements of Christian morality; and stamp the whole religious portion of their writings with a mark either of delusion or of hypocrisy. It is miserable, indeed, to hear the nonsense which we often hear uttered in defence of the grossness and violence of other days. Doubtless outward manners, and forms of speech, and rules of artificial decency, vary considerably in different stages of civilisation; but we must not forget that there is a limit to these variations; and that there are certain transgressions of the strict rules of morality, which it is preposterous to palliate on any ground of popular taste of the day, and which nothing on earth can ever justify. And just such are the extravagances and abominations of the English Puritan writers of Queen Mary's days. Their ideas and expressions are not only unpolished, but immoral; not only rude, coarse, and rough, but filthy, impure, and bloodthirsty. If they had been guided by the spirit of Christianity, they would have so far overcome the habits of the age as to have adopted at least a style of writing not flagrantly violating the fundamental laws of the Gospel. Perhaps no English writer ever equalled Luther himself in his horrible profaneness and indecencies; but still Luther had **many** a worthy follower in this island; many a disciple who lacked rather the ability than the will to rival him in the wickedness of **his** expressions. Dr. Maitland's remarks on this subject are so **much** to the **purpose,** that we shall make no **apology for** quoting them at length.

"I cannot help thinking, that none but those who have paid some attention to the works which were written by the exiled party during the reign of Mary,—I mean the works themselves, in contradistinction to selections, extracts, modernisations, and generalising accounts,— can properly estimate the effect which they were calculated to produce on the measures of the English government in Church and State during that period. Before, however, I come to speak particularly of these works, as regards their design and effect, I would offer a few remarks of a more general nature on the style of some of the more popular Puritan writers. It is a matter which has certainly been misrepresented, principally, I believe, though not entirely, by ignorance; but it is one which, if we wish really to understand the history of the period, we must look fairly in the face.

"It must be considered that those parts of the works of writers of **this** class and period which are the most contrary to good taste and good manners, have been very seldom, very sparingly, and then commonly with some preface or apology, brought forward by their admirers;—and further, that through those admirers almost exclusively, these writers are known to Protestants of the present day; and further still, that when any such matter as admirers would not wish to find does come into notice, it is frequently purified from its grossness by the omission of words or sentences, with or without notice **to** the reader, who thus forms a very imperfect and erroneous opinion **of the** author whose work he is reading. Of course I do not mean to find **fault** with such omissions, as things **wrong** in themselves, or as less than absolutely necessary in some **cases.** Occasions may arise on which it may be very right to reprint a work or extract a passage, of an old writer, containing words or phrases **so** obscene or profane that common decency requires them to **be expunged.** This, too, may probably be done without any **injury** to the purpose for which the reprint or extract is made; **and** if it be fully acknowledged, it is hardly likely to lead to any **ill** consequence. But when without notice, or with a notice that is false, and even with the very best intentions, that which would disgust is tacitly altered, or omitted, and a coarse, obscene, or scurrilous writer is weeded and cleared of his offences, and made to look quite innocent, it is obvious that, whatever information or instruction we may gain from his writings thus garbled, we shall get a very wrong idea of himself, his style, and his admirers. But where this expurgation of a writer cannot be fully effected, there is one standing excuse for a favourite writer which may pass current for every thing that is offensive, whatever be its kind or degree—that is, the manners of the age. Only take that with you—take it, perhaps, from some writer who repeats the phrase like a parrot, without knowing any thing about the age or its manners or language—take it only on trust, as a phrase to which you do not, perhaps, yourself affix a very clear idea, and it is sufficient to cover any sin against propriety and decorum, and almost religion. With this salvo you may be expected to read with edification such things as if spoken or written in the present day would be considered absolutely ungodly and profane.

"If, however, we wish to form a true judgment, this point must be looked into and settled. It is quite clear that some words and phrases which were in common use three hundred years ago, and which had then no character of coarseness, would be considered intolerably gross in the present; but this, really, has nothing to do with the matter now under consideration. No more has any notion that may have been set on foot respecting the free, blunt, plain speech of our forefathers. It is not with coarse words or plain speech as such that we are concerned; though, at the same time, the use of coarse language in particular circumstances and to particular persons must be taken into account. I suppose, for instance, that there never was a period in the history of the united Church of England and Ireland when it would have been thought quite common-place and Christian for the Bishop of Ossory deliberately, and in print, to address the Bishop of London as a "beastlye belly-god and damnable donge-hille." But one of the most material, and in an historical point of view most injurious, effects of this sort of misrepresentation is, that it comes to be taken for granted that the fierce and virulent scurrility of some of the Puritan libels, which cannot be entirely concealed or defended, even by the most through-going partisans, was not characteristic of the writers, but of the times. Bishop Burnet is even kind enough to make a sort of an excuse for Sir Thomas More, by saying, "he wrote, according to the *way of the age*, with much bitterness;" and so the bishop's readers may naturally infer that, whatever may be meant by "*much* bitterness," and whatever degree of it may be found in Sir Thomas More's works, it belonged not to the man, but was "the way of the age"—that it was the way of people in those days; very wrong, no doubt, but at the same time as good for one as for another; the Puritans abused the Papists, and the Papists abused the Puritans, tit for tat. As if Sir Thomas More and John Bale were as like as two peas.

"Now, as far as I have yet been able to learn, this is really a false view of things. It is true enough that each party abused the other, and that many keen, severe, false, and malicious things were put forth by the Romish party; but for senseless cavilling, scurrilous railing and ribaldry, for the most offensive personalities, for the reckless imputation of the worst motives and most odious vices; in short, for all that was calculated to render an opponent hateful in the eyes of those who were no judges on the matter in dispute, some of the Puritan party went far beyond their adversaries. I do not want to defend the Romish writers, and I hope I have no partiality for them, or for the errors, heresies, and superstitions which they were concerned to maintain; but it really appears to me only simple truth to say that, whether from good or bad motives, they did in fact abstain from that fierce, truculent, and abusive language, and that loathsome ribaldry, which characterised the style of too many of the Puritan writers. Specimens will frequently appear as other occasions may require; but here, and merely for the sake of illustrating what I have already said on the subject of *style*, I will give a few extracts from the works of three eminent Puritan writers, who may fairly be classed among the leaders of the party, not only on account of the eminent stations which they held, but for the talents and learning for which they have had credit, both among their own contemporaries, and from more modern writers. These extracts may probably suggest a good many things of various kinds to the reflecting reader, but it must be observed that they are here given only as specimens of *style*, denoting the character of certain writers; and those who are previously acquainted with the works of the writers in question, will be aware that, for obvious reasons, I do not quote passages which would but too broadly confirm what I have stated.

"As I have already alluded to John Bale, Bishop of Ossory, and as he may perhaps be on the whole the fittest person to take the lead on such an occasion, I will first give some passage from his pen. Let not the reader who knows him be startled. I am not going even to mention some of his filthiest productions, or to extract the worst parts of that one work from which I now take specimens of his style."

Here, then, we have the distinctly expressed testimony of one of the most learned men in the Anglican communion to the purity and Christian spirit of the Catholic writers, as compared with their Protestant opponents. Our readers will observe that Dr. Maitland positively denies that the rules of Christian morality and charity were, as a general rule, broken through by the Catholic controversialists ; and that though instances of comparative impropriety may be named among them, yet their writings are faultless in comparison with the productions of the Reformers. And we have ourselves no hesitation in asserting that, in the whole range of Catholic literature, the same moral superiority is clearly and undeniably manifest. We do not pretend to claim for our writers, who have written controversially on any topic in theology, science, or literature, an absolutely immaculate purity. Far from it ; the visible Catholic Church is composed of men of all varieties of character, from the saint to the sinner. Nevertheless, on the whole, we have conducted our disputes among ourselves, and those which we have maintained with non-catholic writers, with a forbearance, a charity, and **a decency** of thought and language, which stand out in striking contrast with the reckless excesses which characterise almost every non-Catholic controversialist on any subject whatsoever.

A further subject, bearing upon our knowledge of the Reformation period, is the degree of credulity due to the authors on whose records **the** Protestant opinion of the times is based. " For the history **of the** Reformation in England," says the author before us, **" we** depend so much on the testimony of writers **who** may be considered as belonging, or more or less attached, to the Puritan party; or who obtained their information from persons of that sect; that it is of the utmost importance to enquire whether there was any thing in their notions respecting *truth* which ought to throw suspicion on any of their statements. " In a word, were not many of these sources of history, liars by their **own** confession, and on principle ? Accordingly, Dr. Maitland has two chapters on "Puritan Veracity," **in** which he very satisfactorily shews that with these men the end constantly was held to sanctify the means; and that therefore we have little or no guarantee that many of their stories of Protestant piety and Catholic cruelty were not fictions of the imagination, invented by these new apostles for the propagation of their new Christianity, and to be ranked among the most impudent of pious frauds with which priestcraft has ever deluded a credulous generation. We cannot, however, linger on this part of our subject; and can only recommend Dr. Maitland's graphic stories and extracts to those who are not convinced that lying and perjury were accounted no sins by many of the founders of the Established Church of England, and by those writers on whose chronicles our knowledge of the period is for the most part based.

We now turn to the *ribaldry* of the Protestant party. This was a favourite weapon with the party, whose aim it was to bring the old religion into discredit with the people at large. Every one knows that though the multitude cannot reason, they can laugh. In our own days we have known a woman of notoriously infamous character in Paris, after braving successfully public opinion (such as it was) for years, finally driven from the field by falling into a scrape in which she became personally ridiculous. And if vice itself suffers from ridicule, still more fatally are its poisoned shafts made to tell upon that pure truth which, being bound to a more sparing and conscientious use of that cutting weapon, too often suffers bitterly in a contest of sarcasm. The Reformers, however, were bound by their notions to no such cautions and careful application of satire and scoffing. Insult and mockery were among their favourite instruments of warfare; and cleverly and systematically were they turned to account by the leaders in the movement, and by all that influential party of men in office whose interest it was to overthrow the Church and seize upon its spoils.

First in this fierce onslaught against all that was holy was Thomas Lord Cromwell.

"He," says Dr. Maitland, "was the great patron of ribaldry, and the protector of the ribalds, of the low jester, the filthy balladmonger, the alehouse singers, and hypocritical mockers in feasts," in short, of all the blasphemous mocking and scoffing which disgraced the Protestant party at the time of the Reformation. It is of great consequence in our view of the times, to consider that the vile publications, of which too many remain, while most have rotted, and the profane pranks which were performed, were not the outbreaks of low, ignorant partisans, a rabble of hungry dogs such as is sure to run after a party, in spite even of sticks and stones bestowed by those whom they follow and disgrace. It was the result of design and policy, earnestly and elaborately pursued by the man possessing, for all such purposes, the highest place and power in the land."

Burnet, in his *History of the Reformation*, describes one species of ribaldry thus employed against the Catholic religion.

"These were the stage-plays and interludes which were then *generally* acted, and *often in churches*. They were representations of the corruptions of the monks, and some other feats of the Popish clergy. The poems were ill-contrived, and worse expressed; if there lies not some hidden wit in these ballads (for verses they were not) which at this distance is lost. But from the representing the immoralities and disorders of the clergy, *they proceeded to act the pageantry of their worship. This took with the people much,* who being provoked by the miscarriages and cruelties of some of the clergy, were not ill-pleased to see *them* and their *religion* exposed to public scorn. The clergy complained much of this; and said it was an introduction to Atheism, and all sort of irreligion. For if once they began to mock sacred things, no stop could be put to that petulent humour. The grave and learned sort of Reformers *disliked and condemned* these courses, as not suitable to the genius of true religion; but the political men of that party *made great use of them, encouraging them all they could*; for they said, contempt being the most operative and lasting affection of the mind, nothing would more effectually drive out many of those abuses which yet remained, than to expose them to the contempt and scorn of the people."

The statement made in the last sentence, Dr. Maitland looks upon as a direct falsehood. His own researches have furnished him with no proofs that these insulting mockeries were generally disapproved by the Reformers; and he looks upon Burnet's interpretation of their motives as a piece of pure invention of his own.

"To say the truth," says he, "I cannot but think that any one who observes how Burnet himself, when not particularly engaged in performing the sincere historian, relates the profane and irreverent pranks which some of "the party" indulged, will doubt whether, if he had lived at the time, he would have been very forward or very fierce in trying to stop or to punish "these courses." For instance, he relates an incident which occurred shortly after the accession of Queen Mary, in a tone which reminds me very much of the "mixture of glee and compunction" with which Edie Ochiltree dwelt on the exploits of his youth. The passage, not only for this, but for the historical fact itself, is much to our purpose, and quite worth quoting : "There are many *ludicrous* things every where done in derision of the old forms and of the images : many poems were printed, with other ridiculous representations of the Latin service, and the pageantry of their worship. But none occasioned more *laughter* than what fell out at Paul's the Easter before; the custom being to lay the Sacrament into the sepulchre at even-song on Good Friday, and to take it out by break of day on Easter morning : at the time of the taking of it out, the quire sung these words, "S*urrexit, non est hic*, He is risen, he is not here :" but then the priest looking for the host, found it was not there indeed, for one had stolen it out; which put them all in no small disorder, but another was presently brought in its stead. Upon this a *ballad* followed, That their God was stolen and lost, but a new one was made in his room. This raillery was so salt, that it provoked the clergy much. They offered large rewards to discover him that had stolen the host, or had made the ballad, but could not come to the knowledge of it."—Vol. ii. p. 270.

"I do not know where Burnet got this story, because, as in too many other cases, he gives no authority. Fox relates the same thing as happening on the same day at St. Pancras in Cheap, and perhaps it is the same story; and in the next paragraph Fox tells us a story that should not be separated from the other, and which Bishop Burnet might have considered equally "ludicrous : " "The 8th of April there was a cat hanged upon a gallows at the Cross in Cheap, apparelled like a priest ready to say mass, with a shaven crown. Her two fore feet were tied over her head, with a round paper like a wafer-cake put between them : whereon arose great evil-will against the city of London; for the Queen and the Bishops were very angry withal. And therefore the same afternoon there was a proclamation, that whosoever could bring forth the party that did hang up the cat should have twenty nobles, which reward was afterwards increased to twenty marks; but none could or would earn it."—Vol. vi. p. 548.

"It is needless to say that the story is told by Fox without any mark of dislike or condemnation, for he has given ample proof that he enjoyed such things amazingly. Indeed, it seems probable that his troubles first began, while he was yet at college, from the indulgence of that jeering, mocking spirit which so strongly characterises his martyrology. Take a specimen that occurs only ten pages after the story of the cat, and which he introduces by saying, "But one thing, by the way, I cannot let pass, touching the young flourishing rood newly set up against this present time to welcome King Philip into Paul's Church;" and having described the ceremony of its being set up, he proceeds : " Not long after this, a merry fellow came into Paul's, and spied the rood with Mary and John new set up; whereto (among a great sort of people) he made a low courtesy, and said : Sir, your mastership is welcome to town. I had thought to have talked further with your mastership, but that ye be here clothed in the Queen's colours. I hope ye be but a summer's bird in that ye be dressed in white and green, &c."

"Another brief specimen may be found in a story of a "mayor of Lancaster, who was a very meet man for such a purpose, and an old favourer of the Gospel," who had to decide a dispute between the parishioners of Cockram and a workman whom they had employed to make a rood for their church. They refused to pay him, because, as they averred, he had made an ill-favoured figure, gaping and grinning in such a manner that their children were afraid to look at it. The "old favourer of the Gospel," who seems to have been much

11

amused by such a representation of his Saviour being set up in the church, recommended them to go and take another look at it, adding, "And if it will not serve for a god, make no more ado, but clap a pair of horns on his head, and so he will make an excellent devil." This the parishioners took well in wroth; the poor man had his money; and divers laughed well thereat—but so did not the Babylonish priests." Strange that the priests did not join in the fun; and stranger still that those blind Papists did not seize on the skirts of the "old favourer of the Gospel, and say, "We will go with you, for we see that God is with you."

Ballad-singing against the Church was one of the favourite devices of the "Gospellers," as they were called. Dr. Maitland gives specimens of this and similar schemes for bringing Catholicism into disrepute.

"A more open and more flagrant manifestation of this spirit was given by Henry Patinson and Anthony Barber, of St. Giles's-without-Cripplegate, who were presented "for maintaining their boys to sing a song against the sacrament of the altar," and Thomas Grangier and John Dictier, of the same parish, were "noted for *common singers* against the sacraments and ceremonies." Nicholas Newell, a Frenchman, of St. Mary Woolchurch, was "presented to be a man far gone in the new religion, and that he was a great *jester* at the saints, and at our Lady.' Shermons, Keeper of the Carpenter's Hall, in Christ's parish, Shoreditch, 'was presented for procuring an *interlude* to be openly played, wherein priests were railed on and called knaves.' 'Giles Harrison, being in a place without Aldgate, merrily jesting in a certain company of neighbours, where some of them said, 'Let us go to mass : 'I say, tarry,' said he; and so taking a piece of bread in his hands, lifted it up over his head : and likewise taking a cup of wine, and bowing down his head, made therewith a cross over the cup, and so taking the said cup in both his hands, lifted it over his head, saying these words, 'Have ye not heard mass now?'' for the which he was presented to Bonner, then Bishop of London.' I presume, however, that Giles Harrison was one of those who became bail for each other; and certainly there was a moral beauty and fitness in making that good office mutual—indeed, a sort of necessity; for if they had not done it for each other, how would they have got it done at all?"

Let us now proceed to Bishop Bonner, and commence with Dr. Maitland's view of his real character. The common idea which Englishmen entertain of this prelate is founded upon what they read in that book of legends, termed *Fox's Book of martyrs*. In Fox's estimation, Bonner was a ravening wolf, only happy when gorging himself with victims, and frantic for blood. Yet see what even Fox's *facts* come to, when rigidly examined, apart from his own deductions and colourings. In Fox's book, says Dr. Maitland,

"The rage and fury of prelates and persecutors is of course a constant theme, and affords many ludicrous specimens of nonsense and falsehood; none perhaps more so than the following. If the reader turns to vol. v. p. 765, he will find that, at the 'third Session against Bonner,' after Cranmer had been addressing 'the people,' and telling them how Bonner went about to deceive them, and had appealed to the said people, to judge of the denunciation against him, which he ordered to be read to them by Sir John Mason : ' This done, the Archbishop said again unto the audience, 'Lo ! here you hear how the Bishop of London is called for no such matter as he would persuade you.' ' With this,' continues the Martyrologist, ' the Bishop being in a *raging heat*, as one *clean void of all humanity*, turned himself about unto the people [whom the Archbishop had made his judges], saying'——Now, what does the reader suppose he said ? of course, such a torrent of oaths, and brutal blasphemies, as no scribe, though ' clean void of all humanity,' unless he were also in a ' raging heat,' could set down in writing. Not at all—nothing of the kind—the story of the mountain in labour is clean outdone, unless we can imagine a volcano and a dormouse. Fox's own words are literally what follow : 'The Bishop being in a raging heat, as one void of all humanity, turned himself about unto the people, saying : ' Well, now hear what the Bishop of London saith for his part.' But the commissioners, seeing his *inordinate contumacy*, denied him to speak any more, saying that he used himself *very disobediently;* with more like words of reproach.' This is only given as one of many specimens continually recurring, and producing, often insensibly, by dropping on the minds of thoughtless readers, fixed and obstinate, though obscure and unfounded, ideas, that they have read dreadful things about shocking rage, and passion, and inordinate contumacy, and disobedience, and merited reproach, when in fact they have merely been duped by a tale ' full of sound and fury'— not indeed ' signifying nothing,' but signifying something very different from what they have understood, or were meant to understand by it. "

What, then, is our author's own opinion of Bonner, as deduced from the writings of his bitter foe, the Martyrologist ? The bloody wolf is transformed into something like a good-tempered mastiff, who might be safely played with, and who, though he might be teased into barking and growling, had no disposition to bite, and would not do it without orders. Bonner's character is throughout that of a man straightforward and hearty, familiar and humorous ; sometimes rough, perhaps coarse; naturally hot-tempered, but obviously (by the testimony of his enemies) placable and easily entreated, capable of bearing most patiently much intemperate and insolent language, much reviling and low abuse directed against himself personally, against his order, and against those peculiar doctrines and practices of his Church, for maintaining which he had himself suffered the loss of all things, and borne long imprisonment. At the same time he was not incapable of being provoked into saying harsh and passionate things, but generally meaning nothing by the threatenings and slaughter he breathed out, but to intimidate those on whose ignorance and simplicity argument seemed thrown away. In short, we can scarcely read with attention any one of the cases detailed by those who were no friends of Bonner, without seeing in him a judge who (even if we grant that he was dispensing bad laws badly) was obviously desirous to save the prisoner's life. The enemies of Bonner have very inconsiderately thrust forward and even exaggerated this part of his character, and represented him as a fawning, flattering, coaxing person, as one who was only anxious to get those submissions, abjurations, and recantations, which would have robbed the wild beast of his prey. That he did procure a great number of recantations there can be no doubt, and as little doubt can there be that "Puritan veracity" has by no means recorded all the effects of his persuasion. Such is the opinion of the late librarian of the Archbishop of Canterbury, respecting that Bonner who is held up to the infant Protestant mind as the incarnation of every thing that is murderous and diabolical. We cannot follow Dr. Maitland through the various passages he quotes from Fox and others in justification of his defence of the Bishop, but it is impossible to read them fairly and not be convinced that the estimate he has formed of Bonner's personal character is substantially correct, and that, as a true Christian Bishop, he was more anxious to save their souls than to burn their bodies. One specimen of the style in which he conducted the examination of the accused will shew the extraordinary impudence which he bore from them with all the good nature which Dr. Maitland attributes to him. It is a fragment of the examination of one Robert Smith.

"*Bonner.* 'By the mass this is the most unshamefaced heretic that ever I heard speak.'
"*Smith.* 'Well sworn, my Lord; ye keep a good watch.'
"*Bonner.* "Well, master comptroller, ye catch me at my words: but I will watch thee as well, I warrant thee.'
"' By my troth, my Lord,' quoth Master Mordaunt, 'I never heard the like in all my life.'—*Fox*, vii. 351.
"The argument went on, however, without much interruption or variation of style, until the Bishop, thinking enough had been said respecting the sacrament of baptism, went on.
"*Bonner.* 'Well, sir, what say you to the sacrament of orders?'
"*Smith.* 'Ye may call it the sacrament of misorders; for all orders are appointed of God. But as for your shaving, anointing, greasing, polling, and rounding, there are no such things appointed in God's book, and therefore I have nothing to do to believe your orders. And as for you, my Lord, if ye had grace and intelligence, ye would not so disfigure yourself as ye do.'
"*Bonner.* 'Sayest thou so?' Now, by my troth, I will go shave myself, to anger thee withal:' and so sent for his barber, who immediately came. And *before my face* at the door of next chamber he shaved himself, desiring me before he went to answer to these articles.

* * * * *

"'With this came my Lord from shaving, and asked me how I liked him?'
"*Smith.* 'Forsooth, ye are even as wise as ye were before ye were shaven.'
"*Bonner.* 'How standeth it, master doctors, have ye done any good?'

" *Doctor.* 'No, by my troth, my Lord, we can do no good.'
" *Smith.* 'Then it is fulfilled which is written, How can an evil tree bring forth good fruit?' "

Another extract will serve as an example of our author's mode of dissection of the stories by which the deeds of Bonner have been distorted and misinterpreted. It is but a sample of many such. Fuller tells us that the bloody wolf Bonner scourged one John Fetty, a lad of eight years old, to death as a heretic. Let us now hear Dr. Maitland's examination of the fact.

"John Fetty, the father of the child in question, was a simple and godly poor man, 'dwelling in the parish of Clerkenwell, and was by vocation a taylor, of the age of twenty-four years or thereabout.' He seems to have married at an age when he could not be expected to shew much discretion in choosing a partner; for this (not his only, and perhaps not his eldest) child was ' of the age of eight or nine years.' He suffered for his youthful indiscretion; for his wife, disapproving his resolution 'not to come into the church, and be partaker of their idolatry and superstition,' was so cruel, or so zealous, as to denounce him to 'one Brokenbury, a priest and parson of the same parish.' Accordingly, 'through the said priest's procurement, he was apprehended by Richard Tanner, and his fellow-constables there, and one Martin the headborough.' Immediately after doing this the poor woman was seized with such remorse that she became 'distract of her wits.' Even the pitiless Papists were moved; the Balaamite priest and the constables, and headborough, all agreed, for the sake of her and her two children, that they would 'for that present let her husband alone, and would not carry him to prison, but yet suffered him to remain quietly in his own house; during which time, he, as it were forgetting the wicked and unkind fact of his wife, did yet so cherish and provide for her, that within the space of three weeks (through God's merciful providence) she was well amended, and had recovered again some stay of her wits and senses.' But strange to say, 'so soon as she had recovered some health, her cruelty or zeal revived, and she 'did again accuse her husband.' The steps are not stated; but we may reasonably suppose them to have been the same as before. Now however, as there was nothing to interrupt the common course of things, John Fetty was 'carried unto Sir John Mordaunt, Knight, one of the Queen's Commissioners, and he upon examination sent him by Cluny, the bishop's sumner, unto the Lollards' Tower.' On what charge (except so far as may be gathered from what has been already stated) Sir John sent him to prison we are not told; but there he lay for fifteen days, and probably Bonner knew no more of his being there, than he knew of Thomas Green's being twice as long in his own coal-house.

"Perhaps while her husband lay in prison, the poor woman, who may so peculiarly be termed the wife of his youth, relented, and thought herself happy that, owing to their early marriage, they had already a child of an age to traverse the streets of London, of 'a bold and quick spirit,' who would make his way in search of his father; and at the same time, 'godly brought up,' and knowing how to behave himself before his elders and betters at the Bishop's palace. I own, however, that this is mere supposition, and that I find no particular ground for supposing that his mother knew that he was gone out upon what may have been only a spontaneous pilgrimage of filial piety; but, to come to facts, it is clearly stated that he 'came unto the Bishop's house to see if he could get leave to speak with his father. At his coming thither one of the Bishop's chaplains met with him, and asked him what he lacked, and what he would have. The child answered, that he came to see his father. The chaplain asked again who was his father. The boy then told him, and pointing towards Lollards' Tower, shewed him that his father was there in prison. 'Why,' quoth the priest, 'thy father is a heretic.' The child being of a bold quick spirit, and also godly brought up, and instructed by his father in the knowledge of God, answered and said, 'My father is no heretic; for you have BALAAM'S MARK.'

By this notable speech the unhappy child has gained a place in the holy army of martyrs. At least (so far as Fox tells us) he said and did nothing else; though perhaps we may take it for granted that the precocious little polemic shewed his 'bold and quick spirit,' and his godly bringing up, in some other smart sayings, and gave some other 'privy nips' to the Balaamite priest, such as Bishop Christopherson and Miles Hoggard would not have approved, before he got the whipping, which he is said to have received ere he reached his father in the Lollards' Tower. For 'the priest took the child by the hand, and led him into the Bishop's house,' says Fox; and he adds, with the absurdity which so often and so happily neutralises his malice, 'whether to the Bishop or not I know not, but *like enough he did*.' 'Like enough'— is that all? and is there the least likelihood of such a thing? especially when Fox proceeds to state that the child as soon as he had been whipped was taken to his father in the tower, and fell on his knees and told him his pitiful story, how 'a priest with Balaam's mark took him into the Bishop's house, and there was he so handled;' but not a word did the child say of ever seeing the Bishop. Fox himself dared not put more in his marginal note than 'The miserable tyranny of *the Papists* in scourging a child.'

"The historian, however, tells us that they detained the boy (whom they probably considered as a go-between) for three days; and the end of that time Bonner makes his first appearance in the history. And then we are introduced to him, not burning heretics, but 'basting of himself against a great fire' in his bedroom. There is nothing to shew that he had ever before heard of either John Fetty or his child; but on that occasion the father (and as far as appears the father only) was brought before him. He quickly shewed by his conduct and discourse that he was either a sort of half-witted person, or else that finding himself in awkward circumstances he wished to pass for one. In that character, whether natural or artificial, he talked some sad nonsense and impertinence to the Bishop, who having, of course, gone through the necessary preliminaries of being in a '*marvellous rage*' and a '*great fury*,' and then again being in 'fear of the law for murdering a child,' (for all at once it has come to be quite certain that the child *was* killed, and by Bonner too, and therefore he) 'discharged him.' It is remarkable that on one point Fox says absolutely nothing, —there is not a word of the prisoner's being asked to abjure, or recant, or submit, or amend his evil ways—no hint of his being offered, or signing, any bill (as Fox calls it), or of any thing of the kind, so common on such occasions. I think, however, that every well-informed reader will suspect that so far as prudential reasons and 'fear of the law' might weigh with a 'bloody wolf,' Bonner must have known that it would have been safer for him to whip two tailor-prentices to death, and hide them in his coal-house, than to discharge one prisoner committed under the warrant of Sir John Mordaunt without a recantation or submission, or some sort of voucher, to lay before the Council. But nothing, I repeat, is said about it.

"Our business, however, is rather with the story of the unfortunate little creature, whom, for his impertinence, Fox has made a martyr. Within fourteen days after he had been taken home by his father the child is said to have died; and Fox most characteristically adds, 'Whether through this cruel scourging, or any other infirmity, *I know not;* and therefore I refer the truth thereof unto the Lord who knoweth all secrets, and also to the discreet judgment of the wise reader;' discreet and wise historian—he gives no hint how he picked up the story, and does not venture to insinuate that the boy, or the father, or any body else ever said that the Bishop even knew of the whipping. Such is the authority for Fuller's bold, brief, and, I suppose I may add. false statement."

Bonner, then, and Gardiner (for the same conclusions apply to him as to Bonner) must, in all truth and fairness, be looked upon merely as representatives of the principle of their age. They were administrators of the laws of the land, which were not different from the laws of the rest of the world, and were based on the same ideas of justice and mercy as the laws of Protestant kingdoms. Whatever be our theory as to the lawfulness of persecution in itself, or as to the advisableness of carrying it to the severe extent to which it was carried under Queen Mary, it is preposterous to speak of Bonner as a monster who was a disgrace to our common humanity. The closer we look into facts, the clearer does it appear, that so far from desiring to push a cruel law to its utmost possible extent of harshness, he repeatedly strove to strip it of its terrors, and to administer it in the most lenient spirit that would be permitted by the secular power. Indeed, it is certain that so far was he from revelling in needless bloodshedding, that on one occasion he was reproved by the court for his slowness in executing the laws, and stimulated to a more prompt and rigid adherence to the letter and spirit of the statutes against heresy. He shed blood because he was compelled to do it, partly by the commands of his own conscience, and partly by the urgency of the lay authorities of the time.

But now let us proceed a step further, and "clearing our minds of cant" a little more thoroughly, inquire dispassionately, how far the age in which Bonner lived was really to be blamed for burning heretics in Smithfield. If we are willing, indeed, to adopt the popular fancy on the question, as people now with parrot-tongues repeat the worn-out theme, religious persecution is monstrous, wicked, absurd, and anti-Chistian in the utmost extreme. If we are to give credit to the prevailing sentiment,— the reader will mark well that we say nothing of the prevailing *practice*,—it was a horrible act in Queen Mary and her advisers to put the "martyrs" to death, not merely because the punishment was excessive, but because one man has no right whatsoever to persecute another for the sake of his religious belief. Such is the general theory now upheld by the vast majority of the Protestant world, while the idea is countenanced, or at least timidly assented to, by many persons in the Catholic Church itself. From speeches in Parliament down to penny tracts, the whole voice of the nation joins in one loud cry against the lawfulness of religious persecution; orators, pulpit, parliamentary, forensic, and from the tub; fathers of families, smitten with horror at the very name of " bloody Mary;" school-teachers, lecturers, and governesses; the whole race of Englishmen and Englishwomen denounce all persecution as an infringement of the rights of man, and a violation of the first principles of the Gospel of mercy and peace. Far from contenting themselves with condemning the Smithfield burnings as needlessly and cruelly severe, they pretend that it is wrong *ever* to persecute, and that they themselves consistently repudiate all persecution in their own conduct towards others.

For ourselves, on the contrary, we are prepared to maintain, that it is no more morally *wrong* to put a man to death for heresy than for murder; that in many cases persecution for religious opinions is not only permissible, but highly advisable and necessary; and further, that no nation on earth, Catholic or Protestant, ever did, ever does, or ever will, consistently act upon the idea that such persecution is forbidden by the laws of God in the Gospel. Let not our readers be amazed; we are not about to propose the erection of a gibbet in Smithfield, so soon as the wisdom of the enlightened citizens of London shall banish the cattle from that notorious locality, or to bring forward a plan for burning the worthy aldermen who now regard cleanliness and Catholicism with equal horror. We abhor all such frightful exhibitions; and were it ever our duty to put an unbeliever to death, would take his life with the utmost possible gentleness. But at the same time we cannot re-echo the cant of the day, which condemns the Marian persecution as utterly vile and wrong, however cordially we may agree with those who think that it was most injudicious, most needlessly severe, and most unfortunate in its results. All we allege is, that a secular government is perfectly justified in inflicting penalties and punishments for religious opinions *in certain cases, and under certain circumstances;* and though in the present state of the world, and especially of the English world, persecution, even of the slightest description, is generally, if not always, undesirable and indefensible, yet that instances do incessantly occur in which persecution, in some form or other, is both wise, merciful, necessary, and Christian.

There are two points of view from which the question may be considered. We may look at the secular power either as bound to promote the spiritual as well as the temporal welfare of its subjects, or as concerned merely with their present happiness and prosperity. We are not disposed, however, to enter at present upon any topic which would assume the former of these theories, as we wish to narrow the discussion as much as possible, and to shew that all men, *upon their own principles,* are bound to admit that persecution is not in itself and in all circumstances *wrong.* If it be granted, indeed, that a body of men forming a nation, or exercising the rights of a secular authority, are bound as a body to promote those religious interests which they hold sacred and uphold as individuals, then it is plain, without further argument, that if I, as a private person, am right in excluding blasphemers, adulterers, and infidels from the society of my children and servants, lest they corrupt them by their evil example, I am also bound, in any magisterial or legislative capacity which may belong to me, to use similar measures for banishing blasphemers, adulterers, and infidels from all communication with the people at large over whom I exercise authority. Whatever steps are lawful to the individual, are lawful to the society; and if I am justified in dismissing a nursery-maid because she would teach my child that the Christian religion is a falsehood, though the dismissal would plunge her into the deepest poverty, I am equally justified in inflicting fines and imprisonment upon any public teachers who insist upon promulgating similar doctrines, however solemn be their assertion that they are conscientious in the belief they would propagate. We shall however, not press this view of the question, but confine ourselves to its necessary bearings, on the supposition that civil government is a purely secular institution, which is bound to protect and further the temporal happiness and enjoyment of mankind, and this alone.

No sensible person, then, can deny that a good secular government will apply itself to the correction of *every* evil which may work mischief to the people over whom it bears rule. It matters not what may be the theoretical *origin* of any social mischief, its existence will be sufficient to call for the exercise of the authority of the law for its extirpation. A scoundrel who robs or swindles his neighbour is not to be let off from the treadmill or the hulks, because he has a plausible metaphysical hypothesis to urge in favour of robbing and swindling. The state must not be scared from putting forth its strength to crush every species of enemy to its prosperity and comfort, by any real or imaginary difficulty in drawing the line between what is theological and what is secular, between what is temporal and what is eternal. It must do its duty vigorously and consistently, though at the expense of trenching upon the domains of religious creeds, and of wounding the conscientious belief of some section of its subjects. This we may assume will be granted by every man of sober sense and real candour.

When, however, this principle is brought into action, at once it appears utterly impossible that the secular power should refuse to take cognisance of the differences in men's religious creeds *as such*. There is not a creed in existence which does not powerfully affect the *temporal* happiness of mankind. Whichever among the opposing divisions of Christianity be true, it is undeniable that a man is a better or a worse member of society according to the creed he professes and acts upon. We know that this is an unpalatable opinion in the present day, and that the popular voice proclaims that all creeds are equally advantageous to our social well-being, provided their followers do but conscientiously act up to their professions. Toleration is defended upon the ground that a pious Catholic, a pious Anglican, a pious Lutheran, a pious Socinian, and a pious Jew, will all be equally good citizens and members of the great brotherhood of humanity, notwithstanding the dissimilarities in their dogmatic belief and religious practices. But they who say this really know nothing whatever either of the actual differences which exist between various creeds, or of the extent of their influence upon their followers. Facts are so diametrically opposed to the theory, that the notion of the indiscriminate toleration of all sects vanishes before the first sight of their real character. A man of one creed *is* a better citizen than a man of another. There are religions which tend more powerfully to overthrow the foundations of civil society than the most inflammatory speeches of the most seditious of demagogues. There are interpretations of Scripture which call for the interference of the police as loudly as the wildest fanaticism of the Socialist, the Communist, or the Red Republican. Just now these things may be so far dormant as not to strike the public eye; but they may wake into life and activity in a moment, and demand a rigorous crushing from the might of soldiers, policemen, and acts of Parliament.

Short of these extreme excesses also, it is preposterous to deny, that the temporal well-being of a state is materially affected by the creed of its members. We know very well that the most elementary laws of social morality are better observed by persons of one religious faith than by those of another. We no more think of forgetting the differences in people's creeds in the business of private daily life, than of obliterating the distinctions between sex and age, between the governor and the governed. If I have any pecuniary dealings with a Catholic, I am more confident that he will not try to cheat me than if he were a Protestant. I am much more afraid of being swindled or libelled by an "evangelical" than by a Puseyite. I would rather make a bargain with a Socinian than with a Baptist; and would let my furnished house to a Wesleyan rather than to an Independent. And why? Because I know well that the morality of all these sects does practically vary according to their theological belief; and that an Anglican, who believes that good works are necessary to salvation, is much less likely to be a rogue, than a Lutheran who thinks that he is justified by faith, without any good works at all. What is it to me, that the Lutheran is as sincerely convinced of his creed as the Anglican, and as conscientiously acts up to it? His very creed itself tempts him to sin, and makes him a worse subject and a worse citizen, a worse dealer and a worse servant, than if he looked forward to a judgment to come, when he will be tried according to his deeds.

How absurd, then, to suppose that the moment we are called to make laws and execute them we are to set aside these pregnant truths, and treat all creeds as if all were equally favourable to social happiness and civil government! It is mere cant to condemn Catholic sovereigns or Catholic parliaments for enacting decrees to stop the progress of opinions which they regard as hostile to all honesty, sobriety, and peaceableness. If the House of Commons conscientiously believed that the taxes would be better paid, and the gaols emptied, by inducing all Englishmen to go to confession to a Catholic priest three or four times a year, what conceivable reason is there to forbid their taking such steps for the promotion of the Catholic religion as might be in their power? If the nation could be set free from some millions of taxation now expended on prisons, courts of law, police, and military, by the propagation of the Catholic religion and the forcible silencing of the preachers of Protestantism, can any man be so simple as to believe that Parliament would hesitate to clap the Rev. Hugh M'Neile into gaol, and to bind over Sir Robert Inglis to keep the peace against the Pope? In very truth, we should be sorry to change places with these celebrated anti-Popish orators, were the Tories, Whigs, and Radicals of the House of Commons once convinced that Catholics are better subjects than Protestants, and that a man who goes to confession is less likely to be a swindler and a thief than one who boasts of being a Bible Christian and calls the Pope Antichrist. Whatever might be the private convictions of our lawgivers themselves, could they once see that the peace of society, the happiness of families, and

the treasures of the national exchequer, would be materially
benefited by the cessation of all the anti-Popish declamations
now so rife amongst us, we should be sorry to expend a solitary
sixpence in insuring the liberty of speech which would be
granted to Sir Peter Laurie and other notorious apostles of
Protestantism from our very liberal and very tolerant Parliament. We do not think that the Government would proceed to
burn Sir Peter, or to whip Sir Peter, or to hang Sir Peter; but
we have no doubt that they would take as effective measures
for making Sir Peter hold his tongue as they have taken for
quieting the unfortunate Smith O'Brien, and for putting an end
to the demonstrations of the belligerent Cuffey.

All this, however, it will be said, is very different from committing men and women to the flames for denying transubstantiation. Granted; it is different—*but only in degree;* the
principle involved is one and the same. An Act of Parliament
empowering magistrates to silence summarily all men who in
word or writing maintain that civil authority has no claim to
our obedience, is founded on the very same principle of
government as the Acts of Parliament under which Bishop
Bonner burnt the "martyrs" in Smithfield. There is persecution for opinions involved in both alike—the dissimilarity is
only in the measure of the punishment. Were some wild fanatics to follow about the judges, and at every assize town gather
together a mob, and harangue them on the unlawfulness of all
oaths and the sinfulness of hanging men for murder, of course
the Home Secretary would ferret out some dormant law empowering him to transfer the offenders from the platform to the
treadmill, or from the cart from which they preached to the bar
of the court of justice whose authority they impugned. And
just such were the measures of Queen Mary for the extirpation
of Protestantism. They were *repressive* measures. There is
not a particle of evidence to shew that if the Protestants had
peaceably held their tongues they would have suffered the loss
of a hair of their heads. They provoked the persecution they
endured. They insulted and defied the civil government of the
land. They preached sedition and treason as a part of their
religious creed, and dared the Queen and her Ministers to their

face. Of course they were punished, as they deserved. Mary would have been an idiot to endure their proceedings. She might as well have descended at once from her throne, and plunged the whole kingdom into anarchy and ruin.

As to the peculiar bloodiness of her punishments, she only acted upon the received notions of the time. In those days people thought no more of killing a man than we now think of killing a sheep. We are now tender-hearted, civilised, and refined. In those days the world was rough and rude, and the law slaughtered offenders for the slightest crimes. Such laws, we grant, were absurd, severe, and generally failed of their object. No man has a deeper horror than we have of the bloodthirsty Draconian spirit of the old English jurisprudence. We look upon our grandfathers as little short of insane, when they hung people by hundreds for sheep-stealing and forgery. But still we cannot forget that this murderous spirit did actually animate the whole criminal law of this country. We cannot put down the burning of heretics under Mary, and the executions and torturings of Catholics under Elizabeth and James, and even down to the reign of George the Second to any thing but the rude ferocious ideas of the times; or look upon Bonner as a whit more blooby-minded a persecutor than Sir Herbert Jenner Fust, when he enforces the laws of the Church of England upon refractory parsons, or the Right Rev. Dr. Philpotts, when he puts the Rev. James Shore into Exeter gaol. Now-a-days we are sensitive almost to effeminacy. Maudlin tears are shed over murderers' pangs, and the suffering housebreaker extorts the pity which our ancestors would have refused to a city given up to military plunder and outrage. Consequently we now persecute for religious opinions with a delicate forbearance, and even cloak our unwilling severities with the guise of toleration. And so long as modern civilisation wears its present aspect, so long will religious persecution be restrained to political disqualifications, moderate fines, dormant penalties, decrees of the Court of Arches, and the hospitalities and amenities of Exeter gaol. Should that very improbable state of things which we have supposed ever come to pass, and the British Parliament do homage to the social advantages to be derived from the practice of auricular confession, the Lauries, the Inglises, the Plumptres, and the Tyrells who may still survive, need fear no rack or torture, no floggings or faggots; they will be chastised and restrained with the same courteous moderation which we now shew in feeding the condemned felon with better food than the toiling peasant, and in contriving to make the **penitentiary a place of** recreation for our starving millions.

Apart, then, from all **idea of the spiritual** and religious duties of any secular government, **we conclude that** the time never will come when the civil power can for any length of time treat all religions on an equal footing, because a **man's** conduct as a citizen is powerfully affected by the doctrines and customs of the creed he professes. The only state of things in which we can approximate to such an indifference to the character of different sects is such as that which now prevails in our own country, where the population is so equally divided between different religions that it becomes impossible for any one division to be alone favoured and supported. While Catholic and Protestant, Christian and Unbeliever, Anglican and Dissenter, are on the whole so equally balanced as to numerical and personal preponderance, the councils of the nation will confine themselves to such petty and unfair artifices as the exclusion of Jews from Parliament, and the bullying of recalcitrant curates. But should any one creed again succeed in winning the affections of the great heart of the nation, we hold it ridiculous to suppose that Parliament would hesitate to discourage all opposition to that creed, though solely on secular grounds, by such penalties as it may then be the fashion to inflict for offences in general. If northern barbarism has by that time swept over the fair face of Europe, and brought back the untamed savage feelings of other days; if human life is again held cheap among us, and a pecuniary fine is thought ample compensation for the blood of a fellow-creature; then shall we see the ruling creed supported by severe, and it may be by bloody, laws. But if our present feelings on the nature of all punishment still have root amongst us, the refractory theologian will be merely visited with **gentle fines and comfortable imprisonment;** or perhaps will be sent across the seas to preach his heresies to the few aboriginal savages who shall still be found in the forests of America or the plains of Central Australia. Meanwhile, let us clear our minds of cant for ever, and cease, if we are Protestants, to revile, and if we are Catholics, to be ashamed of, Queen Mary and Bishop Bonner, as if they hardly deserved the name of Christians.

ANCIENT IRISH DOMINICAN SCHOOLS.

(From the Dublin Review.)

A glance over the leading periodicals and more elaborate works, with which the Anglican press has been teeming for some time past, satisfies us that at no former period of our literature, was there a more willing mind amongst the most learned of our separated brethren than at the present moment, to receive information and pronounce impartial judgment respecting the claustral character and social influences of the various orders of the ancient regular clergy. People of education are likely before long to be shamed our of the phrases, "monkish ignorance" and "dark ages;" than which no terms have been more conventional in ordinary discourse, and more hackneyed in every path of literature. Of late a spirit of historical enquiry is struggling through these masses of popular, literary, and sectarian prejudices and misrepresentations. Maitland has done good service in the cause of justice to "the monks of old."[a] Beckoned on by the honoured shades of Mabillon and his cloistered brethren, the librarian of Canterbury has forced a passage for truth through heaps of misquotations, and cleared away much of the accumulated rubbish of protestant traditions; and with learned toil and clerical intrepidity, has shown how malignant or illusive are the common notions about the state of literature, as well as of religion, in the ages, still called with pertinacious ignorance, "the **Dark** Ages." But his researches

[a] "The Dark Ages," &c., by Rev. S. R. Maitland, 1844.

range only from the ninth to the twelfth centuries. We regret that his subject did not extend beyond the glorious eras of the Benedictines and Cistercians, and that he did not trace the literary zeal and services, of the renovated form of monasticism, which sprung up in the thirteenth century, when the active life was combined with the contemplative spirit, and the impersonation of all the ascetism of the cloister, and the charity of the apostleship, was embodied in the conventual missionary, or "Friar Preacher." Then it was that new alliances were formed throughout Christendom between the sciences and the religious orders. That was the most interesting and eventful period of collegiate history, when the learning that had been nursed and fostered by monks and churchmen from the most remote antiquity, went forth under the auspices of religion from amidst the consecrated shadows of cathedrals and abbeys, and centralized the higher studies in universities; incorporating faculties, endowing halls, privileging scholars, and marshalling graduates from all nations, and in all costumes; scarlet cloaks, black cassocks, academic gowns, mingling picturesquely with bleached scapulars, dark cowls, and all the prismatic variety of monastic habits. At that time the great intellectual movement commenced, to which even our present collegiate agitation must be referred for its primary impulse, if not direction; then was the republic of letters, after a pure Catholic model, organized and founded; and amongst the leaders of the educational reforms—the constructors of all that is most solid and beautiful in the learned institutions—the high intellects who were seated in the first chairs of the universities—history gives a prominent place to the members of the orders of St. Dominic and St. Francis. In the extension to our own country of the scholastic improvements then maturing on the continent, the regular clergy were also eminently conspicuous and useful. "We find," says Mr. Wyse, in his speech at Cork, for the establishment of Provincial Colleges, "a similar spirit animating the religious as well as the secular clergy. I cannot instance nobler proofs than were exhibited by the Benedictines, the Dominicans, the Franciscans, the Augustinians, the Jesuits. The Dominicans, in particular, signalized themselves in this country by their devotion to the cause of academical and collegiate education;" and then the eloquent speaker proceeds to state a great effort made by the Dominicans in the 17th century, for the foundation of provincial colleges in Ireland, of which we shall have occasion to speak at another time.

It was the perusal of this passage, bearing such honourable testimony to the literary devotedness and exertions of the venerable monastic orders, which determined the subject of our present paper, not only for the purpose of vindicating those ancient associations from the charge of checking the growth and expansion of the human mind by systematic resistance to every form of intellectual culture, but also under the irrepressible promptings within ourselves of a hope, that the atonement so auspiciously commenced towards the Alma Mater of Catholic Ireland might be extended in an enlarged spirit of tolerance and generosity, not to speak of strict restitution of rights, to those suppressed and spoliated, and once more doomed, monastic establishments, which, in former ages, were not only sanctuaries of holiness, but also nurseries of learning in our country.

For the illustration of our subject, we select the Dominicain order, rather than the Benedictines, or Jesuits; not only because these have been so often brought in this Review before our readers, in connection with learning; but also because the Dominican is more intimately connected with the history of education in Ireland, and its intellectual character and inappreciable services in the reform of early university education, are as familiar as household topics with the writers of the new Anglican school of scholars and divines.[a]

The culture of the sciences, divine and human, entered as an elementary idea into the first construction of the order of St. Dominic. The blessed founder spent many an anxious, devout, and penitential vigil on the steps of the altar, organizing in his mind such a society of learned missionary priests, as the actual state of the church and of society then peculiarly required. He determined that the chief and characteristic func-

---

[a] See, for example, British Critic, January, 1843. Article "Dante and the Philosophy of the 13th Century."—Sights in Foreign Churches, by Faber, pp. 14, 353, &c.

tion of the new association which he contemplated, should be public instruction in faith and morals. The patriarchal man of God would impress the character of his own well-educated mind, and the movements of his own glowing zeal, on the religious order which Providence designed to be the offspring of his spirit and the inheritor of his name. In his own ministry he combined the attributes, and discharged the duties, of a doctor and a missionary. He publicly expounded to the pontifical household the sacred Scriptures, in which he was extensively and profoundly learned; and was therefore honoured by the pope with the office and title of "Master of the Sacred Palace," which privilege continues to be an heir-loom in his order; and for his preaching and labours in the south of France amongst the Albigenses, he was venerated, even during his life, as the apostle of the thirteenth century. With such views and qualifications he instituted the monastico-canonical body, which the reigning sovereign pontiff designated as the "Sacred Order of Brothers Preachers"—Sacer Ordo Fratrum Prædicatorum.

To sustain the character and efficiency of such a society in the church, no inconsiderable share of learning and talents was requisite in the body and the members. Constitutions,[a] luminously impressed with the spirit of the apostolic Dominic, were soon framed in the general chapters, for promoting, not merely the personal sanctification of the brethren under the discipline of cell and choir, but also to form them as preachers for the mission, and teachers for the schools. Individually, they were obliged by their rules to study, as well as to pray; to learn or instruct, as well as to fast and meditate. Every convent was to contain within its precincts a school, as well as a cloister; a library, as well as a choir. In fact, the portraiture of a primitive Dominican did not fully express the marked pecularity of his sacred profession, unless scholarship and zeal for public instruction were its brightest and most prominent features. He should be always prepared to be sent by his

---

[a] Our extracts are taken from "Constitutiones, &c. Capitulorum Generalium S. Ord. Prædicatorum Auctore P. F. Vincentio Maria Fontana."—Romæ, MDCLV.

superiors, either to a college or conventual school as a lecturer; or to a congregation or mission as a preacher.

The whole life of a Dominican, from his noviciate to the highest offices in the government of the institute, was a life of study, as well as of prayer, zeal, and mortification.[a] The proposed end of all studies was the acquisition of sacred knowledge.[b] Other learning was sought and cultivated as subsidiary, illustrative, or ornamental of the divine sciences, which it was his professional duty to treasure up in his mind.[c] In admitting persons to the habit, strict care was taken that they should be apt for learning.[d] During the first probationary year, before solemn inauguration in the order, the novices were exercised in the knowledge of such portions of the liturgy as regulated the service of the choir, attendance on the ministers of the altar, the recitation of the divine office, and in the obligations of the religious state. During this period of trial, they were, however, allowed to learn languages.[e] In every convent there was a grammar school, preparatory to the higher departments, in which the liberal arts were taught, and a regular master was appointed for the training of the younger brethren in knowledge.[f] Even out of school they were accustomed to

---

[a] "Taliter debent esse in studio intenti, ut de die, de nocte, in domo, in itinere legant aliquid, vel meditentur, et quidquid poterunt retinere cordetenus nitantur." Dist. 2. cap. 14. text 1. "Priores et Lectores, Fratresque omnes ad studii promotionem incumbere tenentur."—Parisiis A.D. 1276. ord. 10.

[b] Nec propter studium artium Fratres a studio Theologiæ retrahantur. Mediolani, A.D. 1278. ord. 1.

[c] Sacrarum litterarum studium Religioni nostræ quam maxime congruit—Dist. 2. cap. 14. in declarat. text 1.

1st. Because the order professes the contemplative life, and study of sacred subjects is necessary to give a proper direction to the consideration of things divine and spiritual. 2dly. Because the order is designed for teaching others the sacred knowledge its members must have acquired by learning. 3dly. Because such studies restrain the sensual passions. 4thly. Because sacred studies quench the lust of riches, &c. Melius est philosophari quàm ditari, &c.

[d] Ordinamus, ut nullus ad habitum clericalem in nostro ordine recipiatur, vel ad professionem admittatur, nisi sciat distinctè et claré legere, bene intelligat ac declaret quæ legit et latinam calleat linguam—p. 533.

[e] Confirmamus item, ut Novitii intra probationis annum non occupentur in studio litterarum præter quam linguarum, sed in exercitiis spiritualibus devotionis, addiscendis ceremoniis, cantu, Regula, Constitutionibus, &c. (522) Ibid.

[f] Confirmamus, quod in Conventu ubi sunt Juvenes, sit aliquis Lector qui eos doceat Grammaticam, vel artes juxta eorum capacitatem.—Ibid. 355. The seven liberal arts taught in these schools were divided into *trivium* and *quadrivium*, viz. three of grammar, and four of physics—music, dialectics, rhetoric, grammar, mathematics, astronomy and geometry.

converse and write in Latin.[a] In Spain, special provisions were made for learning the Arabic language.[b] In all the provinces of the order it was commanded that the Greek and Hebrew languages should be taught.[c] Three years were spent in philosophy. In some places it was customary that the students who had completed their philosophical course, should pass three years more in teaching the same branch of study to the junior members of the community, before they were admitted themselves to take their seats in the theological hall. Against the bias of the age for heathen studies—which, when uncontrolled, sad experience had proved to be most dangerous to faith and morals—the youth of the order were solemnly warned and sedulously guarded; though under certain restrictions they were permitted to read the works of the pagan philosophers.[d] Classes were held every day. Examinations were daily, weekly, and yearly. The most distinguished of the students in their own cloisters, were selected for a higher order of scholastic exercises in the Houses of GENERAL STUDIES; but as an indispensable qualification for their admittance into the highest schools of their province, they should have previously spent at least an entire year in the study of the Bible, under a professor of the sacred Scriptures.[e]

"Besides the particular school in each convent," as a well informed

[a] Ordinamus quod omnes studentes et studii officiales non nisi Latino Sermone loquantur et scribant, etiam extra litteraria exercitia.—*Ibid.* 607.

[b] Injungimus Priori Hispaniæ, quod ipse ordinet aliquod studium ad addiscendam linguam Arabicam, 619.

[c] Ordinamus, ut post sex menses a præsentium notitia Priores Provinciales singuli in suis Provinciis teneantur studium linguarum præsertim Hebraicæ et Græcæ instituere, perquirendo doctissimos harum artium præceptores: quos si in ordine habere nequiverint ex sæculo accersant, discipulisque præficiant, decernendo illis annua stipendia ex communibus sumptibus suorum Conventuum. De Studentibus Cons. Dis. 2. ch. 14. *a.*

[d] Declaramus quod *quamvis liceat* fratribus nostris studere scientiis sæcularibus, non tamen *diu* in illis versari debent, et *omne ætatis suæ tempus consumere, sed potius scripturarum studio*, atque eis quibus consulere possunt saluti animarum, debent se assidue ac solicite exercere, a curiositate et inani gloria cavendo, atque ex illis non sibi solum, sed etiam aliis ad bene sancteque vivendum documenta capere.—*Ibid.*

Admonemus etiam ne per speciem bonarum, ut ferunt, humanarum artium et excultioris atque ornatioris linguæ, libros maxime a Canone prohibitas legent, ex quibus corruptos mores et dogmata perversa facile possunt imbibere.—*Ibid.*

[e] Ordinamus quod nullus Frater antequam per unum annum in studio Bibliæ Biblicum audierit, assignetur alicui studio Generali, sive in sua Provincia, sive extra; quod si secus actum fuerit, sit irritum et inane.—*Page* 606. In Cap. Gen. Neapoli, A.D. 1311.

writer in the British Critic relates, "every province had a general school, to which the promising students were sent; each province also sent a certain number of its most distinguished members to Paris. Certain indulgences were allowed to the students at the discretion of the Magister Studentium; for instance, private cells were assigned to those who wished for solitude; they might, if they pleased, write, read, and pray in their cells: they were even allowed lights to watch there by night for the purpose of study."—*British Critic,* "*Dante and Philosophy of* 13*th Century,*" No. LXV.

In the beginning of the Institute, there was but one such conventual collegiate establishment, or House of General Studies, as it was called, "Studia Generalia," for the rising talent of the entire order, that of Saint Jacques at Paris, to which three students of superior merit and promise might be sent from each province. At the General Chapter, held at Paris in 1246, it was proposed, and subsequently ordained, that four others of a similar kind should be erected at Bologna, Oxford, Cologne, and Montpellier, to which each provincial could send two of his subjects. At these great normal schools of the Dominicans, literary degrees were taken by the most distinguished amongst the professors and students. When this number of central establishments for higher studies was found insufficient for the crowd of scholars in the order, who were qualified by their proficiency and abilities for admission; it was judged necessary to open an establishment, with the same advantages and privileges, in each of the provinces into which the society of Brothers Preachers had already spread. From some cause which we have not examined sufficiently, probably from the troubled state of the countries exposed to the incursions of Saracens and Tartars, the provinces of Greece; of Dacia, lying at the east of Europe, south of the Danube; and of the Holy Land, were excepted. Ireland at that early period was not a distinct province, but was dependent on England, in consequence of which, Oxford was as yet its chief house of studies. It might, however, as we shall show more particularly send some of its cleverest students to Paris, Cambridge, London, &c.

To enable the reader to form some idea of the manner in which studies were conducted in these provincial colleges, it may be sufficient to remark, that at the Dominican school of

Cologne, Albert the Great was Head Master, St. Thomas
Aquinas Assistant, and such youths as Thomas Joyce [a] disciples. The teachers and office bearers of all these chief houses
were, the Regent of Studies—in some places he was assisted by
a Vice Regent—the Bachelors, or second lecturers in theology;
and the master of students, who united the offices of a modern
Dean with occasional teaching as a professor. It was a rule
of the order most strictly to be observed, that merit alone, and
not age or seniority of profession, entitled to those situations.
It was required that the Master of Studies should have previously taught theology at least for six years, the Bachelor ten
years, and the Regent twelve; and that each should have
maintained, at least, five public acts or solemn disputations in
the schools before the assembled doctors, graduates, and
scholars.

The students of the Monastic orders in the middle ages, who
were sent far from their own conventual homes to the
universities, were not left without a place of security on their
arrival in the great cities, as the writer in the British Critic,
already referred to, judiciously observes.

"Lest the students (who were sent to Paris, Oxford, or elsewhere)
might become unsettled, or even fall into vicious excesses by mixing
with the world, it was provided, that during the time of their studies
the students were members of the convent in the place where they
studied: that they might not wander from their own province, after
three years' absence they returned to the convent in which they had
first taken the vows, if the place to which they had first been sent was
out of their province. Thus the Dominican student was at home and
under discipline wherever there was a society belonging to his order;
but at the same time, his affections were specially concentrated in his
own province, whither he always returned at a given time, 'ut magis
studium suæ provinciæ vigorari possit.'"

What superior advantages must have been enjoyed by the
Dominican student in those provincial colleges of his order, the
halls of which, it must not be forgotten, were thrown open also
to lay and ecclesiastical scholars, whom the fame of the

---

[a] One of six brothers, all of whom became Dominicans; they where English
by birth. Thomas was created Cardinal of St. Sabina. Walter was Confessor of
Edward the Second, Professor in *the public schools* (as we read in the History of
Oxford) of the Brothers Preachers at Oxford, consecrated Archbishop of Armagh,
and subsequently he resigned the Primacy of Ireland.

professors attracted in crowds to their lectures! There the whole circle of the sacred and secular sciences was taught, and the most eminent doctors were located, and the sharpest young intellects exercised in scholastic collision, regulated by laws more courteous than those of chivalry. But far beyond those mental advantages was the moral discipline which flourished in those institutions. The Dominican student at Paris, Oxford, or Bologna, found in his collegiate conventual cloisters, a sanctuary for his innocence, a home of enjoyment more pure and holy, and no less cheerful in its associations than all the social influences which radiate from the domestic hearth. Not so in those early days of the universities was the condition of the secular clerk, whether lay or ecclesiastical. Then there were no colleges except those possessed by the regular clergy in their convents,[a] which suggested the expediency and the plan of erecting similar collegiate homes for the secular students.[b] Inns and hospices and hostels abounded in all the streets and alleys, where youths of gentle blood and varlets of low degree congregated for brawls and carousals; and the peace of the community was disturbed by frequent day outbreaks and midnight feuds, between turbulent academicians and officious bailiffs and sturdy burghers; and serious issues therefrom arose between the authorities of the universities and the magistrates of the cities, for violated privileges on the one hand, and municipal order broken, and public officers maltreated on the other.

From the "Houses of General Studies," the students who had been honoured with distinctions in their own cloisters, passed on to graduate in the Universities. The connexion of the Friars Preachers with the most ancient Universities, was coeval with the foundation of the Order, and almost as early as the period when these famous schools of Bologna, Paris, and Oxford, assumed the name of Universities.[c]

[a] On appelle ici Collèges les Maisons où les religieux vivaient en communauté, comme les Jacobins (Dominicains), &c.—Hist. Eccles. tom. xii. 169.

[b] Les premiers (Collèges) furent des hospices pour les religieux, qui venaient étudier à l'Université, afin qu'ils pussent vivre ensemble, séparés des séculiers. Institution au Droit Ecclésiastique.—Page 198.

[c] The general Study of Paris, as the Parisian school was first called, was founded by Charlemagne about the year 800. Under Louis VI. in 1110, the

The favourite conventual home of St. Dominic, in which he resided after his various missions and visitations, was at Bologna; it was the centre from which he governed the entire order, and sent forth colonies of the brethren to form new provinces; and there, to this day, his blessed ashes are enshrined, for the veneration of the faithful, under the mingling shadows of the university and his own venerable cloister. In Oxford he planted the first affiliation of the institute which he sent to our northern islands. He personally visited Paris, "to set in order a regular house, with cloister, dormitory, refectory, and cells for study." It was the University of Paris, conjointly with the Dean of St. Quintin, which, in the generosity of its attachment to the young and struggling community, bestowed the celebrated convent of St. Jacques on "the Brethren of the Order of Preachers, studying the sacred page at Paris," as they were styled by Pope Honorius III.—thus testifying its desire of early fraternization with a society already beginning to shine forth with a singularly intellectual character.

"The privileges accorded to the Friars of this House of Studies in Paris," as we are informed by the writer already quoted, "were much more extensive than those possessed by King's College at Cambridge, and new College at Oxford, but not in their nature unlike them. It appears that a member of the convent of St. Jacques, could demand a degree without being within the pale of the University, or subject to its laws; and that they could license two of their own Doctors to lecture without consulting the authorities, though the number of professors allowed by the University was limited."

Fleury, in his fifth discourse on Ecclesiastical History, describes the manner in which the Friars Preachers graduated in the University of Paris; and from their mode of procedure, in taking degrees, infers what the usual practice in all cases of the kind must have been. *a*

studies grew very flourishing, and the establishment obtained the name of *Academy*. In the century following the same institution became so important, by embracing within its circle of teaching all the sciences and arts, that the more pompous and significant title of UNIVERSITY was bestowed upon it. The University was a literary incorporation, composed of masters and scholars, and was not originally an aggregate of colleges, which, as we have already shown, did not exist in the beginning, unless in the communities of the regular clergy. The University of Oxford, properly so called, is probably of equal antiquity.

a Il est à croire que les frères Précheurs suivirent l'ordre qu'ils avaient trouvé établi dans l'Université.—Tom. xi. p. xxix.

The Dominicans were aggregated to the University of Paris from the beginning of their institute, and they observed the following order in advancing to the degree of Doctors in Theology. The Friar named for Bachelorship [a] by the General of the Order, commenced by expounding "the Master of the Sentences," in the school of some Doctor, for none other than a Doctor was authorized in those days to keep a school for the higher studies.

When the Bachelor had spent a year in teaching from "the Master of the Sentences," the Prior of the convent and the Doctors of the community presented this assistant teacher to the Chancellor of the church of Paris, and attested upon oath, that they deemed him qualified for his *license*, or faculty, to open a public school on his own account. After certain public examinations, and the observance of prescribed formularies, the Bachelor so recommended was elevated to the higher grade of doctorship; and then, in his own school, passed a second year of teaching the same scholastic book of divinity. During the third year of the process the new Doctor was allowed to have for his assistant a Bachelor, whom at the close of the year he presented, as he had been himself, in conjunction with the other persons above-named, for the Chancellor's license. The career was complete at the termination of three years. No one was raised to the rank of "Master of Sacred Theology," or "Doctor of Divinity," who had not thus publicly taught. So jealous was the order of St. Dominic for its character of orthodox teaching and its scholastic reputation, that no

---

[a] Scholastics were established in the cathedrals so early as the 11th century. They were often head masters in the Diocesan schools. In the 12th century it was regulated that no person should teach without their license. In the same age academical degrees were introduced for the purpose of thus licensing teachers. The degree of *Licentiate* was first given at Paris in the twelfth century. In conferring this degree a wand or *bacillum* was delivered, a school rod, whence the name "Baccalaureus or Bachelor." The title was some time after made an inferior and distinct degree. Peter Lombard, Archbishop of Paris, reduced theology into a science about the middle of the 12th century, and may be called the first of the Schoolmen, as St. Bernard has been styled the last of the Fathers. Both classes of writers treated of theology, but with this distinction, that the latter expatiated on the subject without being restricted to the method or terms of any regulated system; whereas the former laid out all the doctrines of revelation on a plan suggested by the philosophy of Aristotle. The standard work in the schools, at the time of which we are writing, was the "Four Books of Sentences," composed methodically by Peter Lombard.

degree, though conferred by an Apostolic Brief, was considered valid, unless the aspirant for the university honours had passed through the prescribed ordeal of examination, and finished the appointed period of professorship in the schools, and been presented by the proper authorities.^a

"The effect of this compact and severe system," as an Anglican observes, "thus thrown upon the chief universities of Europe was electric; it seemed to be the very thing which the church wanted, and it so filled up a void felt by the pious students of the time, that numbers immediately took the vows in Dominican convents. Nothing but the pure love of God could have actuated them; in addition to the hard life of ascetics, they had to struggle with poverty and with all the disadvantages of a newly established order."

Such was the system of studies and degrees under which arose, not only to competition, but to pre-eminence amongst the most illustrious Doctors of the University, many of the devout and humble members of the Dominican community of St. Jacques at Paris, such as Albertus Magnus, and Vincent of Beauvais, so remarkable for their knowledge of the exact and physical sciences; St. Thomas Aquinas, the angelic doctor, the great reformer of Christian philosophy and expounder of theological science; Hugh of St. Char, the eminent biblical scholar, and first author of the Concordance of the Bible—but to mention names we should describe the glories of an intellectual galaxy. Suffice it to say, that the Dominican Order, though yet a new institute, might boast of possessing for its colleges and schools, a "cursus completus," in some departments never excelled, written exclusively by its own professed members.

It was in the full vigour and earnestness of its intellectual growth and apostolical expansiveness, that the Institute of Friars Preachers stretched forth its young giant arms from the continent, to embrace our islands within the widening circuit of its zeal and enlightenment. From the second General

---

^a Declarantes etiam quod illi qui per Bullas aut Brevia apostolica, sine licentia et favore Reverendissimi Magistri vel Capitulorum Generalium promoti sunt, vel de cætero promovebuntur ad quoscumque gradus in Theologia, sive Biblicatus, sive Baccalaureatus sive magisterii, nullis libertatibus, exemptionibus, gratiis, preeminentiis hujusmodi graduatis ab ordine concessis gaudere possunt sed solum pro simplicibus Conventualibus haberi debent. Mandantes Præsidentibus Conventuum, et omnibus Fratribus Nostri ordinis sub poena *Gravioris culpæ*, ne tales sic per saltum et furtivò graduatos pro graduatis habeant, aut eos graduatos nominare præsumant.—Const. apud Font. 290.

Chapter, held at Bologna in 1221, St. Dominic sent thirteen of the Brethren to our northern shores. These men of apostolic meekness and humility, travelled in the suite of Peter de Rupibus, or Roche,*a* Bishop of Winchester, on his return from the Holy Land. Arriving at Canterbury, they presented themselves before the Archbishop, the celebrated Stephen Langton, the assertor of Magna Charta, and reformer of education in the English University.*b* The illustrious Prelate received the religious strangers with paternal benignity; and as their profession was to announce the Gospel, he commanded the Prior of the Pilgrim community, Gilbert de Fresnoy, to preach forthwith in his presence in a church where he himself had promised to deliver the sermon on that occasion. The Primate was so pleased and edified with the words of light and unction which fell from the lips of the zealous missionary, that he ever after most graciously cherished the new order, both in its convents and on its missions. Thence they proceeded towards London, and without much delay, for that city was not marked out as their first resting-place, they continued their journey towards Oxford, the place of their destination. It was on the Feast of the Assumption of the Blessed Virgin, the Patroness of the Order, that "the Friars of the Virgin Mary," as the Dominicans were first named,*c* arrived at this famous seat of learning. At once they erected an oratory in honour of the Mother of God, and dedicated their schools under the invocation of St. Edward the Confessor. Thus the first house of the Dominicans in England arose near the walls of its chief university, and the learned convent at Oxford became the mother house of the English and Irish affiliations; for the establishments of the Institute in both countries were, for a very long period, administered by the same central government in England, and were subject to the authority and visitation of the same Pro-

---

a "Des Roches."—*Lingard.*

b It was by his aid principally that Fulk of Neuilly effected the "prelude to that greater reformation, wrought not long after by Reginald and the Dominican preachers; all of them instruments in God's hand to save souls f.om the perils of study."—*Life of Stephen Langton*, London, Toovey, 1845.

c "In principio Fratres ordinis dicebantur Fratres Virginis Mariæ."—S. Anton apud Touron Vie de S. Dominique, p. 291.

vincial. In England and Ireland, the Brethren of the Order bore the same popular designation of "Blackfriars," from the dark flowing cloak they were accustomed to wear on public and solemn occasions over their conventual habit of spotless white; while in Scotland, as in France, they were distinguished from other fraternities by the name of "Jacobins," because the first colony planted in Northern Britain, came direct from the Convent of St. Jacques, (Conventus S. Jacobi,) in Paris.

Friar Reginald, or Ronald, of Bologna, whom some writers suppose to have been an Irishman, is specially named as one of the number sent to these countries by St. Dominic. Leaving his fellow travellers in England, he passed over to our island. He is the reputed founder of the Order in Ireland, was subsequently appointed Papal Penitentiary in Rome, and died Archbishop of Armagh and Primate of the Irish church. He must have been soon joined by other brethren, for communities were formed in Dublin and other places in 1224. The first convent of the Order was St. Saviour's, which occupied the present site of the Four Courts in Dublin. This house had been a monastery of the Cistercian order, and such was the fraternal sympathy then existing between the two orders of St. Bernard and Dominic—who was then dead but three years—that the monks of the former surrendered as a present to the friars of the latter, their own abbey. The institute thus introduced into the country, was admirably suited to the character of the people, and hailed as likely to confer great blessings on the church and nation, in the distracted condition of both. Before the end of the century, very many of the great cities and towns possessed Dominican convents and schools. The system already described as prevailing in the continental houses, was extended to all the establishments in this country, in all its fervour, regularity, and strictness; so that a special account of the ascetic life and yet public usefulness of the institute in Ireland, would be little more than a repetition of the same facts with merely some incidental varieties. The architectural beauty and extent of their earliest foundations in this kingdom, may be conceived from the ruins of these ancient structures yet standing in magnificent desolation, such as the Belltower of Drogheda, the Black Abbey of Kilkenny, the ruins of Kilmallock Friary; and as to the learning and other high endowments which illustrated the Irish communities of the order within the first century of his existence amongst our forefathers, a pretty fair estimate may be drawn from the brilliant and numerous array of Dominican Prelates, who were raised to the highest ecclesiastical dignities and offices in our national church in that limited period; a number which, instead of diminishing, rather increased in succeeding ages. To name only the Metropolitans, there were of Armagh, Archbishops, Robert Archer, 1237; Henry, 1245; Reginald, 1247; Patrick O'Scanlan, 1261; Raymund, 1286; Walter Joyce, 1306; Martin of Bologna, 1307; Roland Joyce, 1313: of Dublin, Archbishops, John of Derlington, 1279; William de Hothun, 1297: of Cashel, David Mac Kelly, one of the venerable fathers of the first General Council of Lyons. A long list of names equally illustrious, linking the Dominican order with the episcopal succession in various sees of Ireland, may, within the same short period, be traced; and this circumstance is the more singular, as the spirit of the institute was adverse in those days to such promotions, and vehemently protested against them as injurious to the best interests of the society, and seldom was known to yield to the imposition of such honours, unless when overruled by the authority of the Holy See. It might be difficult to account for such a number of eminent men in an order just emerging from its first difficulties, if we did not know that, as on the continent, so here in like manner, ecclesiastics of rank and merit took the habit and mingled with the novices of the order. It was thus that the last-named prelate, Archbishop Mac Kelly, had been Dean of Cashel before he took his solemn vows as a Friar Preacher in "St. Mary's of the Island," at Cork.

The cultivation of learning which so strikingly marked the character of the order in foreign countries, ever since its institution, soon illustrated it also in our own island. A connection was maintained from the beginning between the Irish branch of the Dominicans, and the English and continental universities and houses of general studies. In the year 1314, the head superior of the order, Berangerius de Landorra, addressed a letter from the General Chapter held in London, to the priors, sub-priors, and brethren in Ireland, granting them, with the approval of the Deffinitory, that they might keep at free charge two students of the Irish province at Oxford, two at Cambridge, a third in addition to the two already maintained at Paris, two at London, and as many others as they might be entitled (secundam ratam terræ vestræ) to send to the houses of general studies in various parts of the world. The general recommended at the same time, that some students specially qualified for philosophical pursuits, should be sent to the particular houses appointed in England for that department of science. By this intercourse the Irish Dominicans were enabled to enjoy, from the earliest settlement of the order in this country, the most choice and ample opportunities of mental culture afforded in the middle ages.

By the reflux of such talent to our shores, bringing back the purest and most profound learning of the age, it is easy to comprehend how the intellectual character of the entire country must have been influenced and elevated. The friars, who had graduated on the continent and in England, opened schools in various parts of this kingdom. Their houses of studies must have been in a very flourishing state in Dublin, previously to the erection of the first Irish university. In the document published by Archbishop de Bicknore, on the 10th of February, 1320, for the establishment and administration of the new university, the schools then in actual operation under the conduct of the Dominicans and Franciscans, were specially noticed, as having been recognized as canonical, "Scholas Fratrum Prædicatorum ac Minorum duximus canonizandas."

The Dominicans of Ireland became at once connected with the learned body of the university. No sooner were its doors thrown open, than the Friars Preachers entered with others to claim a share in the freshest honours of the first Irish academy. Four on that solemn occasion were admitted to the degree of doctorship—three in theology, and one in canon law : viz., William Roddiart, the dean of the cathedral, who was appointed chancellor of the university; Henry Cogry, a Franciscan; and two Dominicans, namely, Edward of Caermarthen, who subsequently was consecrated Bishop of Ardfert, and William de Hardite. De Hardite was, in precedence of time, *the first honoured with the Doctor's degree;* a distinction conferred, no doubt, for some acknowledged superiority. However indifferent the circumstance may now appear, it was thought to be an incident so memorable, that it has been handed down in various records of the time. Thomas Carve, in his Irish annals, informs us, that he was not only the first Master and Doctor of the Irish university—" Universitas Dubliniensis............cujus primus Magister seu Doctor fuit Gulielmus Hardite ordinis Prædicatorum"—but also that he promoted a great number of others Doctors in Divinity—"qui sub prædicto Archiepiscopo plurimos Doctores Sacræ Theologiæ creavit." (page 205.)ᵃ We shall be pardoned for lingering with complacency on this apparently trivial event. We wish that "our own" young Ireland, brought up as it ought to be in a healthy state of Catholicity, intelligence, and patriotism, should, in the present revival of literary national recollections, be reminded that the primacy of collegiate honours in this country was conferred on the shorn head of a member of a religious order, which, perhaps, is now foredoomed to suppression—that the first chair of the sacred sciences erected in an Irish university, was occupied by a Dominican Friar—and that from a priest of the order of Preachers, the highest graduates who have been ever since admitted to their degrees in this kingdom, must trace their academical descent.

As long as the university which was annexed to St. Patrick's cathedral was properly supported, the different orders of the regular clergy participated in its honours and privileges, and contributed to its efficiency and reputation. It has just been observed that the Dominican and Franciscan orders had representatives amongst its first professors; and as we proceed in our historical outline, we may be permitted incidentally to

---

ᵃ Annals of Ireland, in 4th volume of Camden, p. 488.
Annals of J. Grace, translated for Irish Archæological Society. By Rev. R. Butler, p. 96.

mention, that in the year 1364, a chair of theology was endowed for a member of the Augustinian order, also in the college of the cathedral, by the Lord Lieutenant of Ireland, Lionel Duke of Clarence, who gave for that purpose an acre of land at Stachallane, and the advowson of the church charged with an annual stipend of ten marks for the lecturer. From the inadequacy of its funds for the maintenance of masters and scholars, the university declined gradually, until, in progress of time, it became almost practically extinct. This failure in the working of the only incorporated literary institution in the country, must have been a heavy discouragement to the aspiring youth who would crowd its halls. Such was the state of collegiate learning in the metropolis, when the devoted and disinterested zeal of the Dominican fathers for the advancement and support of public education, was exerted to meet the critical emergency, and, as far as it might be, to supply from the resources at their own command, the means of academical improvement. They erected a college for instruction in all branches of knowledge, from grammar to theology, and admitted to its advantages all classes of students, lay and ecclesiastical. This institution is described in the historical note annexed to Mr. Wyse's Speech on Academical Education.

"A. D. 1423. As a preparatory academy, or high school to the University, or to meet the scantiness of the education there afforded, the Dominicans of Dublin opened a 'Gymnasium,' as it is called by the chronicler of the order, on Usher's Island, which was then a populous suburb of old Dublin. It was dedicated under the patronage of St. Thomas Aquinas, the angelic Doctor of their schools. To this seat of learning, youth crowded for instruction.[a] The full attendance of masters and scholars was not unfrequently interrupted. The Liffey divided the convent of the Dominicans from their seminary. The former occupied the present site of the Four Courts; the House of Studies was on the opposite side of the river. When swollen by floods, the river was impassable. There was no bridge. That which had been built at a remote period, had fallen forty-three years before. The professors and students of the convent, and the secular youth who lived in the neighbourhood of Ormond Quay, (Juvenes Ostmanorum burgi), (Oxmantown), were thus often prevented from attending the schools. With the perseverance and munificence characteristic of the ancient regular orders, the community of St. Saviour's, as the Dominican Friary was called, at their own expense and that of the benefac-

---

[a] Quo confluebant juvenes pro philosophicis et theologicis disciplinis.—Heb. Dom. 193.

tors of their house,ᵃ erected the stone bridge of four arches, which was called 'Old Bridge,' or 'Dublin Bridge,' and was the only structure of the kind in the Metropolis for more than two centuries. It is an interesting fact in the history of education in Ireland, that the only stone bridge in the capital of the kingdom was built by one of the monastic orders, as a communication between a convent and its college, a thoroughfare thrown across a dangerous river for teachers and scholars to frequent halls of learning, where the whole range of the sciences of the day was taught gratuitously.ᵇ On it stood a Font for Holy Water, long undisturbed by the spirit of later times.ᶜ The bridge fell in the floods of 1802."

Unsatisfied with their exertions and sacrifices in the cause of education, while anything remained to be done that might be effected by energy, the regulars of Dublin aimed at the accomplishment of a nobler project than they had yet collectively, or in separate communities, undertaken. These professors of monastic vows—the adoption or observance of which is, in the evil days on which we are fallen, proscribed under penalty of fine and banishment—displayed in the year 1475 an act of glorious audacity in the application they presented to the Holy See for powers to erect a university; that of St. Patrick's having been allowed by this time to fall into inefficiency and decay. From the same source which supplied our last extract, we derive the following interesting information: —

"Third Period, A. D. 1475. In this year a fresh and vigourous effort was made for the restoration of the University, or rather for the foundation of a similar institution, unconnected with that of St. Patrick's cathedral. This movement originated with the four mendicant orders, and was headed by the Dominicans.ᵈ They addressed a memorial to Pope Sixtus IV. for the canonical authority to found such an establishment in Dublin. In this petition they set forth, that no house of General Studies was then flourishing in the kingdom of Ireland, (nullum *viget* Studium Generale), where degrees might be taken or studies prosecuted, though the youth of the country were most anxious for learning, and Professors qualified to teach theology and the arts abounded in the four orders;ᵉ that they were obliged to cross the sea

ᵃ Sumptibus Fratrum Prædicatorum Suorumque Benefactorum—*Ibid.* ut supra.
ᵇ Walsh and Whitelaw's History of Dublin.
ᶜ Puerque vidi vas pro aqua lustrali.—De Burgo, p. 195.
ᵈ Dominicans, Francicans, Augustinians and Carmelites.
ᵉ "Licet in Civitatibus et Villis muris munitis, in dicta Insula consistentibus, quæ Guerris perspe affliguntur, Multitudo præfatorum Quatuor ordinum professorum propter eorum exemplarem vitam, et Verbi Dei prædicationem admittantur, tamen scholares et studere volentes, de facile in illis non recipiuntur; quod que in dicta insula reperiantur quamplures dictorum ordinum Professores Magistri et Baccalaurei in Theologia et Artibus sufficienter instructi, et quamplures scholares ad hujusmodi scientias bene dispositi, qui in eis proficere cupiunt, et quorum ingenia de die in diem decrescere et torpore cernuntur, in maximum reipublicæ Christianæ et Fidei Catholicæ detrimentum, eo quod eis tutus non patet accessus ad aliquod studium generale," &c. &c.

with great risk of life, many of their brethren having suffered shipwreck—and to encounter expenses which they were not able to meet in foreign universities; and that, moreover, in foreign universities they had to endure a cold reception, and to combat national antipathies. 'In Universitatibus alienis—frigescente caritate multorum, et pullulante discordia nationum.'

"The Pope assented to this prayer, and published a Brief, bearing date 5 Kal Maii, 1475, empowering the memorialists to erect a University for the cultivation of the liberal arts and theology, (studium generale artium et theologiæ), with all rights and privileges appertaining thereto, similar to those enjoyed by Oxford.

"History does not inform us, whether special buildings were erected for the purpose of carrying out the powers given to the religious orders by this pontifical diploma. It is most probable, that as the first University was located in St. Patrick's cathedral, so the new institution was formed in connexion with the convents of the four orders, the halls of each being raised to the rank of a College of the University.

The statement put forward by the historical annotator, in the concluding passage of this extract, is reserved and cautious, as it should be, in the absence of documentary evidence respecting the manner in which the regular clergy, when authorized to establish a university in the Irish metropolis, accomplished their enlightened project. That the attempt was an instant and utter failure, we cannot, upon any presumptive ground, be persuaded to admit. It appears to us most improbable that, having obtained from the Holy See the boon which they so anxiously sought, prospective of so much honour to themselves, and auspicious of so much advantage to men of learning and studious youth in general, the religious orders should fling such a prerogative incontinently to the winds. Such inconstancy of mind, such recklessness about their own privileges, such indifference to the public good, were never the temper, or the practice characteristic of monastical corporations. If the undertaking proved abortive, not from any lack of zeal or disinterestedness on the part of the regular communities, but from crushing opposition, or irresistible obstacles encountered at the onset, is it not strange that no record to which we can have access in the archives of the four orders, bears any trace of such a struggle? Our deliberate opinion is, that the University, privileged by Sixtus IV., started noiselessly and in the fulness of its stature into life and activity, as soon as the bull for its institution was accepted in this country; and that, from its birth, it silently waxed strong, and flourished in connexion with the monasteries until their suppression; and in this opinion we are confirmed by a passage in Campion's History of Ireland, which we shall have occasion immediately to cite.[a]

Dr. Todd, of Trinity College, thinks otherwise.[b] He treats the whole affair, discourteously enough, as " a vox and præterea nihil " of a papal bull. But what are the grounds on which he thus lightly discards the supposition that the university of Pope Sixtus ever obtained "a local habitation or a name?" Forsooth, he says, because first, "His bull provided it with no endowment;" and secondly, because " no buildings were ever erected." But he forgets to inquire whether the memorialists applied to his holiness for funds to raise a grand structure, or to enrich learned chairs; and, in the next place, whether special buildings, or additional fixed revenues, were indispensably requisite for the opening and maintenance of the University under consideration. We opine not, on both queries.

It was not for leave or means to build up from the ground a *material* university with stone and timber, brick and mortar, that the good men who originated this movement applied to the sovereign pontiff, but for powers to institute a literary body,[c] a university incorporate for all faculties and studies in their own country, wherein, for the causes recited in their petition, they might be enabled "to graduate at home as licentiates, bachelors, and doctors, with all and each of the privileges, immunities, graces, favours, exemptions, and concessions, in general and in particular, as granted to the rector, masters, doctors, scholars, and persons of the University of Oxford." We cannot see either, that there was an absolute necessity for the construction of such buildings in the present case. Why might not the senatus academicus solemnly hold its commence-

---

[a] Page 40.

[b] Remarks on some statements attributed to T. Wyse, Esq. M. P. in his speech in Parliament on Academical Education in Ireland, July 19, 1844, by James Henthorn Todd, D. D., V.P.R.I.A., Fellow of Trinity College, Dublin.

[c] Taking up the first book at hand on the subject, Institution au Droit Ecclesiastique, tom. 1. p. 195. (Fleury), we find that Universities are defined to be Companies of Masters and Scholars. This body was not at first an aggregate of colleges, but was composed of masters who were scattered and gave their lessons in particular places. They were not lodged in collegiate houses until towards the middle of the 15th century, when instruction was transferred to these establishments.

ments and terms? Why might not the students pursue their ordinary courses within the spacious halls, which were the ancient schools of the conventual establishments of Dublin, at least *pro tempore*, until, if found expedient and attainable, more appropriate and concentrated structures should be raised? Was there a single stone laid for the University of St. Patrick? Were not all the universities, at home and abroad, originally schools enclosed within the precincts of churches? Why might not, in like manner, the new university have been aggregated to the religious houses? Is there anything impossible, unusual, or absurd, in the assumption that such was the fact?

But the pope promised no income?—Assuredly not : his holiness was not asked to tax the apostolic treasury, or to commission the mendicant friars to quest or levy an impost on their friends and benefactors for the purpose of creating rich fellowships, paying stipendiary professors, and furnishing chambers and commons to poor scholars. Then, argues Dr. Todd, how could the studies of such a university be provided for? We will tell him. There was a time when pious and learned priests were honoured in college, church, and cloister, for their strict observance of the vow of evangelical poverty —men truly independent "titulo paupertatis"—men who were doctors, bachelors, and licentiates, though in cowls and scapulars, with leathern girdles and discalceated feet, and who, without fee or reward, could have filled the professorial chairs with as much unaffected dignity and sterling talent—who could have conducted their scholars through the college course with as consummate skill and complete success—and who, entrusted with the powers of the university, could as discreetly and legitimately confer degrees and honours, as any board of provosts, fellows, masters, &c., established in the modern seats of learning, upon which church and state have lavished with emulous profusion the wealth and patronage of this world. In the four religious orders as then existing in Ireland, the memorial addressed to Sixtus the Fourth, states that such professors were numerous. These men loved learning for learning's sake, and because they loved it, were zealous for its diffusion. They were not influenced by base lucre, as modern professors of science, of whom Sir H. Davy speaks. "There are," says the philosopher, "very few persons in England who pursue science with true dignity; it is followed, as connected with objects of profit."—*Consolations in Travel*, 1830.

Though unendowed with vested property, nevertheless the safety and permanence of this academical institution were sufficiently secured by its connection with the religious houses. With them it was, thenceforward, to stand or fall. And amidst the turbulence of lawless times, what shelter more sacred and shaded than the cloisters within which this literary establishment was planted? What preservative more certain against the poverty with which the university of 1320 was so often shaken to its roots, shorn of its honours, and was then actually withering away, branch and stem, than the stability of the monastic state upon which the university of 1475 was engrafted and intended to be supported?

The suppression and plunder of these convents in the succeeding century, we hold to have been tantamount to the disfranchisement and spoliation of the second Irish University. So identified was academical education in those days with the monastic system—both were felled together by the same sacrilegious and tyrannical violence—both were stript together by the same act of unmerited confiscation. When will the day of retribution come? We ask not for restitution of property, but of rights—freedom of religion and **education** upon which we boldly insist.

It is not to be supposed **that the** older university had been utterly extinct, before the regular clergy so energetically exerted themselves for the restoration of studies, by the establishment of a similar and independent institution. It certainly may be said, that it languidly existed, so reduced had it become in reputation and usefulness under the pressure of poverty. To this cause alone Sir James Ware ascribes its insensible decay. "The maintenance of the scholars failing, the university likewise by degrees came to nothing."[*] He acknowledges, however, that " there remained indeed some footsteps of an aca-

---

[*] Antiquities of Ireland, chap. xv. p. 38.

demy in the time of Henry VII. For in the provincial council held in Christ Church, in Dublin, before Walter Fitzsimons, then Archbishop of Dublin, the archbishop, suffragans, and the clergy of the province of Dublin granted certain stipends to be pay'd yearly to the *readers[a] of the* UNIVERSITY." This timely and generous effort for the revival of studies, and the renovation of the university in St. Patrick's, occurred in 1496, twenty-one years after the first appearance of its younger and more vigorous competitor within the monastic cloisters. Could the success of the latter have excited and encouraged her elder sister to make this last recorded appeal, for her restoration to the almost forfeited honours and the almost forgotten preeminence to which she was entitled over all other schools in the metropolis and in the kingdom? That the venerable Irish university of the cathedral never lost its privileges, we have undoubted proof—that, in the hour of its need, its wants were largely supplied by the conventual schools—and that when *these* were closed under Henry VIII. *that* languished and died we have the testimony of a[b] Protestant historian who lived in Dublin, and was deeply interested in the cause of academical education, as is evident from his report of the speeches delivered at the meeting for the erection of a university[c] before Trinity College was founded. Campion, in his "Historie of Ireland," says, "Neither was the same, (to wit—the Universitie ordained in Develin by Alexander Bigmore, archbishop) ever disfranchised, but onely through variety of time discontinued, and *now since the subversion of monasteries utterly extinct, wherein the divines were cherished,* and OPEN EXERCISE MAINTAINED," p. 123. The reader will judge for himself whether Dr. Todd is warranted in winding up his argument against Mr. Wyse in the following sweeping statement in a tone rather oracular:—" It is unnecessary to pursue any

---

[a] Lecturers.
[b] Campion was not at this time a convert to the Catholic faith. (A.D. 1570.)
[c] " Whereof comming home to my lodging I tooke notes, and here I will deliver them, as neere as I can call them to minde, in the same words and sentences that I heard them." We refer the reader to the perusal of them, as most interesting and instructive on the subject of founding colleges, particularly the speech of James Stanihurst, an esquire of worship, Recorder of Develin.—p. 194.

further the history of those transactions, since it must be now sufficiently obvious that the whole story of an endowed university—or any *university at all, endowed or not endowed*—which was confiscated and destroyed at the suppression of monasteries is *an absolute fiction:* and consequently, that the argument, if it be an argument which Mr. Wyse would found upon such a misrepresentation, must fall to the ground." To make out his case, Dr. Todd lays great stress on the words in the memorial to Sixtus IV. "Quod in dicta insula *nullum* viget studium generale." We have as good a right to underline *viget* which proves our view—that the university was not then in a *flourishing* condition though *existing*.

The older university was kept up until the suppression of the cathedral under Henry the Eighth. In the chain of historical testimony by which we have been endeavouring to trace down to the time of the introduction of Protestantism into Ireland, the continuous existence of university education in the cathedral, correlatively with general studies in the religious houses, we may bring forward as a terminating and important link, the provision in the charter of Philip and Mary for the restoration of St. Patrick's church, eight years after its interdict by the royal usurper of ecclesiastical jurisdiction; wherein it is specially recited that amongst the most lamentable consequences of the dissolution of the collegiate and cathedral church, was the closing up of its halls of learning for youth, "verum etiam quod dolendum magis est, pueritiam solitam educationem non habuisse," and that one of the principal motives by which their majesties were influenced in the re-establishment of the cathedral, was to revive its collegiate character, by the re-opening of its schools, in which the youth of Ireland might be trained in moral conduct and the arts and refinements of social life. "Ut hujus regni nostri Hiberniæ pueritia in morum civilitate et virtute erudiatur."

From what has been said, we may collect that there were two universities in Ireland, that of the cathedral, and the other of the monasteries. Even so late as 1584, seven years before the foundation of Trinity College, there appears to have been an impression yet lingering in the public mind, that there ought to be erected two universities in Ireland—a notion originating, most probably, in the popular recollection and belief, that before the confiscation of church property and the suppression of monastic institutions, there had been two independent academies in the capital of the kingdom. In the letter of the Lord Deputy, Sir John Perrot, to the Lord Treasurer of England, on the disposable property of St. Patrick's, and the public purposes to which its revenues might be applied, it is stated, that its yearly income amounted to about four thousand marks; and " this sum," he writes " would serve to begin the foundation of *two* universities, and endow a *couple* of colleges in them with £1000 per annum apiece."

If the more ancient university had not flourished uniformly in every stage of its progress up to the time of the establishment of Trinity College, it was owing mainly to the pressure of the poverty which checked its expansion from the beginning, as has been already stated on the authority of Sir James Ware, and not from any lack of zeal or disinterestedness on the part of the clergy, secular or regular, for upholding the dignity and usefulness of the national institution. In its struggles from its infancy to its decrepitude and final decay, the helping hand of royal bounty was not extended to it with the promptitude and munificence to which it was justly entitled. It strikes us, also, as rather strange, that history records no very energetic measure proposed, no large sum contributed for the maintenance of the Irish university by any of the intervening bishops of Dublin, between the founder and Fitzsimons. Might such indifference be traced to the fact that the prelates who occupied the metropolitan see during that long period were, almost without exception, Englishmen by birth and education; each having but a life interest in his see; each proud of his own alma mater, Oxford or Cambridge; having perhaps little sympathy with the native clergy, regular or secular, for the establishment or endowment of a National Irish university, which under proper encouragement might develop Irish talent and become a rival to the English seats of learning?

When it became the policy of the foreign rulers to Protestantize Catholic Ireland, then grudging parsimony, cold neglect, and national antipathies were laid aside. The royal and Anglican-church solicitude for extending all the lights, honours, and emoluments of the highest university education to the hitherto unendowed mind of Ireland, became marvellously anxious and liberal. A new spirit sat in the high places, and it held out the glory of learning and the gifts of the state, as temptations that might allure the young aspiring intellect of this country to fall down and adore, after a modern fashion unknown in the Island of Saints. To buttress up the tottering universities of Ireland, or rather to build up from its foundation a new national academy, the queen bestowed upon it **great** wealth, (no matter **now** how that wealth had been got,) and built it colleges like palaces, and encircled it amidst spacious fields, and planted it round with pleasant gardens. "But at last," says Sir James Ware, after relating the withering parsimony of former times, "Queen Elizabeth restor'd the honour of the university, and built the colledge dedicated to the Blessed Trinity, and *indowed it with revenues* and priviledges," xv. p. 38. The spot on which the truly magnificent structure arose was once holy, lifting up its proud pinnacles over the ruins of the monastery of All Hallowes. Upon that place, in the chanted offices of night and day, the protection of all the saints of God's church used, before the hand of sacrilegious spoliations was stretched forth upon it, to be devoutly invoked. In all this there was something mournfully ominous of the change that had **taken place**. The new college and doctrine **were** based **on** the subversion **of** Catholic principles **and institutions. What** a large measure of the evils—**religious,** moral, intellectual, and social—which have befallen **our afflic**ted country for the last two centuries and a half, still lies accumulated—as yet an unexpiated sin—at the gates of Trinity College, Dublin! It is not easy to think of the legalized ignorance to which the mind of Ireland had been consigned for so long a period without calling up the apparition of the grim spectre of Old Trinity. How can we read, without shuddering, the dread records of soul-murder—worse even than death or exile—and all the laws proscriptive of education, which the fell demon of apostacy inscribed in dark characters on the portals of that royal citadel of bigotry and exclusiveness? Was it not on that threshold of high-church Protestantism, that hecatombs of the children of saints were sacrificed to the Moloch of an overshadowing pitiless sectarian ascendancy?

Amidst the political and religious troubles which succeeded the expulsion and outlawry of the parochial clergy and monastic orders, we can catch, but at intervals, and from scattered spots, the fitful glimmerings of the torch of Catholic science, now escaping through chinks of caverned rocks and other hiding places, where aged priests and friars, unable or unwilling to flee, lingered about to teach the poor persecuted children of the land; and at another time gleaming dimly, like expiring beacon-lights on the creeks of the sea-coast, when learning, banished from all its accustomed haunts, was forced to take its mournful departure from the shores, on which, in days of old, it had welcomed the strangers who had come in quest of knowledge, from every clime, to the schools of Lismore, Armagh, Cleonard, Ross, Clonfert, and Bangor. Now the Irishman is to be the exile and wanderer, in quest of learning denied him at home, and every Christian land, save that which was nearest, returns the rights of hospitality; and every university, college, school, and convent abroad, emulously contending for the honour of enrolling the poor homeless Irish student amongst its doctors, scholars, or brethren, throws open wide its gates, and compels him with generous violence to enter, and throw aside his pilgrim's staff, and rest his weary feet, and abide in peace, as in more ancient times, strangers were wont to find a home in the schools and cloisters of his fatherland. Spain, France, Italy, Portugal, Belgium—may it never be forgotten how each of your people succoured Irish genius in the hour of its need, and sheltered it when harbourless, and slaked its thirst for knowledge at the fountains of living waters, and broke to it the bread of every science.

We would on the present occasion follow the fortunes, so replete with mournful interest, of our exiled countrymen, who matriculated in foreign literary establishments; but the space we have already occupied reminds us, that we must close our lucubrations at the most dismal period of our educational history in Ireland, when the persecuting legislation of its English Mistress sealed up the doors of every college, convent, and school, in which a Catholic might instruct his mind without sacrificing his conscience. Our narrative has already extended beyond the bounds prescribed, and we cannot but regret that it has dragged its slow length along with, perhaps, an unavoidable wearisomeness of detail, and has been marked by a dry and methodical style of composition, so much less attractive than the matchless simplicity of the monastic legend, or the discursive and salient literature that should characterise an Irish periodical. But our subject lay more with the schoolmen, than with ancient chroniclers or modern reviewers. Our object in pursuing the line of inquiry now brought to a close, was to convict of ignorance or misrepresentation, the outcry so often heard within parliament, and repeated in a multitudinous variety of ways abroad, in print and speech, during the debates on the Maynooth, Academic, Trinity College, and Catholic Disabilities bills; that the Catholic Church, in all the grades of its priesthood, from the highest pontiff to the lowest levite, has been at all times unfavourable to the culture and spread of gospel knowledge and scientific acquirements. To overwhelm such dark prejudices and calumnies with utter discomfiture, by opening up the whole historical subject of Catholic university, collegiate, and academical education, such a guide should go before our readers, as the author of the Mores Catholici, holding a lamp filled with the purest and most fragrant oil which may be extracted from every branch and fruit and flower of the tree of knowledge, and trimmed by the genius of every art and science and language. Then, indeed, would historic truth be unveiled in all its lustre and beauty; then would the temple of learning, reared by Catholic hands, be lighted up in all its glorious splendours, and shown in all its sacred harmonies of symmetry and strength and taste; and every shrine would be illumined, which has entombed for ages the honoured and blessed memories of hooded scholars; and every mural tablet of stone or brass, would be made legible with its mystic inscription, and made fresh with its emblems of the schools intertwined with monastic symbols; and all the rows of niches solemnly shadowing the statues and images of bishops, chancellors, clerks, monks, civilians, who were once the most celebrated doctors, or the most munificent founders, patrons, and benefactors of colleges and halls still called after Catholic saints, would be revealed and shine out amidst the rich and varied erudition with which the multifarious reading of Kenelm Digby colours and illustrates every subject upon which his mind is poured out, like tinted glories streaming up through an ancient minster. As for our part, we must content with carrying our small taper into one nook, as it were, of such a spacious topic as is the connection of the regular clergy with the rise and advancement and reformation of the higher departments of studies. From one isolated spot, but sufficiently luminous and prominent in the history of the literary world, we have endeavoured to dissipate some dark and malignant prejudices, which gathered most densely upon that particular quarter. The Dominican Monk, or the Black-Friar was— as popularly imagined and fictitiously drawn— a horrid spectre which could scarcely be supposed to dwell or be at rest amidst a blaze of intellectual illumination. Yet so it was—the Dominican—whether doctor of the university, student of the college, preacher of the temple, missionary of the world, artist of the studio, rapt with ecstasy as a saint, or with visions of transcendent loveliness as a poet, or with inspired dreams as a prophet—*his* ordinary home and choicest repose were to abide and rejoice in the encircling and spreading light of all sciences divine and human. This is not the too vivid colouring of an admiring partiality—it is the truth reflected upon our convictions from the many illuminated pages which we have read, concerning the objects, laws, pursuits, services, of a society, which in all the writings of the learned, is usually called "the illustrious order of St. Dominic." Had we put forward in front of our argument in defence of the contributions rendered to literature by the religious orders, the Benedicdines, for instance, already so honoured, even by infidel writers, such as Gibbon, for their immense accumulation of learning, the most recondite and extensive ; or had we given the prominence—so deservedly due to their company—to the Jesuits, whose superiority in every compartment of elegant and instructive knowledge, and inappreciable services in the conduct and improvement of school education, their bitterest enemies durst not gainsay; we would be only reproducing evidence already known to the public, often through the pages of this Review; but to drag forth from the obscurity in which it has been shrouded by circumstances, of which none has been so influential as its own constant and avowed dislike to the blowing of the unevangelical trump of self-laudation, an Institute little known to literary fame in these heretical countries, and in these modern times; such testimony, however scantily we may have supplied it, and feebly put it forth, is, notwithstanding, novel, and may not be without its special weight and impressiveness in the mass of evidence that has been already collected, and so variously exhibited in proof of the services and zeal of the monastic bodies generally, in promoting the cause of mental cultivation and progress.

OLIVER CROMWELL.[a]

(From the Rambler.)

PURITANISM is that form of religious delusion which clothes the spiritual pride of its intentions in the most grotesque assumption of scriptural phraseology. It makes hideous faces at the world, the flesh, and the devil, remaining all the while by no means on bad terms with any one of them; but it stipulates with all three that its ordinary language must always seem to be that of vernacular inspiration. Its visage is long, and its looks are sour. By its ordinary admirers little is seen but the whites of its eyes; nor would common spectators imagine, if history had not spoken, that those hands, folded so meekly on its bosom, could wield the sword of the soldier or the sceptre of sovereignty. Owen, Baxter, Howe, Flavel, and

---

[a] History of the English Commonwealth, from the Execution of Charles I. to the Death of Cromwell. By M. Guizot. Translated by Andrew M. Scoble. In two volumes. Bentley, London.

Manton, were its pundits and prophets, so far as pen and paper, prayer, doctrine, and preaching, were concerned; yet to have a living personification before us of what the system really was,—of what it professed to do, and what it actually perpetrated, it will be necessary to study with closeness and care the subject of these pages. Oliver Cromwell may teach us many lessons. His lot was cast in extraordinary times. An ecclesiastical revolt from the Holy See, such as the world had never witnessed since the days of Arius and his imitators, had convulsed Europe and desolated the Church. On the continent the tide of error had begun to retire; in England it was otherwise. Her crown had pushed aside the tiara; whereby Erastianism, selfishness, and absolute power had triumphed. The people had lost the liberties upon which they once lived and revelled, as derived traditionally from their Saxon forefathers. Henry VIII. had trampled them under his feet with the same ruthlessness which he manifested in the decapitation of his wives: nor were the Stuarts better than the Tudors; except that their follies and absurdities might be considered less formidable than the occasional abilities of their predecessors.

Elizabeth was still on the throne when Oliver Cromwell was born at Huntingdon, in a large Gothic house, to which the brewery of his father was attached, on the 25th of April, in A.D. 1599. Robert Cromwell, a gentleman of good lineage but narrow fortune, had purchased the property of one Philip Clamp, whose fermentation of malt and hops had established a creditable business on the premises,—far too profitable an affair to be sneezed at by the new-comer, although his wife, a sensible lady, originally named Steward, the widow of William Lynne, and rejoicing in a jointure of 60*l*. per annum, claimed her descent from the royal family of Scotland. This highly respectable couple had three sons, of whom Oliver was the second, and the only survivor growing up to manhood. There were also six daughters, who lived to be well married; besides another, carried to her grave in early life. The mother could have been no ordinary woman, as was shown by her entire conduct through life, manifesting as it did a combination of simple tastes with great energy of mind. A portrait of her may still be seen at Hinchinbrook, with a small and sweet mouth, betokening not less firmness than gentleness of character; the light pretty hair over her forehead is modestly enveloped in a white satin hood; she wears a velvet cardinal, with a rich jewel clasping it. Her brother-in-law, Sir Oliver Cromwell, stood godfather to the future Protector, on the fourth day after his birth; holding the child at the baptismal font, and giving him his own name. Alison has not failed to remark, that Napoleon was brought into the world upon a sofa covered with tapestry representing the Iliad of Homer: about as sagacious a nonjuror, who subsequently bought and inhabited the house of the Cromwells at Huntingdon, used to point out a curious figure of the devil wrought in the hangings of the bed-chamber in which the conqueror of Dunbar and Worcester first gladdened the hearts of his parents. They had soon some trouble with him. Without noticing the legends of his being carried off by a monkey, and saved from drowning by the worthy curate of Cunnington, it is certain that his early tastes were for the excitements attending personal peril, and that his temper was wayward and violent. He was eighth or ninth cousin once removed on the maternal side to his rival Charles I.; and when only five years old is said to have had the honour of being a playmate with that prince, and in some boyish quarrel inflicting on him a bloody nose. There was a royal palace in the neighbourhood, to which, no doubt, on one of the progresses of the court, Sir Oliver Cromwell had taken his nephew in right of the distant relationship. What King James said to this premature onslaught on a son of the Lord's anointed we are not informed; but Forster observes, as well as Guizot, that for an instant "the curtain of the future was uplifted here."

Robert Cromwell transferred his hopeful progeny to the care of one Doctor Beard, who kept the free grammar-school of the town, and flogged his pupils after the most approved fashion of Solomon and Dr. Busby. But Oliver had the loosest notions of what constituted the rights of property with regard to fruit and poultry, pippins and pigeons. The fear of the rod never restrained him from any nocturnal raid upon the dovecots and orchards of his neighbours. He came to be called the " appledragon " of the district, in which he was devoted to practical jokes and unseemly frolics. His inclinations at this period present a singular contrast of what may be described as nastiness mingled with the sublime. Puritanism must have relished and fostered the strange combination; so that we may smile at, rather than admire, the magniloquence of Milton, when, in apologising for the coarseness of his patron, he assures us that the genius of such a hero was as much above refinement as it was superior to ordinances; " that it did not become a right hand to be wrapped in down amongst the nocturnal birds of Athens, by which thunderbolts were to be hurled thereafter at the eagles which emulate the sun. " That there were extraordinary movements and presentiments in his mind during the hey-day of youth may be well imagined. He had laid himself down on one occasion to sleep, when the curtains of his bed were withdrawn by a gigantic female figure, which, gazing at him silently for a while, informed him that before his death he should be the greatest man in England. He remembered, when he told the story, that the apparition made no mention of the word king. His father seems to have received so marvellous a narration very much as Jacob the patriarch listened to the visions of his son Joseph; with remonstrance at least, as well as interest, since he wrote to the pedagogue, requesting that this ambitious and dreaming scholar might be soundly whipped for his presumption, which was done accordingly. Flagellation only strengthened his impressions ; for he carried them to his uncle, Sir Thomas Steward. The latter, however, merely repaid his confidence with loyal and suitable assertions that " it was traitorous to entertain such thoughts."

From the hands of Dr. Beard, Oliver Cromwell passed at seventeen to the University of Cambridge, where he was entered at Sidney-Sussex College as a fellow-commoner. He had picked up a respectable stock of Latin, yet preferred his sports to his books. But in June, A.D. 1617, his father died. His good mother found herself still obliged to carry on the brewery, in an age, happily for her business, guiltless of the follies of teetotalism. Her son, instead of helping to work the domestic oar, betook himself to the easier task of assisting to sink the family. Abhorring the protracted sermons and dismal practices of the godly people at Huntingdon, he degenerated into a rake of the first water. Few roysterers were a match for him at the boisterous game of quarter-staff. The tinker, or the pedlar, or the cow-doctor of the parish, had an equal welcome to a black eye or a broken skull,—whichever the young spark might happen to inflict, and afterwards heal with deep potations of the maternal ale. What could the poor widow do, in the loneliness of her heart, and with her six young and comely daughters, but apply to those apostles of hypocrisy, who boldly shook the pulpits of their conventicles and the purses of their disciples with weekly hurricanes of faith without works, and the impossibility of falling away from grace? They conselled her to transfer the gay prodigal to London, where he might enter at an inn of court, and apply himself to the study of the law. The fact probably was, that his debaucheries, both as to wine and women, had gone to such a height at Huntingdon, that the credit of the brewery was at stake, to say nothing of the glimmering hope that a change of scene might break off certain inconvenient and dissolute connections, which, so long as they lasted, rendered even external reformation altogether out of the question.

If the Puritans ever slept at all over money-matters, it was with one eye open. Oliver had not mended his manners or morals in the metropolis, as a nominal student in Lincoln's Inn, where, the remainder of his patrimony having been wasted, he attempted to raise further ways and means by drawing upon the indulgent liberality of his uncle Steward. With his godfather at Hinchinbrook he had long quarrelled; but Sir Thomas Steward appears for a time to have bled more freely; at length, however, even this eccentric worthy buttoned up his pockets, and would yield no more. The nephew thereupon immediately applied for a commission of lunacy against his relative and benefactor, whose habits were rather peculiar, although by no means such as to warrant the ground taken up by his ungrateful and ungracious favourite, that he was incapable of managing his own affairs. King Charles refused the application, and is admitted by the admirers of Cromwell to have acted justly in so doing. Soon after reaching his majority, Oliver married an admirable wife in the person of Elizabeth, daughter of Sir James Bourchier, of Halsted in Essex, a kinswoman of the Hampdens. With such plain good sense as to be perfectly contented with an humble station, she had spirit and dignity sufficient for the loftiest. Her felicitous influence assuaged the passions of her husband, lifted him up out of the mire of his profligate courses, and reconciled him to his family; his house became notorious as a refuge for persecuted Nonconformists and their pastors. Here he practised his first lessons in yoking fanaticism and hypocrisy to the fiery chariot of ambition. Every religious grievance was listened to and brooded over, until it was hatched into some magic talisman for influencing the minds of men. Discourses on knotty texts of Scripture protracted to almost interminable dimensions; details of spiritual experiences, seasoned with such unction and fervour as Bunyan might have conceived or Quarle envied, alternated with the agitations of confession, effusions of tears, and the more substantial relief of hot suppers, sack-possets, and warm nightcaps. The home of the future hero was heated into a religious furnace, in which was forged many a weapon of genius and puritanical power, before which, in after times, his enemies fled from the field of conflict, and his friends bowed down their faces to the ground in respectful or reluctant homage. There was even then no resisting the prowess with which the apparently repentant profligate wrestled in prayer, or unveiled in the mystic pages of prophecy an apocalypse of the New Jerusalem. His eyes were perfect sponges, fountains of pious waters flowing at command, edifying beyond expression the ministers, women, and servants kneeling in amazement around, and weeping themselves into correspondent floods either in their sincerity or through mere force of sympathy. Such enthusiasm, in ascending to higher and still higher degrees of heat, no doubt produced some temporary state of external purity and improvement. The clouds of smoke generated and developed occasional flames. We find more than one instance of full and fair compensation being rendered by Cromwell to the uttermost of his means for gambling debts; with respect to which his conscience smote him, as he said, for having had recourse to unfair play. His acute understanding quickly discovered the hollowness and tyranny of national episcopacy, revelling as it then did in the plenitude of its pretensions. His fellow-townsmen began to discuss his abilities, whilst they admired or patronised his beer. They drank his health in every pothouse, canted over his last exposition, and at length ripened into realisation an offer which they had volunteered of returning him as their representative at the next election. The attempt was first made in A.D. 1625, and failed; but three years later the star of the brewery culminated, and Oliver Cromwell took his seat at Westminster, in the third Parliament of the unfortunate Charles, as member for the borough of Huntingdon. A family of children had now begun to gather around him.

Such were some of the circumstances under which he emerged from private into public life. His gait was clownish, his dress ill-cut and slovenly, his manners harsh and abrupt, his features such as people look at with dislike, but from the contemplation of which it seems impossible to turn away. The author of *Hudibras* says, that one might have thought "he had been christened in a lime-pit and tanned alive!" Yet his very warts and wrinkles told, mingled as they were with firm-set lips, a fair large front, shaggy eyebrows, a threatening forehead, and a conspicuous ruddy nose. This last lineament of his face afforded immense **fun to** the **wits** and cavaliers of his day, who **were** divided into comparing it with **a** blazing beacon or a burning coal. Whenever he gazed at any one thoroughly, the object of his attention was not merely looked at through and through, but weighed, measured; analised, classified, and never forgotten. His relation Hampden soon introduced him to Sir John Eliot, Sir Robert Philips, Colonel Hutchinson, Pym, and Vane. They were all men of an iron stamp and strength; patriots in the popular sense of patriotism, banded together in heart and will for the abolition of secular abuses, full of suspicions as to the crown and constitution, and compounded of the narrowest and basest prejudices as to religion. The last, perhaps, was not altogether their own fault. The system of which they were the spawn was in itself neither more nor less than a spiritual rebellion ; the crisis at hand was only about to demonstrate that society must have solid foundations to rest upon, or else it only sinks from one depth of degradation to another, until, in a bottomless chaos, it resolves into its original elements ; and that the basis of the material fabric is in reality a living religious principle of obedience to a religious authority. The grand impertinence which just at that particular moment roused up and mustered together these masterspirits of the age, happened to be the presumption of English prelacy. Cromwell and his contemporaries looked upon it with the earnestness manifested by one set of mountebanks watching the impostures of another, and availing themselves of the popular gale against their adversaries. There was an obscure preacher named Mainwaring, protected by the bishops, who had preached up the depreciation of parliaments ; for which the Commons impeached and punished him. Of course the ultimate results were a royal pardon and an Anglican mitre. Such martyrs would be sure to spring up like mushrooms, until the king and his establishment had come to form a more correct idea of the enemy with whom they had to deal. Puritanism then raised the howl of "No Popery;" a cry which has always succeeded in England and Scotland, from the reign of Elizabeth to that of Victoria. Mainwaring had not as yet reaped the wages of his servility, when the harsh and broken but piercing tones of the member for Huntingdon electrified the House. It was the maiden effort of a voice which knew exactly what note to sound. He accused one Dr. Alabaster of promulgating the doctrines of the Roman harlot in a sermon at St. Paul's Cross, by the express orders of the prelate of Winchester. Furthermore, the same spiritual peer had just presented Mainwaring to a rich living ; so that the road to preferments, as the orator instructed his hearers, was to turn the realm into a land of Papists and slaves. Immense was the sensation produced. Pym registered thereupon his famous vow in heaven against the Church of Laud, Williams, and Andrewes; of which he and his adherents thought as Sydney Smith did of

Puseyism, that it was " all illusion, delusion, and collusion." A dissolution speedily followed; and Sir Oliver Cromwell took measures, in his hall at Hinchinbook, effectually to prevent any future return of his nephew for the borough, which in his opinion, as a Royalist and Episcopalian, had been so scandalously misrepresented. He was appointed indeed a justice of the peace for the town, on the score of his formidable popularity; but within three years he sold part of his property in the neighbourhood, and removed to a small farm at St. Ives, which he stocked and cultivated. The sum he raised by the sale amounted to about 1800*l.*

Fanaticism was here also his familiar spirit. The few vestiges of Catholicity still permitted to adorn our rural districts were to him fantastic sources of scandal and secret agony; even the beautiful symbol of redemption, erected by the loving faith of antiquity in the market-place at Huntingdon, had thrown him into " the strangest phantasies!" On his farm and in the neighbourhood he sowed those seeds of doctrine and discipline which subsequently grew up into his invincible regiments of Ironsides. The greater portion of every day fomented the spiritual inflammation of red-hot devotional exercises. We may understand the curious recollection of the clerk of his parish, who used to remember that Farmer Cromwell came to church "with a piece of red flannel round his neck, since he was liable to soreness in the throat;" possibly from its natural wryness of direction, as well as the torrents of puritanical lava of which it was the source and issue.

Meanwhile his agricultural prosperity languished. In his particular case prayer and preaching failed to speed the plough; when, in A.D. 1636, he inherited at last the long-conveted property of his much-aggrieved maternal uncle Sir Thomas Steward. It consisted chiefly of some tithe-leases held under the dean and chapter of Ely Cathedral; to the glebe-house of which, near the churchyard of St. Mary, he lost no time in removing with his family. Golden opinions were earned by him here as elsewhere, from the rising sectaries. The grand struggle drew on between prerogative and constitutional right; the High Commission and Star-Chamber were slitting the noses and cropping the ears of the Bastwicks, Burtons, and Leightons, besides enabling the Crown to enact the part of Rob Roy with regard to the liberties, lands, and moneys of the lieges. The interval between the last and the Long Parliament gathered together the materials whose explosion overturned the throne, prostrated the aristocracy, and convulsed the three kingdoms for half a century. It is not true that Cromwell, with Hampden and others, contemplated an emigration to the colonies. On the contrary, the future Protector was watching every sign of the times, and bathing his soul in the Stygian lake of his own gloomy and bitter enthusiasm. He foresaw the tempest when it was no bigger than the fingers of a human hand. His prescience anticipated that some genius might be found capable of riding upon the storm; while a mysterious gleam of idea every now and then flashed through the darkness, that possibly he might be that man. This seems evident from what has since transpired of his correspondence, conversations, and contemplations. The affair of the Bedford Level brought him out at once as a champion for the people against the king. He came to be worshipped by the commonalty throughout the counties of Cambridge, Huntingdon, Northampton, and Lincoln, under the title of "the Lord of the Fens." No sooner had Strafford fallen before his foes, than even Hampden predicted the probable greatness of his kinsman. He directed with invisible, yet not less certain guidance, that series of marvellous measures and events which are to be found in all our histories; nor will it be necessary that we should touch upon the parliamentarian war, which was the subject of a previous work by M. Guizot, and therefore is not included in the publication now on our table. Suffice it to remind our readers, that his management of what was termed the self-denying ordinance, the lustre of the military achievements, which blazed throughout the country down to the decisive battle of Marston Moor, his still greater victory at Naseby, the masterly skill with which he had formed an army bound up in the promotion of his own personal advancement, the genius with which he cajoled the parliament, and erected his party of Independency upon the ruins of Presbyterianism, the audacity with which he contrived the total suppression of royalism and the execution of Charles I.,—altogether led to the establishment of the commonwealth, with its sovereign power intrusted to himself ultimately under the modest title of its Protector.

The newly-created commonwealth for a time grumbled and blundered on; working the will of the enchanter its master, whose potent spell had called it out of anarchy into an ephemeral existence for his own purposes. This legion of Puritans had to serve a tyrant after all, as they discovered to their cost. Their internal anxieties already tormented them far more than their enemies could have done. Conquerors as they were, they always found a far greater mind in the midst of their own circle, overshadowing or eclipsing their fame, appropriating at every crisis the whole amount of credit and renown that might seem to be gained in getting the state out of its difficulties, and rendering them in return for their hard and abominable labours only smooth professions and scanty wages. Scotland and Ireland both remained also convulsed or discontented; though under peculiar and different circumstances, such as made utterly nugatory the respective dispositions of a party in each of them favourable to the pretensions of Charles II.

Not that the Royalists in either of these kingdoms could have reasonably expected any other result than that which really followed. In Ireland, Lord Ormonde had proclaimed the young Stuart with the best formalities in his power. Cromwell was offered the supreme military and civil command against him, as he expected would be the case; yet before he accepted it, profound was the dissimulation practised both by himself and his nominal employers. Puritanism could never move in direct and honest line, even to accomplish any object nearest and dearest to its own hollow heart. At this distance of time it is impossible to view without loathing and horror the falsehood and fanaticism with which the new lord-lieutenant prepared for his crusade. In the first place, two officers from each corps were to meet him at Whitehall, that they might seek to know the will of Almighty God in prayer for a fortnight. He then consented to "submit his shoulders to the burden," with professions of preparatory fastings, wrestlings of spirit with the King of Saints, and unutterable travail of soul. He then secured 12,000 cavalry and infantry selected from his own veterans, plentiful supplies of provision and ammunition, and 100,000*l.* in ready money for the public service. For himself, he stipulated that there should be allotted him 3000*l.* for an outfit, 10*l.* sterling per diem as general whilst remaining in England, and 2000*l.* per quarter in Ireland, besides his pay in his new function. His body-guard was to consist of fourscore young men of quality, several of them holding commissions as majors and colonels. His appointments invested him with dictatorial authority; and his state-carriage was drawn by six Flemish mares of whitish-grey. On the morning of his march he expounded the Scriptures, with a couple of other generals, " excellently well and pertinently to the occasion;" whilst three ministers invoked a blessing on his banners, proceeding as they were " to fight the battle of Heaven against the blinded Roman Catholics." And truly if ever hell could boast of a human champion, Oliver Cromwell enjoyed and exercised that dreadful honour.

He reached Dublin on the Assumption, A.D. 1659. Three-fourths of the island appeared to have been brought under the sway of the Marquis of Ormonde, in the name of Charles II. With lips pouring forth a torrent of texts perverted from holy writ, and waving in his grasp " the sword of the Lord and Gideon," the hero of Protestantism and Independency set forth to shed blood like water, and extirpate, should it be possible, the persecuted Church of Christ. At Drogheda, after the entrenchments had been carried by storm, and quarter offered and accepted, the pledge given was violated as soon as resistance ceased. An indiscriminate massacre ensued; for five days the streets ran with gore; an impious fury stimulated the passions of the soldiers. From the garrison they turned their weapons against the inhabitants, of whom above a thousand were immolated within the walls of the great church, to which they had fled for protection. Two thousand had been already slaughtered in the assault; for, as Cromwell himself wrote to the President of the Council and the Speaker of the House of Commons: "**I** forbade our men to spare any that were in arms in the town; and the next day, *when they had submitted*, their officers were knocked on the head, every tenth man of the soldiers killed, and the **rest** shipped for Barbadoes. *I believe all their friars were knocked on the head promiscuously. I am persuaded that this is a righteous judgment of God upon these barbarous wretches!*" Such are the tender mercies of expounders of the Apocalypse.

The Puritans, flushed with slaughter, pushed on to Wexford. Its unfortunate citizens fared no better than those of Drogheda, where the aged, the sick, the infirm, together with women and children, had been sacrificed in cold blood. No distinction was drawn between the defenceless burgher and the active warior; nor could the shrieks and prayers of three hundred perfectly helpless females, congregated for refuge round the market-cross, preserve them from the death they dreaded. Cromwell, in fact, abhorred crosses. They then, **as** now, were believed to be the marks of the Beast; nor were the followers of the Protector in the seventeenth wiser than the audiences of Exeter Hall in the nineteenth century. Five thousand innocent individuals perished in the two sieges. Oliver wiped his weapon with the coolest internal satisfaction. They were all Papists and idolaters, and he thought it, to use his own words, "a marvellous great **mercy!**"

Cork, Ross, Youghal, and Kilkenny, submitted without resistance; but Callan, Gowran, **and** Clonmell, made bold and glorious defences. Waterford manifested such vigor that Cromwell was baffled in his advances. Every cruelty, the more fearful ones not excepted, sullied the puritanical successes. A bishop was hanged in his episcopal robes before the walls of a fortress, subsequently to its surrender upon articles. In another case, and with similar disregard for the laws and customs of war, after troops had capitulated all their officers were brutally murdered, evidently on the ground of their being Catholics. "These last," as Guizot observes, "were always pompously excepted from his promises of Christian toleration;" whilst, strange to say, this ingenious Protestant historian describes him as "not bloodthirsty, but only determined to succeed rapidly, and at any cost, from the necessities of his fortune." We will extract a brief passage to illustrate the indulgent touch of an artist in softening down the characteristics of a conqueror, when his admirer cannot forbear fancying them a little too red and sanguinary :

"His great and true means of success did not consist in his massacres, but in his genius, and in the exalted idea which the people had already conceived of him. Sometimes by instinct, sometimes from reflection, he conducted himself in Ireland towards both his friends and enemies with an ability as pliant as it was profound; for he excelled in the art of treating with men, and of persuading, or seducing, or appeasing, those who even naturally regarded him with the greatest distrust and aversion. At the same time *that he gave up to murder and pillage the towns which fell into his hands*, he maintained in other respects the severest discipline in his army."

The italics are ours, and are of course intended to imply our cordial condemnation of that inconvenient delicacy, which seems to have restrained so able and amiable a writer as the author of these volumes from denouncing the savage monster who could preach, and weep, and whine, and pray over the pages of the New Testament, whilst bigotry and ambition swept on their remorseless way, beneath his stern command, over the mangled corpses of infancy and innocency, or youth and old age. By an arrangement with France and Spain he got rid of 45,000 Irish soldiers, who consented to take service under those powers and relieve his own cause of just so many opponents.

Scarcely, however, was Ireland conquered, or rather crushed by Cromwell, when the affairs of Scotland summoned him to another field of action. The wild expedition of Montrose terminated in the defeat, arrest, condemnation, and cruel execution of that magnanimous chieftain. But Charles Stuart had arranged matters with the commissioners at Breda, and landed on the Scotch coast in May 1650. Oliver Cromwell, quietly superseding the over-scrupulous Fairfax, who had been nominated his colleague, proceeded agaist this fresh enemy at the head of about 15,000 men. Crossing the border, he addressed two proclamations, one to the inhabitants of the kingdom generally, and the other "to all that might be saints and partakers of the faith of God's elect." He kept near the sea-coast, that he might the more easily feed his troops, and obtain from time to time the necessary supplies from England. His antagonists withdrew every where before him, to avoid a collision if possible, and starve him out. The Presbyterian Royalists, nearly double his own numbers, had Lesley for their general. This officer never dared to advance until the English had fallen back upon Dunbar, when at length he occupied the pass of Cockburnspath, cutting them off, as it would seem, from any return home by land to their own country. Never was invader surrounded with more imminent peril.

Thus far Cromwell had gained nothing by his long march but disappointment, mortification, and short commons. It was now the 2d of September, and a most rainy season; Lesley had hemmed him in between the hills and the sea; when, partly provoked by the reproaches of some fanatical ministers, and partly piqued by the remarks of a "stout prisoner whom his skirmishers had captured, and who had but a wooden arm," and partly compelled by his real want of forage and water, he formed the fatal resolution of "having the English army dead or alive, by seven o'clock on the morrow." That army wished for nothing better, and spent the entire night in noiseless preparation for combat. On the 3d of September, after hours of wild storm and darkness, a thick fog at daybreak postponed the attack, although only for an interval. As it cleared away, volleys of musketry awoke ten thousand echoes, with booming artillery roaring on both sides; for the fight was loud and long, amidst cries of "the Lord of Hosts" from the English, and "the Covenant,"—"the solemn League and Covenant," from the Scotch. Cromwell reserved the onset of his invincible Ironsides until the propitious moment when the mists dispersed, permitting the full beams of sunshine suddenly to illuminate the scene from the heights to the ocean. "Now let God arise," said he, and "His enemies shall be scattered; for they that hate Him shall flee before Him." His well-known voice sounded through the ranks like a trumpet. Each battalion caught up his solemn and sonorous words; for enthusiasm is as contagious as discouragement. "Indeed," observes one of his contemporaries, "he was a strong man in the dark perils of war; and in the high places of the field hope shone in him like a pillar of fire when it had gone out in all the others." Once and again Oliver and the English charged with redoubled vigour; the Scottish cavalry at length gave way; and even a body of infantry, which had remained unmoved, like a rock, was at last broken through, and scattered by the assailing squadrons. "After the first repulses," wrote the triumphant victor, "they were made by the Lord of Hosts as stubble to our swords." The struggle was over before nine. Three thousand enemies had been slain. More than 10,000 prisoners were taken, with all their cannon, baggage, and 200 standards. Leith, Edinburgh (except its castle), and the adjacent country, submitted at once. Charles II. withdrew northwards to Perth; not over-sorry that some of his subjects had received so severe a lesson. Until now he had been treated as a mere puppet, with an allowance of 9000l. per month for his civil list. Lesley, with the wreck of his late gallant array, went westward to Stirling. Scotland had nevertheless to bend her neck to the yoke of Cromwell and the Commonwealth, very much as Ireland had done. The coronation of the king at Scone produced only a slight effect upon the course of events; notwithstanding the sudden illness of the English lord-general, and various plots against republicanism, which broke out somewhat later. Charles, however, soon took the command of his army in person, and then indeed there came a change over the spirit of the drama.

Oliver had recovered, and laid siege to Perth; upon which the hunted Stuart resolved to give his adversary the slip, and invade England. On the last day of July 1651, he was on the road to Carlisle, backed by forces estimated at 11,000 to 14,000 soldiers. London quaked with terror on receiving the intelligence; while Vane, Scott, Robinson, and Henry Martyn set their shoulders to the wheel of preparation. Cromwell wasted no time either; for he overtook the royalists at Worcester, within four weeks after they had started from Stirling. His own followers, with the militia collected for him by his active adherents, amounted to 24,000 infantry and 10,000 cavalry.

He encamped on the left bank of the Severn on his arrival; and that same afternoon pushed a portion of his lines across the river, that he might attack the city on either side. The anniversary of his victory at Dunbar was close at hand: accordingly, on Sept. 3d, his favourite and fortunate day, as he ever afterwards called it, the western suburbs of Worcester were assailed by Lambert and Fleetwood: the lord-general himself directed the principal attack against the city, at the eastern extremity; while Charles was on the tower of the cathedral, surrounded with his staff, all looking about them. Thunders of artillery, as the clock struck one, announced that the republicans were battering the approaches. Windows rattled, houses fell, or were riddled as the iron shot went through them. The king mounted his horse, rushed to the defence, and manifested among his generals no lack of personal courage. But Cromwell had surrounded him, like a lion in a lair. The battle lasted for five hours. Charles, with his body-guards, fell so vigourously upon the republican militia-men, that the latter recoiled, until Oliver rallied them; showing that, with ordinary firmness on their part, the laurels of victory must be won. The Royalists, on the other hand, got discouraged; they **were** outnumbered; their ammunition began to fail; their officers were too numerous, and with no master-mind to combine or concentrate their efforts. Lesley, with 3,000 cavalry, remained motionless **at** the critical moment; **and the** brave Cavaliers shouted **in agony** " for one hour of Montrose!" It **was in vain.** The heads of Cromwell's columns had now fought **their** way into one street after another in almost every quarter. " Shoot me dead," exclaimed the defeated monarch, "rather than let me live to see the sad consequences of this fatal day!" When his valiant friends formed themselves into a compact body, in order to cover his retreat, he at length left the city by St. Martin's Gate, and took **the** northern road. Falling in with some Presbyterian cavalry, who were flying without having fought, considering, as they evidently did, how sore a temptation of Providence it must be to abide the brunt of danger, he would fain for a moment have led them back again into pretended action. "But no," he said to himself; " men who deserted me when they were in good order, would never stand by me now they are beaten." Common sense had not as yet quite deserted him—the romance of the Boscobel Papers had to be acted out; and Charles II. was reserved for the Restoration.

Meanwhile, Cromwell was enjoying his crowning victory. Three kingdoms seemed to be in the act of falling down to worship the idol which their own follies, in conjunction with his then unparalleled genius, had thus wonderfully set up. The palace of Hampton Court was assigned him for a residence, with a landed estate of 4000*l.* a year. Fanatic as he was, he never intended to serve God, even in his own way, for any thing short of solid pudding as well as empty praise. Both were now overwhelming him upon rather a sublime scale. As to his gaping supporters, he must have often recalled the proverb, *Decipiantur qui volunt decipi.* It was therefore that he had canted so intolerably amidst the splendours of his military career. From Ireland he had written to one of his correspondents in the full glow of conquest: "The Lord is wonderful in these things—it is His hand alone that does them. Oh, that all the praise might be ascribed to Him! I have been crazy in my health; but the Lord is pleased to sustain me. I beg your prayers; I desire you to call upon my son *to mind the things of God more and more. Alas! what profit is there in the things of this world? except they be enjoyed in Christ, they are snares!"*. When the Speaker and House of Commons, with the Lord Mayor and Aldermen, met his triumphal entry into London, amidst the firing of the troops, salvoes of cannon, and the acclamations of the people, he acted his humility to a turn; although Hugh Peters, with a few others, understood him thoroughly, and even whispered to each other: "This man will be King of England yet!" His lieutenants, Ireton and Monk, had perfectly carried out his intentions, and completed the subjugation of Ireland and Scotland. The fleet and troops of the Parliament had regained possession of the Channel and Scilly Islands, Sodor and Man, Barbadoes, and the various colonial dependencies. The throne, or what was equivalent to it, loomed out in the perspective distinctly before the writer of such sentiments as these: "Lord, deliver me from this very vain world! Oh, how good it is to close with Christ betimes: there is nothing else worth the looking after. Great place and business have come upon me, a **very** poor worm and **weak** servant!" After the battle of Dunbar, his pious inspirations were as follow: "We lay fearfully near the enemy, and therefore there came over us a weakness of the flesh, because of their numbers; **because** of their advantages; because of their confidence; because of our frailty; because of our straits. But we were in the Mount, and on the Mount the Lord would be seen; and He shall send the rod of His strength out of Zion!" and finally applying to himself the Scripture, *Dominare in medio inimicorum tuorum.*

In fact, the general blasphemy of the entire age should never be forgotten, since it helps to explain the curious rounds of that ladder of impiety by which the Protector ascended to his elevation. Beneath the warm sunbeams of unexpected prosperity he had stealthily returned to his earlier sensualism and indulgences. But what were these to a blinded partisan and sectary, who could trace out a parallel from the pages of the Bible between himself and Moses; dwelling upon the marvellous and princely perfections of them both, "ascending in their respective ages through thirty degrees to the height of honour." The German apostle of Protestantism had said *Pecca fortiter* to one of his adherents; **nor could some** of the Puritans in the seventeenth century bring themselves to forbear saying out *Amen* to the precept. All sense of real reverence towards Almighty God had vanished from these islands; and where was morality to be sought for when genuine faith was gone? The counterfeits of both were of course multiplied in the most disgusting forms. We will venture on two or three specimens of their pulpit eloquence. The blasphemy of some of them is so shocking, that we almost doubt as to the propriety of introducing them; but they are necessary as illustrations of the spirit of the times.

At **Perth a** military preacher avowed in his prayer before the army, that "unless God delivered them, He should not be their God." A Presbyterian wrestled, as it was termed, in his Sabbath prayer,—"O Lord! when wilt Thou take a chair, and sit among the Peers? When wilt Thou vote among the honourable Commons? Another said, "We know, O Lord, that Abraham made a covenant, and Moses made a covenant, and David a covenant, and our Saviour a covenant; but the covenant of Thy parliament is the greatest of all covenants!" Oliver had once to listen to a regular roarer in England, who addressed his Maker thus: "Lord! what wilt Thou do with the malignants, the prelatists, the papists, and the rest of them? I'll tell Thee:—e'en take them by the heels, and roast them in the chimney of hell. Lord! take the pestle of Thy vengeance, and the mortar-piece of Thy wrath, and make their brains a hodge-podge. But for Thine own bairns, Lord; feed them with the prunes and raisins of Thy promises; give them the boots of hope and the spurs of confidence." His own chaplain, Hugh Peters, already mentioned, when alluding in his sermon to the late struggle between the English and Dutch, informed his audience that the conflict really "lasted so long that Almighty God was thrown upon *His hums and His haws* as to which side He should cast the victory." And when one of the fifth-monarchy enthusiasts mentioned to this puritan Boanerges, or as another account has it, to his friend and fellow-secretary, Streater, that Jesus Christ was soon coming in person to reign with the saints in London,—the preacher confidentially replied, with more seriousness than reverence, that "unless He came before Christmas, *it would be too late!*"

In truth, to all intents and purposes Oliver Cromwell was from this time the real regent or sovereign of the realm. It was resolved in October 1651, that the forces should be placed upon such an establishment as would reduce their expenses by 35,000*l. per mensem*. The parliament also proposed an amnesty, as well as a new electoral law, with various projects of civil and religious reform; when it presently appeared that its days were numbered. The members remained purblind to a most amusing degree, whilst their master was only giving them rope enough to strangle what yet remained to them of reputation. There were individuals amongst them of spotless integrity; but the majority had manifested little else than selfishness, narrow-mindedness, hypocrisy, and an utter incapacity for honest or effective government. Cromwell and his creatures had so managed public opinion, that the clamour for a dissolution appeared unanimous at the very period when the parliament was idly attempting to perpetuate its own existence. At length the crisis arrived; and the well known scene occurred on the 20th of April, 1653, in which the sword of the executive overcame and put to flight the mace of the Speaker, with such a sentence as "Take away that bauble!" "When I went down to Westminster," said the mendacious lord-general, "I did not think to have done this. But *perceiving the Spirit of God so strong upon me, I would not consult with flesh and blood.*" The Council of State was dissolved on the same afternoon. Hatred and contempt for that political gimcrack, the Commonwealth, which the foot of a conqueror had now kicked to pieces, aroused many partial movements of popular admiration, such as an audacious and successful line of conduct will almost always inspire. Congratulatory addresses awaited the dictator from various quarters: from the mystical sectaries, who hoped that the fall of the Parliament might introduce a reign of Christ and His saints (meaning by the latter term themselves); from the army in Scotland, whose leaders cordially approved the whole measure; from the army in Ireland, which at least signified its acquiescence; from the fleet, careless as it seemed of politics, and intent alone upon the acquisition of naval glory; from the City of London, where a few scrupulous aldermen lifted up their voices in vain; and generally from the richest and most influential towns in the three kingdoms. Cromwell nevertheless condescended to justify his conduct in a long manifesto; convoked the Barebones assembly; demonstrated to its component members, as well as to the world, their unfitness both for counsel and action; accepted from them a resignation of the government into his own more able hands; and finally, on the 16th of December, 1653, assumed openly the office and powers of the Lord High Protector over England, Scotland, and Ireland, with all their colonies and territories. He was solemnly installed in a grand chair of state with extraordinary festivities, and after a very long sermon in the banqueting-hall. His town-residence henceforward was the palace of his late decapitated sovereign.

It had been newly furnished for the reception of the protectoral family upon a magnificent scale. The style and etiquette of a regular court were once more revived. Ambassadors were presented to his Highness, as he stood upon a platform raised three steps above the floor. They had to make a profound reverence thrice; the first time on entering to saloon, the second when they had advanced midway, and the third when they approached the foot of the elevation; where Cromwell, having given to each of their homages a slight inclination of his head, then allowed them at last respectfully to kiss his hand,—at least such a permission was sometimes awarded, though by no means as a matter of course; for on occasions he withheld such a mark of his condescension, and waved the representatives of foreign powers out of his presence with more than a royal bow. The expenditure of his household was 140,000*l. per annum*, equivalent to the civil list of Queen Victoria, when the differences in the value of money are taken into consideration. His equipages must have appeared truly regal: his wife, and his mother, with the junior members, all received the attention exacted by princes and princesses; whilst, notwithstanding the occasional coarseness which might now and then deform the manners of Oliver, or the coaxing familiarities which policy induced him to tolerate with " certain godly vessels of grace " booked on their journey to the New Jerusalem, there was an external grandeur throughout the entire affair which gratified superficial observers, and soothed the national pride. It contrasted strangely with the profligate and pitiful exhibition of Charles Stuart at Paris, a pensioner of the proud king, and wasting his allowance of 6000 francs a month upon Lucy Walters;—his grand lord-keeper the Marquis of Ormonde, and his equally grand chancellor of the exchequer Hyde, besides other right honourable officers and privy-councillors, being all the time without a pistole in their pockets, and cheating the poor woman who boarded them through never paying her bills. Shoes and shirts even were not too plentiful with these proud and beggarly exiles; on account of whom, the bitter but honest Andrew Marvel compared their master to Saul the son of Cis, " in looking after the asses of his father."

In vain were base plots of assassination hatched against the Protector. He organised a system of espionage which let him know what Charles whispered in his bed-chamber; how that royal ladies were between their sheets for the hottest hours of a summer's day, because the laundress was washing the single linen garment they were so happy as to possess; how that an emisary from Mazarin was in London to confer with Gerrard and his fellow-conspirators; and in one word, exactly what was going forward against or in favour of the government throughout astonished Europe. He restored the finances, repaired the roads, reformed both law and equity, mitigated the sufferings of prisoners for debt, improved the jails, established a good police, regulated public amusements, prohibited duels, restrained the madness of Presbyterianism as well as the follies of fanaticism, did his best for a new representation of the people, nominated able judges, and, of course, persecuted Catholics. In so doing, he only worked out the natural instincts of his creed. Dyed red as he was with the purple martyrdoms of his Irish compaigns, he barbarously put to death a pious and elderly priest named Southworth, simply because **he** had fallen into the clutches of one of his **officers, and had been** convicted thirty-seven years be**fore, at Lancaster, of** no other crime that Papistry. Yet what was to be done? This worthy gentleman had since been to Rome, and taken holy orders. For this the fierce sordid sectarians demanded his blood, as a proof that Cromwell was sincere in professing himself a " Bible Christian." The French and Spanish ambassadors repeated their solicitations for mercy with incessant yet fruitless urgency; while such was the respect and sympathy displayed towards the innocent and reverend sufferer, that 200 carriages, with a multitude of gentlemen on horseback, followed the hurdle on which he was drawn to his glorious agony. On the scaffold he meekly mentioned the satisfaction with which, through the grace of God, he was enabled to lay down his life for the sake of truth; but he also pointed out the enormous inconsistency of his murderers, who, having pretended to take up arms for liberty of conscience, could nevertheless inflict such cruel penalties upon persons differing from themselves in religious opinions. And so this holy victim was hanged, disembowelled, and quartered, by the very potentate about to be enshrined in the false flattery of anti-Catholic historians, for his subsequent interference on behalf of the Calvinistic insurgents at Nismes, and the Waldenses of Piedmont.

In less than nine months, the active and able Protector had issued above four score ordinances, bearing upon almost every part of the social organisation of the country; but the boasts of his domestic policy were such events as the execution of the brother of the Portuguese minister for riot and homicide, or the incorporation of Scotland and Ireland with England. Even these achievements, however, might subside into obscurity, as compared with the skilful management of foreign affairs. Schemes had been started for that sort of union between Holland and the three kingdoms which circumstances, little anticipated, at length effected for an interval of thirteen years, through the Revolution of 1688. No sooner was the helm openly in the grasp of Cromwell, than he set himself to effect what alone was at all possible under the then existing state of things : he aimed at a reasonable peace with the United Provinces, recognising indeed their national independence, but securing the trident of the ocean for his native land. Vane had superintended the Admiralty with the most prescient and disinterested ability. By uprooting abuses, and surrendering enormous emoluments, he contented himself with the modest salary of one, insteed of thirty thousand pounds per annum; and at the same time laid deeply and immovably the foundations of our maritime greatness. True indeed it is, that for nearly a quarter of a century the Dutch maintained a struggle for naval supremacy with their more fortunate rivals; yet equally certain it also is, that they never recovered from their efforts, and that from the age of the protectorate, and the subsequent administration of James Duke of York, the British flag has permanently maintained its superiority.

Oliver's next object was a general Protestant alliance, by which Denmark, those of the Swiss cantons which were not Catholic, as also several of the petty Lutheran princes in the north of Germany, were included in the negotiation with the Batavian republic. With Sweden he had a more difficult part to act; for the subjects of Queen Christina were practical as well as theoretical opponents to the precepts and doctrines of religion, and their sovereign was contemplating a return to the fold of the faithful. Whitelock, the envoy of Oliver, and far from being a strict Puritan himself, any more than his master, was absolutely scandalised at their laxity of morals. The propositions from London, followed up by suitable instructions from the Protector, were nevertheless acceded to at Stockholm, just one month before the daughter of Gustavus Adolphus ceased to reign. They placed Oliver Cromwell, with regard to the Protestant interests of Europe, exactly in the position in which a confederation in our own age placed Napoleon with regard to the Germanic principalities. He became thereby an almost absolute umpire over the foreign relations of numerous adjacent states. Another special treaty with the court at Copenhagen opened the Sound for English commerce, depriving the merchants and herring-busses of Amsterdam and the Brill of their long-cherished monopoly.

France and Spain meanwhile were bidding against each other for the honour of his friendship. With Portugal he also effected an arrangement most beneficial to the trade of his people; so that, thus caressed and feared by the whole of Christendom, and victorious over all parties at home, he thought he might face without danger the seventh article of the Protectoral Constitution, which called upon him to issue writs for the convocation of a new parliament. No general election had now happened for fourteen years; but the former plan of Sir Harry Vane was adopted, and the summonses were made returnable for the 3d of September, 1654. Four hundred members were allotted for England and Wales; thirty for Scotland, and the same number for Ireland. Yet the expectations of the great autocrat were disappointed. After wearisome speeches which satisfied nobody, and party hostilities no longer possessing a shadow of interest, he dissolved the assembly in anger, that he might endeavour to govern alone. This proved no easy task; he had to baffle the royalist and republican conspiracies, resulting as they did in the insurrections of Salisbury, under Colonel Penruddock, and the northern counties, where Lord Rochester was to have carried all before him. Then followed his system of major-generals,—a set of satraps, who were to exercise all political and administrative powers, and to a certain point all judicial authority, in their respective districts, which were twelve in number. From their decisions there was to be no appeal but to the Protector and his council. The object was to overawe some legal attempts at resistance against the usurpations of Cromwell, and at the same time support a local militia devoted to the government, for which the ways and means had to be found in an income-tax of ten per-cent, levied on the Royalists alone. Connected with such arbitrary measures was an interference with the liberty of the press; but, as M. Guizot justly observes, Oliver Cromwell thus " tyrannically involved his power in a course of revolutionary violence, and set parties once more at variance, not by civil war, but by a system of oppression. He appealed to necessity, and doubtless believed himself reduced by circumstances to act as he did; if he was right, his was one of those necessities inflicted by the justice of God, which reveal the innate viciousness of a government, and are the inevitable sentence of its condemnation."

Henceforward his administration was neither more nor less than a naked despotism, compared with which that of Charles and James, kings of England, had been the mildness of milk-and-water,—excepting that the former was so lost in the latter that the evil sank into the social constitution like the poison of a spring, which happens to be tasteless, though not the less deleterious. His endeavours to preserve popularity by a one-sided religious toleration could have deceived no one, not even himself, any more than his conduct towards Oxford and Cambridge. There might be hope through the dazzling effects of foreign conquests; and he had now made up his mind to act with France against Spain. Cardinal Mazarin and the Protector proceeded in the execution of a project which was destined effectually to humble the court of Madrid. Blake sailed into the Mediterranean, and performed wonders of policy and valour before Leghorn, against the Barbary States, and off the port of Malaga. But in the West Indies Admirals Penn and Venables failed against St. Domingo; and the capture of Jamaica, then estimated far beyond its genuine value, remained their only trophy. Yet still the popular mind seemed to some extent gratified. On the continent the prowess of Great Britain had never been so felt and lauded. External testimonies of respect reached the Protector from various parts; since, independently of the foreign ministers who had their usual residence in London, ambassadors-extraordinary were sent from Sweden, Poland, Germany, and Italy, to present him with the homage or overtures of their masters. Sagredo, the Venetian envoy, presents us with a picture of his impressions in 1656 :—" I am now in England," he says : " the aspect of this country is very different from that of France; here we do not see ladies going to court, but gentlemen courting the chase; not elegant cavaliers, but cavalry and infantry; instead of music and ballets, they have trumpets and drums; they do not speak of love, but Mars; they have no comedies, but tragedies; no patches on their faces, but muskets on their shoulders; they do not neglect sleep for the sake of amusement, but severe ministers keep their adversaries in incessant wakefulness." There appears little of the attractive in this portrait; and Cromwell himself, surrounded as he seemed to be with secular grandeur and glory, must have inwardly recognized the skeleton that marred it all, or dreamed of the sword of Damocles terrifically gleaming in the air. There could be no rest for his soul, as it mounted from **one** splendid misery to another.

Stern necessity at length compelled him to venture upon another parliament; nor could he complain this time of its results. The exclusion of nearly 100 members left the remainder at liberty to strengthen the sceptre of the Protector, and even tender him the real crown for his acceptance. We may well conceive how tempting must have been the offer; yet, after an agony of suspense, he declined it, accepting in its stead the *Humble Petition and Advice*, which was soon followed by the famous pamphlet entitled *Killing no Murder*. Colonel Saxby was probably its author; but it did not prevent a second installation of Oliver Cromwell, who by the new constitution, as arranged between himself and the commons, now enjoyed the right of appointing his successor, and governing with more concentrated powers. An upper house was also restored,—the illusive shadow of a peerage. It has been thought by some, and perhaps with justice, that he was never the same man again after the vain vision of recognised royalty had for ever withdrawn from his view. He still enjoyed the reality, it was true, or at least with regard to prerogative, and the extent of his renown and influence in Europe; but the golden circlet of a diadem, that symbol of venerable authority, with its hallowed associations of 1000 years, worn as it had been by Alfred, by the Conqueror, by the Henries and Edwards of English history, —that crown which confers the title of majesty, which religion consecrates and which the world worships, and which the representatives of an admiring people had positively pressed upon his brow,—had now vanished even from his imagination. The hard, cruel scruples of a few intimate friends had alone intervened between the dreams of an ambitious manhood and their fullest realisation. How bitterly he strove to overcome those scruples, to what humiliations and hypocritical artifices he condescended for that purpose, Whitelocke, in his Memorials, has almost unconsciously informed us.

"The Protector," he says, " again and again advised with us about this affair of his accepting the title of king, and would sometimes be strangely cheerful with Lord Broghill, Pierrepoint, Sir Charles Wolseley, Thurloe, and myself ; yea, now and then laying aside his greatness, he would become exceeding familiar, and by way of diversion would make verses with us, so that every one might try his fancy. He would then commonly call for tobacco, pipes, and a candle, or would now and then even take tobacco himself ; *then he would fall again to his serious and great business,"*—that vanity of vanities; in other words, of enjoying the name as well as the substance of sovereignty.

On another occasion, he invited himself to dinner with Colonel Desborough,—a very Brutus among the opponents of the proposed revival of avowed monarchy,—and after the meal he "drolled with the party present about kingship. Speaking slightingly of it, he said, *it was but a feather in the cap of a man, and therefore wondered that folks would not please the children, and permit them to enjoy their rattle.*" This incident is mentioned by Ludlow. But all the tricks of the arch-actor were useless; so that the apex of his aspirations dissolved finally into air: and thus foiled in that single point he felt himself defeated. His health undoubtedly began to fail, whether from this particular cause or not can now scarcely be ascertained. He was getting into years, after a life of labour and care which would have told upon the energies of a Cæsar or a Samson. Henceforward he is said to have worn armour under his clothes, and to have seldom slept two nights consecutively in the same apartment. The Parliament which had so flattered him began to get restive: in its second session it openly quarrelled with him; nor could the upper house long stand its ground. The old ancestral peers would not sit, or at least would not work with the new lords, some of whom had once been cobblers, clothiers, woollen-drapers, dry-salters, and little shop-keepers. His Highness at last dissolved his refractory chambers. The agitation of parties out of doors augmented **every** day. Payment of taxes was now and then resisted; the exchequer was getting low, particularly through the heavy expenses of the Spanish war. Admiral Blake had also died, after gaining the most brilliant of his naval victories in the Bay of Teneriffe. Some galleons had been taken at an earlier period with considerable, although exaggerated, treasures on board; but the public convoy which carried them from the sea-coast to the vaults of the Bank and the Tower deeply impressed the populace, and seemed to render the general burdens more tolerable.

Plots, however, revived with increasing frequency. The

Protector, indeed, suppressed them, and entered with greater cordiality than ever before into the objects of his alliance with France. In fact, on the continent his policy had immense success, while the capture of Mardike and Dunkirk threw gleams of transitory radiance upon the sinking sunset of his reign. He had sent his son-in-law, Lord Faulconbridge, on a splendid embassy to Louis XIV., and received the Duke de Cregin as representative of that potentate in London. Already was the convocation of another Parliament occupying his mind, when family misfortunes, in connection with the cares of state, undermined his strength, and laid him more open to attacks of intermittent fever, which had been his old disorder in Ireland and Scotland. He had removed for change of air, after the death of his favourite daughter, Lady Claypole, to Hampton Court, but was induced to return to Whitehall on the 24th of August 1658. From this day his danger became visible. It is to be feared that fanaticism alone upheld him in his last struggle. He had named his successor, and yet still clung to life. With all his crimes gathering around the ghastly recollections of the past, there seemed scarcely a semblance of any repentance, or humble apprehensions for the future. The Calvinistic and monstrous delusion, that, having felt himself to have been once in the grace of Almighty God, it was impossible for him ever to have fallen away, was the mermaid which held before his eyes her false and fatal mirror of hope, a hiss soul vainly battled with the awful billows of eternity. He expired on the 3d of September, between three and four o'clock in the afternoon, with a deep sigh, amidst the wailings of his family and attendants, the half-frantic amazement of his chaplains, the shudder of three nations, and the roar of a violent tempest, which had been raging all through the previous night, with innumerable disasters over the sea and land.

Such was Oliver Cromwell, the hero and personification of Puritanism, and certainly one of the most remarkable men in the pages of British history. His funeral was performed with the pomp and parade which have usually accompanied the obsequies of our sovereigns. In some worldly respects, he truly towered amongst them as a giant amidst the great ones of the earth; conspicuous as he had been for military achievements, successful policy, and governmental talents. He had, moreover, carved out his own fortunes; and in doing so, had availed himself both of the strength and weakness of his fellow-countrymen. But the grand spell of his life, with which so many wonders had been wrought, it must be admitted, was a system of imposture. Astonishing genius was indeed, in his peculiar instance, the soul and essence of the fraud; yet there it glittered, an enormous cheat, after all. The personal character of the Protector, from his cradle to his grave, strikes the eye of the mind as a vast congeries of curious contrarieties; the grand mingles strangely with the base, and the grovelling with the sublime. He was generally coarse, yet could be most refined: at times full of tricks and antics, and making the most hideous grimaces in his prayers, or turning his eyes into fountains of tears, or filthily soiling the dresses of his ladies with practical jokes which ought to have brought him to the pump and the whipping-post, he could nevertheless mould a senate to his will, or direct for his own purposes the waves of rebellion and the thunders of war. Beneath the garb of godliness he concealed outrageous vices; the less pardonable after his marriage with a lovely and pureminded lady, who had too solid grounds for her jealousy, not perhaps against the Queen of Sweden, but certainly against other women.

It is remarkable that, as in the case of several enormous sensualists, no drugs of embalmment could preserve his body from overpowering and rapid corruption. The sere-cloths, though six times doubled, yet swelled and burst, with an offensiveness so far worse than the fetor of disease or the work of the worm, that immediate interment became necessary; and the final solemnities, both at Whitehall and Westminster Abbey, as is well known, presented, instead of the real remains of the deceased, a mere effigy to the public gaze. It was made of wax, fashioned to an admirable likeness, apparelled in rich velvet, laced with gold, furred with ermine, and adorned with purple. The kirtle was girded with an embroidered belt carrying a sword. In the right hand of the image was a sceptre, in the left a globe; and behind the head, when it lay in state, was a rich chair of tissue surmounted with an imperial crown. Surely this singular pageant affords an instructive hieroglyphic of the character and destinies of the personage whose portrait we have been attempting to draw.

Guizot observes, "that he departed in the plenitude of his power and greatness: having succeeded beyond all expectation, far more than any other of those men ever succeeded, who by their genius have raised themselves, as he had done, to supreme authority; for he had attempted and accomplished, with equal success, the most opposite designs. During eighteen years, he had alternately sown confusion and established order, effected and punished revolution, overthrown and restored government in his own country. At every moment, under all the circumstances, he distinguished with admirable sagacity the dominant interests and passions of the time, so as to make them the instruments of his own rule,—careless whether he belied his antecedent conduct, so long as he triumphed in concert with the popular instinct, and explaining the inconsistencies of his conduct by the ascendant unity of his power. He is perhaps the only example which history affords of one man having governed the most opposite events, and proved sufficient for the most various destinies." The wonder is, that he was never assassinated, nor his life ever actually attacked. The greatness of his family began and died with him; for neither widow nor children could find favour, or even justice, amidst the popular frenzy of the Restoration. Yet his administration involved and partially developped the noblest germs of our national and naval prosperity. His name will never be forgotten. Abroad he intimidated Holland, humiliated Spain, overawed Sweden, overreached Mazarin, and punished the Barbary corsairs; whilst at home, in three kingdoms, he coerced their aristocracy, bridled their religious establishments, and subdued their factions. Walter Savage Landor declares, that "no agent of equal potency and equal moderation had appeared upon earth before him. He walked into a den of lions, and scourged them growling out: his imitator in modern times was pushed into a menagerie of monkeys, and fainted at their grimaces!" Napoleon, however, was a Cromwell upon a European scale; but then the latter *preceded* him. We owe much, beyond the possibility of doubt, in the way of mere worldly welfare, to the Great Protector: yet clearly enough it appears that, upon the **whole, he** was a bad man, who reaped, under the auspices of a lie, the rewards in this lower scene of enormous iniquity; whose soul, though endowed with so many gifts and talents, yet revolved in lonely selfishness upon its own centre; and who lived through a generation of hypocrisy, to leave his subjects no better alternative than a choice between anarchy or the Stuarts.

MASTERS AND WORKMEN IN THE MIDDLE AGES.

(From the Rambler.)

A thousand years ago, when England was ruled by Ethelred the Anglo-Saxon king, the law of the country was thus declared:

"We all zealously hold one Christianity; and the ordinance of our Lord and the 'witan' is, that just laws be set up, and that every man be entitled to right; and that peace and friendship be observed; and let every injustice be carefully cast out from the country; **and let** fraudulent deeds and hateful wrongs be earnestly shunned; and let God's law be zealously loved by word and **deed**: then will God be merciful soon to this nation. And let Sunday's festival be rightly kept, and marketings and workings be abstained from on that holy **day**; and let all St. Mary's feast-tides be strictly honoured, first with fasting, and afterwards with feasting; and **at the** celebration of every Apostle let there be fasting and feasting; and let the other festivals and fasts be observed; and the holy tides of the Ember-days and Advent **(until** the Octave of the Epiphany), and from Septuagesima until fifteen days after Easter. And let us diligently turn from sin, and confess our misdeeds, and strictly make compensation. And let every man, poor or rich, be considered worthy of right; and let every man do **to** others the justice which he desires shall be rendered to to him, according as it is reasonable. And ever as any one shall be more powerful here in the world, so shall he pay for every misdeed more dearly; because the strong and the weak are not alike, and cannot raise a like burden; nor is the hale like unto the unhale; and discreetly are to be distinguished rich and poor, weak and strong. And if a money-penalty arise, let it belong, by direction of the bishops, to the behoof of the poor. And let mercy be shewn for fear of God, and those be protected who need it, because we all need that our Lord oft grant his mercy to us."

Similar was the character of the laws of Alfred, who in his ordinances recited the precepts of the Mosaic law, marked as it was by the most careful consideration for the poor, and a systematic favouring of poverty as against property, and commanding that the same judgment be given for rich and poor; the king also incorporating in his code the New Testament precepts, embodying them all in the comprehensive principle that every one should do unto others what he would wish done unto himself.

Asser, in his *Life of Alfred*, shews that his example amply illustrated his laws; for he gave a great part of his revenues to the poor, and was to their interests wonderfully attentive. The biographer adds: "The poor had beside him few protectors in the country, for the powerful turned their thoughts rather to secular than heavenly things, more bent on their own profit than the common good." So, Guizot says, that the principles of justice and beneficence acted on by the Church, explain why the people were always so anxious to be placed under her domination: lay proprietors being far from watching so carefully over the interest of the inhabitants of their domains, looking chiefly to their own profit. These instances exhibit the different ways in which the Church and the world deal with the poor,—that is, those who live by their labour: a difference displayed in all ages down to the present time, at which, indeed, perhaps it is more marked and more important than ever.

When the Church first founded her divine kingdom in this

realm, there existed the institution of serfdom as respects the labourers in husbandry, which was not absolutely abolished, but which was deprived of its evil by the influence of her benign principles, as above expressed, and embodied in the law. Another view which the Church inculcated is conveyed in the ordinance of Louis le Hutin abolishing such servitude in France. "Since according to the right of nature every one should be born free, but by certain usages and customs which have been kept from great antiquity in our kingdom, many of our common people have fallen into condition of servitude, which greatly displeases **us**, we ordain that such servitude be abolished, and freedom given on good and just condition to all who are fallen **into it.**" But so contented were the people under Catholic lords, that they **scarcely cared** for the offered enfranchisement. And the spirit which in this country characterised the system under the influence of the Church is shewn in the simple fact, that if a serf were made to work on a Sunday or festival, he was *ipso facto* emancipated.

The author of *Mores Catholici* truly says : " In the middle **ages the** social state was no doubt imperfect : Christianity had not terminated its work ; but was it not better to be one of the people then, than to be so now, in the nineteenth century ? He was a *serf*, it is true ; but is he not now a *workman ?* " It is our object to answer these questions, by shewing that the workman now is worse off than the serf was then.

The same author observes : "**The peasant** then held to something : a moral tie attached him to his master and the Church ; **at whose** door he assumed all the dignity of a man and of a Christian ; and which offered him an asylum against the world. There was a community of faith and feeling among **high** and low, rich and poor.

"In a Catholic state one might have looked upon every person in every rank as one of a great but closely-united family, possessing the same feelings and acting from the same motives : the poor labourer, the young apprentice, the student, the artisan, the soldier, and the sovereign, all had the same sources of instruction and consolation as himself. In the tribunal of penance they had all been taught the same lessons, and had been directed to the same end. In every other state, heathen or modern, each man has his own motives, his own end in view; perhaps he thinks virtues what you regard sins; and sins what you regard as virtues. In Catholic states there was only one standard of morality; there was only one faith. What an increase of public and social happiness resulted from such unity!"

The same author shews how the spirit of the Church, so essentially social, led to the formation, from a very early period, for all trades and manufactures, of confraternities or societies, which included *both the masters and the men ;* and which regulated, by amicable arbitrament, all those questions that have, for a long course of years, proved in this country fruitful in fatal dissensions between the employer and the employed,—the case of unskilled labour, the admission of apprentices, the amount of wages, and the hours of work. Guardians were actually appointed to see that the men had their meals properly, and worked neither too early nor too late. These "guilds" or confraternities are of very ancient origin, and are mentioned in our Anglo-Saxon laws. They were of a religious character; and all their rules were based upon religious principles. The common condition of admission was to "work well and honestly;" and any misconduct forfeited the **privileges attaching** to them. The men were not to work late : **why? because** the work could not be so well done at night. **The** masters could not employ men who had not been brought up to the business : why? because the work would not be well done. So again, the master could not have more than a certain number **of** apprentices with each workman : why? because otherwise they **would not** be well taught. It will be seen how the principles of honesty and equity were applied; and with what truth our author observes, "that under such a **system** there could not exist (as in our own age and country) **a state** of continued (concealed or open) war between masters **and men.**"

It **will be** observed that the Church did not leave the masters and the men **to** settle all matters separately, each individual for himself ; **or as two classes,** each class for itself ;

but blended both the masters and the men together in common confraternities, with a common interest and fellow-feeling: so favourable was the Church to association, so hostile to separation. Guizot testifies to the marvellous unity produced by the Church in the middle ages; and the latest of his productions proves isolation to be identified with infidelity, and destructive of the greatness and happiness of man. And De Haller truly says, that the Catholic religion alone secures a union of hearts and minds; being founded on that reciprocal sacrifice of one for another, which is the bond of all society; not on egotism or selfishness, which is its solvent and destruction: on the bond of **an** immense community united by the same faith and law; not on a principle of hatred, isolation, and law. It is obvious how admirably all this was illustrated by these confraternities; and how much the reverse of all this is exhibited in a system of hostile combinations of masters and men as separate classes, with opposite interests; each acting unrestrainedly on the selfish instincts of human nature. Under these associations it was not allowed to any master, for his selfish aggrandisement, to make his men work later than others; nor for any man, from the same selfish motive, to offer so to work; as it was considered that thereby an unfair advantage would be gained at the expense of the general good. It is obvious that the Church alone, with her supernatural system, could induce men to sacrifice their selfish interests, and act in concert, instead **of each seeking " his** own."

And, indeed, as already has been intimated, these societies were essentially religious, having each its patron saint: the embroiderers, Our Lady; the carpenters, St. Joseph; the tent-makers, St. Paul; the bookbinders, St. John; and so on; the feasts of the Saints being kept with great devotion. The law no further acted than by enforcing among the members of the confraternities the engagements they had thereby contracted to each other; just as to this day penalties levied by "byelaws" are recoverable **at common law.** But the erection of these confraternities, and the entering into them, were purely voluntary; and the work of the Church, who infused into society the spirit of fraternity, which led to their formation. In our

Statute-book many references may be seen to these " guilds " or " fraternities," as simply recognised by the law ; and in one act they are described as having been erected by the people " merely out of devotion ; " which is a clear legislative recognition of the credit of their establishment being exclusively due to the Church; the " devotion " she had created and kept up among the people.

And thus things were, so long as society continued true to the Church; and thus they would have remained, had not the Church been interfered with, or rather checked, controlled, and counteracted, and all her good work of unity and peace marred, defeated, and defaced, by the selfish legislation of the State. Prompted by the selfish feelings of those who " cared not for the poor," nor for the Church, who was their protector, " Jeshurun waxed fat and kicked." An evil generation arose, who, wearied of the Church, envied her her endowments, which she shared with the poor, and hated the power she exercised for their protection ; and when this evil spirit of covetousness and selfishness was in the hearts of the " great men, it was inevitable that they should assail the poor and the Church together ; that they who coveted the property of the Church should grudge the wages of the poor ; that those who sought to cripple her power, should seek also to enslave those on whose behalf she exercised it. And it was so. It cannot be merely a coincidence : it is an important, instructive, and pregnant fact, that at the period when took place the first formal legislative encroachments on the Church, arose the first legislative aggression upon the poor. So it is. The first statute of mortmain, directed against the religious houses, to prevent their acquiring land, passed in the reign of Henry III. ; in whose reign the Parliament made the first declaration of a feeling adverse to the authority of the Church. To appreciate the significance of the statute of mortmain upon this subject, it is requisite to remark that the precepts and example of the religious led to the greatest liberality towards the poor, and of course tended to keep up the rate of wages. The voice of history, and the recitals of the acts of Parliament themselves, alike attest that these resources were principally expended in charity and hospitality; and although, of course, the obligations of religion, and dictates of reason, would prevent them from maintaining in idleness those who were able but averse to work, their alms would protect the poor from that pressure of poverty which compels them to take whatever wages are offered, however inadequate. Hence, the statutes of mortmain, though directly and immediately affecting the religious houses, indirectly and remotely, but not the less really, bore upon the poor, and affected the rate of wages; for the more the resources of the religious houses were restrained, the less relief could be dispensed to the poor, the greater would be the pressure upon them, and the more unfavourable the condition of labour.[a] It **was** not long, however, ere direct legislation was resorted to against the poor, precisely in the reign in which passed the first **act** against the Holy See.

In the reign of Edward III. an act was passed against alms-giving, reciting, that "Because many valiant beggars, as long as they may live of begging, do refuse to labour, giving themselves to idleness and vice, and sometimes to theft and other abominations; none, upon the pain of imprisonment, shall, under colour of pity or alms, give any thing to such which may labour, so that thereby they may be compelled to labour." This was quite of a piece with the statutes of mortmain: both were acts against alms-giving; the one against alms (of land) to the Church, the other against alms (of money or meat) to the poor. The object, nature, and effect, were much the same in both cases and as to each class of statutes, viz. love of money. In a former series of papers, *On the Encroachments of the State upon the Church*, we shewed that this "root of all evil" was the "root of bitterness" which wrought and rankled into the fatal schism of the Reformation. And **we** shall see the

---

[a] An act of Henry V. **recites** "that many hospitals founded by the kings of this realm, and lords spiritual and temporal, to which the founders had given a great part of their moveable goods, and lands and tenements, to sustain impotent men and women, and to nourish, relieve, and refresh other poor people" (*i. e.* those not impotent—"able-bodied" labourers), "be now for the most part decayed, and the goods and profits of the same, by divers persons, spiritual and temporal, withdrawn and spent on other uses, whereby many men and women have died in great misery, for default of living, aid, and succour." Of course the effect of this must have been to increase the competition for wages, along with the poverty and distress of the poor.

same spirit actuating the legislation designed to depress the poor beneath the rich.

Concurrently with a series of acts of Parliament directed against the Church, commenced another series directed against the rights of the labouring classes. An act of Edward III. recites, " Because many, seeing the necessity of masters, and the great scarcity of servants, will not serve unless they may receive excessive wages, and some rather willing to beg in idleness than by labour to get their living; we, considering the grievous incommodities which of the lack especially of ploughmen and such labourers may come ; " and then proceeds to enact, " that every man and woman able in body, and not having of his own whereof he may live, if he be required to serve, shall be bounden to serve him who shall so him require, and take only the wages which were accustomed to be given in the places where he oweth to serve in the twentieth year of the king's reign, or the five or six common years next before; and if any such man or woman, being so required to serve, will not the same do, he shall be taken and committed to the common gaol, there to remain in strict keeping until he find surety to serve." That is, the poor are to be forced to work, but, as some protection, their wages are fixed; for it is provided, " that no man pay, or promise to pay, any servant any more wages than was wont to be paid in the twentieth year of the king's reign " (or the five years before), and " that saddlers, skinners, white tanners, cordwainers, tailors, smiths, carpenters, masons, tilers, shipwrights, carters, and all other artificers and workmen, shall not take for their labour above the same that was wont to be paid in the twentieth year of our reign, or other common years next before ; and if any man take more, he shall be committed to gaol." It is obvious that the wages which were " wont to be given " at the time referred to, were less than the labourers now claimed, and there is every reason to believe less than they had a right to claim, *i. e.* less than the wages which would be just and fair and reasonable. It appears that it was difficult to enforce the act ; for a subsequent act recites, that, " forasmuch as it is given the king to understand that the said servants having no regard to the said ordinance, but to their own ease and singular covetise, do withdraw (*i. e.* decline) to serve great men and other, unless they have double or treble of what they were wont to take the said twentieth year;" it is enacted, "that carpenters, masons, and tilers, shall not take by the day above so much, and 'their knaves' so much. And that cordwainers and shoemakers shall not sell boots nor shoes, nor none other things touching their mystery, in any other manner than they were wont the said twentieth year; and that goldsmiths, saddlers, horse-smiths, tanners, tailors, and other workmen, shall be sworn to use their crafts in the manner they were wont to do the said twentieth year; and if any refuse, they shall be punished by fine and ransom and imprisonment, at the discretion of the justices."

These "justices" were of course the "great men" who complained of the "excessive wages" of the labourer; and one may imagine the "justice" the poor labourers got at their hands, and may suspect the "singular covetise" of those who framed it. The act was too iniquitous to last in that form; so, after a few disturbances, which the student of history will perhaps recollect or refer to, the act was altered as to the "penalty," and it was "accorded that labourers shall not be punished by fine and ransom," and imprisonment at discretion, but by imprisonment for fifteen days. Nevertheless the labourer did not gain much; for by the same act it is provided, that a labourer "departing from **their** service" might be branded and "burnt in the forehead with an iron made in the form of the letter F, in token of his falsity."

In the reign of Richard II. we find it ordained that these statutes be firmly held and "put in execution." The result all our readers are aware of—the formidable insurrections under Wat Tyler and others, which, though ascribed by historians (so carelessly is history written by **men** not acquainted with the laws) only to the pressure of taxation, were obviously excited chiefly by these arbitrary enactments. In the year 1381 (in the same reign) the king, in an act of pardon, speaks of the "insurrection of villains, which of late did traitorously rise in outrageous numbers against God, good faith, and reason; but we suspect that there was more ground to say that the laws against which they rose were against "God, good faith, and reason." Such, however, were the "strikes" of the middle ages. In the same reign, in the year 1388, it is again ordained, that the statutes of labourers and artificers be firmly kept and holden, and that there be a pair of stocks in every town to *justify* the said labourers and artificers, as is ordained in the said statutes. **And it is** " ordained " that no labourer shall depart (even) **at the end** of his term (of service) out of the hundred where **he** is dwelling, to serve **or** dwell elsewhere, or by colour to go thence in pilgrimage, unless he have letters patent, &c. It is also " ordained" that, because labourers will not labour without outrageous and excessive hire, they take no more than so much, or " less in the county where less was wont to be given," " without clothing, courtesie, **or other reward,** (even) by contract." So that even if the employer promised any thing more, he need not have given it. We may imagine how the poor working-people would be "justified," however, under this act, if they complained of low wages! It would appear that the operation of these acts was obstructed by the guilds and confraternities we have before described; for we find an act " against unlawful orders made by masters of guilds, fraternities, and other companies," **which** it will be recollected had for ages been recognised by the law, and allowed by Church and State to regulate the rate of wages. The present act recites "that, whereas the masters, wardens, and people of the guilds, fraternities, and other companies incorporate, oftentimes by colour of rule and governance, and other terms in general words to them granted by these charters make themselves **many unlawful and** unreasonable ordinances "— (*i. e.* against the " ordinances " of **the** statutes of labourers, which we have described ; and any thing which the " great men " considered as against " good faith and reason ")—it is then enacted, that no such guilds or fraternities make any ordinances not approved of as reasonable by the " justices!" Afterwards, however, it is enacted, that the " justices shall fix the wages to be paid"—*i. e.* if not by themselves, by their tenants! This iniquitous provision is repeated in the reign of

Henry VI., with a revival of the infamous enactment empowering the justices to inflict punishment by fine and imprisonment at discretion! Thus, then, the justices could force the labourers to work for whatever wages they (the justices) pleased to fix; and on refusal could punish them by fine and imprisonment at pleasure! Such was the slavery which the State substituted for the holy and happy liberty which the Church had conferred; such the fetters forged for those whom she had made free! Still let it be remarked that, bad as all this was, the employers had not the power of fixing the wages they were to pay; and the poor had at least the protection of some intermediate power. In the same reign (of Henry VI.) we find an act reciting, "that, by the yearly congregations and confederacies made by the masons in these general chapiters and assemblies, the good (?) course and effect of the statutes of labourers be openly violated and broken, in subversion of the law, and to the great damage of the commons;" (*i. e.* the great men who complained of having paid "excessive wages,") and it is enacted, that "such chapiters and congregations shall not be hereafter holden; and that if any such be made, they that cause them to be assembled shall be judged felons; and all other masons coming to such chapiters and congregations be punished by imprisonment, and make fine and ransom at the king's will."

These acts are curious, because directed against the very combinations which, in our own times, have caused such commotions.

It was manifest that after the suppression of religious houses, the **numbers of the** poor and the pressure of their poverty would be greatly augmented; and the character of Protestant legislation against them, even in this reign and that of the pious Edward, is revolting and savage. In the 27th year of Henry was passed an act, that governors of shires, cities, or towns, shall find and keep every aged, poor, and impotent person, by way of voluntary and charitable alms, with such convenient alms as they shall think meet; and shall compel every sturdy beggar to be kept in continual labour; and a " valiant beggar or sturdy vagabond (*i. e.* an able-bodied labourer without work) shall have the upper part of the gristle of his right ear cut off; and if, after that, he be taken wandering in idleness, or doth not apply to his labour, or is not in service with any master, he shall be executed as a felon!" This, be it observed, might be merely because the man refused to work for unjust wages; and, to close the door of charity against him, this act prohibits any " dole or alms," except to the common boxes and gatherings of the parish!

It need hardly be said, that under the last of the Henries, especially after the breach with the Holy See, the legislation against the poor was still more oppressive. Thus, one act provides that " the justices of peace in every county shall give license under their seals to such poor persons to beg within a certain precinct as they shall think to have most need" (so some, who had less need, were to be refused license); "and if any do beg without such license, he shall be whipped, or set in the stocks three days and nights upon bread and water." And a vagabond " taken begging shall be whipped, and then sworn to return to the place where he was born, or last dwelt by the space of three years, and there to put himself to labour." These last words expressively indicate the drift of all these statutes, so uncatholic in their character, even if passed in Catholic times; the object being, in fact, to force the poor to labour for such wages as the rich thought proper. There was no provision made to prevent a man being dealt with as a "valiant beggar" or "sturdy vagabond," who was not in work simply on account of his refusing to work for wages less than what would be fair and just.

An act of Edward VI. recites that "the multitude of people given to idleness and vagabondry hath always been very great," and that the "kings of the realm had 'gone about' and essayed with godly statutes to repress the same; yet not with that success which hath been wished;" and, "partly by foolish pity and mercy, the number of idle and vagabond persons hath increased, and yet do increase;" and then follow cruel enactments, denouncing, for the first offence, branding and slavery; for the second, branding and perpetual slavery; and for the third, death. These were the dooms for simple begging! Such was the legislation of our "Reformers" for the poor!

Well they realised the Scripture promises to those who "consider the poor!"

Of course such savage **and** barbarous statutes could not long be enforced in a country yet more than half Catholic in character. They were repealed in the reign of Mary, and an "**act** touching weavers" recited, that the "weavers have complained **at** divers times, that the rich and wealthy clothiers do many ways oppress them: some by employing persons unskiful, to the decay of a great number of artificers which were brought **up** to the said science of weaving: some by giving much **less** wages and hire than in times past they did."

This preamble is **curious,** as shewing that in those days precisely the same complaints were made (and especially, be it observed, as to the employment of unskilled persons) which are at this moment made by the manufacturing artisans. And it is also important as a parliamentary testimony, that after the Reformation people began to give less wages than they had been **wont to** pay; and less than Parliament deemed just. And it is pretty plain that the " godly statutes" passed by the Puritans had tended very much to the prejudice of the working classes, **and** the profit of the men of money, **who of course** pocketed the difference between just and unjust wages. It is important to observe here, that the two complaints, of the employment of unskilled persons, and the payment of unjust wages, are closely connected, and placed in juxtaposition; for of course the employers' **only** object in having unskilled workmen was to pay them **less wages; and of** course the only objection of the regular workmen was, that these unskilled men were employed **to do** skilled work, for which they were not properly fitted, **while** the regular workmen were; a system clearly prejudicial **to** the purchaser, as tending to the production of inferior articles; and Parliament, which had enacted many statutes to prevent the sale of such inferior manufactures, now decidedly pronounced *against* the system of employing unskilful men to do skilled work, merely in order to enable the employer to pocket more profit. The act provides, that a weaver shall have but two apprentices; and that none shall be a weaver unless he have been apprenticed. The principle of these provisions was upheld in the reign of Elizabeth, very early in whose reign (in 1562) an act was passed reciting that there remained in force a great many acts on the subject; and that "the wages limited in many of them were too small;" and could not, "without the great grief and burden of the poor labourer," be enforced. It is obvious, on the one hand, that the "poor labourer" had been gradually getting the worst of it, and that as the legislature bore harder upon the Church, it had also borne harder upon the poor. Still England (as we have already observed) was half Catholic in character, and therefore this act again exhibits a great deal of the old Catholic feeling as respects the working classes. It confirms, as before intimated, the principle of the two provisions of the act of Mary, extending it unto all "crafts" or "mysteries;" and enacting that no person shall exercise them without having been apprenticed; and that for every three apprentices a workman shall be employed. It also enacts that no workman shall be retained for less than a year: a most important provision, leading to prevent that fluctuating and fleeting character which now, it is universally complained, too often attaches to the relation of employer and employed. It then enacted that the hours of work should be in winter from "spring of day" till "night" (*i. e.* eight and six), and in summer from five till between seven and eight, *i. e.* about twelve hours, deducting two hours and half allowed for meals. And, for the regulation of wages, it was provided, that the justices in counties, and mayors in towns, should assemble yearly, and calling unto them "grave and discreet persons," and conferring with them, fix the amount of wages in the several occupations for the ensuing year. It is apparent that this act is, to a great extent, equitable towards the labouring classes. Ten years more, however, of Protestantism and pauperism produced a great deterioration in the character of the legislation on the subject; and, enraged by the increase of vagrancy (that natural consequence of the confiscation of the monasteries), Parliament relapsed into the barbarism of the first year of Edward VI., passing an act directing that a vagabond should be "grievously whipped" and burned through the gristle of the right ear with an hot iron

of the compass of an inch, unless some credible person will
take him into service for a year ; and " if he fall again into a
roguish life, he shall suffer death as a felon."

The object of this act could not have been only to force
the labourer, by terror of greater penalties than before, to
take such wages as were offered him, according to the standard of wages settled under the previous act by the justices in
conference with the " grave and discreet persons ;" for the
acceptance of such wages, if the act were fairly complied with,
could scarcely be otherwise than very willing on the part of
the workmen, and could not have required to be forced on
them by such dreadful penalties. But the object plainly was,
to hold over the working classes the terror of such terrific punishment in case of refusal of work, as to enable the justices
to fix, or the employers to offer, a far lower rate of wages
than it would otherwise have been safe to proffer. The act, in
short, exhibits the savage selfishness of the Puritan spirit,
struggling to subdue and supersede the half-Catholic character
of the previous statute for settling the standard of wages, as
some protection to the poor, and at all events an effective arbi-
trement between them and the rich.

Towards the end of the reign of Elizabeth, however, it was
found that such severe measures were certain to be failures,
by reason of what the puritanical Parliaments were fond of
calling " foolish pity and mercy of those who should enforce
them ;" so, in 1597, the inhuman enactments alluded to were
repealed, and the comparatively mild coercion of houses of
correction invented. How puzzled the Parliaments of Reformed England were (then as ever since) by the problem of
labour, and what a medley of ideas confused the Protestant
mind on the subject, can be seen in a subsequent statute for
encouraging the erection of " hospitals, *maisons de Dieu*,
houses of correction, or abiding places for the poor ;" *i. e.* any
" abiding places," prisons, or hospitals, so as only to get rid
of the " great difficulty " of Protestantism, *poverty*.

The difficulty evidently was, how to deal with such as were
temporarily unable to get work. The Catholic system was
charity ; the Protestant system was *cruelty*. The Catholic

system was to *relieve* by alms; the Protestant system was to *refuse* relief, from a selfish apprehension that men who could get any alms would not be so anxious to work, or would be less ready to accept *any* wages that might be offered. The Protestant plan has been to put a pressure upon the poor, to leave them in as much poverty as possible, in order that they may be more at the mercy of the employers.

It is easy to see that the act of Elizabeth, settling a standard of wages, would be an obstacle in the way of such a system, supposing it to be fairly enforced, which probably it often was not; and even if it were, why, it would be easily evaded when there was no fund of relief for the poor to fall back upon. And to deprive them of any such resource, or any means of relief, was clearly the primitive policy of Protestantism, *i. e.* to let the poor be at the mercy of Mammon. It was found, however, that the system could not be quite enforced without greater outrages upon humanity than the nation would bear. And so, at the end of Elizabeth's long reign, in 1591, was passed the original poor-law, which provided that the parish officers might levy rates for "setting to work" such as had "no means to maintain themselves." Such was the basis of our present poor-law system, substituted by the Protestant Parliament, after half a century of barbarous proscription, for the old Catholic way of dealing with the poor; such is the only resource for relief or support to which the working classes can resort; and to that they cannot, unless the parish officers, representing the very classes who pay both rates and wages, deem that there **are no means** of maintenance; which they are hardly likely to deem, **if any work, for** any wages at all, have been offered. It serves to **shew very significantly** the spirit in which Protestantism has all along dealt **with the** poor, to state, that under this act, wages, avowedly insufficient for the labourer's support, used to be eked out by relief from the rates! *i. e.* by collusion with the parish officers, employers paid less wages than the labourer could subsist upon, and made up the deficiency out of rates levied on the rest of the parishioners! Under such a system, of course the working classes were virtually in the power of their employers; and the statute of Elizabeth, for arbitrating wages, could scarcely be much protection to them, when liable to be **compelled** to take any wages they might be offered.

The only way the workmen had of protecting themselves against the injustice of inadequate wages was, of course, to refuse to work at all; or to agree to work, and then claim the fair wages on the ground that the act of Elizabeth had not been observed, and the rate of wages had not been arbitrated upon.

From the language used in the recitals of numerous acts of Parliament passed in the last century, it seems that great difficulties had arisen on the subject in the manufacturing districts, where the workmen, more intelligent than the agricultural labourers, were not so easily to be imposed upon, and would not willingly submit to see themselves defrauded of part of their just wages to swell the profits of the capitalist. There is reason to believe that the act of Elizabeth was often appealed to by the artisans; and it is obvious that the Protestant legislature must have found themselves in considerable perplexity on the question. The act, while it existed, gave the artisan a right to an independent arbitration of wages; and it could scarcely be seemly to repeal so fair and equitable an enactment. The course pursued, accordingly, is most evasive. An act is passed, empowering justices to **enforce** any contracts of employment, although the rate **of** wages may not have been arbitrated. **The effect of course** was, that the act of Elizabeth, **although not** expressly repealed, was quietly got rid **of**; for if the workmen once accepted employment at any wages, they could be compelled to work, however unjust the terms; and so they were reduced to this sole resource, the refusal of work. *i. e.* to what is **called a** "strike."

Of course strikes ensued, **and the** combinations, without which strikes could not **be effective.**

And it is recited by a statute passed in 1725, that "great numbers **of** weavers and others have lately formed themselves into unlawful clubs and societies, and have presumed, contrary to law, to enter into combinations, and make by-laws or orders, by which they pretend to regulate the trade and prices of goods, and advance their own wages unreasonably; and many other things to the like purpose." And then the act declares such combinations illegal, and imposes the penalty of imprisonment on those who take part in them. We have already said these combinations on the part of the workmen were (and are now deemed to be) quite legal; being only combinations to settle between themselves what wages they would take, just as masters agreed among themselves **what wages** they would give; and as no one **ever** imagined the latter combinations illegal, there was no pretence **for** supposing the former to be so. **And** the reason for the combination of workmen is obvious enough from the recital of an act in the same reign, that "divers controversies and disputes had arisen between the clothiers and makers of woollen goods, and the manufacturers employed by them;" which disputes and controversies, when arising about wages, there were then no means resorted to for the purpose of adjusting and determining, as there would have been under the act of Elizabeth, or under that act of Mary, which our readers will recollect recites, that "rich and wealthy clothiers do many ways oppress the weavers;" a statement not less true now than then.

The regulation of wages, from the time of George I. to the present, has **been left** to be adjusted by the masters and men among themselves.

Such is the state in which Protestantism, **after three centuries** of shifting legislation, places the question at **this moment**. We have seen recently the practical result.

The statutes referred to passed since the Revolution—doing away tacitly or expressly with the old Catholic or semi-Catholic acts, which provided protection of some kind for the working-classes as well as for their masters—were all passed under the influence of the masters, *i. e.*, of the men of money; whose "interest" became then paramount, and was always the main support of the Whigs. Consequently, they are all for the protection of the masters, and not at all for the protection of the **men**. Amidst a long series of statutes, from the Revolution **to** the present time, passed for the encouragement of every manufacturer, there has not been any enactment for the protection of the men. There are, it is true, provisions for deciding disputes between them and their masters; but that of course was necessary **for** the sake of the masters. What we mean is, that while there is an enormous accumulation of enactments in favour of capital, there is not one in favour of labour; while there are innumerable provisions for the protection **of** the masters' interest, there is not a solitary one for the protection of the men's. And, in particular, though there are plenty of clauses to make the men do their work, and not combine for greater wages, and so forth, there is none to secure them a fair rate of wages, nor reasonable hours of work. And, above all, no provision is made for a tribunal of arbitration upon these important points, such as was established by the act of Elizabeth, **in accordance** with those of Edward III.

Now, we repeat, these modern acts were all passed by the masters, the men of money; and this consideration at once occurs: if they deemed any arbitration would be for their interests or for their protection, they would have taken care to restore or provide it. Their not doing so, coupled with their **obstinate opposition to** it **at** this moment, and the earnestness **of the men in** asking for it, is clear proof that the masters known the practical result of leaving them to deal with the men upon the questions **of** wages and hours of work must be, that they, the masters, will get the best of it; that is, that the masters will eventually get the men's labour for less wages than under any fair system of arbitration—that is, less than fair and just wages. This, we repeat, is clearly the conviction of masters and **men**.

How **can it** be otherwise? The most clear advocates of the masters know the reason why, viz. that the masters have (in Lord Cranworth's language) "an immense advantage over the men," inasmuch as the masters are not obliged to employ the men, while the men are under a necessity of being employed by the masters. The employers can do without the work, the employed cannot do without the wages; the masters are men of money, the artisans are men without money; the former can wait, the latter cannot (at least it is not likely they can wait so long as the masters); in a word, the former are capitalists, the latter are labourers; and the effect of the Protestant system is to force the labourers to work for the capitalists on such terms as the capitalists choose to offer. It is not so enacted, but it is virtually effected. It is the necessary result of leaving two parties to contract, one of whom is not in reality, though he may be nominally, free to elect whether to accept or reject the terms offered by the other.

Such (we repeat) is the way in which Protestantism has dealt with this social problem: such the state to which it has brought the working classes and their employers! We do not desire to enter into the controversy between them; but, in order to illustrate our observations, let us quote a passage or two upon each side of the question. The *Morning Herald*, the advocate of the workmen, says, "The demand of the men is for the abolition of systematic overtime and piece-work; but they are ready to submit their case to any impartial tribunal. The masters will not allow of this, and call it 'dictation.' Yet what is there in the demands which those who have the welfare of the labouring classes at heart do not desire? seeing their poorer brethren ground down, ground to atoms, as beneath the upper and nether millstone; and those who ought to help them, perverted by false theories of political economy, refusing to regulate labour; *i. e.* to protect the weaker against the stronger, so that the whole frame-work of society is being reduced to a mere cotton-mill, tearing and roaring on, and on, and on, until the stuff, sinew, and substance which supplied it are consumed." "If (say the men) there were a fairly-constituted board of masters and men to fix prices and see justice done to both parties, the piece-work would be best; but the men ought not to be called upon to labour from morning until night for sixteen hours, from six till ten; while the masters exercised an arbitrary power of fixing the prices, and compelling them to accept them under pain of being cast on the streets."

The gist of the men's complaints is, it is clear, that the masters, under the present system, exercise a kind of moral coercion over the men, and practically regulate what wages shall be given for the work, and what work shall be done for the wages. On the part of the men themselves their grievances are thus stated by one of their spokesmen : " **If a** mechanic asked to leave at the close of a regular day's **work**, he was discharged. This was a sample of the compulsory system of ' overtime. ' Men were morally compelled, by the fear of losing their employment and having their **families** left destitute, **to** accept their employer's terms. Then **as to** piece-work, there was no **objection to** it, if on terms equitable and fair **to** both parties. **But the master,** knowing the measure of a **day's** work, if he **found on the** completion of a job done by piece-work, that the man **made more** than the regular day's wages, on the next occasion offered **a** reduction ; the man was forced to take it, and worked yet harder to keep **up** his wages at the former rate ; and it **was clear** that this **tended to** excessive labour, and lessened remuneration. There had been reductions to the extent of one-half thus effected."

The masters, in their manifesto, say, " **All** we want is to **be let** alone. With every respect for noble and distinguished **referees,** whose arbitration has been tendered, and with no reason to doubt that their award would be honest, intelligent, and satisfactory, we must take leave to say that we alone are the competent judges of our own business, and masters of our own establishments, and it is our firm determination to remain so. Ours is the risk **of** loss ; ours the capital, its perils and engagement. We **claim, and are** resolved to assert, the right of every British **subject, to do what** we like with our own ; and **to** vindicate **the right of the** workmen to the same constitutional privilege. Artisans and their employers are respectively individuals, each legally capable of consent, each severally entitled to contract. Our agreements for their services are made with them in their separate, not their aggregate capacity. They have labour and skill to sell, we have capital to employ and to pay. Who, then, shall stand between these two parties to a lawful contract, and dictate to us what we **shall** pay ? "

It is obvious that all this proceeds upon that principle of isolation—in other words, of selfishness—which we have shewn, even upon Protestant testimony, is so identified with infidelity, **and is** so utterly opposed to Catholicity,—which tends, as it has been seen, to counteract the selfish in man's nature by means **of the** principle of association. The principle of Protestantism, or of isolation, is, as developed in the argument of the advocates of the masters, that each man is to act, employer or employed, only as if he were the only individual affected by his actions ; as though, for instance, if he worked overtime, other persons would not be obliged to do so too, or to suffer loss, and so of every thing else. Thus the masters contend for the uncontrolled right of every employer to contract for the services of any British subject he pleases; by which they mean, "on any terms they please," for such, as we have shewn, is the practical result, if the man be obliged to accept whatever terms are offered, or to lose employment altogether ; **and** the effect of his acceptance be, to impose on all the others the same alternative. Such is the inevitable result of the principle of isolation, which, we have seen, is the principle of Protestantism—that is, of sectarianism, of egotism, and of atheism.

The real character of these principles we will state in the words of a Protestant journalist. The *Herald* says : " Of the disunion which exists in our manufacturing districts between masters and men we have had very striking and fatal proofs within the last few weeks. That disunion is not confined to the engineers. It runs through all the ranks of mechanical labour, and is almost inevitable on a state of things where men come and go, where property rapidly changes hands, and where nothing, in fact, binds master to man, except the weakest and most shifting of all bonds—mutual interest. Other than this there is no tie of union between them ; there is nothing to appeal to, not only when their respective interests seem incompatible, but when, as in the present case, they are thought to be so. Nothing, then, remains but the annihilation of one or the other, so far at least as regards their relations of master and **man ; and** nothing can shew this more clearly than the present dispute, wherein the only arguments used, by one side at least, had reference only to self-interest."

Thus, upon Protestant testimony, we convict Protestantism

of the curse of a system of organised selfishness, of which the essence is, "Every man for himself, and only for himself;" instead of the old Catholic and English feeling, "Live and let live."

And the result—what is it? We will shortly state, in the language of the *Debats*: "We believe that the contest going on at present in England between the masters and workmen, between capital and wages, is more connected than is imagined with general politics, and may be attended with consequences of interest to all other countries; and that there is at the bottom of this agitation of the working-classes a principle of social revolution is what is not contested, and men begin to admit it, even in England. It is not generally known what formidable progress the Socialist doctrines have made among the working-classes in England. It is probable that the workmen who are in coalition will be obliged to capitulate, because starved out. But on that account will peace be established? The workmen will return to the factories with feelings of humiliation and hostility, and the war of the two classes will be perpetuated silently until a new explosion takes place. That cannot be a sound social state which presents the spectacle of two great classes arranged in battle array, one with numbers on its side, the other with money. If the struggle should continue for some time, immense losses must ensue on both sides, and eventually it is the country itself which will lose by the contest. The position assumed at present by the two parties, workmen and masters, leads to a double suicide. This antagonism of interests and classes assumes in England proportions more and more alarming; and the peril of such a situation is augmented, when the upper classes, the governing ones, afford the spectacle of a radical inability to solve the great social problem."

Such is exactly the conclusion to which we contemplated conducting our readers,—that Protestantism cannot settle the question how the rich are to satisfy the poor; how the wealthy class is to live with the working class in unity, harmony, and peace. We have appealed to history to shew how Catholicy did this. These passing events conclusively shew how lamentably Protestantism fails to do it.

KING WILLIAM III.

(From the Rambler.)

OTHER people besides the worshippers of mere stocks and stones have had their idols both political and religious, before which they have bowed down with homage and offerings not less wonderful than they appear disgraceful. When the great ecclesiastical revolt of the sixteenth century had shaken European society to its foundations, moral standards assumed the form of sliding-scales, adapted in the hands of Protestantism to suit every emergency: so long at least as they seemed to measure the mark of the Beast, or square with the mystically perverted numbers of the Apocalypse. Heroes were, therefore, either angels or devils, not as their conduct fulfilled or fell short of the requirements of the Gospel, but rather as they opposed or favoured a certain line of human politics—the projects of a Spanish monarch, or the ambition of a king of France: more especially when, under the guise of religion, worldly gear was to be gained, or the robbery of monasteries defended. Hypocrisy rapidly rose to an ascendency over the master-spirits of the age. Just in proportion as heresy waxed rampant in Christendom, rebellion and licentiousness sported among its fairest fields; at first with unblushing effrontery, but latterly under some decency of masquerade. Amidst the confusion, men elected their leaders, followed them, crowned them, fought under them, sold their own souls for them, and even honoured them after death with a sort of secular apotheosis. The Whigs of England have distinguished themselves in this line; they glory in a political calendar canonising the names of knaves, who in the lower ranks of life might have illustrated the cells of Newgate, and ascended the ladder of Jack Ketch at Tyburn. To recount them would be long and tedious; yet surely at the head of them all stands that royal figure to whose immortal memory the Orange clubs of Ireland still pour out their annual libations of claret, William III.; eulogised by the most brilliant of living reviewers, for the instruction of our fellow-countrymen, **at an** expense of thirty thousand pounds sterling, paid this very year as the price of volumes which will **be justly denounced** by our posterity under the **denomination of** *plaustra mendaciorum*.

A count of Nassau, called Willliam the Silent, had become Prince of Orange, by the will of his cousin Renatus; that personage being heir, on the maternal side, to Philibert, of the house of Chalons in Upper Burgundy. When resistance broke out in **the** Netherlands against the tyranny of Philip II., **the** first William held the office of stadtholder to the provinces **of** Holland, Zealand, **and U**trecht. He was really a great man, barring his unhappy apostasy; wrapt, indeed, in profound reserve, **but** consistent in his **own** principles after he had **once** adopted their errors; and a sincere champion for never subjecting Catholics, however deeply he differed from them, to any civil disabilities. He shines in history as the Washington of his day and generation, achieving the independence of his country by the compact of Utrecht, A.D. 1579, **which** united the seven Dutch states into one republic. On **his** assassination at Delft by Balthazar Gerard in A.D. 1585, **his son** Maurice succeeded him, memorable for his connection with **the** Arminians and Gomarists, the Synod of Dort, Grotius, **and** Barneveldt. Henry Frederick, brother to Maurice, was the next stadtholder, dying prosperous and rich as to the things of this world, having never really troubled himself about that **which is to come.** His **son** and successor, William II., married **a daugther of our Charles I.;** through her becoming father **to a** posthumous representative, whose genuine character **we** would fain attempt to draw in these pages. Astrology gloated over his horoscope, as was common in those days; but the plain fact was, that his mother brought him into life about **a** week after she was a widow, and **at least** a month before his time. From the cradle he seemed puny in health, size, and constitution. **His** birth occurred **A.D.** 1650, amidst political **storms and social confusions,** when the Seven Provinces were at the height of their commercial grandeur, but when faction could insult patriotism with safety, and authority was only mentioned to be despised.

Two leading parties at that crisis enjoyed the intense pleasure of trying to tear their young country into pieces; the republicans, not unfairly represented by the famous brothers De Witts, and the adherents of the Orange family. The former were for some years a little disposed **to admit French** influences; so long, at least, as their indigenous **liberalism was** let alone, and their independence **uninvaded. The latter** were more aristocratical, not to say monarchical**, in their** tendencies, and abhorred the Perpetual Edict passed **by their** antagonists, that the princes of the house of Orange should be excluded from the stadtholderate for ever. Every form of heresy which could originate or exist in the phlegmatic temperament of Dutch consciences multiplied like frogs from one end of the land to the other; rendering the religious chaos a perfect paradise of Calvinistic and Arminian conventicles. Burgomasters contended about the five points of divinity, buried as to their nether members in so many pairs of trousers, that the kick of a horse might be almost as innocuous as the thundering argument of a rival. Severed moreover from the Church of God, the very genius of mammon had entered into the soul and body of the Seven Provinces. Money and merchandise drove out every other idea; except as to **the** verbal form in which it might be expressed, which was **generally** borrowed from **Scripture,** and therefore sounded **most sanctimoniously** to the external ear. The statue **of Erasmus, on one of the** innumerable bridges at Rotterdam, looked down upon **countless** disputants, fierce defenders of free will, reprobation, or indefectible grace; but whose hearts were as cold and hard as its own copper metal; ready at any moment to trample for gain upon the holy coat at Treves, or violate the sanctity of a crucifix in the distant regions of Japan. Their ledgers were their real Bibles; rich argosies constituted their floating churches; guilders seemed dearer to them than guardian angels; whilst ten thousand pillar-dollars, or a place in the customs, **or a** successful voyage to India, or the abasements of the **various co**ntroversialists, each in succession identified with the attainment **of power** or profit **to** one or another, stood in profane yet insepara**ble connection with** the absolute decrees of an Almighty Providence. William III. was educated from his nursery amidst such subjects **and** circumstances. He was **a** minor at the mercy **of a** greedy multitude, quarrelling, from his birth, about the management of his household and estates, encumbered as the latter were with heavy debts and obligations to needy courtiers or dependents, besides the enormous jointures to his mother and grand-mother, which had of course **to be** paid **out** of them. Prudence and caution, therefore, may **be said to have** been among the necessities of his existence, as **they** undoubtedly **proved** the main ingredients of his subsequent culmination. He inherited the talent of taciturnity from his ancestors; but then, in his mind it was the silence of deep and dark waters, which not even the eye of the cormorant can pierce, but from whose unfathomable abysses the spectres **of** Might and Mischief may be expected at any moment to to emerge. Beneath the still waves of such an intellectual Avernus, his soul learnt no very Christian lessons from the difficulties of his childhood and youth; while he watched over the **events around** him, as his abilities developed, with the most **ambitious aspirati**ons for the future. His religion, if it de**serves** that name, seems to have been a kind of Calvinistic infidelity, not at all restraining him from sensualism or vice, but leading him to trust in his destiny, after the manner of those who believe in the Koran.

The portraits of his countenance and person pretty well agree. He had **brown hair,** a strongly-defined aquiline nose, bright **sparkling eyes, wi**th a large brazen brow, grave as the **monotony of a Dutch** polder, yet relieved in some degree by **the** clearness **of** his complexion, until this last grew sallow; upon which the face of William became as ugly as that of his mistress, Elizabeth Villiers,—a wicked woman, whose influence over him combined the double elements of carnal and mental sorcery. His stature was that of an attenuated body, too often panting for breath, through constitutional asthma, to be princely or grand in its movements, as Louis XIV always appeared, although not favoured by nature for that purpose. William, on the other hand, seemed a dry formal Hollander, with the dregs of the small-pox thrown in upon his lungs; uncheerful and unimpressive; without conversation or the least shadow of attractive manners; a royal prig when not aroused into passion or violence; taking care moreover, whenever that happened, that none below a certain rank should ever see him fall foul of his servants, either with the cane he might hold in his hands, or the stool he had caught up from the floor. Habitually, however, he stood much upon his guard, as to which his inherent reserve helped him not a little; and the pensionary John De Witts had taught him betimes rarely to betray his sensations, but to see and get by heart every thing without seeming to take ordinary notice. His memory is declared to have been almost unlimited in its range and accuracy. For war and foreign policy he conceived an early and ardent admiration; and, if his talents in the cabinet and on the field were not first-rate, they were nevertheless so sharpened and intensified by his education and ambition, that they did more for himself, and told more against others, than those of far superior generals or statemen have sometimes done. His powers of observation and combination were the keenest; whilst all his physical senses, through nervous excitability, had become acute, and critically exquisite. The gaze of the seven provinces never forsook him from the commencement of his career. His dull countrymen looked upon him as a prodigy destined some day to extend their dominions, promote their commercial interests, and perhaps preserve their liberties. John and Cornelius De Witts probably considered him in another light; in fact as a serpent, uncoiling from feebleness into strength, in the bosom of their darling republic; nor will an honest and impartial historian ever aver that they were really mistaken.

The prime object with the youthful prince of Orange was to recover the high office of stadtholder; to which he presumed to feel, without of course at first saying so, that, as the lineal representative of his family, he was fairly entitled. The grand obstacles in his path were the pensionary and his brother Cornelius at the head of the republican party. John De Witts governed for many years with great personal simplicity and disinterestedness: but it was in an evil hour that Holland threw down the gauntlet to England for the sovereignty of the seas, since their trident was at that period wielded by the potent and steady genius of Oliver Cromwell. The protector proved too powerful an adversary for the pensionary: the Dutch acknowledged the loss of 1122 men-of-war and merchantmen; nor were their expenses less in two summers than they had been during the entire struggle of more than **twenty** with Spain. In the pacification of A.D. 1654, Cromwell not merely asserted the supremacy of the British flag, but, to **prevent** Charles II. from ever obtaining assistance through foreign alliances, he attempted to enforce by treaty the perpetual exclusion of his nephew William from the stadtholderate. The Dutch were indignant at this attempt on the part of Oliver; to which, however, under the rose, the De Witts were not unfavourable: but they visibly lost popularity from that hour, through the dislike with which the people viewed the interference of a foreign potentate, or rather, as they termed him, **of** an usurper, in the internal arrangements of the republic. As William grew up, his adherents fanned this flame in many ways. The prince himself had listened, as an obedient pupil, **to** the instructions of the very man whom his ambition would have to destroy before a road could be cleared for realising the object of his aspirations. It must have been a curious spectacle to have seen the future sovereign learning from his hated preceptor the arts of statecraft and kingcraft, involving as they ultimately did such tissues of crime and hypocrisy. Meanwhile the good pensionary fattened into personal portliness upon his modest salary, varying from 300*l.* to 700*l.* per annum: notwithstanding the cares of state extending over more than half a generation, to additional fierce conflicts with England, the encroachments of France, the fanaticism of the clergy spouting sedition and controversy from a thousand pulpits, and the ripening maturity of the Orange viper. William, on the verge of manhood, initiated himself into every plot and intrigue which might serve his own purposes; based as they one and all were upon maintaining and inflaming the nascent hatred of the nation against a couple of prominent yet most useful officials. He had entered upon his eighteenth year, when the pensionary carried his point in establishing the Perpetual Edict A.D. 1667; whereby it was fondly conceived that the republic would never be again plagued with the bugbear of a regal prerogative vested in an hereditary president. Alas for the folly of human anticipations! William rallied round him in profound secrecy, and with consummate skilfulness, every element of revolution which might be ready to explode at any signal made by himself. Innumerable coincidences seemed to fall in with his design: **the De** Witts and their followers had not worn the laurels of their political successes very meekly, nor were the undercurrents of public opinion really in their favour; they were now branded as the traitorous allies of Louis, whose armies in A.D. 1672, like a torrent, rushed across the frontiers, and overwhelmed three out of seven of the provinces; slanders of the vilest description, worse than the subsequent one of the warming-pan at St. James's, and equally successful, poisoned the populace; invisibly, yet effectually, the Orange party wound up the passions of the mob, and then let them loose upon their victims; nothing was heard from Amsterdam to Dordrect but one wild outcry for an immediate repeal of the Perpetual Edict, passed only five years before; since the salvation of the country, as it was now averred, could be achieved in no other way than by declaring Wiliam III. stadtholder. That princely adept in hypocrisy performed his **part** to admiration. He had prepared and pronounced the spell which raised the storm, and at the same time perfectly veiled his own share in the transaction. With mingled coyness and alacrity, after various abjurations, denials of his real object, and multiplied perjuries, he at length permitted those powers, honours, and offices to be, as it were, thrust upon him, for which he and his partisans had been plotting through a lustrum of years. In the month of July A.D. 1672 the Prince of Orange was declared captain-general of the army, supreme admiral of the fleet, and finally, hereditary stadtholder. All classes, from fear, inclination, or prudence, acquiesced in what could no longer be avoided. The goal of guilt was won, and success commanded admiration.

Not that the new master of the republic had triumphed

without massacre and bloodshed, for the reverse proved to be the truth of the case. The patriotic brothers De Witts were offered up as sacrifices to the vengeance of excited throngs, hounded on to their sanguinary work by the suspicions of commercial selfishness, and the sly suggestions of a victorious faction. The late pensionary, for he had resigned his functions, was assaulted by four ruffians, and left almost **dead in** the streets. Cornelius had the house, in which sickness confined him, attacked, and only not pulled down because a Protestant inquisition awaited him, on the false charge that he had offered an enormous sum of money to a barber-surgeon, named Tichelaar, for the assassination of William. Cornelius endured the tortures of the rack with unflinching constancy; repeating one of the odes of Horace, like an old Indian singing his death-song, whilst his wounded brother wiped the tears of agony from his eyes, and consoled him with their mutual consciousness of unsullied innocence. After some treacherous calm in the political tempest, the billows of popular and polemical turbulence broke out beyond all bounds. The Orangemen whispered, from head-quarters, that reaction might be at hand, unless it were anticipated by necessary firmness. Drums and trumpets gathered together multitudes of irritated burghers at the Hague, where they surrounded the prison of the De Witts, broke down the doors, dragged out both John and Cornelius from their dungeon, trampled them to death under their wooden sabots, and then deliberately, like wild-beasts, mangled every member of their victims. The two fingers of those hands which, according to the Dutch form of solemn swearing, had been held up in taking the oath of adherence to the Perpetual Edict, were now severed, and sold publicly at the rate of twelve stivers a joint: less than half an ear of one of the brothers fetched twenty-five stivers. The bodies remained hung up by the heels from a gibbet all through the night; their garments were, of course, rent off to rags; the cannibals continuing to cut horrid morsels from each carcass until the blushing daylight banished to their dens the perpetrators of these deeds of darkness. Their rage had been maddened by a demand of Louis XIV. for the free exercise of Catholic worship, with which requisition it was no doubt imagined that the late obnoxious leaders of the French party were more or less identified. Nor must be it forgotten, that William, instead of punishing such disorders, as he was bound to do in his mere capacity of governor, effectually screened all the criminals from legal penalties; and even directly or indirectly rewarded several of them so soon as it could be done without too startling a violation of Dutch decency. He now avowed himself a champion for the Reformation, raised up by the grace of God to overthrow Popery, and rescue from ruin the independence of his country.

In this latter labour of love he unquestionably succeeded; nor are we denying the secular merits of the Prince of Orange in so far as they possessed a real existence. Our object is simply to call attention to the genuine facts of history, to place them in their true perspective, to unmask the hollowness of Protestant Whiggery, and withdraw the false lights thrown upon its favourite idol. The stadtholder now fought a good fight, in the sense of local patriotism, against the domineering ascendency of France; but surely he never meant to serve either his native provinces or the cause of high Calvinism for stinted wages. When, therefore, he placed his encumbered estates at the service of his government, it was only throwing out sprats to catch whales. His pecuniary and political interests happened to be happily identified at a particular crisis of European affairs with the limitation of French absolutism; whilst he exerted himself zealously in that career of general usefulness which conferred upon his extraordinary courage and abilities magnificent worldly rewards. But such a course, however important, by no means constitutes the personage called upon to follow it, a hero of the first water. It gives him no title to adulation and worship when the grave has closed over his bones, and is already sullying the gilded crown or coronet upon his coffin. William III. was all the while a very bad man; although he liberated Holland from invasion, restored order, reduced Naarden, laid large districts under water to save them from an enemy, resolved to die in the last ditch of his flat and foggy yet wealthy meadows, baffled the mighty

monarch of the age with all this marshals, and invited Burnet
to his court, where, long before the arrival of that doubtful
divine, fresh dreams of grandeur had begun to drawn upon his
imagination. His uncle James, Duke of York, was paying a
tremendous penalty of unpopularity in England for having
conscientiously abandoned a false for the true religion. The
infamous Cabal, as well as the hateful genius of the celebrated
Lord Shaftesbury, one of its most Satanic members, assisted
to bring matters in our own island to the simple issue, whether
Catholicity or heresy should become predominant : the latter,
moreover, being enabled to impregnate the British mind with
those horrible prejudices which resulted in the judicial murders
of the Popish plot and Titus Oates, its ostensible contriver.
When the Duke of Monmouth, as the natural son of Charles,
appeared too coarse a leader for the Protestant party, Shaftesbury, retaining in his grasp its most secret springs of action,
had looked across the water towards William, the next in succession to the sceptre of the Stuarts after the death of James
and his children. Several of the most profligate agents of
Protestantism had not hesitated to pledge themselves to his
service, and advocate his interests, even at a time when he was
openly waging war with their own sovereign. This treasonable correspondence passed through the hands of Du Moulins,
who, on suspicion of such treachery, had been dismissed from
the office of Lord Arlington, and obtained in Holland an appointment of private secretary to the prince. A plan seems
to have been arranged as early as A.D. 1674, between Frymans, William Howard a member of Parliament for Winchel-
sea, and the Earl of Shaftesbury, that the Dutch fleet should
suddenly appear at the mouth of the Thames, when the howl
of " No Popery " was suddenly to be raised, and a Protestant
deliverer demanded before the panic of the people had subsi-
ded. The conclusion of peace then prevented the attempt,
but did not dissolve the connection between the stadtholder
and his British adherents. The latter were perpetually encouraging the former still to hope for success through exaggerated statements of the national discontent : advising him
meanwhile to hold himself always in readiness for taking ad-

vantage of any revolution, which must, they said, be more or less imminent in the three kingdoms.

A marriage was at last openly proposed by Arlington between William and the Princess Mary, which it was reserved for Lord Danby to bring about at a later date. The stadtholder at first declined it, distrusting Lord Arlington, who was supposed to have become a Catholic, as he actually did before his death; and guided also by instructions from Shaftesbury, that just at present the nuptials were an artifice of the enemy for the destruction of his popularity as Prince of Orange; for it would then be given out that he had joined in a league with the king and the Duke of York against British liberty and the Protestant religion. William, therefore, rested upon his oars, and waited for another opportunity, which fell out quite soon enough in October A.D. 1678. The lord-treasurer and Sir William Temple were now devoted to his interests; and returning with his not unhandsome consort to the Hague, he there laid himself out for supplanting his relatives, as well as overreaching his opponents. The Dissenters, rather than the high Anglicans, were the polemical janizaries on whom he mostly relied, and for whose sake, as the twaddle of the Bishop of Salisbury informs us, he became "most examplarily decent and devout in the public exercises of the worship of God; only on week-days being somewhat too seldom at the services. Yet he was an attentive hearer of sermons, constant in his private prayers, as also in reading the Scriptures; and whenever he spoke of religious matters, which he did not do often, it was always with a suitable gravity. He was much possessed with the belief of absolute decrees; and he once said to me, he adhered to these because he could not see how the doctrine of a Providence could be maintained upon any other supposition. His indifference as to the forms of ecclesiastical government, and his being zealous for toleration, together with his cold behaviour towards the episcopal clergy, gave them generally very ill impressions of him." It will be remembered, that the toleration of William went no further than the narrow and wavering limits of Protestantism, which seemed the more unpardonable from the nobler traditions on that subject which he might have inherited from his ancestor and namesake William the Silent. Meanwhile the only difference between the immoralities of the court at the Hague and those of Charles and James was, that at London no mask was worn. The Prince Orange, behind a curtain of concealment which proved far thinner than he supposed, violated the matrimonial vow, and revelled in abominable vices. It was not for beauty, since the most influential of his women could scarcely be brought to pass muster upon canvas even through the art of Sir Godfrey Kneller. He had an end of his own to gain by appearing to be what he was not; while so great was the gullibility of his admirers that they gaped and were satisfied. Both Covel and Skelton, comparatively respectable persons, **lost** his favour, simply for daring not to be blinded by **the dust** attempted to be thrown in their eyes when the complaints of the weak-minded Mary could no longer be restrained. In one word, the amours of the royal champion of Protestantism were simply disgusting; compounded at once of brutalism and depravity, notwithstanding the cant and courtliness of Burnet, who cannot deny the facts which he and others were dishonest enough to palliate, although their inherent passion for gossip prevented the maintenance of a somewhat less undignified silence. Thomas Ken, afterwards the famous nonjuror, made some effort on behalf of at least external morals, even when William had kicked the communion-table in the chapel, **or rather** prayer-room of his consort, to curry favour with the nonconformists in England. One of the gay favourites at court had seduced a young lady in the train of Mary through a promise of marriage, which Ken compelled him to perform, and for which the prince got rid of so rigid a chaplain with all conceivable expedition. Yet nothing would bring the genuine truth home to the consciences of Puritanism and Whiggery. They went forward plotting in the name of Protestantism,—now against Charles, at least as to his worthless and disgraceful policy, then against the heir-apparent, **and always** against the religion of both sometimes on behalf of Monmouth, and then again in favour of William, who managed to reap the real harvest from their advances, partly through his superior artifice and abilities, as also from the visible and palpable unsuitability of an instrument so vile and wretched as the bastard of Lucy Walters.

It is notorious at the present day, however the Orange-party contrived to conceal the truth from the bulk of their contemporaries, that William secretly promoted the unjust scheme of excluding the Duke of York from succeeding to the throne of the Stuarts. Van Lewen was his agent in treating with Charles; and Frymans undertook to open clandestine negotiations with the country leaders, as they were termed, in Parliament. Godolphin, Sunderland, Hyde, and others, were effectually won over to enlist themselves in nefarious intrigues, subsequently developing into the revolution of A.D. 1688. On one occasion, in the summer of A.D. 1681, the prince came over to England, under the specious pretext of prevailing with Charles to unite himself in an alliance with Spain and the States against the encroachments of France. Nothing could be more popular, with a certain class of partisans, than this timely visit. His antechambers in London became to him what the cave of Adullam was to David: "Convenerunt ad eum omnes, qui erant in angustiâ constituti, et oppressi ære alieno, et amaro animo; et factus est eorum princeps" (1 *Reg*.xxii.). The merry monarch meanwhile suspected nothing; but even pressed him to return again the following year, when there occurred an opportunity of his meeting James, which William decidedly declined, as he did not think it at all for his peculiar interests in England to stand on good terms with his popish father-in-law. His game was of a deeper nature; for even with the Duke of Monmouth and the Earl of Argyle he dealt as much as he dared. On the peaceful accession of James, an external reconciliation ensued between the new sovereign and his nephew, more particularly after the victory at Sedgemoor; but in fact these near relatives only disguised, or rather, endeavoured to disguise, their cordial mistrust of each other, beneath worthless expression of the warmest attachment. It became a struggle between two masters in mendacity, as to which of them could push into general circulation the greatest amount of false professions. James was in possession of the prize: William gasped for it in secret expectancy. The precise mode, indeed, in which it fell to him at last perhaps took him by surprise; since it was impossible for him to conceive that any religious convictions whatsoever should exist among princes, except as stepping-stones to power. When, therefore, his antagonist really held fast to the Catholic faith, in the face of certain political failure, the astonishment of the vigilant stadtholder seemed only exceeded by his satisfaction. The machinery for effecting an ultimate realisation of his hopes had been preparing for several years: his favourite counsellors, Fagel, Bentinck, and Halweyn, were in the closest correspondence with the foreign enemies and domestic traitors of the King of England; the six British regiments, in the pay of Holland, were weeded of every officer and private refusing to be subservient to William; rumours were carefully spread that James intended to set aside the hereditary rights of Mary in favour of the Princess Anne, upon condition of her secession from Protestantism; or, if that were out of the question, his illegitimate son, the popish Duke of Berwick, would be the substitute; but the Prince of Orange could never have imagined beforehand that his royal father-in-law would draw together, with incredible diligence, the very elements for achieving his own ruin and dethronement. When at length he really beheld and this passing before his eyes, he only marvelled at the kindness of fortune. Smiles and flatteries were lavished on his doomed rival with greater profusion than before; embassy followed upon embassy, attesting the filial submission and obedience, nowhere else so rife or edifying as at the Hague; whilst, at the same time, Dutch agents dug a thousand mines of mischief throughout the upper, middle, and lower classes in this country; charging them with the gun-powder of anti-Catholic prejudices, identified as such errors unhappily happened to be, at that crisis, with the love of liberty and attachment to an ancient constitution. Not less crafty and energetic were the efforts of William to get Anne into his possession, well aware that her strength of mind was about as small as that of his consort, her sister Mary. It was through an apparently accidental alteration of plan, on the part of James, that

he was thwarted; although the subsequent treason of the
Churchills more than atoned for the temporary disappointment.
In fact, madness and folly hurried forward the ultimate catas-
trophe with an abundant sufficiency of precipitation.

His majesty had despatched William Penn, the Quaker, to
sound his son-in-law as to whether he would sanction an abolition of the Test Act, in connection with at least some modification of the other penal oppressions against both Catholics
and Dissenters. Now the prince had at that precise moment
two parties with whom he wished to stand particularly well:
namely, the Emperor of Germany and the King of Spain, his
grand allies against France, on the one hand; and his own
Protestant adherents in England, who were to support his
pretensions to the royal prerogative of James, on the other.
His highness, therefore, presented himself to the former as the
main supporter of monarchy within the British islands, the
existence of which would be imperilled, were he not to support
the Test Act against Popery; since its relaxation, he told
them, would let in the Dissenters to supreme power, who were
all bitter republicans. Dyckveldt, his ambassador, cajoled the
latter, by assuring them, that the Prince of Orange would
never submit to any measures not perfectly agreeable to the
paramount interests of Protestantism. Honesty and straightforwardness might well be lost in amazement at the profound
duplicity with which each faction was duped in its turn, so
only that all would but unite in the single object of advancing
the political projects of the stadtholder. Anglicans were
taught to believe that he would never weaken the ascendency
of an establishment which had rescued from Rome, and intended to hold fast, such good things as opulent bishoprics
with empty cathedrals, large livings with small duties, tithes,
emoluments, rank, prestige, position, peerages, and parso-
nages, to say nothing of a clergy with wives, and a laity relieved from the restrictions of superstitious discipline. Nonconformists had a rather more difficult dose to swallow, so that
it had to be sweetened with the greater caution and subtlety:
*cosi a l'egro fanciul porgiomo aspersi di soave licor gli
orli del vaso.* They were assured that, under the rose,

William could not bear episcopacy, however necessary it might become to him that he should trample upon his predilections for the sake of saving Dissenters from another series of fires in Smithfield; but they were respectfully advised to keep aloof from the contest for the present, and receive from the successor of James a more legal and permanent toleration. Some lumps of sugar were even thrown out to the Catholics themselves, in the shape of whispered promises, that *if they would only deserve it by their conduct*, they might find in a Dutch deliverer the best protection from the future vengeance of their enemies. Dyckveldt, in the meantime, faithful to his instructions from the prince, lost no opportunity of learning the genuine spirit of the army and navy, the state of the royal finances, the respective positions of parties, the wishes of various sections in the population; thus fulfilling to a nicety the objects of his mission, which was that of an accredited spy behind the screen, and armed with the privileges of an ostensible ambassador. Zuyleistein followed in the same footsteps, and with similar results. Upon the perverse obstinacy and judicial blindness of the lawful sovereign counsel and remonstrance were alike urged in vain. The Catholic peers at this period were the Duke of Berwick, the Marquis of Powys, the Earls of Salisbury, Peterborough, Portland, Cardigan, and Derwentwater, the Viscount Montague, the Lords Abergavenny, Audley, Stourton, Hunsdon, Petre, Gerard of Bromley, Arundel of Wardour, Teynham, Carrington, Widdrington, Belasyse, Langdale, Clifford, Jermyn of Dover, an Waldegrave. Not one of them could help listening to the roar of those breakers ahead, which Pope Innocent XI. foresaw, and kindly condescended to indicate. A letter written by Fagel at this time, and published as a state-paper, in Dutch, French, English, and Latin, of which 45,000 copies were circulated in these kingdoms, was considered as the composition of William himself. Lingard most correctly remarks upon it, that by its tone of deceitful moderation, "the Pope, the Emperor, and other Catholic powers, were all of them brought to imagine that William was prepared to grant to their co-religionists in Great Britain and Ireland every indulgence which they were entitled to expect; whilst, by pointing out to the British Protestants the prince and princess as defenders of the Test Act, it constituted them in effect the leaders of that party. On the one hand, it allayed the jealousy of his allies; on the other, it encouraged the timid amongst his friends, confirmed the wavering, and stimulated all to resistance and exertion."

Some Catholics, not well informed as to the mysteries of diplomacy towards the close of the seventeenth century, have expressed wonder at the countenance which the court of Rome in reality gave to the machinations of the Dutch stadtholder. The fact, however, was, that for many years the bitterest enemy to the Church of Almighty God had been no other than the House of Bourbon, with Louis XIV., the grand monarque of Europe, at its head. It is no less melancholy than true, that the pretended patron of what have been styled the Gallican liberties, not merely insulted the Holy Father of Christendom in his own capital, but grievously persecuted genuine Catholicity throughout those vast dominions over which he ruled with a rod of iron. Both Innocent and his successor Alexander VIII. braved his fury and insolence in the true spirit of good shepherds over the flock of Jesus Christ. The French king had presumed to invade the papal prerogatives, and appoint prelates to their sees independently of the Chair of St. Peter. With the cordial approbation of all sound divines, the Popes refused them institution: so that a fourth part of the dioceses of France had merely nominal bishops, incapable of performing episcopal functions. The entire policy of the tyrant, during a considerable interval, realized what Sallust says of the latter Romans; *proinde quasi injuriam facere, id demum esset imperio uti*. To such arrogance it was necessary to set bounds; for not only was Louis aiming at universal secular as well as spiritual dominion, but he was suspending the operation of sacraments, and urging his wretched subjects to the verge of open schism. His Holiness therefore called in a Dutch cat to extirpate Gallican vermin, without in the least vouchsafing any sanction to the naturally wicked propensities of Grimalkin. William was to an immense and most useful extent the enemy to the enemies of St. Peter; whose representatives, in consequence, stroked him with their temporary patronage, from his ears to his tail, as the cunning contriver of the League of Augsburg, which brought Louis at last to his senses. Towards James the utmost commiseration was always manifested, falling, as he had done, through his own fault and folly, from an altitude where, had he been able to retain his position, he would have probably proved a tool of France, another sword in the hands of her already too powerful sovereign, as well as a thorn in the side of orthodox and genuine Catholicity. Misfortune, whilst it contributed to mend his private character, could never teach him any substantial amount of wisdom; so that to the end of his days he illustrated the proverb of Solomon: *Si contuderis stultum in pila, non auferetur ab eo stultitia ejus*. Nevertheless he latterly shone in his adversity as a luminary of religion and morals, compared with his competitor, whose prosperity, founded upon artifice and slander, never failed to betray its origin; nor could remorse of conscience remain altogether extinguished, even amidst the splendours of the purple, or the plaudits of Protestant nations.

History solemnly avouches that, necessary as the revolution of A. D. 1688 might have become, it was brought about, so far as William was personally concerned, as much by feline contrivances as by the more noble exercise of courage, energy, and astuteness. It was by a ladder of lies that the stadtholder ascended his throne, planted upon Protestant prejudices, and supported by a combination of circumstances. Forged correspondence between the Jesuit fathers Petre and La-Chaise, relative to the designs of Catholic sovereigns in general, and those of Louis and James in particular, emanated on a large scale from the Hague; inflaming public apprehension with the most absurd vagaries and chimeras. It was averred in these false documents, that the rights of freedom, property, and conscience, were all about to be sacrificed at the feet of the Apostolic Church; and that from Holland alone could safety be sought for, in the persons of William and Mary. The queen of James, at this crisis, was declared pregnant, being the favourable answer from heaven to a maternal vow made at

Loretto to **Our** Blessed Lady. From that moment, an ocean of slander seemed to rise up, and overflow the land with its Stygian deluge. Delicacy, not to say decency, vanished from the mind of Mary towards her own father and mother-in-law. It would disgust the purlieus of Covent Garden or Drury Lane **to** wade through the pamplets, pasquinades, and multiplied publications, levelled at all that is most dear, tender, **and** sacred in the conjugal or domestic relation. At length Maria d'Este reached her **hour of** trial, violated and outraged as it was to be by the **falsehood** of the warming-pan story. It was affirmed by grave divines calling themselves bishops, as also by statesmen then willing to be styled champions of Protestantism, that a supposititious Prince of Wales was introduced into the royal bed, and passed off as an imposture upon the British people. Both Burnet and William rendered themselves direct accomplices in this nefarious yet successful fable; for it figures prominently in the memorial pretended to be presented to the United Provinces from the persecuted Protestants in England, which Burnet in reality composed, and which the Prince of Orange suggested and promoted. It is notorious, **also,** that neither of these personages for one moment believed **it,** at the time when the celebrated invitation arrived, calling upon William and Mary to come over, **and** pluck the crown from the brow of their once indulgent **parent.** Meanwhile every engine of art and intrigue had been set in motion **to** rouse the passions of the populace into a state of frenzy. Moderate men felt themselves condemned to silence, simply through fear of a fate like that of John and Cornelius de Witt; and unfortunately the most inflammatory libels acquired a portion of their force and popularity from the aspect of foreign affairs abroad, not less than from the madness and fatuity of a dissolving government at home. The result is too well known to need a recapitulation in these pages.

But what we want to record is simply the genuine nature of Whiggery, in for ever falling down and worshipping such a **hero** as William. Is it that the latter is neither more nor less than an impersonation of the former? We much fear so. The Prince of Orange mounted the throne of these realms,

amongst other purposes, **to purify the** various departments of
administration. With a thousand pretences of doing so, **he**
pensioned Titus Oates, and appointed the legal adviser of that
worthy to the confidential and lucrative post of solicitor to the
Treasury. Corruption in high places thenceforward became
an organised system of bribes to members of parliament, and
all that mysterious disposal of patronage, secret-service money,
or dispensation of golden ointment, which served as a salve to
sore consciences in bringing the Lower House under the management of the minister. What is to be said of the artful
manner with which William balanced one section of concealed
political thieves against another—Tories against Whigs, or
Whigs against Tories,—right honourable robbers and scoundrels every one of them, and who would have been described as
such, had they not worn coronets upon their heads, and been
wrapped in robes of scarlet, ermine, or fine linen? The predecessors of William had shown themselves negligent in their
royal duties, in giving orders without due consideration, and
then sheltering their agents behind the broad buckler of their
prerogative. But what shall be said of the massacre at
Glencoe,—merely as a specimen of what we mean, and taking
the merciful view of it, that the whole catastrophe was an accident? Here we have an acute, laborious, constitutional
sovereign signing a paper without reading it, but which in its
operation sanctioned the commission of between thirty and
forty distinct murders. " One or two women," says Macaulay, " were seen amongst the number, and a yet more fearful
and piteous sight,—a little hand, which had been lopped in
the tumult of the butchery from some infant." The assassins,
it must be remembered, had been enjoying for days and nights
all the rites of hospitality at the hands of their victims. A
child only twelve years old, clinging round the legs of Captain
Glenlyon, was shot dead then and there by a ruffian named
Drummond; some of their hosts were actually dragged out of
their beds, bound hand and foot, and slaughtered like sheep;
an old man above seventy, too infirm to fly, was found alive
after the onset, and ruthlessly slain in cold blood; the chief
Mac Ian received a bullet in his head whilst getting up to order

the breakfast for his dastardly murderers, whom he had been
entertaining as his guests; his wife dying the next day, through
the violence of the soldiers, one of whom tore away the golden
rings from her fingers with his teeth! These sanguinary
crimes were perpetrated under a royal order from King William, subscribed, his apologists say, through an error to which
he was frequently liable; even Burnet mentioning, that his
majesty had the dreadful habit of suffering matters to run on
" till there was a great heap of papers, when he suddenly
signed them as much too fast as he was before too slow in
despatching them." Macaulay doubts his procrastination, but
coolly observes, that feeling an interest in continental affairs
exclusively, " he attended to English business less, but to
Scotch business the least of all." When this dreadful affair
had actually happened, the entire blame was meanly thrown
upon the Master of Stair; and still more meanly, when public
indignation demanded punishment, William, finding it inconvenient to visit with heavy penalties so high a functionary,
beyond dismissing him from office, permitted the storm to fall
upon the humbler instruments; thus endeavouring to stifle
the matter with a real act of indemnity as to himself and his
favourites:

"So little villains must submit to fate,
That large ones may enjoy the world in state."

But the Prince **of Orange was enthroned**, we are told, to
save the constitution, **limit** royal prerogatives, establish ministerial responsibility, suppress standing armies, and blot
out that scandal in our commercial history of the Stuarts having
once shut up the Exchequer. Whatever the great fact of the
Revolution itself may have more or less indirectly achieved, it
is only fair to glance at what was the personal conduct of its
mighty leader. Surely his genuine regard for the British
constitution bore about that proportion to his selfishness which
the dry bread of Sir John Falstaff did to the quantity of sack
which he imbibed. To what had William sworn more
solemnly than to the Bill of Rights, which declared that, without
consent of Parliament, the maintenance of military forces was
to be thenceforward illegal? Yet we find him coolly and deli-

berately, in A.D. **1697, when** the Commons had reduced the troops to 10,000, leaving sealed orders with his ministers, before he went to Holland, that 16,000 men should be kept up,—orders which those ministers, professedly responsible to parliament alone, as unconstitutionally obeyed. What pickpocket **ever cut** a purse, we would ask, with greater nonchalance than William displayed in his appropriation of the immense Irish forfeitures, of which he granted away a million of acres, contrary to his solemn promises, for the mere enrichment of foreign favourites, male and female; one of them the hideous courtesan whom he had created Countess of Orkney? What can be said of his perpetually acting as his own minister, with as much arbitrariness as Louis **or the** Emperor, in foreign affairs, except that, as the British **kingdoms** sometimes love to be deluded, they were thus gratified **to the** top of their bent throughout a long series of years? **So** also, instead of shutting up an exchequer, he left his successors and their subjects the rather dubious blessing of a national debt, which exceeded in its origin about twenty times the iniquity of the Cabal, and has grown in our times to the amount of eight hundred millions sterling. To **all** which must be added the introduction of a permanent excise upon the system **still** existing, and which has swollen into **colossal** dimensions as to mere extent, and which rivals the labyrinth of Crete in its deceptive sinuosities and ramifications. To the Protestant deliverer we are still further indebted for the use of hollands, or that vile form of alcohol which has summoned from the infernal pit our gorgeous gin-palaces; where the house **of** the harlot opens " the way to hell, reaching even to the inner chambers of death."

But above all other objects was the British sceptre consigned to the care of William—if we may believe the hollow voice of patriotism and nonconformity—that the *rights of conscience* might be at rest for ever from secular interference, as well as the oppression of penal laws. Translated into the language of truth, this statement means, that the Catholic Church of Almighty God was to be bound, were it possible, naked and helpless to the rock of Protestant prejudice, where, like the exposed Andromede of antiquity, she might become a prey to the monsters of the deep. Religious toleration, it cannot be too often repeated, signified, in the mouth of the Revolution of A.D. 1688, *just this and no more*. Witness the violation of the Treaty of Limerick, and the acts passed by the crowned Dissenter against Roman Catholics. What renders his conduct in this respect so much worse is, that he had actually incurred obligations to his Catholic allies, when standing in need of their assistance, that he would really relieve the faithful children of the Church, so soon as he had the power to do so; nor, moreover, should it be omitted, that these breaches of honour occurred against the light of his internal convictions, based upon his own individual knowledge and experience. He had come to learn that the traditional policy of his family was the sound and right **one** to adopt; his Dutch **armies** were always in great **measure composed of** Catholics; many **of** that profession had served under him in his invasion of England, on the faith of his professions given, or at least implied, to their officers; he had now and then, in earlier days, even played with the dulness of James himself, in secretly declaring, whenever there seemed something to gain by it, that the penal persecutions of papists ought in reality to be repealed. Yet, after the Peace of Ryswick, some **few** priests having come **over,** King William assented to the **statute** against **the** growth of Popery, A. D. 1700, **which** Hallam, **in the full** fervours of Whiggery, cannot forbear denominating **as** " disgraceful." Its admitted **aim was to** expel **the** Catholic proprietors of land, comprising **many very** ancient and wealthy families, by rendering **it necessary for** them **to** sell their estates. It offers a reward **of 100l.** to any informer **against** an ecclesiastic exercising his functions, **and adjudges the penalty to the** party in orders of perpetual imprisonment. " **It requires every** person educated in the popish religion, or professing the same, **within** six months after he shall attain the age of eighteen years, to **take** the oaths of allegiance and supremacy, and subscribe the declaration **set** down in the act of Charles II. against transubstantiation and the worship of saints,"—in other words, to apostatise from the faith; in default of which he stands incapacitated, **not** only from purchasing, but from inheriting **or** taking lands under any devise or limitation whatsoever. *The next of kin, being a Protestant, was to enjoy all such estates during his life.* This measure existed for fourscore years: a mere specimen of the code of persecution which William of Nassau knew to be wrong, yet which he sanctioned, after oaths and protestations to the contrary, *as being right.* And lo, this is the monarch whose usurpation the Anglican liturgy commemorates as an era of deliverance from thraldom, although he had no belief in its doctrines, or admiration for **its** discipline; whilst **his name** survives as a watchword for bigotry,—when it **can do so** with impunity,—to abuse for the worst purposes of Toryism; **nor less as** a theme **for the** eulogy of such reviewers or historians **as the Right** Hon. Thomas Babington Macaulay. Notwithstanding **the** benefits **which** resulted from the rejection of the Stuarts—and they are not **to** be denied—we nevertheless are bold to affirm, that the boasted Revolution of A.D. 1688, looking at the spirit in which it came unhappily to be accomplished, constituted, or rather involved, **an** enormous fraud upon the credulity of these kingdoms. **It originated** from necessity; but was founded, as well as fashioned, **upon** the most thorough misrepresentation and hypocrisy. Instead of emancipating nations, it enthroned at first a usurper, and then an aristocracy; the latter as selfish and unprincipled as the artful stadtholder himself. The peerage from that **moment,** either through their **own Chamber** or the Lower House, **to which in** effect they could generally nominate a **majority, at once trampled upon** the liberties of the lower classes, and dictated **their own** terms to the crown. Nor did **they** care **to** imitate either the profound policy of Solon **in** Greece, or the just arrangements of Servius Tullius at Rome. Taxation was arranged so as to press lightly upon the rich and heavily upon the poor. Meanwhile government has presented, for a century and a half, a series of shams, illusions, shifts, and juggles. Its system formed **an** immense procession of littlenesses and low **impostures,** dependent for success upon ignorance, prejudice, falsehood, and calumny; base crawling artifices constituting the very spiders and centipedes of human politics. Bishop Burnet may be said to lead the march, with his warming-pan flourishing in the air; whilst Lord John Russell and the Earl of Derby bring up the rear, the one with his Durham Letter, and the other with his proclamation against the appearance of religious habits in public. Their master, King William, by whom they are always ready to swear, must be content to take his place in impartial history as one of the most royal rascals that ever reigned.

A CHAPTER IN THE HISTORY OF THE REFORMATION IN IRELAND.

Elizabeth's first Irish Parliament.

(From the Rambler.)

IN discussions on the re-settlement of Church property in Ireland, advocates of the Established Church frequently assert that this property was transferred to its present uses by an act of the Irish nation assembled in Parliament in the second year of Elizabeth, January 12, 1559-60. The Irish Bishops, it is maintained, were present; and not only did not oppose the spoliation of the Catholic Church, but conformed very generally to the Anglican heresy. A settlement of this historical question can influence very slightly, we fear, the conflicting claims of the rival Churches at the present day. If one hundred Irish legislators voted the establishment of **Pro**testantism three hundred years ago, their votes cannot prove that the Irish Church has not been ever since an injustice unparalleled in the annals of nations, civilised or savage; if these legislators did not vote its establishment, if the Irish statutes of 1560 never received their assent, Drs. Whately and Beresford would not, therefore, be more easily induced to resign their princely palaces and broad acres to the nation, much less to Archbishops Cullen and Dixon. If, then, we undertake to discuss the point, it is purely as a matter of history; and we shall the more carefully abstain from exaggeration or vituperation, as we think we have something important to communicate, not **generally known to our readers.**

An act of Parliament, old or new, is a very good thing when it falls in with our prejudices, and fills our pockets with money; and Anglicans, therefore, very naturally cherish Elizabeth's first Irish Parliament as being the very keystone of their Church in that country. But they can throw a veil over the proceedings of that Church when opposed to acts of Parliament. They had no act of Parliament for their heresies introduced into the Irish Church by Edward **VI.**; **their first Bishops**, Brown of Dublin, Staples of Meath, Bale of Ossory, and Casey of Limerick, took wives, not only against the canons of the Church, but also against an existing act of Parliament; Edward's heretical liturgy was introduced into **a few** Irish cathedrals in spite of all law both civil and ecclesiastical. All these innovations were brought about **solely by the authority of a king's letter in council**; nor has any Anglican writer ever attempted to assign any other sanction for them.[a] Elizabeth herself, before she ever summoned an Irish Parliament, commanded her English servants in Ireland to use her liturgy in their houses, and by her high prerogative exempted them from impeachment for thus violating acts of Parliament and the laws of the Church[b]; and even though she had pursued this line of conduct uniformly to the end, though she had never summoned an Irish Parliament at all, but had robbed the Church by a letter in council or by royal proclamation, we feel confident that her measures and her memory would have been just as zealously defended by those who now plead her acts of Parliament. And, for our own part, we think that the bolder would have been the better course; for her Parliament, such as it was, only added fraud to force, treachery to tyranny. It represented neither the nobility, nor the commonalty, nor the clergy of Ireland; the great majority of those who are said to have assisted at it never approved its enactments, or certainly never observed them; it was not an act of the Irish

---

[a] Dr. Mant's History of the Church of Ireland, vol. i. pp. 188-192.

[b] Shirley's Original Letters, p. 90. These Letters, lately published (London, 1851), confirm all that was generally believed of the uncanonical and purely secular means adopted by Edward VI. to suppress the Catholic religion in Ireland.

nation; and it left the Protestant clergy, what, for the most part, they have been ever since, chaplains to a garrison of English adventurers and landlords. Never, even for one hour during Elizabeth's reign, could they be called the clergy of the Irish people. Our adversaries themselves admit the truth of this assertion with regard to the last thirty years of her reign. In the following paper, therefore, we shall restrict ourselves to the first years, and shew that it is equally true of them also.

And first, let **us** speak of the House of Commons in this vaunted Irish Parliament, which is said to have voted for the establishment **of** Protestantism. According to the published list,[a] it consisted of seventy-six members; twenty from ten counties, and fifty-six from twenty-eight cities or boroughs. There was no county member for any part of Ulster or Connaught, though parts of both provinces had been represented in preceding Parliaments. These provinces, comprising fully one-half of Ireland, had only six borough members; two from Carrickfergus, and two each from Galway and Athenry. Of the six counties of Munster, two only were represented, namely, Tipperary and Waterford; and even in Leinster, four of the present counties, namely, the King's and Queen's Counties, Longford, and Wicklow, were not represented. Thus the *county* representation in this Parliament included little more than one-fourth of the island. Of the borough members the great majority were returned from places in eight Leinster counties. Munster sent only sixteen members, from Cork, Waterford, Limerick, Dungarvan, Youghall, Fethard, Clonmel, and Kinsale; while Leinster sent thirty-four members from seventeen boroughs or cities. Thus, of the whole representatives **in the Commons,** two-thirds were returned from a part only **of the present province of Leinster.** Will any one pretend that the votes of such a Parliament can with any propriety be considered the will of the Commons of Ireland?

Moreover, if it is true that these members consented to the establishment of the Protestant religion, it can only have been

---

[a] Tracts relating to Ireland, vol. ii. p. 135. Irish Archæological Society.

in order that both themselves and their constituents might have the luxury of violating all the enactments which they are said to have made; for, according to these enactments, attendance at the Protestant worship was prescribed under penalty of fine, the Catholic worship was prohibited, and the oath of supremacy required as a qualification for all offices, both civil and religious. Now, in the first place, attendance at Protestant worship was simply an impossibility in all the counties, except half the counties of Louth, Meath, Dublin, and Kildare, beyond which the Irish language alone was understood.*a* The Protestant Prayer-book was not translated into that language.*b* The reformers, it is true, convicted themselves of dishonesty by dispensing in what they said was God's law; they sanctioned the translation of the Prayer-book into Latin (an unknown tongue) for the use of those places in which the English was not understood; but even this self-convicted imposture was not carried into effect.*c* If, then, the county members voted for this Protestant Prayer-book, they voted for what they knew was at the time an impossibility for their constituents, and which continued so during the whole reign of Elizabeth. This argument does not apply with equal force to the boroughs, in some of which, especially in Leinster, the English language was understood; and the Protestant service therefore was possible, if the people wished to attend it. That they had no such wish, however, is perfectly clear from the unexceptionable evidence of the first reformers themselves, who declaim against the blindness and obduracy of the Irish, with as much pathos and violence as the most accredited organs of English bigotry at the present day. Brown, Bishop of Dublin, complained that the Irish were as zealous for the Papacy as the

---

a These half-counties were the English pale in 1515. The pale was becoming even more Irish in the course of Elizabeth's reign, if we may believe English writers. Craik, first Protestant bishop of Kildare, complains that even in that diocese "neither I can preach to the people, nor the people understand me." Shirley, Original Letters, &c. p. 95.

b Irish types were sent over in 1571; but the Irish Testament was not printed until 1603.

c Shirley has proved that the "whole service of the Communion" had been translated into Latin, by order of the Lord Deputy, in the year 1549 or 1550; and that it was his intention to have it speedily printed. Original Letters, p. 47. But there is no proof that this intention was carried into effect.

saints and martyrs ever were for the truth.[a] Cromwell's name was as odious to their ears as that of his too-famous namesake Oliver was to their descendants; and they gave an unequivocal testimony of their detestation of his measures by preserving the Church and monastic lands of three provinces for their lawful owners, notwithstanding Henry's confiscations and grants.[b] Bale of Ossory, another of those so-called reformers, who was sustained in Kilkenny during Edward's reign by the trimming Ormondes and the influence of government, was hunted from the city as soon as Edward's death was known. The old canons of St. Canice purified the cathedral, " flung up their caps to the battlements of the great temple " in the exuberance of their joy, and issuing in procession from its portals, cheered the hearts of the citizens in the thronged streets with the Catholic melody, " Sancta Maria, ora pro nobis."[c] Staples, first Protestant Bishop of Meath, strikes the key-note of that lugubrious howl which his brethren have sustained during three centuries against the martyr-fidelity of the Irish Catholics : " A beneficed man of mine own promotion," he writes, " came unto me weeping, and desired me that he might declare his mind unto me without my displeasure. I said I was well content. 'My lord,' said he, ' before ye went last to Dublin you were the best-beloved man in your diocese that ever came into it, and now you are the worst-beloved that ever came here.' I asked, why. 'Why,' said he, ' for ye have taken open part with the state, that false heretic, and preached against the Sacrament of the Altar, and deny Saints, and will make us worse than Jews : if the country wiste (knew how,) they would eat you; you have,' he said,

---

[a] Cox, Hibernia Anglicana, vol. iv. pp. 246-257.

[b] "How many frère (friar) howses and others remayne using the old Papists sort?"—*Answer*. "All Munster, in effect; Thomond, Connaght, and Ulster." State Papers, 1548, Append, Shirley, p. 22.

[c] Bale's Vocation, "They rang all the bells in the cathedral, minster, and parish churches; they flung up their caps to the battlements of the great temple, with smilings and laughings most dissolutely; they brought out their copes, candlesticks, holy-water stocks, crosses, and censers; they mustered forth in general procession, most gorgeously, all the town over, with "Sancta Maria, ora pro nobis," and the rest of the Latin Litany. They chattered it, they chaunted it with great noise and devotion; they banqueted all the day after, for that they were delivered from the grace of God to a warm sun."—*Mant*, ii. p. 228.

'more curses than ye have hairs of your head; and I advise you, for Christ's sake, not to preach at Navan, **as** I hear you will do.'"[a] This letter was written before Christmas in the year 1548. If Staples did preach at Navan, it was his first and last Protestant sermon. To the day of his death he had more curses from his flock than hairs on his head. The national hostility to the reformed doctrines had in **no** degree been mitigated. The Lord Deputy, Sept. 27, 1550, "never saw the land so far out of good order; for there is this three years no kind of divine service, neither Communion nor yet other service; having but *one* sermon made in that time, which the Bishop of Meath made, who had so little reverence at that time, *as he had no great haste eftsones to preach there.*"[b] From numerous other evidences, too copious to be cited here, it is manifest that through the whole of Edward's reign the Anglo-Irish spurned the Reformation, and with no exception. If, therefore, a great change had not taken place, their representatives from the twenty-eight boroughs in the Parliament of 1560 must have known that in voting the abolition of the Catholic worship they were acting against the will of their constituents. But there is no evidence of any such change; rather there is abundant evidence of the contrary; and we shall see that the reformation effected by Elizabeth was that of Robespierre and Marat,—the suppression of all public worship in some parts of Ireland.

We have said that the three principal enactments of the Parliament of 1560 concerned the oath of supremacy, attendance at Protestant **service,** and the abolition of the Catholic **worship.** We will speak of each of these in turn; and first **with regard** to the oath of supremacy. So far from complying **with this** leading point of the reformed enactments, the boroughs continued during the whole reign of Elizabeth to retain the old Catholic oath; it alone, and no other, was administered to their civic officers. And it must be remembered that that oath was not a mere profession of civil alle-

---

[a] Shirley, Original Letters; p. 24.
[b] Ibid. p. 41.

giance; it was also a profession of the Catholic faith, and renounced and execrated all heresies and schisms contrary to that faith. We do not deny but that now and then some slippery aspirant for corporate honours may not have paid his court to the crown by taking the oath of supremacy against his conscience; but we repeat what was asserted at the time, without contradiction, by Catholic writers,[a] and what the boroughs themselves asserted when James I. required the same oath, namely, that during the whole reign of Elizabeth the oath of civic officers was the old Catholic oath that had been in use before the reign of Henry VIII. The truth is, that Elizabeth more than once checked the imprudence of some of her over-zealous officers when they wished to enforce the new oath;[b] for all the boroughs and cities, without exception, were loyal to her throne, against the old, or, as they were called, the "wylde" Irish, and she could not afford to drive them to desperation, and was compelled therefore, for the time, to be satisfied.

The enactment which enjoined attendance on the Protestant service met with no better fate than that which concerned the oath of supremacy. From the temper of the public mind in religious matters, as shewn already, during the reign of Edward VI.; from the bitter complaints of the English governors against the Irish Bishops, as "blynd and obstinate bishops," for not introducing the English Prayer-book,—it is antecedently in the highest degree improbable that the Parliament of 1560 could at once work so great a miracle as to draw the people to the Protestant service. Were there no evidence on the point at all, it might still be safely assumed that they would not go to such a service unless the law were strictly enforced. This could not be without the machinery of an ecclesiastical commission. No such commission was appointed until May 23, 1561, and even then for the county

---

[a] Peter Lombard, Archbishop of Armagh, Commentarius de Regno Hiberniæ, p. 236. This work was composed about the year 1601, though not published till many years later. O'Sullivan, Historiæ Catholicæ Compendium, p. 281, Dublin, 1850.

[b] Cambrensis Eversus, vol. i. p. 22, note.

of Westmeath alone. In the December of the following year a second commission was appointed for the province of Armagh, including the diocese of Meath; and in October 1564 it was extended to the whole kingdom.[a] These commissions were signal and miserable failures, as the commissioners themselves admit; there is not the least evidence that even a serious attempt was made to enforce them, except in parts of the three dioceses of Armagh, Meath, and Dublin. In July 1565, "instructions" were drawn up for Sir Henry Sydney, ordering him to report on the state of religion. Two draughts of these instructions are extant. Both directed him to inquire into the state of the clergy of the realm in general; both refer to the ecclesiastical commission lately issued, and give orders about it, but of a very different kind. The first draught states that within the English pale, both in private places and in the churches, the Catholic worship was exercised; and it peremptorily prohibits such toleration in future. The second draught, corrected by Cecil's hand, is by no means so confident; it leaves the execution of the commission entirely to Sydney's discretion.[b] A report was presented the following year, April 15, 1566, in which Sydney and the three reforming bishops virtually confess that they know nothing of any dioceses except Meath, Dublin, and Armagh, for that "with the residue order cannot yet so well be taken, until the countree be first brought into more civil and dutiful obedience."[c] Now this civil obedience, which was an indispensable preliminary to the church reformation, was not attempted till four or five years later; that is, until the appointment of English presidents for the provinces of Munster and Connaught. Moreover, they confess that even "within the three said dioceses the work goeth slowly forward, by reason of the former errors and superstitions *inveterated and leavened in the people's hartes.*" This is merely a repetition of the report presented by the commissioners of 1562, who stated that

---

[a] Liber Hiberniæ, vol. i. part 2, pp. 181, 182.
[b] Shirley, pp. 206, 209, 211, 213.
[c] Ibid. p. 233.

the people were "unwilling to be taught" the Reformation, and ordered the judges not to meddle with "the simple multitude," but to punish a "few boasting massmen" in every **shire** of the pale. As for the Reformation beyond the pale, "the bishops," they add, "be all Irish; we need say no more;"[a] that is, they were not Protestant reformers.

But we may go still further, and justly question the truth of the report that the Reformation was making any real progress even in these three dioceses of Armagh, Dublin, and Meath. It is true, indeed, that the official report says so; but then the bishops of these dioceses signed the report,[b] and of course they would give a good account to the queen of their own proceedings. This testimony, however, will appear still more suspicious when we examine more closely who **these** bishops were. On the repeated evidence of two of them, we know that the third, Curwen Archbishop of Dublin, was "an unprofitable old workman;[c] that he hardly ever preached the reformed doctrines;[d] that he frequently did not require the oath of supremacy from the clergy whom he promoted to benefices;[e] that he and *all* his canons of St. Patrick, who were also parochial clergy,[f] "were old bottles, and could not hold this new wine" of the Reformation, "dumb dogs, neither teaching nor feeding save themselves;[g] that he never exacted conformity from many of those canons, who retained their places to their death;[h] and that, in fine, Sydney deemed it absurd to think of reforming the rest of the land so long as the city of Dublin itself remained unreformed, under the go-

---

[a] Shirley, p. 140.
[b] Ibid. p. 237.
[c] Ibid. p. 201.
[d] Ibid. pp. 275, 162, 136.
[e] "He placeth in sufficient livings those that he never saw, nor never come there, *open enemies*." Loftus to Sir William Cecil; Shirley, p. 275.
[f] Shirley, p. 152: "The prebends be paroch churches, having cure of souls." Their churches were all within five miles of Dublin. Ibid. p. 258.
[g] Shirley, p. 162.
[h] The ecclesiastical commissioners, appointed in 1562, requested the Lords of the Privy Council, March 16, 1563-4, to devise some plan "how the prebenders that will no be conformable may be, without wrong, by law compelled." Shirley, p. 141. They suggested a special commission to visit both St. Patrick's and Christ Church, but obtained neither. For, in 1565, Cecil writes, "I am sorry to hear no good done in the survey of St. Patrick's, which now serveth for lurking Papists." Ibid. **p. 160.**

vernment of such a bishop. When **he was** removed at his own request to the see of Oxford, in 1567, and the Archbishop of Armagh had been brought to Dublin, then only do we find the Lord-Deputy Sydney closing one of his letters with the significant words, "now comes the hour for reforming **the** Church;"[a] the hour that has been coming for three hundred years, and in expectation of which English governors keep Ireland still in agony. From the new Bishop of Oxford's letters it is, in fact, evident that he troubled himself very little about matters of doctrine; he never says one word about them, except inasmuch as they were the royal will;[b] his sole petition is for a pension, or a bishopric equal in revenue to that **of** Dublin, which would support his family and enable him to keep as good a table as before. So much, then, for the Protestant Archbishop of Dublin. We come next to the Archbishop of Armagh. All accounts agree in representing Loftus as having been zealous for the Reformation from the time of his promotion to the see of Armagh in 1562 to his removal to Dublin in 1567. But what progress could he make in the former diocese, whilst far the greater part of it was **under the** dominion of John O'Neil, who, for a large portion of the time, had with him the true Catholic Primate of Ireland?[c] Loftus himself expressly acknowledges his failure. He petitioned to be removed from Armagh, "because it was neither worth any thing to him, nor *was he able to do any good in it*, as it altogether lay among the Irish;" a fact of which he does not appear to have made the discovery until John **O'Neil deprived him** of the little reverence which he had **previously received.** There yet remains to be considered the **diocese of** Meath. In this diocese resided most of the lords

---

[a] Shirley, p. 294.

[b] See his Letters in Shirley, pp. 143, 147, &c. &c. They breathe very little indeed of the spirit of a Christian reformer. He prided himself on being a faithful servant of the crown; and, singular enough in a bishop, reminds Queen Elizabeth of his fidelity to Queen Mary. Loftus, Archbishop of Armagh, gives a bad character of him. "In open judgment [he was Lord Chancellor], loth I am to say it, and I say it not but constrainedly,—in open judgment he will swear terribly, and that not once nor twice." Shirley, p. 275.

[c] Primate Creagh, whose interesting examination, taken in the Tower of London, has been published, for the first time, in Shirley's "Original Letters."

of the pale, who, as we shall presently see, adhered to the old religion. They were sustained also in their fidelity by the example of their bishop, Walsh, who had been present in the Parliament of 1560, but certainly did not vote for the Reformation, and who a few months afterwards was deprived of his see for preaching against the Book of Common Prayer. On the 13th of July, 1565, he was committed to the castle of Dublin by Loftus : " he refused the oath, and to answer such articles as we required of him ; and besides that, ever since the last Parliament he had manifestly contemned and openly shewed himself to be a misliker of all the queen's majesty's proceedings ; he openly protested before all the people the same day he was before us, that he would never communicate or be present (by his will) where the service should be ministered, for it was against his conscience, and (as he thought against God's word ; he is one of great credit among his countrymen, and *upon whom as touching causes of religion, they wholly depend.*" [a] Brady, the intruded Protestant bishop, who had not been appointed, however, until the see had been (professedly) vacant for two years and a half, confesses that the people imitated this example. In a letter dated March 14, 1563-4, he protests that he would rather be a stipendiary priest in England than Bishop of Meath in Ireland ; that the lawyers were the sworn enemies of the truth, and the ruin of the country by not executing the laws ; that the clergy were stubborn and ignorantly blind ; that he had little hopes of their conforming ; that the simple multitude were "hardly to be won;" and that though some of them, especially at his native place Dunboyne, were " greedy hearers," his success had as yet only amounted to a *hope* " that they will be unfainedly won." [b] Two years later, May 16, 1565, his hopes are disappearing ; " things are rather worse than otherwise, and without speedy redress the whole body will be so sick, that it shall with difficulty recover, so frowardly be men disposed here." He was able to hold his ground solely by keeping an

---

[a] Shirley, p. 229.
[b] Ibid. p. 135.

open house and a good table; "**for these** people," he says, "will have the one or the other; I mean, *they will either eat my meat and drink or else myself*."[c] So critical was his position, that in 1566 he excuses himself on prudential grounds for not having executed the ecclesiastical **commission** as zealously as his colleague Loftus expected.[b] Down to this period, August 19, 1566, these two men were the only persons "willing to reform the clergy, or able to teach any wholesome (Protestant) doctrine."[c]

Thus, on the evidence of the reformers themselves, on the same evidence by **which** we know that the Reformation was attempted in Ireland, we know that it was from the commencement a total failure, even **in the towns** and among the Anglo-Irish of the pale, **and in** those three dioceses **in** which alone it could be said to have been attempted. We acknowledge, indeed, that in the first five years of Elizabeth's reign some of the Anglo-Irish frequented the Protestant churches, but it was in ignorance of the change of religion, and with all the usual externals of Catholic faith, Catholic crosses, Catholic rosaries, Catholic litanies and images;[d] but as soon **as they** learnt that it was unlawful, they universally refused to go any longer; or some went to church for mere sport, or at least made sport when they were compelled to go.[e] With these facts before him, Sussex early foresaw the impossibility of reforming Ireland except by penal laws. "The people without discipline, utterly void of religion (Protestant), come to divine service as to a May game. The ministers, for dishability and greediness, be **had in contempt;** and the wise fear more the impiety of **the** licentious professors than the superstition of the erroneous Papists. These matters be so far come, as they be not, I think,

---

[a] Shirley, p. 189. Is not this the same system **of** proselytism which has been attempted during these few years past in the west and south of Ireland?

[b] Ibid. p. 272. "If he say, I have drawn backward; I only say again, he (Loftus) hath drawn too fast forward, as the circumstances shall well declare." Meath was becoming too hot, even for a *hospitable* Parliament bishop, after Walsh's banishment.

[c] Ibid. p. 265.

[d] Peter Lombard, Comment. de Regno Hibern. p. 282.

[e] Sometimes they put their fingers in their ears, and raised a general shout **in the** church. See O'Sullivan, Hist. Cat. Comp. p. 135.

to be helped by private commissions, but rather by Parliament, wherein limits in religion and discipline may be appointed, with such severe orders for the punishment of the breakers thereof, as men may fear to go beyond or come short. God hold His hand over us, that our licentious disorders and lack of religious hearts do not bring in the mean time His wrath and revenge upon us!" (July 22, 1562.[a]) This is not the report of a man who saw, as Protestants pretend, the churches crowded with people during the first years of Elizabeth. The Pope's nuncio, who was then residing at Limerick, intimates, it is true, that in some parts of Leinster some persons stood in need of the extraordinary faculties which he had received from the Pope; and as they could not come to him in person, he delegated his jurisdiction, in December 1563, to Father Newman, who was residing in Leinster. But in that delegation there is not the least confirmation of the assertion so confidently reported by some writers, that there had been in Leinster a considerable secession from the Catholic Church.[b]

With this evidence of the state of Ireland, both before and immediately after the first Parliament of Elizabeth, regarding two of the most practical and prominent features of the new religion, namely, the oath of supremacy and attendance at Protestant worship, it is hard to believe that the Commons of that Parliament, representing the wishes of their constituents, had voted for the proscription of the ancient faith. It is hard to believe that in one session, almost without adjournment and without debate,[c] members from different parts of Ireland, who had never availed themselves even of the enactments of Henry VIII., the most tempting to human cupidity, would now unanimously vote, without one word of remonstrance, the suppression of the ancient worship ; a measure which, unlike

---

[a] Shirley, p. 117. It is strange to find this Lord Deputy, who had held the Parliament of 1560, now calling for another.

[b] The Pope's nuncio, David Wolf, arrived in Ireland in August 1560, and resided there, especially at his native city, Limerick, until his death. Shirley, p. 171.

[c] The Parliament was held on the 12th of January, according to Liber Hiberniæ, vol. ii. part. 6, p. 10; but on the 11th of that month, according to the record above referred to (Tracts relating to Ireland, vol. ii. p. 135); it was prorogued to February 1st, and dissolved on same day.

the oath of supremacy, affected all their constituents alike, from the richest citizen to the meanest beggar. There are records of the debates of preceding and following Parliaments, but none of this; and there is an old tradition that the great majority of this Parliament were opposed to those enactments: that by the artifice of the speaker, Richard Stamhurst of Corduff, a clandestine session was managed, in which a few only were present who were known to be favourable to the reform; that the others, on discovering the cheat next day, vehemently protested, and were not pacified until they had received a solemn assurance that the enactments would never be enforced.[a] That Elizabeth's Irish advisers were capable of such a manœuvre, no man can doubt; that they really contrived it is exceedingly probable, both from the prevalence of the tradition even in her own reign, and from its being confidently cited before James I. by the Irish delegates[b] as a plea against his persecution, as well as from there having been no attempt in either of her subsequent Parliaments either to pass new penal statutes, or to exact the oath of supremacy from the members.

In one point alone do the statutes of 1560 appear to have been invariably executed; that is, in the prohibition of public Catholic worship wherever and whenever the government believed it safe to enforce such a prohibition.[c] This was within their power; for it is far easier to destroy than to build up. The parish churches[d] in the towns and in the country of the pale were gradually closed. As in the reign of Edward VI., there was no public divine service, the churches fell to ruin, and in a few years, according to the unvarying reports of lord deputies, roofless and desecrated churches saddened the eye in

---

[a] See some of the authorities for this tradition, cited in O'Connell's Memoir of Ireland, p. 141.

[b] Analecta Sacta, by David Rothe, Bishop of Ossory, p. 431. He lived near enough to the time to attest the prevalence of the tradition.

[c] In the English town of Galway, however, public Mass was not suppressed until the year 1569.

[d] Under the short administration of the famous Earl of Essex, Mass was allowed in chapels (sacellis), but never in public churches. Lombard Comment. de R. Hibern. p. 413. The Anglo-Irish civic and military officers accompanied the English governors to the church-doors; and "then run," says an English eye-witness, "like wild cats." Hardiman's Jar Connaught. p. 395.

all quarters of the pale, even in those which had escaped the ravages **of war,** but not the zeal of the reformers. It was a great triumph to the Evil One to suppress the Christian sacrifice; a triumph, as an Irish preacher of the day pathetically **laments,** which converted many churches of God into haunts **of** prostitutes and robers. When the towns of Cork, Waterford, Kilkenny, &c. &c. rose at the death of Elizabeth and opened the churches for Catholic worship, such of them as had survived the decay of those dreary forty years of her reign were found to be loathsome dens of filth.[a]

Such **is a** true account of the Reformation effected by Elizabeth **in her** Irish dominions; and it sufficiently demonstrates the falsehood of the received Protestant account of the vote of the Irish Parliament by which it professes to have been established. Had her first Parliament really been so obsequious as is pretended, she would not have evinced so marked a repugnance to summon another.[b] Neither would such care have been taken to pack her second Parliament, A.D. 1569. The Catholic members in that Parliament complained that some persons had been returned to the house for places not incorporated, that in others mayors and sheriffs had returned themselves, and for others non-residents had been returned, contrary to law. After four days' warm debate, the matter was referred to the judges, who decided in favour of the Catholics on the first two points, and ruled on the third that the returning officers had subjected themselves to penalty, but that the non-residents could take their seats.[c]

On a future occasion we may examine what was the conduct of the lords spiritual and temporal in that same Parliament of 1560, **since it** has been said of these too that they voted in favour of the Reformation.

---

[a] The writer published in Duffy's *Catholic Magazine* a manuscript account, by a contemporary, of the rising of the Catholic towns, especially Waterford, after Elizabeth's death. It gives a good key to the feelings of the Anglo-Irish during her reign. See Duffy's *Catholic Magazine* for November and December, 1848.

[b] Hardiman's Statute of Kilkenny, Introduction, p. xvi.

[c] Cox, Hibernia Anglicana, i. p. 329.

THE CHANCELLORS OF ENGLAND.[a]

(From the Rambler.)

LIVES of Lord Chancellors must be a subject of interest to Catholics, since almost all our chancellors up to the period of the Reformation were ecclesiastics; the most eminent of them archbishops, and many of the greatest of them cardinals and papal legates; and among them have been numbered not merely such splendid geniuses as Wolsey, but the illustrious martyr More, and the canonised martyr, St. Thomas of Canterbury. For this very reason it is not to be expected that 'lives' of our old Catholic chancellors should be written with impartiality by Protestant authors. Moreover, the chancellors were in ancient times really prime ministers; their history is the history of the country, and to do justice to them is to do justice to their policy and to the Church. To do this—to do justice to the premier and to the primate, to the chancellor and to the cardinal archbishop of Catholic England—is too much to expect from Protestant biographers. To conceive of it being done by the Presbyterian Lord Campbell is of course purely chimerical. But prejudice and partiality are really the least of his disqualifications. It is impossible to express his unfitness for the task. For Lord Campbell to portray the characters of the Langtons and the Mortons, the Wykehams and the Waynefleetes, has really almost the aspect of an insult to those magnificent men; we are persuaded they would, if aware of it, resent it as an unpardonable indignity. We consider his book as utterly unworthy of the subject, and should not have mentioned it (as it has been some time published) except by way of contrast to the work of Mr. Foss, which is still incomplete, but which, so far as it is at present carried down, is the only one which is at all to be relied on. Its pretensions are not

---

[a] *Lives of the Lord Chancellors.* By John Lord Campbell. Murray.
The Chancellors and Judges of England. By Edward Foss, Esq. F.S.A., of the Inner Temple. Vols. i.-iv. (from the Conquest to 1485.) Longmans.
Life of Lord Langdale. By T. D. Hardy. Bentley.

so high as Lord Campbell's; it does not profess to give 'lives,' but only sketches of lives: but the sketches of Mr. Foss are far more correct and interesting than the lives of his noble and learned rival; indeed, the carefulness of the one as to facts is as remarkable as the recklessness of the other. It is really ludicrous to remark how monstrous are the misstatements of Lord Campbell; and Mr. Foss corrects them in a caustic and sarcastic style, which renders these portions of his book particularly racy and piquant; especially as Lord Campbell's mis-statements, while having all the unscrupulousness of invention, have less ingenuity than stupidity.^a

From the subjoined specimens, we conceive few Catholic readers will have any desire to read more of Lord Campbell's book than they find in that of Mr. Foss, who we hope will not fail to continue and conclude his valuable labours. At present he has only just reached the era of the Reformation. That, however, brings us to More, whose character even Protestants revere; and after him no chancellor was so morally great as to render his life very important.

Before reviewing the history of our Catholic chancellors, we will recur to Lord Campbell's book for the purpose of shewing in a striking way not only the merits of their Presbyterian biographer, but to exhibit a choice specimen of that

---

[a] Writing of the reign of Henry I., Mr. Foss says: "Flambard, afterwards Bishop of Durham, is introduced into Spelman's list of Chancellors. That author refers to William of Malmsbury and Bishop Godwin, neither of whom, however, say any thing of him that will bear that interpretation.

The last authority, repeats the name, but says nothing to justify its adoption;" unless the addition of the minute detail of Flambard's amazing his enemies by appearing at court "with the great seal in his hands" may be so considered. Lord Campbell, in telling the story, has copied the language of Lingard, with the slight addition of these words! If his lordship had kindly referred to the author from whom he culled this interesting incident, which has more the appearance of modern colouring than antiquarian truth, some reliance might have been placed upon his subsequent assertion, that "at all events he appears to have held the great seal till the end of this reign;" an assertion of which the audacity may be estimated, from the fact that there is no trace of his ever having held it at all.

In speaking of a chancellor of the reign of Edward II., Lord Campbell notices a grant of safe conduct to "the chancellor's poulterers," whom he had appointed to provide poultry for him and his clerks; and he draws attention to it by a prominent marginal note, "Epicurism of the Lord Chancellor." Upon this stupid and laboured levity the piquant comment of Mr. Foss is: "This is scarcely fair. Would Lord Campbell deem himself liable to this accusation for eating a pullet?"

species of misrepresentation or invention of which Protestant history is made up. Speaking of a judge named Billing (temp. Henry VI.), Mr. Foss says, in a passage which may serve as a specimen of his style as well as Lord Campbell's:

"Fuller inserts Sir F. Billing among his 'worthies;' adding, that 'he had his habitation in great state.' Unsupported by any authority, Lord Campbell, in his biography of the judge, represents him as in every respect a contemptible and worthless person. He remarks, that Fuller is silent as to his ancestors and descendants; but this omission is not uncommon with Fuller; nor is there any thing in his account of Billing to indicate, as Lord Campbell asserts, that he is evidently ashamed of introducing such a character among his worthies. In truth, no memorial of Billing's ancestors, or of the personal history of his early years, has been found; nor does any authority exist for the supposition made by Lord Campbell, that he had been clerk of an attorney. A letter in the *Paston Correspondence* speaks of him as a Fellow of Gray's Inn; and it appears that he not merely 'contrived to be called to the Bar,' as Lord Campbell insinuates, but that he was so well reputed as to be made lecturer in that society. And we must suppose that he distinguished himself in his early professional career, since he was returned by the citizens of London as their representative, and was elected recorder. If this do not raise a sufficient doubt of Lord Campbell's assertion, that his business was not of the most creditable description, we may find further proof in the *Paston Correspondence* that he had already acquired a high reputation, and that his personal position was such as to produce an intimate **intercourse** with the families of Paston and Lord Grey de Ruthyn. As **we** have never seen nor heard of Billing's treatise on the subject of the claims of the royal antagonists, which Lord Campbell quotes, but does not enable us to refer to" (we need hardly say, it never existed, and that this is a delicate but sarcastic accusation of a barefaced fabrication), "we are prevented from judging of his private aspirations or his political sentiments. Having lived from his infancy under the mild sway of an amiable monarch, we hope he was 'outrageously loyal' (as Lord Campbell calls him). We do not find, however, that the Rolls of Parliament mention his name as appearing at the bar of the House of Lords as counsel for Henry VI., leading the attorney and solicitor general" (Lord Campbell had forgotten that it is doubtful whether there was at this time any such office as that of solicitor-general!) "and on that occasion 'it was remarked that his fire had slackened much, and that he was very complimentary to the Duke of York, who was virtually master of the kingdom.' We acknowledge our ignorance of any work (except Lord Campbell's) in which the observation is recorded. On the contrary, it appears by the Rolls, that not only the judges, but the king's serjeants and attorneys (none of whom are mentioned by name), excused themselves altogether from giving any opinion on the question. It would have been more satisfactory to his readers if Lord Campbell had stated his authority for saying that on the accession of Edward IV., 'instantly Sir Thomas Billing sent in his adhesion; and such zeal did he express in favour of the new dynasty, that his patent of king's serjeant was renewed, and he became principal law-adviser to Edward IV.' We might then, perhaps, have comprehended why his lordship designates him as 'this unprincipled adventurer;' though Coke speaks of him 'as among other excellent men who flourished at the time.' But it does seem unjust" (and absurd) "to single out Sergeant Billing from his brethren with such harsh terms, when the only evidence of his 'turning.' is, that he did exactly what not only the serjeants, but every one of the judges except Fortescue, very naturally and very properly did on the change of dynasty —he retained his legal position in the courts of law. In the very first Parliament of Edward IV., we find that besides Billing, the famous Littleton and Laken, serjeants in precisely the same position, were nominated by Parliament as referees in a case between the Bishop of Winchester and his tenants; but the Rolls do not supply us with any authority for the very improbable fact which Lord Campbell introduces, that 'Serjeant Billing assisted in framing the acts by which Sir John Fortescue and the principal Lancastrians, his patrons, were attainted;' or that he 'took an active part in the subsequent measures of hostility against King Henry and Queen Margaret.' We have no materials which would justify us in ascribing to Billing the private suggestions of which Lord Campbell makes him the author, or in judging of the correctness of the motives assigned for his elevation to the bench. Neither can we find any evidence of his presumed dissatisfaction with the office of puisne judge, nor of his resolution that 'mere scruples of conscience should not hold him back from the woolsack.' Discarding every thing but the simple fact, it is enough to say, that on August 9, 1464, he was added to the three judges of whom the court of King's Bench then consisted. Lord Campbell, quoting from Baker's *Chronicle* and Hale's *Pleas of the Crown*, mentions Billing as the judge who tried one Walter Walker for saying that he would make his son, 'heir to the Crown,' meaning his inn so called; and gives the judge's ruling on the case, with the conviction and execution of the unfortunate prisoner. It is curious, however, that his lordship, when citing Sir N. Throgmorton's address to Lord Chief-Justice Bromley, omits the chief-justice's answer, referring to this very case, by which it appears that Markham was the judge, and that an acquittal was the consequence of his honest ruling. But if this omission is curious, what will our readers think when it turns out that neither Baker nor Hale state the case as occurring in Billing's time; and further, that Stow gives the time of the trial (March 12, 1460) four years before Billing was on the bench! Billing was selected for Markham's successor as chief-justice, and received his patent January 1468-9. The trial and conviction of Sir Thomas Burdet, for wishing a favourite buck of his (which the king had killed in hunting) 'horns and all, was in the king's belly,' is said by Lord Campbell to have taken place before Chief-Justice Billing in the very next term after his appointment, and that a rumour was propagated that the late virtuous chief-justice had been displaced because he had refused to concur in it. We cannot discover whence Lord Campbell has extracted the ruling of Billing in this or Walker's case, which he has printed as quotations; but we are surprised that with his lordship's known experience and great knowledge, he was not aware that Burdet's case had been lately referred to in Westminster Hall; and that the record of his attainder was searched for and found in the *Baga de Secretis;* and that this labour might have been spared by looking into Cooke's reports, where the proceedings against him are published. The result of all would have proved that the whole story of the buck and the belly was a figment; and that the charge against Burdet was for conspiring to kill the king and the prince, by foretelling the speedy death of both, and scattering papers containing the prophecy among the people. By the record it appears also, that instead of the trial taking place in the 'very next term' after Billing became chief-justice, no part of Burdet's crime was committed before 1474; he was not tried until 1477. What, then, becomes of Lord Campbell's charge against Billing, of justifying his promotion by the renegade zeal he displayed for his new friends? What becomes of the 'rumour,' that Markham, who had retired nearly ten years before, was 'displaced for not concurring in the conviction?' Little more than two years after Billing had attained the chief judicial seat, Henry VI. was restored to the crown, which he retained for about six months, when he was again expelled by his successful rival.

It is a strong proof of the seat of justice being considered exempt from the consequences of the civil strife, that on both these occasions the judges, with few exceptions, were replaced in their seats by new patents, issued immediately after each of these kings had gained the ascendancy; so that all the conjectures as to Billing's deportment, at either crisis, in which Lord Campbell indulges, must be deemed applicable, if at all, to his brethren as well as to himself; and it seems more natural to infer, from Billing's double reinstatement, that he had not made himself obnoxious to either party by 'extreme partiality' or 'outrageous loyalty.' Lord Campbell states the latter re-appointment took place 'about a twelvemonth after Edward's return in 1471; but the patent is dated June 17, 1471, a few weeks, instead of a year, after Edward's return. Thus Lord Campbell's statements, that Billing 'found great difficulty in making his peace,' that 'he was dismissed from his office, which was allowed to remain vacant about a year,' and that 'he is supposed to have been hiding during the interval,' are at once deprived of the groundwork on which they rested. For the one good deed he did, in advising Edward IV. to pardon Sir John Fortescue, we should feel obliged for Lord Campbell's authority, with an explanation why he attributes to Billing the imposition upon Sir John of the condition to publish a retractation of his former sentiments, which he had in his previous life of Fortescue ascribed to the king himself. Sir Thomas Billing presided in his court up to the day of his death, which took place in 1481; and he was buried in Bittlesden Abbey, under a large blue marble slab, on which are the figures of the chief-justice and his lady,—he being represented in his official robes, and she in a plain dress with short waist. This slab, after the dissolution of the monasteries, was removed to the church of Weppenham, in Northamptonshire, where it now remains."

This extract is long, but is really worth inserting at length, as an instance of the way in which Protestant histories are written. It is, however, we confess, an outrageous instance, and we cite it particularly as a specimen of the character of Lord Campbell, and an interesting illustration of that plastic power of dealing with facts which he displayed in the case of Achilli. It is evident that these are not accidental blunders or vagaries; they are characteristic of the man; and probably no more severe or discrediting exposure was ever inflicted on any writer with more justice **than in** the passage we have quoted.[a]

The names of chancellors are not mentioned until after the Conquest. They were **at** first always ecclesiastics, and usually men who attained episcopal rank; but it was not then usual for them to hold the offices of bishop and chancellor together. Hence, in the list of William the Conqueror's chancellors, all are mentioned as "afterwards" bishops. So of the reigns of William II. and Henry I. One of William's chancellors, Bloet, " afterwards Bishop of Lincoln," is described by Henry of Huntingdon as mild and humble, a raiser of many, a depressor of none, the orphan's father, and the delight of his family. And Matthew Paris testifies to the beauty of his person and the sweetness and affability of his manners and conversation. One of Henry's chancellors, Gifford, "afterwards Bishop of Winchester," when nominated to that see, at the time when St. Anselm was expelled the country by the king, nobly encountered the royal wrath by refusing to be consecrated by the Archbishop of York, and had the honour of not only being deprived of his office, but banished from the kingdom. However, he had his reward in this world as well as the next for preferring the wrath of an earthly sovereign to the displeasure of Christ's Vicar and the anger of the Heavenly King; for he was a few years afterwards consecrated by St. Anselm, and held his see twenty-one years, during which he introduced the Cistercian order into England, and founded an abbey for them at Waverley, Surrey. He also erected a priory at Taunton, and was founder of the priory of St. Mary Overy, Southwark.

The King's Chancellor (*Cancellarius Regis*), says Mr. Foss, was an officer of the *Curia Regis*, an office traceable to

---

[a] Yet though Lord Campbell's is an extreme case, the character it exemplifies is not confined to him, but pertains to all Protestant writers; and curiously enough, his sarcastic censor and critic, Mr. Foss, falls into the very fault (though in a far less degree) he so severely exposes in his learned rival. To use his own expressions as applied to Lord Campbell, we should like his authority for the assertion (a specimen of many similar), "that Pope Paschal granted absolution to a prelate on condition of his proving his penitence by enriching the Church." We might then be better able to judge whether the "condition" were not simply one of restitution, and precisely of the same kind as Mr. Foss would apply to one of his footmen who had stolen his plate.

the time of Ethelbert, the first Anglo-Saxon king who embraced Christianity. He was originally always an ecclesiastical person, and, Madox says, was in truth " the king's chief chaplain ; " which looks remarkably like a confessor, and reminds one of the familiar phrase of our own time, which merely embodies an ancient tradition, as to the office of " keeper of the king's conscience."

The first really bad chancellor of whom we have any record appears to have been Ranulph (temp. Henry I.). He has a king's chaplain, but seems to have been far more of a layman than a priest, and we do not read, indeed, of his holding any benefice or bishopric. Even he, however, was a benefactor to the abbey of Reading. Roger de Wendover describes him as ready for all kinds of wickedness; and Henry of Huntingdon speaks of his impiety, oppression, and avarice. The first truly great chancellor we find mention of was Roger, afterwards Bishop of Salisbury (temp. Henry I.). He was chancellor at the beginning of the reign, and until 1103. He was appointed bishop 1102; but as he was one of those whose consecrations were in abeyance pending the contest between the king and St. Anselm, and his scruples could not be removed till that dispute was accommodated, he was not consecrated until 1107. He retained his see for thirty-two years, and at last afforded an example of the true worth of the favour of a king, for he died of grief or fatigue suffered in some piece of royal outrage and oppression. His memory was regarded with such estimation, that he is usually named with the addition of Magnus.[a]

The great chancellor, however, of this, and indeed of any other age, and the one whose history and name sheds most lustre upon it, is St. Thomas of Canterbury. And Fitzstephen, in his life of St. Thomas, archbishop and martyr, says, " he was remembrancer in his chancery, and when he sat to hear causes, reader of the bills and petitions," the very phraseology now employed in chancery proceedings. Our readers need

---

[a] Foss, vol. i. p. 159, citing Madox's Ex. ch. i. p. 33; Godwin de Præsul. 37; Wendover, vol. ii. p. 183.

hardly by reminded that St. Thomas resigned his chancellorship when elected archbishop, and that this was the first occasion of offence to the king. In the schools of London and Paris he acquired scholastic education; in those of Bologna and Auxerre a knowledge of civil and canon law; and his high abilities were at once exhibited and exercised in several important embassies. In a merely human sense, it is perfectly plain that no one ever sat in chancery with a greater diversity of knowledge or a higher degree of ability; and perhaps it would be difficult to name any holder of the great seal so well qualified for the office. It is amusing to see how even an unusually enlightened Protestant like Mr. Foss is puzzled to discover the explanation—to a Catholic perfectly easy and plain—of that alteration and elevation of character which took place upon St. Thomas's elevation to the episcopate. " The king had reason to consider himself deceived when Becket sent in his resignation of the chancellorship, on the pretence of his incompetence to discharge the duties of the two offices."[a] " As this doubt of his own powers could not have been the result of experience, inasmuch as sufficient time had not elapsed to try them, and as the two offices could not be considered incompatible" (how easily this is assumed!), "Henry might be justly indignant at a primate declining to be premier." For Mr. Foss had previously informed his readers most truly, that in those days the chancellor was virtually prime minister. How essentially secular the Protestant Church-system must be, which thus positively disables an intelligent member of that Church from perceiving any incompatibility in such offices, and prevents his seeing the monstrosity of one person assuming to exercise the entire charge of the whole spiritual and temporal interests of the nation! But above all, how utterly does it appear to disqualify a man from appreciating the awful character of the episcopal office, and from understanding the deep humility and sense of responsibility with which it ought to be assumed, and by Catholic prelates ordinarily has been assumed! Very different from St. Thomas was his successor in

---

[a] Foss, vol. i. p. 202.

the chancellorship, Geoffroy Plantagenet, Henry's gay and gallant illegitimate son, who gave up his bishopric for the chancellorship, as his sainted predecessor had given up the chancellorship for the bishopric. He, at all events, understood his vocation was not spiritual; for when compelled by the Pope to elect between being ordained and abandoning the See of Lincoln (the temporalities of which he held), he chose the latter alternative. His military propensities were so overpowering, that he appears to have been almost as unsuited for the office of chancellor as bishop. A still greater contrast to St. Thomas is to be found in the celebrated Longchamps, Bishop of Ely, the first remarkable instance we have of a bishop retaining the chancellorship. Here, at least, was a man who had no distrust of his own powers, and no pretended scruples as to the incompatibility of temporal and spiritual offices; the precursor of men like Beaufort and Wolsey. Longchamps held together the offices of chancellorship, chief justiciary, and papal legate, thus uniting in his own person the whole civil and spiritual jurisdiction of the realm! What was the result? "He engrossed all the ecclesiastical patronage, and accumulated vast sums by appropriating the rents of the vacant abbeys and bishoprics. He affected royal state, never travelled without an enormous attendance, and the churches and monasteries where he was entertained were nearly ruined. The people suffered severely from the taxes he imposed, the clergy were oppressed, the nobility disgusted, and all classes eager to rid themselves of so tyrannous a ruler."[a] Well, will any pious Protestant prefer such a man to St. Thomas? Will any sensible person suppose he made a better chancellor or a better bishop?

Up to, and until the end of, the reign of Edward I., which forms an era in the legal history of England (as that of Edward III. does in its ecclesiastical history), the chancellors, or keepers of the great seal, were almost exclusively ecclesiastics. And so of the Masters of the Rolls, whose office is mentioned in that reign as ancient. The preference for ecclesiastics was, however, purely politic, on account of their being the only

[a] Foss, vol. i. p. 390.

persons possessed of the requisite qualifications in point of education; and unhappily there was no difficulty in finding plenty of them sufficiently secular in spirit, **though** it is to be observed that still the instances were **rare of bishops** holding the office of chancellor.

Throughout the greater part of the long **reign** of Edward III. bishops held the great seal; but while it was **in the** hands of the illustrious William of Wykeham, the Commons objected to the great offices of the State being held by **the** clergy, and he was displaced. This **was** after the statutes of præmunire; and there can be no question that the motives **of** the Commons in this representation **were as mean** and as miserable as those which dictated those **celebrated statutes : motives of** mere mercenary jealousy; jealousy in **the one case of natives** for foreigners, in the other of laymen for **clerks.** The ecclesiastical chancellors were, as a body, admirably qualified for the office; possessing, of course, a good acquaintance with the civil law, which some of the best equity lawyers of our own day are known to regard as **the** best possible teaching of equity.

However, at the end of the reign of Edward III. there were **substituted for a** short time lay chancellors,—the first being **Thorpe,** chief justice of the Common Pleas. We shall see whether the lawyer chancellors were as good as the ecclesiastical. One thing is clear,—the ecclesiastics were almost universally liberal **and generous in** the disposal of their wealth, and there **were few of** them **who** did not found colleges or convents or churches : [a] **and let it** be recollected, that in an age when the Church was the Church of the people, liberality to the Church was charity to the poor. The very names of William of Wykeham and William of Waynefleete (who are only specimens, albeit illustrious ones, of our ecclesiastical chancellors), may suggest to **us the sort** of men they were.

---

[a] Walter de Merton, afterwards Bishop of Rochester, was created chancellor in 1261; and in 1274 he was elected Bishop of Rochester, and thereupon resigned his chancellorship. He held the see only three years, but founded Merton College at Oxford, the most ancient establishment of its kind, and incorporated by charters so wise, that they were consulted as precedents in the foundation of Peter House, the earliest existing college of the sister University.—*Foss*, vol. iii. pp. 130, 131. This is one out of innumerable instances which make this work of great interest.

Let us take at random another instance—Richard de Bury, Bishop of Durham, made chancellor (temp. Edward III.) in 1335. It is true that, finding the chancellorship withdraw him from the duties of his diocese, he resigned it in less than nine months (without in the least forfeiting, by the by, the favour of his sovereign, who seems to have been far more reasonable in this respect than Henry II.); thus, after the lapse of two centuries, imitating the example and vindicating the conduct of St. Thomas. But, as we have seen, originally it was not usual to hold the episcopal office with the chancellorship; and such an instance as this rather shews the unfitness of the chancellorship for a bishop, than a bishop for the chancellorship. Richard de Bury neglected none of the duties of his diocese, and turned all his time to account. He occupied his leisure in forming what became the largest library in Europe, which he bequeathed to Trinity College, Oxford, and was the first public library founded in that University. Mr. Foss thus describes his character: "His virtues and charity were equal to his talents and learning. He was beloved by his neighbours, with whom he lived on terms of reciprocal affection; to his clergy he was an indulgent superior; to his tenants and domestics a considerate master. He was most bountiful to the poor, distributing eight quarters of wheat every week for the relief of those around him, and never omitting in his journeys to appropriate large sums for the indigent in those places through which he passed. The memory of few names, and of none in that age, is more endeared than that of Richard de Bury. His income was so much exhausted by his liberality, that his representatives at his death found little to divide." In this last trait, we fear, little resemblance will be found either to modern bishops or chancellors. Of course, when bishops have children, it would hardly be a virtue to carry liberality to such an extent; and whether chancellors have children or not, they are sure to have prudence enough to preserve them from such an extreme. But there are limits to prudence as well as to charity, and even a proper provision for children has its bounds. We believe it is some centuries since chancellors founded libraries, and many generations since bishops founded any thing but *families*. The last two primates of the State Church left each something like a million behind them; so that their representatives, unlike Richard de Bury's, found plenty " to divide," [a] and their children moreover were amply provided for.

It is remarkable fact, that the first lay chancellor (like the great Protestant chancellor Bacon) was degraded for bribery. And corruption had soon so increased in Chancery, that in the reign of Richard II. we find a complaint exhibited against the Masters (of whom, as already observed, the Master of the Rolls was one), that they were "over fatte both in bodie and purse, and over-well furred in their benefices." [b] The practice of bishops holding the great seal now revived; and Simon de Sudbury, Archbishop of Canterbury, was chancellor at the outbreak of Wat Tyler's riots, in which he was brutally murdered, having resigned the chancellorship only two days before, with the vain hope of appeasing the populace, who had doubtless taken offence at some political or secular proceeding of the primate: had he never taken the great seal, he would not have lost his head. In this reign, however, the illustrious William of Wykeham again had it; and during the two years and a half for which he held it, he restored public tranquillity so effectually, that the parliament thanked the king for his good government; and could he have been induced to remain in office, it is probable (Mr. Foss says) that his wise counsuls might have checked the king's intemperance, and prevented the fatal consequences that followed. We need hardly remind our readers of the foundation of Winchester School, and of New College, Oxford—the great works of this celebrated prelate. Of him, as of so many other illustrious ecclesiastics, we may well say, that it was not they who were unsuited for the chancellorship, but the chancellorship which was unworthy of them. In the reign of Henry IV., out of six chancellors all but one were not only ecclesiastics but bishops; and though this was bad for the Church, it was not deemed bad for the country,

---

[a] See *Speculum Episcopi*.
[b] Mr. Hargrave's *Law Tracts*.

since Henry was particularly careful to comply with any representations of the Commons, especially as to the administration of justice, and none can be discovered to have been made upon this point; which is very observable, and seems to shew that since the Commons complained on this score in the reign of Edward III., the public experience had proved the superiority of ecclesiastics in the office. Certain it is, that lawyers were now in bad odour. Thomas de Arundel, Archbishop of Canterbury, was in this reign chancellor for the fifth time: which appears to indicate, on the one hand, that his administration of office was appreciated; and on the other, that he was not well satisfied with himself for undertaking it. What a contrast to St. Thomas!

This brings us to the age of Cardinal Beaufort, whose name will readily occur to our readers as one of the most illustrious holders of the great seal, and as the predecessor, and in many respects perhaps the exemplar, of Wolsey. To those who have formed their ideas of history upon Protestant authorities, or who have not disabused their minds of the mendacious and calumnious misrepresentations of Shakspeare, the great cardinal of Henry V. will be as much, or more, an object of prejudiced dislike as the great cardinal of Henry VIII.; and both will very much be associated in their minds with aversion to Catholic ecclesiastics in general, and to cardinals in particular. But though very likely Beaufort was not scrupulously careful as to his episcopal duties, no complaint was ever made of neglect in his judicial, and none can be substantiated of misconduct in his political duties. He was unquestionably faithful to the country and the crown; and if failing in fidelity, it was rather to the Pope than to his prince, and it was the Church, not the State, that had a right to complain. Mr. Foss does this illustrious ecclesiastic no more than justice; but in a Protestant it displays a praiseworthy freedom from prejudice when he declares, that "though more attentive to his political than his episcopal duties, there is little that can affect his character as a man anxious at once to serve his sovereign and promote his country's welfare;" and he says, that the imputations against him of being a party to the Duke of

Gloucester's death are not supported even by probability. The cardinal had for some years retired from court, and at the time his own dissolution was rapidly approaching, taking place in six weeks afterwards. His personal neglect of episcopal duties was only during the time he was occupied with others of greater importance, perhaps, to the country at large; and it does not at all appear that he forgot to make full provision for the management of his diocese by vicars-general. Beaufort was not a Borromeo; but taking the whole of his long episcopal career of half a century, he was not a bad bishop. The time during which he was engaged in duties not episcopal he was exerting himself for the benefit of his country (and we may observe, in passing, that these illustrious ecclesiastics constantly did the state good service by embassies of peace), and he expended vast sums in works of piety and charity: in completing the cathedral of Winchester; in the endowment of the hospital of St. Cross; and in gifts to the poor, for whom he made abundant provision in his will. This is the man whom Shakspeare represents as dying a murderer and a **maniac**! No more monstrous instance could be adduced of the **false** traditions by which—as Sir F. Palgrave and Dr. **Newman** have shewn—the people of this country are duped and deluded. Cardinal Beaufort was never chancellor, having resigned the great seal before he received the hat. Some of his predecessors and successors in the chancellorship, with abilities not so striking, yet attained to higher rank. Langley, Archbishop of York, was chancellor, and afterwards cardinal (temp. Henry IV.), and resembled Beaufort, if not in ability, in liberality. **He** resigned all secular offices towards the close of his life to attend to his episcopal duties, and occupied himself in many magnificent and charitable works in his diocese, founding schools and enriching colleges. The successor of Beaufort was Kempe, who was Archbishop of York, chancellor, and cardinal. He was a man of such extraordinary energy and ability, that after resigning the chancellorship, he was, when past the age of seventy, entreated to resume it, and exercised the office at the time of his death, on hearing of which his sovereign said, "One of the wisest lords in this land is dead! And he, at least, is an instance of an ecclesiastic holding these high offices irreprochably, for Mr. Foss informs us that "his character was unblemished." His name is remembered in the University of Oxford, to the schools of which, as well as to his own college (Merton), he was a munificent benefactor. He also beautified the collegiate church of Southwell; and in 1447 founded a college of secular priests, for the celebration of divine service and the instruction of youth; the idea of which seems somewhat of an anticipation of the vocation of the Jesuits and Oratorians.

We now naturally pass to the age of Wolsey, the last in the long line of illustrious ecclesiastics who held the chancellorship. Of him we need not say much. No historian denies the ability with which he exercised the offices he held, or disputes the sincerity of his dying exclamation, "Had I but served my God as faithfully as I have served my prince!" an exclamation clearly implying a consciousness of fidelity to his sovereign and his country; and amply confirming what we contend is a summary of the history of the great seal up to this time, that the possession of it by ecclesiastics was good for the country, though bad for themselves and for the Church. Prejudiced must that man be, who, in spite of the magnificent catalogue of ecclesiastical chancellors—illustrious with such names as Wykeham and Waynefleete and Wolsey, Beaufort and Kempe and Langley,—can cherish the vulgar idea, that ecclesiastical rule is injurious to a nation. England was never better ruled than by these Premier-Primates—or rather Primate-Premiers—whose magnificent minds were equal to the overwhelming duties of prime minister, primate, papal legate, and chancellor. Truly there were giants in those days. These men were great not merely intellectually, but morally. Wealth they valued only as the means of a magnificent liberality and a large-minded charity; and colleges, churches, cathedrals, and schools are monuments of the princely and pious character of our ecclesiastical chancellors.

The successor of Wolsey in the chancellorship was, however, Sir Thomas More; and the first of our line of lay chancellors was the first of martyrs to the Papal Supremacy. What manner of man *he* was, no Catholic need be told. He was one of the few chancellors whose life and character is well known and worth knowing. More was, when a youth, in the household of Cardinal Morton, Archbishop of Canterbury, a splendid specimen of the old race of ecclesiastical chancellors. He had been an eminent civilian and canonist, and was primate and premier during most of the reign of Henry VII., and until his own death, which happened at the advanced age of ninety. He lived to perceive and predict the coming greatness of More, who thus described his venerable predecessor in the chancellor's chair: "He was a man of great natural wit, very well learned, and honourable in behaviour."[a] "He was venerable for his wisdom and virtues, and for the high character he bore. His looks begot reverence rather than fear; his conversation was easy, but serious and grave; he spoke gracefully and weightily; he was eminently skilled in the law, and had a vast understanding and a prodigious memory; and those talents with which nature had furnished him were improved by study and experience. The king depended much on his counsels, and the government seemed chiefly supported by him."[b]

It is to be noted that More, infinitely the most illustrious of the long series of lawyer-chancellors which commenced with him, was in early youth brought up in the house of the venerable Morton, and was the immediate successor of Wolsey. He seems to have imbibed something of the grandeur of character which belonged to these cardinal-chancellors and the age they had adorned. He was certainly very unlike his successors, not one of whom can compare with him. His immediate successor, Audley,—who was such a striking contrast to him, and who is remembered merely on that account,—far more fairly represents them, marked as they are by selfish servility and clever mediocrity.

It is interesting to observe how the first of lay-chancellors spoke of the last of ecclesiastical. On his installation, More said of Wolsey, "When I looke upon this seate; when I thinke

---

[a] More's *Hist. Rich.* iii.
[b] More's *Utopia.*

how great and what kind of personages have possessed this place before me; when I call to mind who he was that sate in it last of all—a man of what singular wisdom, of what notable experience; what a prosperous and favourable fortune he had for a great space, and how at the last he had a most grievous fall, and died inglorious,—I have cause enough to think dignity not so grateful to me as it may seem to others; for it is a hard matter to follow with like grace or praises a man of such admirable wit, prudence, authority, and splendour, to whom I may seem but as the lighting of a candle when the sun is down." [a]

The class of men of whom such a one as More could thus speak could not but have merited eulogium and admiration; and a modern Protestant biographer thus speaks of Wolsey's chancellorship: "We possess unquestionable evidence of the ability and general impartiality of the Cardinal's administration in the Court of Chancery, in which he spared neither high nor low, but judged every one according to their merits and deserts. He established courts for protecting the poor against the oppression of the rich; and his ingenuity and influence were sedulously applied during his entire career in rendering the laws intelligible, simple, cheap, and respected." [b]

Of the successor of More, the infamous Audley, it is enough to say, that he (with such a man as Spelman, to his shame be it recorded) sat on the commission which condemned the illustrious lawyer as a traitor for not submitting to the blasphemy of the royal supremacy. And it is the most simple, though the most severe way of describing the moral calibre of the successors of Audley, to say that they resembled him rather than More, and have upheld that blasphemy and all its hideous consequences with courtly servility, and down to our own days with crafty cruelty. This is true of them all; from Bacon to Hardwicke, from Hardwicke to Eldon, from Eldon to Cottenham and Langdale,—all have remorselessly carried

---

[a] In a letter to Erasmus, More speaks of "the Cardinal of York" (Wolsey) discharging the duties of the chancellorship so admirably, as to surpass the hopes of all.
[b] Lardner's *Lives of British Statesmen*.

out the penal policy of the royal supremacy, so long as public opinion would permit them, by proscription, and even in our own times by confiscation. A new system had now sprung up; the great seal now became the prize of the ablest practising lawyers of the day, men whose hearts were hardened by the keen pursuit of wealth in the practice of the profession, and generally depraved by the bloody training which the holding of office as crown-lawyers under the Tudors and Stuarts too often involved. Under such men Chancery became corrupted into that execrable and abominable system which for generations has been a curse, a scandal, and a shame to the country; and to which the public hope (perhaps vainly) that a death-blow has been dealt in the Chancery Reform Act of last session. Such a system could never have been the growth of true greatness. It never could have been constructed under the auspices of men either intellectually or morally meriting the epithet of great. The popular idea, the notorious truth, as to the Court of Chancery, must be in itself a monument and epitaph for the Protestant chancellors who made it what it was.

Let all our readers remark this plain historical fact, that all this system grew up under Protestant governments and Protestant judges, and ripened into its rank luxuriance of injustice and iniquity under the fostering care of the House of Hanover. This might dispense with any further notice of the Protestant chancellors in the interval. Truly, indeed, if we wished to say much of them, it would scarcely be possible; and if it were possible, they would not be worthy of it. For they were for the most part—almost universally—a mercenary race: narrow-minded among statesmen (even such as were counted large-minded among lawyers), insomuch that they soon ceased to be premiers, and often were not even leading ministers,—indeed, not unfrequently were the least influential members of the Cabinet. In a word, so soon as England ceased to be Catholic, her chancellors ceased to be statesmen, and sank into mere lawyers. No trace can be found of the magnificence of character which marked our ecclesiastical chancellors. The Protestant lawyer-chancellors have lived but for themselves, "to put money in their purse," or at the utmost dispense patronage. They left no monuments behind them of a grand and princely charity. The only one among them intellectually great was morally mean; and the name of Bacon is degraded by bribery.

The old English chancellors were remarkable for their princely charity, and spent the wealth they acquired upon the country. The modern race of chancellors spent their money only on their own families, and not only were the loss of charity themselves, but caused the loss of it in others. Let us look how **they dealt with one branch, one of the** most important branches, of the jurisdiction of the laws—charity. The Court of Chancery is guardian of charity. How have Protestant chancellors dealt with charity? We have seen how Catholic chancellors practised it, and it may be conceived how they cherished it. And even for a century or so after the Reformation (as Catholicism did not die out suddenly in the land, but left some leaven in its laws), the chancellors, at all events, encouraged charity.

In the age of Bacon, parliament passed the celebrated act of Elizabeth as to gifts for charitable uses; an act (in the words of Chief-Justice Wilmot) "with such medicinal properties in it, as to heal every imperfection in a charitable donation;" and the chancellors construed it most largely and most liberally in favour of charity, and in furtherance of the liberal policy of the legislature. Such was the course taken by the Protestant chancellors of that age, who in some degree lived under those Catholic influences which continued until the Revolution. It was the course taken by Bacon, who was a giant compared with his successors, as he was—at all events morally—a dwarf compared with his predecessors. He encouraged charity, if he did not practise it. [a]

Lord Bacon accordingly held, in 1617, that a devise void at common law should be valid for charitable uses. A century afterwards, however, when the corrupting influences of Protestantism had perverted the judicial conscience, Lord

[a] Of course we are speaking of Protestant charities; "Popish" were proscribed.

Cowper held the contrary, observing that "the judges had carried several cases on the act of Elizabeth to very great lengths in favour of charity."

So again, in 1714, Lord Harcourt reversed a decision of the commissioners of charitable uses, declaring a devise good "to pious purposes under the act of Elizabeth, although void as a will at common law." The doctrine laid down by Bacon was thus reversed and repudiated by Cowper and Harcourt; so much had the national and judicial mind become deteriorated and narrowed in the interval between the reigns of Elizabeth and Anne.

In 1720 a case occurred, shewing that the chancellors decided on questions of charity rather in accordance with the coarse, selfish spirit of the laity, than with the feelings of the clergy and the more religious portion of the community. A Court of law had upset a decree of the commissioners of charitable uses (in favour of charity) on some purely legal point, and the case came by appeal into the House of Lords, where Lord Harcourt presided as chancellor. The law-lords differed, and the bishops made a majority for reversing the judgment of the Court below, and affirming that of the commissioners in favour of charity. Lord Harcourt shewed the bent and bias of his mind by citing an expression of Mr. Justice Twisden (a puritan judge), who, when pressed on behalf of a claim for a charity which he thought against law, said, "I like charity well, but will not steal leather to make poor men's shoes;" a saying the value of which depends, of course, upon its application in any particular case, but which has passed into a judicial proverb, of very easy application, by a class of judges who are more disposed to rob charities than to run any danger of countenancing stealing for their benefit. Indeed, it is a confessed fact, that since the Revolution our chancellors have become more and more hostile to charity, although their court is by theory its guardian. Alas, the very juxtaposition of the terms now appears a sarcasm! Chancery and charity! The ancient race of chancellors were magnificent examples of charity; their successors of the Elizabethan age at least encouraged it; the modern chancellors have done their best to destroy it. Catholic chancellors were rivals in charity. Protestant chancellors have been robbers of charity. They have been so upon principle, and have even passed new laws for the purpose. Lord Hardwicke carried the first law ever passed in this country against charitable gifts.

In his evidence before the committee of 1844, Sir F. Palgrave said: "Sutton's case (relative to that fine charity, the Charter-House), as reported by Coke, testifies the joy which Coke felt in overturning the technicalities by which that gift was attempted to be set aside. He considered that charitable donations were as beneficial to the commonwealth as his successors have thought them injurious. Coke's feelings and language form a singular contrast with the opinions of Lord Hardwicke,—a great judge, but one whose narrowed, nay bigoted views, have caused so much mischief to charitable uses." [a]

Hardwicke was a fair specimen of Protestant chancellors. The late Mr. Burge, an eminent lawyer, stated in his evidence before the Mortmain Committee of 1844, that the first cases under the act against charities came before Lord Hardwicke, who gave it a strict construction against charities, and that this construction "has been followed by all his successors;" which simple fact suffices to shew that they were all, morally speaking, little-minded, low-minded, narrow-minded men, as Sir Francis Palgrave most justly describes Hardwicke to have been. The followers of a narrow-minded man must have been narrow-minded; and a melancholy contrast do they present to the

---

[a] In 1754, Lord Hardwicke pronounced a judgment so essentially and shamelessly unchristian, that it seems, long afterwards, his successor, Lord Eldon, was half ashamed of it. A Jew had established a fund for the propagation of Judaism; and the question was, whether the sum should go to the heir (the legacy being void), or be distributed by the court, according to the rule recognised in the reign of Queen Anne, for purposes as nearly analogous as possible. Lord Hardwicke held that the latter course should be pursued; that is, that the testator's design should be carried out as far as it could be consistently with law, and that there should not be a clean confiscation of his legacy; and on this principle the fund would be applicable for a Jewish almshouse or secular shool. But this Christian chancellor said he should hold otherwise of a legacy void under the statute of superstitious uses, and confiscate it; that is to say, the Court of Chancery would do all it could to favour a Jewish legacy, and to confiscate a Popish one. (Da Costa v. De Pas, Ambler's Reports.) Lord Eldon once, in adverting to this decision, tried to do away with this detestable feature in it, but with no success. (Moggridge v. Thackwell, 7 Vezey junior, 76.)

magnificent chancellors of Catholic times. The holders of the great seal in olden times felt it equally their duty, their pleasure, and their pride, to encourage charity to the utmost: modern chancellors have done their utmost to rob charity; and have not scrupled not only to pass bad laws for the purpose, but to press these laws to the strictest possible interpretation, ay and beyond it. They have even warped and altered the law, to make it work more hardly against religion and charity.

As to Lord Eldon, the most eminent chancellor since Hardwicke (as *he* was after Bacon), what need we say of him as to Chancery, but that he was the upholder of all its abuses; or as to charity, further than that he carried out to the utmost the narrow-minded policy of his predecessors? As to the more political portion of the chancellor's functions, what need we say more than the simple fact, that Eldon was the most bigoted opponent of the emancipation of those who held the faith of William of Wykeham and William of Waynefleete, of Langton and Morton and More, and all the other of his innumerable and illustrious Catholic predecessors in the chancellorship? Lastly, of the whole series of Protestant chancellors, we may ask, not so much in scorn as in melancholy, where are their monuments? If we asked their epitaphs, alas, we should read them in the curses of ruined suitors, sick at heart with "hope deferred," and crushed by worse than "law's delays."

The lives of Eldon and Hardwicke have been written within the last few years, forming the only important contributions to the biography of our modern chancellors. The "Life of Lord Langdale" is the life of a modern Master of the Rolls,[a] of course much of the same character as a modern chancellor.

---

[a] The Master of the Rolls was originally only one of the clerks in chancery, and is often in old records so described, long after their appointment to their present judicial office. (Foss, vol. iv. p. 327.)
During the time of William de Barstall, who was Master in 1371, the office of Keeper of the House of Converts (Domus Conversorum) in Chancery Lane was permanently annexed to the Mastership of the Rolls. This establishment was founded by Henry III. as an asylum for such Jews as embraced the Catholic religion. The charter grants 700 marks for their support, &c., until more largely provided for in lands and rents, and a certain place assigned them whereby they might be able to sustain themselves decently to the honour of God and the Blessed Virgin. The church of St. Dunstan's, Fleet Street, was assigned in 1237 as a further endowment for the house. (Foss, vol. iv. p. 323.)

The main merit of Lord Langdale—the only sign of greatness in him—was his declining the chancellorship, partly because he was convinced he should not be able to carry the reforms he saw to be required in the court. For this alone **his** memory deserves respect. There is little **else in** his **history or** character possessing any interest. His was the life **of a** hard-headed practising lawyer realising at last a great prize in the profession, with a certain stern honesty, which prevented him from clutching at the richest prize he could get. With the exception of that honesty, there is nothing in his history worthy of mention, at least by way of admiration. One could mention many things in his judicial career indicating that he zealously carried out the narrow-minded policy commenced by Hardwicke—a policy hostile to charity, and especially to "Popery;" and though he had a seat in the House of Lords for all the years he was on the bench, he never made any effort to alter the law on either subject; so doubtless he approved of it. Cases decided by Lord Langdale could be cited to shew how the Court of Chancery connives at robbery of charity, and which, without presuming to dispute that they were determined according to the modern idea of "equity," prove that this is an idea which would have revolted the minds of our Catholic ancestors.

We must, however, here close. Our object has been attained if we have conveyed a general idea of the contrast between the character of Catholic and Protestant chancellors, and the difference of their conduct and their decisions, above all, as to charity.

THE MARONITES AND DRUSES.[a]

[From the Dublin Review.]

In the marvellous fecundity of our modern literature, scarcely a day passes without bringing before us a notice of some foreign country, and a description, more or less interesting, and more or less elaborate, of the natives of other lands. This is almost a necessary consequence of the extension of our commerce, and the facility of publication which our literature affords. Yet, amid the many objects of attraction which are thus each day presented, we confess that none possess for us so great a charm as those that come from the eastern coast of the Mediterranean, and more especially the neighbourhood of the Holy Land. We have often escorted to the packet-office dear friends who were going to see the splendours of Paris, or to make their long-intended visit to the threshold of the Apostles, and as the steamer bore them away over the hissing waters, we have envied their good fortune only because they were somewhat nearer than ourselves to the land which, beyond all others, we should wish to see. It may be that our temperament is cast in a mould too antiquated for these times, and that the spirit which moves within us is more akin to that which filled men's minds six or seven centuries ago; but the truth is, that the sound of Syria, Palestine, and the Lebanon, have ever kindled within our breast hopes and aspirations, such as we have never felt even for Athens and for Rome. Had we lived in the days of Peter the Hermit, or Bernard of Clairveaux, we should have been the ready instrument of their

---

[a] 1. Notice Historique sur l'origine de la Nation Maronite et sur ses rapports avec la France, sur la Nation Druze et sur les diverses populations du Mont-Liban, par Monseigneur Nicholas Murad, Archevêque Maronite de Laodicée, et Représentant de sa nation près le Saint Siège.—*Paris*, 1844.

2. The Crescent and the Cross; or, Romance and Realities of Eastern Travel. By Elliot B. G. Warburton, Esq. 2 vols. 8vo. *London*, 1845.

3. The Modern Syrians, or Native Society in Damascus, Aleppo, and the Mountains of the Druses, from Notes made in those parts during the years 1841-2-3. By an Oriental Student. 1 vols *London*, 1844.

4. Annals of the Propagation of the Faith. *Dublin*, 1843-4.

zeal, and taken our stand, were it only with our staff and scallop-shell, among the foremost ranks of those who braved the perils of sea and land to lay them down for ever in the consecrated earth of Palestine. We have been often told, that were our fondest wish attained, the feelings that awaited us would be those of disappointment, that few vestiges of its former glory now remain, and that the sword of the Osmanlee, and it may be the visitation of God, have spread barrenness and desolation over those fields which once teemed with luxuriance when they were the heritage of God's chosen people. But the landmark is still upon the plain, and the cedar upon the hills; the rock has not changed its dwelling-place, nor the stream its bed; and the hallowed veneration of ages has perpetuated the memory of those scenes, and determined beyond cavilling the position of those events which have been such as never upon this earth were done. The Mounts of Olives and of Thabor, the towns of Bethlehem and of Nazareth, have never passed away, and "Time's decaying fingers" have not effaced the everlasting tops of Lebanon. No voice that ever spoke in the halls of Athens or the portico of the Parthenon, can be compared to that which so oft was heard on Sion; and even the blood that consecrated the Vatican must yield in holiness to that which purpled the hill of Calvary. It may be judged, therefore, with what interest we take up any work which promises to tell us of those hallowed scenes, and to supply, as far as printed pages can supply, the information we wish to possess; and how we hail with pleasure any tidings that come to us, as these volumes profess to come from the verdant slopes of Libanus, "from the top of Amana, from the top of Sanir and Hermon; from the dens of the lions, and the mountains of leopards."

These volumes contain a description of the present population and condition of the mountains of Libanus, which we bring before our readers the more willingly, that it enables us to continue our sketches of the Oriental Christians, which we have attempted, we hope not unsuccessfully, in the past numbers. The subject of our present notice, the Maronites, should be more interesting than any of the others, as being united to our own communion. It will be impossible to understand their history and condition, without including in our notice another people, their fellow-countrymen and neighbours, though widely differing from them in religion—the Druses.

In the beginning of the fifth century there lived on a mountain in Syria a holy anchoret called Maro. Like all the recluses of that beautiful climate he lived night and day in the open air. He had a small hut, indeed, covered with goatskins, but he seldom needed or had recourse to its protection. In his neighbourhood there was an old ruin, which had once served as a pagan temple, but Maro cleansed and purified it from the foul pollution it had contracted, and made thereof a small oratory, where he prayed and gave spiritual advice to those who sought it at his hands. There, too, he offered the holy sacrifice on being raised to the order of priesthood, to which his virtue entitled him. Theodoret speaks with admiration of his piety. The fathers of the Council of Chalcedon have honoured him with their eulogy, and from the place of his exile Chrysostom wrote to solicit the benefit of his prayers. Surely the man who could obtain such varied and such exalted testimony, must have been an eminent servant of God. After a long and edifying life his divine Master called him to himself, and cities and provinces contested the honour of having his remains among them. Three large monasteries were said to be built over his tomb, but it is now impossible to discover to which that honour is really due; though it has with much probability been assigned to that on the banks of the Orontes, between Apamea and Emesa, which long afterwards was known by his name. These monasteries contained many religious men who were instructed enough or fortunate enough to preserve the orthodox doctrine amid the religious controversies of the time, and in the Eutychian and Monothelite controversies they bowed to the decision of the Councils of Constantinople and Chalcedon. John, a religious of one of these communities, and thence called the Maronite, distinguished himself for his able and energetic defence of these decisions against the innovators of the time, and it is said that from him, still more than from the founder of his order, the national name of Maronite is derived.

Mosheim and several others have asserted that John was a follower of Macarius, bishop of Antioch, who, in the third Council of Constantinople, declared that he would rather suffer himself to be cut in pieces, than admit two wills in Christ. They also maintain, that it was to the opposition and armed resistance offered by the Syrians, at the instance of John, to the decrees of Constantine the Fourth against the Monothelites, that they owe the name of Mardaïti, which is applied to **them** by the writers of these times. This imputation is, however, indignantly rejected by the Maronites themselves, who are proud of what they believe the untarnished orthodoxy of their nation, and who revere the memory of John, as one who suffered and laboured much for the church **of God.** Pagi, Palma, and Benedict the XIV., have given the weight of their authority to this opinion, and Pius the VII. seems to us to have vindicated his sanctity by according the usual indulgences to those who would visit a church of the Maronites on the day that his festival is celebrated. With such authorities on our side, and being also disposed to look with suspicion on those from whom the imputation has come, we believe the origin of this word to have arisen from the contests with the incroaching power of the Saracens. In the seventh century, when the followers of Mahomet had got possession of Damascus, and the whole of Syria seemed about to yield to their victorious arms, the Christians who fled from the dread alternative left by the conquerors to the vanquished, took refuge in the defiles of Libanus, and inspired by the hardy courage of the mountaineers, and also encouraged by the security of their possessions, defied **the** power **of** the caliphs. **By union and perseverance** they not only succeeded in driving the Saracens from the hills, but pursued them with slaughter almost to the gates of Damascus. They compelled the caliph to sue for a truce of thirty years, and bind himself to pay a small tribute to the emperor, Constantine Pogonatus, their nominal sovereign. The mountains of Libanus were thus the first barrier to that tide of conquest which was pouring onward from the sands of the desert, and the successor of Mahomet was compelled for the first time in his career, to bend before the warriors of the mountains. A great number of these warriors were Christians who had retired from the plains of Syria, especially in the neighbourhood of Antioch, under the leadership of John the Maronite. He had been consecrated Bishop of Djebail, by the legate of the Pope at Antioch; and his episcopal rank as well as his personal merit, won for him considerable influence among his people. This influence he exercised to promote union and industry among them. They had a powerful and unscrupulous enemy ever ready to take advantage of their dissensions, on the one side, and from whom, if vanquished, they could hope for little mercy. They had, on the other hand, the degenerate and powerless princes of the tottering empire of Constantine. To rest their hopes on these would be about as wise, as for the gallant natives of Circassia in our own times, to trust for aid to the king of Persia against the legions of the Czar. The Maronite took his determination at once, to put not his trust in princes, but to rely upon the right-arms of his people and on God. He introduced order among them, inured them to military discipline, and provided them with leaders and the necessary instruments of warfare. The divisions of the caliphs themselves which took place after the death of Mahomet, enabled him to carry these changes into effect with more ease and regularity; and such was the success of their arms, that in a few years they became masters of all the mountains nearly as far south as Jerusalem. It was this determined and successful stand that obtained for them in reality the name of Mardaïti. They subsequently exchanged it for that of Maronites, a name which after the lapse of above a thousand years they still retain.

John had been the ablest leader and recognized head of the orthodox in the mountains. When these extended their power over the greatest part of Syria, and had possession of the sea coast from the mouth of the Orontes to the foot of Carmel, it was deemed advisable to invest their spiritual chief with a corresponding dignity, and John was accordingly appointed by Sergius the First, Patriarch of the Maronites.

This nomination took place in 686, in which year the Pope sent him the pallium. Shortly after the death of John, the Maronites were severely visited, not by the Saracens, but by the Byzantine emperor, Justinian the Second, who had the meanness to become their instrument in removing one of the noblest defences of his empire—a brave people upon its frontiers. In 685 the caliph concluded a treaty with Justinian, one of the conditions of which was, that Justinian should free the caliph from the incursions of the Maronites. The degrading condition was carried into effect by means more degrading still, for his Imperial Majesty had recourse to the dagger of the assassin, to rid him of his enemy; and in defiance of every principle of law and honour, the person he employed was his own ambassador. The too confiding chief received him into his house, and he availed himself of the rights of hospitality to plunge his knife into the breast of his unsuspecting host. Notwithstanding the atrocity of this vile deed, the murderer, by means which we cannot now discover, was able to persuade 12,000 men to remove from their habitations, and leave a free passage for the Mahometan arms. Justinian followed up his attempt by sending an army under Marcian and Maurice to lay waste their country. The great monastery of Hama was consigned to the flames, and its inmates, to the number of 500, massacred without mercy. The nation was only saved from total destruction by one of those revolutions which formed part of the daily history of the eastern empire. Justinian resolved to second the operations of his lieutenants in Syria, by a massacre in the capital, but was dethroned by a conspiracy of some disaffected nobles. His successor was differently disposed towards the Maronites, and with his permission they fell upon the army of Maurice, and cut them and their leader to pieces. From this period, and amid the troubles of the East, we lose sight of them, until, three or four centuries later, their history becomes connected with the Crusaders.

In the middle of the thirteenth century, Bandecar, Sultan of Egypt, got possession of the city of Antioch. His cruelty and fanaticism drove into exile the Catholics who had been living there for years, and with their patriarch Elias at their head, and accompanied by the clergy of the city, they took refuge among their brethren of Libanus. Simon, the patriarch of the Maronites, received them with kindness and hospitality. Hospitality has ever been a distinguishing characteristic of this people, and the Christians of Antioch soon found themselves at home among their brethren. They had provisions in abundance, enjoyed the shelter of their roofs, and some received lands to cultivate. Their naturalization became complete when they built and consecrated churches for themselves. The holy father manifested his gratitude for the kindness shown to his afflicted children, by appointing Simon Patriarch of Antioch on the death of Elias a few years after. This dignity was confirmed to the successors of Simon by the pontiffs of later times; and at this day the patriarch of the Maronites assumes the apostolic title, Patriarch of Antioch. He exercises jurisdiction over nine sees: viz. Aleppo, Damascus, Beyrout, Said, Eopoli, Djebail, Eden, Tripoli, and Cyprus. Besides these—the ordinaries, as we may term them, of the nation, there are six others—bishops "in partibus." Two of these are always in attendance on the patriarch, and perform the duties of vicars and assistants, one of the spiritual, the other of temporal department. A third usually resides at Rome, where he acts as the official representative of his nation. The remaining three are intrusted with the care of the more important convents and seminaries of Libanus. They are all nominated and consecrated by the patriarch, who is himself elected by his suffragans, though the election is not complete until it is sanctioned by the Pope.

"The nation of the Maronites," says the archbishop of Laodicea, "which at one period contained near a million of souls, does not amount at this day to more than 525,000, of whom 482,000 inhabit the valleys of Libanus.[a] The remainder are scattered over various parts of the Turkish empire; principally in Aleppo, Damascus, Cairo, Cyprus, a few parts of Africa and Asia, as also at Constantinople, all recognizing for their spiritual head, after the Pope, the patriarch residing in Libanus, where he has three different residences. This population can bring into the field from fifty to sixty thousand fighting men."

[a] Gerambe gives 200,000 only as the number of the Maronites of Libanus.

"The convents of monks and nuns amount to eighty-two. Those for monks, which are sixty-seven in number, contain 1410 religious. The remaining fifteen contain 330 nuns. All these houses have very rigorous constitutions approved of by the Holy See. There are, exclusive of convents, 356 churches in the country. They are served by 1205 priests, who all acknowledge the authority of their respective bishops. The laity also recognize and reverence the power of the clergy, and discharge with piety and exactness their Christian (sacramental) obligations, especially at the time of Easter. There are four public seminaries, each of which contains from twenty to twenty-five pupils. These are gratuitously instructed in the Arabic and Syriac languages, philosophy, dogmatic and moral theology. Those who study theology must, however, previously engage to embrace the ecclesiastical state, promise obedience to the patriarch, and devote themselves to the missions of the country. For some years past, the patriarch has been in the habit of appointing a particular spot, where he collects according to his own desire, and under a superior designated by him, zealous and enlightened priests, who go every year to preach in the different districts. This is called 'The National Mission.'

"The Maronites follow entirely the arrangements of the Roman Calendar, both as to the division of time, and the distribution of the festivals, excepting only a few that are peculiar to themselves. The Syriac is the language of the mass and divine office, but the gospel, epistle, and a few collects, are repeated aloud in the Arabic, that being the language understood by the people, the Syriac being to them what the Latin is to Catholics of Europe. The communion is administered in unleavened bread, according to the Roman rite, and, in fine, the priestly and pontifical ornaments and apparel are the same as those used by the Roman clergy."—*Notice Historique, page* 18.

This is, however, the discipline of the Maronites only of late years and since their liturgy and ritual were revised by the Holy See. Before that event took place, their rite differed in several particulars from that of the Latin Church, and their discipline was not very different from that of the Oriental Christians. The secular clergy were allowed to retain the wives they had married before receiving holy orders. The communion was administered in both kinds, to those who received it publicly in the church, but the sick were accustomed to receive it in one form alone. The host was a small round round loaf of the thickness of a finger, and about the size of a crown-piece. It has impressed upon it the mark of a seal, which part was consumed by the consecrating priest, and the rest being divided into small pieces, was put into the chalice and distributed to the communicants by means of a small spoon. Each village had its chapel and priest, like the villages of France and Italy; and each chapel had its bell, which, as it sent its sweet sounds across the hills on the sabbath morning, carried to every peasant's heart the assurance of his exemption from the evils of Moslem rule, for wherever the Turk has full dominion, this privilege is denied the Christian. It was for a similar reason that he cherished with an honourable pride the right of wearing a green turban, which, except in the fastnesses of his native mountains, would be an outrage on the religious prejudices of the Turk, to be atoned for only by the blood of the sacrilegious offender. For what could be more offensive to a true believer than that an infidel dog, as the Christian was contumeliously called, should arrogate to himself an honour which belonged only to the lineal descendants of the Prophet? Matters have, however, been much changed in the mountains of Libanus by the revolutions of late years.

The intimate relations which have connected the Maronites with the Holy See for the last few centuries, are, in great measure, owing to the establishment at Rome of a college for the youth of that nation. It was founded by the liberality of Gregory XIII. to whose enlightened policy the Christian world is indebted for so many other advantages, and at the suggestion of the Jesuits. It has had the good fortune of producing several men of more than ordinary excellence and distinction. We need only mention the name of Abraham Echellensis, and the three Assemani—Joseph, Stephen Evodius, and Lewis; whose services in the field of oriental literature have never been surpassed, and to whose influence with their people much of their present strong partiality for the Latin Communion is to be attributed. The services of Joseph Assemani deserve particular notice. This great man is better known to the world by his literary labours than by those which he endured in his missionary capacity. Yet were these of more than ordinary importance, for it was under his presidency that the first national council of the Maronite church was held. He was born at Tripoli, on the coast of Syria, in 1647, and was sent to the college of his nation in Rome at the early age of eight years. He was about to leave it in the ordinary course at the termination of his studies, when his proficiency in the Syriac tongue procured him a situation as sub-librarian in the Vatican. Some time after he was sent to Egypt, for the purpose of procuring valuable ancient manuscripts which were said to be still existing in a monastery of that country. His journey was eminently successful, and he returned to Rome, after an absence of a year and four months, with many rare valuable additions to the library. He was soon promoted to the post of prefect, or upper keeper of the Vatican library. To a man of Assemani's habits, whose ruling passion was a love of reading, this situation was the greatest boon he could receive; and if left to his own wishes he would have lived and died within its walls. But the church required his services, and he was called away to preside at the National Synod of the Maronites, which Clement XII. resolved to hold for the reformation of ecclesiastical discipline. His birth, his education, his national connexions, and the confidence that was reposed in his zeal and integrity, pointed him out as the individual best qualified for the purpose. His countrymen were already proud of his fame, and it was thought would yield a ready obedience to his suggestions. Clement gave him full legatine powers, and after several conferences with the patriarch and influential clergy, he succeeded in opening the council on the 30th of September, 1736. It was attended by eighteen bishops, of whom fourteen were Maronite, two Syrian, and two Armenian. The abbots of several monasteries were also present, together with a multitude of the priests and chief people of the country. The state of the Maronite church at this time may be judged of by the subjects that came under discussion. It was complained of by the more zealous and enlightened clergy, that dispensations to marry, excommunications, and even spiritual censures, were sold; that the Eucharist was not administered but in the monasteries; that the clergy, in some instances, married again after the death of their first wives; that the decoration of the churches and the support of the poor were neglected; that the patriarch arrogated to himself the exclusive right of blessing the holy oils, which he distributed to his suffragans and clergy at a fixed price; that in some congregations the Liturgy was performed in the Arabic—the vulgar tongue; and, finally, that the prudent reserve prescribed by the canons, was not observed by the clergy in their intercourse with the nuns. In the East, where females are wont to observe much more reserve towards the other sex, than in our times and country, it is possible that even a trifling deviation from the ordinary etiquette may have given much scandal. However, it is evident from the nature of these complaints, that the church of the Libanus, however it may have fallen away from its first fervour, had not swerved much from the line of essential discipline. The synod held eight meetings, and applied remedies to every one of these abuses. Some of the members were dissatisfied. Even the patriarch thought some of the provisions bore too hardly on his authority; but the legatine character of Assemani bore down all opposition, and at the close of the council he was empowered to embody its proceedings in a series of decrees; which have been since known as the decrees of the Council of Lebanon. The money which was placed at his disposal by the Holy See for such a contingency, enabled him to secure for these decrees the authority of the Turkish government. He also, during his stay in Syria, provided in a spirit of enlightened policy, which was much in advance of his times, for the education of the humbler classes, by establishing schools, which the superior clergy were to support, and where the poor would receive instruction gratuitously. After the successful termination of the great business of his mission, he returned to Rome. Yet, amid the multiplicity of his other avocations, he was not unmindful of the darling passion of his life, and he brought with him from the convents of Syria a large collection of MSS., 2,000 coins and medals, and a curious tablet, which contained the authentic and original record of various civil privileges given to the Egyptians by the Emperor Diocletian. Notwithstanding the success which attended this mission, he had no sooner left the country than, with the inconsistency which has ever marked the eastern churches, the decrees of the synod began to meet with opposition. The patriarch himself was dissatisfied with its enactments. He sent two deputies to Rome, to oppose their confirmation; but their remonstrances were disregarded, and the proceedings were fully and publicly confirmed and ratified by Benedict XIV. on the 14th of September, 1741. This great pontiff availed himself of the opportunity which presented itself, to give his unqualified approbation to the conduct of the legate, and to censure at the same time the conduct of his opponents. This synod exercised a very beneficial influence over the eastern churches, and its decrees have been ever since recognized as the ground-work of the discipline of the Maronites. Assemani lived near thirty years after the conclusion of the synod. They were all spent amid his books and papers, and the mere list of the works published and unpublished in which he was engaged, are, in themselves, enough to fill a good-sized volume.[a]

Before we refer to the present political condition of the Maronites, we must say a word or two about the other inhahabitants of the Lebanon—the Druses and Montualis. In language, government, and mode of life, the three nations are perfectly identified, but they differ widely in religion. With respect to the Montualis, it is enough to the say, that they are Mahometans of the sect of Ali, which is divided from the sect of Omar by as theological an hatred, and, perhaps, by something more, as any two sects are among ourselves. They are computed by the Maronite archbishop to amount to about 800 souls, while the Père Gerambe in his pilgrimage estimates them at 80,000. Perhaps this is a misprint, but it is clear that the first is the more likely computation. They reside at the foot of Libanus to the east, and are almost the only occupants of the valley of Baalbeck. The Druses merit more detailed consideration. In the year 996, which was the 386th of the Hegira, Hakem, the third caliph of the dynasty of the Fatemites, ascended the throne of Egypt. He was only eleven years old. Youth and inexperience, ignorance of the

---

[a] It is said that in the libraries of Rome, besides his printed books, there are still extant enough to fill an hundred volumes in Assemani's own handwriting. A fire which broke out on the 30th of August, 1768, within a year after his death, in the appartments in the Vatican, which had been occupied by him, and were then occupied by his nephew, destroyed whole volumes of his papers ready for the press. Many of the works he published are of vast extent, as, viz. the "Bibliotheca Orientalis," the "Kalendaria," but some were so comprehensive, that no individual industry however great, and no life however long, could possibly complete them.

world, which is almost the necessary result of childhood spent in an oriental harem, and probably the adulation of his obsequious court, soon produced their fruits, and the young caliph began to astonish not a little the good people of Cairo by the eccentricities of his conduct. Perhaps his mind was never of the soundest description, and it was then and since suspected, that he laboured under insanity. He directed, to the horror of the true believers, curses to be publicly uttered against the memory of the first followers of Mahomet in the mosques at the hours of prayer. In a few days he consented to revoke the order. He compelled the Christians and Jews to turn Mahometans, under pain of death, but in a few days he revoked this **edict** also. He made **it a** capital **crime** to manufacture slippers for women, intending, **by** this means, to confine them entirely to their own houses. He would not permit a female on any business, however pressing, to appear in the public streets. Like his imperial prototype among the Cæsars, he burned one half of the capital for his amusement, and to secure the good will of the soldiery, he permitted them to pillage the other. He completed the climax of his absurdities by prohibiting the ordinary and prescribed devotions of the Moslem, and proclaiming that he himself was God. We know not to what convulsions these innovations would have given rise, if the career of Hakem had not been cut short by the fears of an only sister. The tyrant threatened her with a jury of matrons. Furious at the meditated indignity, or afraid of its probable results, she determined to anticipate the blow, and had him privately assassinated, and buried outside the town by some of her own trusty attendants. The followers of Hakem—for what fanatic has not had followers—amounted to about 1600, according to a census taken by him before his death, and were under the guidance of several of his agents, **who pretended to the gift of prophecy. As no** one attempted to account for his disappearance, they gave out that Hakem was gone up to heaven, and that he would soon return to unite and console his afflicted disciples. One of these, Mohammed-ben-Ismael, propagated his opinion with zeal and success throughout Syria and Palestine, especially in the neighbourhood of the sea coast, and being persecuted by the local governors, took refuge with his followers in Libanus. There they still maintain their tenets unmolested by religious persecution. The name of Druse, by which they are popularly known, is derived from El Dorzo, one of the surnames of Mohammed.[a]

From the period of their occupation of the mountains until the beginning of the sixteenth century, they remained almost unknown. The only proofs of their existence and activity we find, are some occasional battles with the Turks, and some desultory skirmishing upon the flanks of the crusaders. About the close of that century, however, they acquired considerable distinction by their success against the troops of Selim and the Second Soliman. After a gallant struggle, however, their stubborn valour had to give way to the superior and overwhelming numbers sent against them by Amurath the Third. Ibrahim Pacha, the victorious general, penetrated the defiles of the mountains, and, aided by their domestic dissensions, succeeded in extorting a contribution of one million of piastres, and imposed a tribute which has continued to the present time. Instead of many independent chieftains, to facilitate the collection of the tribute, and exercise some direct control, he vested the supreme power in one person, and, by this mistaken policy, rendered his tenure of their allegiance more precarious and uncertain; for, by consolidating its civil and military resources, he made the power of the nation more available and effective. This result was soon perceived when the Emir Fakardin attained supremacy, and brought the united power of the Druses to bear upon the Turks. He not only got possession of what his people had lost in the war with Ibrahim, but made himself successively master of Beyrout, Said, Baalbeck, and extended his conquests to the plain of

---

[a] It was rather a fanciful conjecture to derive this name from a certain Count de Dreux, who was supposed to have settled in the Libanus with a party of Crusaders. Deprived of all intercourse with the west by the encroachment of Saracens, their descendants were supposed to have become the Druses of the present day. It is scarcely necessary to say that this conjecture is now universally rejected, for the name is found in the itinerary of Benjamin of Tudela, who travelled before the time of the Crusades.

Ajalon. But the Porte, becoming alarmed at his aggressions, concerted a simultaneous attack, and by forces sufficiently numerous to crush his power, it was thought, for ever. Fakardin took refuge in Italy, where he was favourably received at the court of Florence, and left his son Ali to abide the storm, which he was afraid to meet in person. Victory attended the sword of the young Emir, and, after an absence of nine years, the father returned to take possession once more of the power which was preserved from destruction by the valour of the son. He brought with him from the classic soil of Italy, a love for the fine arts. Splendid baths, sumptuous villas, and ornamented pleasure-grounds, began to adorn the verdant slopes of Libanus, and, in utter defiance of the precepts of the Koran, painting and sculpture began to shed their beauties upon their walls. But even Art cannot call its fair creations into existence, but where it uses the magic wand of gold, and in the sunny sky of Syria gold was only to be had from the sweat and toil of the hardy tillers of the soil. Men soon found that they had a double tax to pay, and therefore more labour to undergo, and they soon murmured and complained. From complaint to disaffection, from disaffection to rebellion, the steps are few, and the transition easy, when men have arms in their hands, and have from their earliest years been taught to love liberty and fight against the tyranny of the rulers. The neighbouring pachas became jealous of his splendour, and the sultan himself was rendered distrustful of his loyalty. Against such odds it was hard to succeed. Ali, whose sword had once averted ruin, was struck down in the heat of a battle he had almost won, and the aged father, dragged from his lurking-place in the mountains, was taken prisoner to Constantinople, where he was strangled by the orders of Amurath, about the year **1631**.

After the death of Fakardin, the principality of the Libanus continued nominally in his descendants, but really in the pachas of Acre and Damascus. His family became extinct about the beginning of the last century, and that of Shehab, which was united to it by marriage, succeeded to the supreme power. The members of this family have been the princes of

Libanus for more than 140 years, and have been struggling with various success against the enmity, open or insidious, of the Turkish authorities. Melhem, who died in 1759, retrieved in some measure, the fallen fortunes of his house, and extended his power over almost all the territory that was possessed by Fakardin. He was succeeded by Mansour, and afterwards by Joussef. The Emir Beschir, whose name must be familiar to most of our readers, is the sixth in regular succession of the family of Shehab. When Joussef became prince of Libanus, Beschir was only in his seventh year. The Emir perceiving in him a more than ordinary share of talent, had him brought up with care, and provided him with all the advantages which his position and future prospects required. In 1784, he accompanied his patron in the expedition against the sanguinary Djezzar, pacha of Acre. He was then only twenty-one years of age, and narrowly escaped with his life from the town of Ryde, of which his own party had just got possession. The Druses were compelled to evacuate the town, and the young Beschir, finding himself surrounded by the enemy, rode at full gallop towards a wall, from which he leaped while the balls were whizzing around him. He received no injury, but the horse was killed. On his return to Libanus, he was employed by Joussef in the financial department of the government. Ambition soon began to take possession of his mind. He ingratiated himself with the principal families, and particularly gained the goodwill of Sheik Beschir, of the powerful family of Kansar. Joussef finding himself unable to resist the power of Djezzar, resigned in favour of Beschir. He wished to keep the ruling power in his own immediate family, and hoped, perhaps, to be able to resume it at some more convenient opportunity. Nor was his hope altogether vain. The avaricious pacha was tempted by a large sum of money to invest him once more with the symbol of authority, but after a short tenure he was again deposed, when his youthful competitor bid a still larger sum. But again —for what will not a lust of power lead men to perpetrate?— he returned to the vile work of corruption, and again was defeated by means more execrable than even he himself purposed to employ.

Beschir promised 4000 pieces, if Joussef were put to death: and the unfortunate emir soon made his appearance for the last time in public. He was hung, together with his minister, Gandour Honry, over the principal gate of Acre. Djezzar affected to disclaim the deed. It was too atrocious even for him. The officer through whom the business was transacted, was drowned by the orders of his ungrateful master, together with all his family; and his property, which was considerable, was added to the blood-money which Djezzar had already received. But the monster wished for more, and Beshir was cast into prison until he should pay a heavy ransom. He was indebted for his liberation from a captivity of twenty months, to the insinuating address of a lady who took a special interest in his welfare, and who tried her powers of fascination on the avaricious pacha. When restored to liberty, he determined to regain his influence in the mountains; and it is not necessary for us here to enter into the full detail of the various measures by which he gained his end. He employed with little scruple or hesitation the ordinary means employed in his time and country. Bribery, intimidation, deception, were all had recourse to. Several of his own immediate relatives were strangled, or for ever deprived of sight, for having opposed, or refused to aid, his advancement. His power was considerably strengthened by his marriage with the widow of a Turkish prince, whom he had himself caused to be slain a few years before. She brought him an immense fortune. In 1804, when Bonaparte laid siege to Acre, he requested Beschir to espouse his cause, and assist him in gaining possession of the town. But the emir, like a man of prudence, replied, that however well disposed he might be, he could not think of joining the French army until it had possession of Acre. Napoleon pretended to be satisfied with his apology, and made him a present of a handsome musket. The events of his later years we shall give in the words of the author of the "Modern Syrians." Our notice would become a book, were we to describe with any minuteness the events in which Besehir has been engaged for more than fifty years:

"Every one of the seven nobles who govern the corresponding number of districts in the mountains of the Druses, may be compared to what the chiefs of a Highland clan were at the beginning of the last century, with a loose allegiance to the sovereign, and arbitrary power over the vassals. Two of these nobles are emirs, (Reslen and Belemma). The other five, (Djonbelat, Abou-Neked, Amad, Talhook, and Abd-el-Malek), are denominated Sheiks, which literally means elder. The Prince of Mount Lebanon occupied a middle station, between these chiefs and the Turkish government. The subordinate houses were generally in a state of feud with each other, and divided into two factions—the Djonbelat and the Yesbeky. In days of yore, when the preponderance of the Druses over the Christian population was absolute, the immigration of Christians for the cultivation of land was much encouraged. The Christians took to the plough and reaping-hook: the Druses stuck to the sword. While the Christians were fruitful and increasing their numbers, the increase of the Druses was prevented by their deadly feuds. Hence we see, that now in all the Druse Mokettas, except Shouf, the Christians form the majority. This in itself was an immense revolution, which was completed by the old Emir Beshir. This crafty man forsook Islamism, turned Maronite, and persuaded the Emirs of Meten (the house of Belemma), with which alone the Shehabs intermarry, also to embrace Christianity, and by his talents and position formed a party which completely overturned the Druse power.

"His great opponent—I might almost say his rival—was the Sheik Beshir Djonbelat, the wealthiest of the Druses. Burkhardt, who visited the Druse country in 1811, speaks of him thus:—'The Djonbelat now carry every thing with a high hand. Their Chief, El Sheik Beshir, is the richest and shrewdest man in the mountain. Besides his personal property, which is very considerable, no affair of consequence is concluded without his interest being courted, and duly paid for. His annual income amounts to about two thousand purses, or fifty thousands pounds sterling. The whole province of Shouf is under his command, and he is in partnership with almost all the Druses who have landed property there. The greater part of the district of Djesin is his own property, and he permits no one to obtain property there, while he increases his own estates yearly, and thus continually augments his power. The Emir Beshir can do nothing important without the consent of Sheik Beshir, with whom he is obliged to share all the contributions which he extorts from the mountaineers.' To counteract this influence, the Emir Beshir sought to develope the power of the Maronites, and had a secret understanding with the Pacha of Acre, in order to get the Djonbelat crushed at the first convenient opportunity. The Sheik Beshir Djonbelat, seeing the position to which the ascendancy of the Emir was likely to reduce his house and his nation, raised the standard of rebellion, was defeated, fled to Hauran, and was subsequently beheaded at Acre. A large proportion of his land was seized by the Emir Beshir, his house at Mokhtara was pulled down, and the marbles that shone in its splendid halls now adorn the palace of the Emir of Betedein. The blow dealt by him broke the back of the Druse power, but the limbs were spared, and the houses of Talhook and Abd-el-Malek, were conciliated. A numerous family of Shouf, called Hamady, who lived in Bahleen, were made sheiks of that district, and affairs went pretty smoothly on until the Egyptian invasion. The Emir Beshir declared for Mehemet Ali, the Druses for the Sultan; and after the battle of Homs and Beilan, several Druse chiefs were exiled to Egypt. The expulsion of Ibrahim Pacha from Syria, in 1840, enabled those exiled Druse Sheiks to return to their homes. Namen, Said, and Ismael Djonbelat, on the death of their father, the late Sheik Beshir Djonbelat, wandered about Turkey, and sometimes lived at Saloniki, sometimes at Constantinople, Broussa, and Smyrna, on an allowance from the Porte, which was gradually diminished, and at last settled in Egypt.

Mehemet Ali, on the news of the success of the British fleet, and the defection of the Emir Beshir, as a desperate venture, invested Sheik Naman, Djonbelat, Sheik Nassif Abou-Neked, and Sheik Hattar Amad, with the dignity of Egyptian Beys, and said, that whoever distinguished himself most in serving his cause should be made prince of the mountain. The Druse Sheiks, too happy to get an opportunity of returning to Syria, made those usual professions of attachment in which Orientals deal so largely, and were immediately sent across the Desert. However, on arriving at Jaffa, finding that Ibrahim had been completely defeated, they swam with the stream, and paid their respects to the new Emir Beshir. This man, endowed with considerable personal courage, was, on the other hand, full of pride and prejudice, and although characterised by a degree of honesty and uprightness, rare in the East, he was altogether destitute of the tact essential to a governor, whose duties are rather civil than military. Beshir received them so badly, that they were thoroughly disgusted. This was a most indiscreet proceeding; for the influential position they occupied, aided by the discipline and secrecy which binds the Druse nation, demanded, at the least, considerable delicacy of management. When the Emir Beshir returned to Mount Lebanon, after the termination of the campaign, and the evacuation of Syria by Ibrahim Pacha, he found that he had no party whatever. The Druse Sheiks were more than consoled for the coolness of their prince, by the enthusiastic reception they met from their own nation. In all the Druse districts the authority of the Emir Beshir was disregarded, and replaced by that of the Sheiks. One would suppose that being a Maronite by religion, he might have made up for it by influence in the Maronite districts of the North. But the Sheiks there were equally anxious to raise themselves, and abase the house of Shehab, while the principal rival of the Emir Beshir was the Maronite Patriarch, whom the bishops were anxious to bring forward, not only as *spiritual*, but as *temporal* Pope of Mount Lebanon. This pretension was resisted by the Druse chiefs as an invasion of their prerogatives. Hence the bloody feud between these two nations, which, fermented by the Porte, ended in the subjugation of both."—*Modern Syrians*, p. 102.

The length of this extract will be pardoned for the important information it contains. It imparts to us the secret of these disturbances which have been agitating the Libanus for the last three years [a], and must inevitably end in the utter prostration of one of the contending parties. We were willing to hope that the numbers of the Maronites, [b] and the strength

---

[a] Written in 1845.
[b] The "Notice Historique" estimates the Maronites, as we have before stated, at 482,500; the Druses, at 18,000. Gerambe gives their relative numbers to be: Maronites, 200,000; Druses, 100,000. We cannot reconcile this discrepancy.

which their party must receive from the leadership of the Emir, and the accessions which he brought in his own family, would have inclined the balance in their favour; but on the side of the Druses there were valour, discipline, secrecy of council, and, above all, unanimity of purpose. Perhaps, we should have included, as the most important item in the enumeration, the length of their purses.* After a desperate conflict of several months, marked by massacre, pillage, and conflagration, the usual consequences of civil strife, and when both parties were weakened to the satisfaction of the Turkish government, it, was thought advisable to terminate the war between them. This cessation was owing, in a great measure, to the kind influence of the British consul at Beyrout, who, at the risk of his life, penetrated into the defiles which were the scene of conflict, and succeeded in obtaining a temporary truce previous to the settlement of their differences. A congress was appointed to be held at Beyrout. Before it was held, however, the Druses kept their hands in practice by burning 4000 houses, killing 700 of the Maronites, and taking away with them immense booty, not only of money and arms, but even clothes and furniture. It is no wonder, therefore, that when the Seraskier Mustapha Pacha landed at Beyrout, as imperial commissioner from the capital, to arrange the differences between them, they should be inspired with the most cheering hopes. They knew with whom they had to deal, and that when under any civilized government, they would be visited with the severest vengeance, they calculated with confidence on obtaining from the commissioner not merely forgiveness, but reward. It was but natural, too, that the hearts of the poor Maronites should be stricken with dismay.

"In my evening walks," says the author of the Modern Syrians, "might be seen now and then some bishop or abbot, pale and haggard, riding into town on his sorry mule, accompanied by some half-starved lay-brother as a servant; while ever and anon on the road to the pines

---

* Another great advantage which the Druses had over their rivals consisted in the possession of arms. When the troops of Mehemet Ali invaded Syria, the Maronites, with the advice of their patriarch, surrendered their arms to the Egyptian General. The Druses, more obstinate, or less confiding, refused to do so. The issue proved that they were right, and in the day of conflict they had, of course, considerably the advantage.

which led to the Druse country, one met a sheik surrounded by his men joyfully singing their war song. The Christians flitter about the streets, long-visaged and poverty-struck. The Shieks paid their way 'like gentlemen.' Hamoud Aboo Neked, when he went to the vizier, gave the men who brought in coffee, a backshish of 500 piastres. In fact, the Christians being squeezed, and the Druses un-squeezed, no doubt existed of the pending suits being terminated according to the must approved rules of Turkish justice. In aid of the long purses of the Druses came the force of their nationality, their perfect union, fathomless cunning, and profound secresy. No one knew what passed at their meetings, while the councils of the Christians became the talk of the whole town, almost before the members had risen from their seats. Mustapha Pacha extracted a large bribe from the Druses, deposed the Emir Beshir, and appointed Omar Pacha, an Austrian renegade, in his place. The Emir was then shipped off for Constantinople."
— Page 127.

After the departure of Emir Beschir, or rather his transportation, for such it really was, and notwithstanding the attempt made to restore tranquillity, the Lebanon continued in a disturbed and unsatisfactory condition. During the negociations relative to the settlement of the Syrian question, the restoration of the Shehab family to the principality of Lebanon formed a prominent and an important topic of discussion. It was opposed by the Porte on the grounds, that Emir Beshir and the Shehab family, being Maronites, could not obtain the full confidence of the Turkish government. If a war broke out between it and any Christian state, it was thought that a Christian prince of Lebanon would be likely to give his co-religionists a free access to these mountain-strongholds, which must ever be the key of Syria. On the other hand, the four European powers were dissatisfied with the manner in which this province had been hitherto governed. In the autumn of 1842, the Druses were goaded into rebellion by the bigotry, tyranny, and bad faith of Mustapha Pacha, who was in consequence recalled, and Assad Pacha, a man of good character, appointed in his stead. The rebellion was quelled only by some vigorous and rapid movements of the Albanian troops. A strong force was conveyed by night from Beyrout to Sidon in steamers sent from Constantinople for the purpose, and fell upon their rear, while Omar Pacha sallied from Betedein where he was besieged, attacked and destroyed Mohtara, the family-seat of the Djonbelats. The Turkish government seeing the unsatisfactory condition of the existing arrangements, consented to a new settlement; and, without restoring Beshir, permitted the Maronites to be governed by a ruler of their own nation; and the Druses, also, to have a similar privilege. The two chiefs were to be subject to the Mushir, or governor, of the now-united Pashalics of Tripoli and Sidon, who has fixed his residence at Beyrout.

The disordered state of Syria, after this evacuation by the troops of Ibrahim, and before the authority of the Porte was fully recognized, was not to be corrected in a day. The entire country was overrun by the Albanian and Turkish soldiery. In the hour of battle they proved cowards, but, as is always the case, they proved themselves ruffians of the darkest dye towards the helpless natives of the country, and the Christian population had no claim on the forbearance of fanatical miscreants who thought it an act of virtue to harass and insult them.

The animosity of the Druses and Maronites, which had been inflamed by civil war and by excesses, the memory of which was still fresh, and the monuments of which were each day before their eyes, has not been yet allayed, and it is only a few days since we saw by the papers, that it was determined to disarm the entire Christian population, and place them henceforward under the authority of the Druses. Thus matters stand at the present moment. What time may yet produce, or what may be their future condition, only the eye of prophecy would be able to determine. The following extract from the "Modern Syrians" will illustrate the state of the Lebanon during the contest, and introduce us to some of the individuals whom we have already alluded to in this notice. It is sad to find, that men's evil passions should disfigure what God made so fair and beautiful, and leave their revolting impression on the loveliest scenery of the earth! Dair-el-Kamar is one of the principal towns of the mountain district, and only a very short distance from Betedein, the residence of Emir Beshir. The population is principally Maronite.

"We now ascended the mountains which led directly to Dair-el-Kamar. Wearily did we toil up another pass, and after emerging from a fig-plantation, we were rewarded with a glorious view of the Mediterranean. The pleasure which one derives from the expanse of azure seen from the heights of Lebanon, if the atmosphere be clear, is so real, that I involuntarily drew up, and my heart would have dilated, had not a dark object caused me quickly to turn about my head and look in the opposite direction. Slowly and majestically rose a thick black column of smoke, to a height far above all surrounding objects, from two considerable villages on the slope of the opposite mountains of Shouf. All my life a peaceable citizen, I saw for the first time the horrors of warfare. Trotting a short way further on, my eyes caught Dair-el-Kamar; but what a picture of desolation it presented, compared with the peaceful and prosperous aspect under which I had seen it a month before! The whole of the lower part of the town, next the Beyrout road, was black, ruinous, and roofless, and a constant fire of musketry was kept up between the parapet of the palace and the upper parts of the town, which were occupied by the Druses. We now entered the town, and were received by the Druses with yells of exultation on their sad victory, and the wildest demonstrations of welcome; but the whole scene and its component objects, were of too horrible a character to admit of making any response which could be interpreted into sympathy with their feelings: their cheers and yells were received in solemn silence. Two men in the middle of the road executed a sort of a Highland fling, and a couple of human heads on the points of pikes were stuck in the wall, eighteen or twenty heads were piled up in a corner, and the horned [a] and veiled women executed the singular trill, which is considered an incitement to bravery. Just at this moment a shot from the Christians struck a great brawny Druze, who rolled down his full length, and several persons cried out, advising the consul-general to keep within the cover of the houses. We turned back a few yards, and at the request of the cadi entered a house, which was in a few minutes thronged with visitors. Next me sat a Christian emir, from the Metten, who was in 'a peculiar position.' Never anticipating the breaking out of civil war, he had come to Dair-el-Kamar, to arrange with the Emir Beshir the preliminaries of a treaty of marriage with his daughter, or niece; and thus found himself in the midst of the Druses, who detained him in polite arrest, out of deference to his rank. Cheers and vociferations outside drew us out to the terrace, and I beheld Sheik Nassif Abou Neked, the commander-in-chief of the Druses, coming down to us. Nothing could exceed the savage enthusiasm with which the people received him. It was said, that he and his men had that morning killed eighty Christians. Sheik Naman Djonbelat, who during all these scenes had remained passive at his own residence, at Mokhtara, followed in about an half hour. The contrast which the demeanour of these men presented did not escape me. Sheik Nassif, the head of the Druse war party, was dressed in Egyptian clothes, of a brown colour, very fully embroidered with black braid, and red shoes. Middle sized, well proportioned, aged about forty. He was in the prime of activity, and his step was remarkably light and springy. Sheik Naman Djonbelat, small in stature, refined in features, but oblique in vision, age about eight-and-twenty, was dressed in dark-green clothes, and yellow shoes. The peace-loving Naman was agitated; a cambric handkerchief, bordered with gold, which he held in his hand, was in perpetual motion from his excitement. This was certainly a critical juncture for him;

---

[a] The females of the Lebanon, both Maronite and Druse, wear a singular ornament projecting from the summit of the head. It is generally of silver, and sometimes near twenty inches in length. It has the appearance of a horn growing out of the head.

as he could not foresee whether death, exile, or confiscation, or peaceable enjoyment of his large property, would be the upshot of these affairs—a severe trial, it must be admitted, for the nerves of any man. With his usual tact, he called out, 'Where is Sheik Nassif?' and on perceiving him, they kissed each other on both cheeks.

"After a short parley, the Pacha and the Sheiks agreed to the proposal of the British consul-general, that a flag of truce should be rigged out, and sent to the Emir Beshir, with a letter. Accordingly a Turkish trumpeter was entrusted with the flag and letter. He mounted his horse, and emerging from the Druse quarter crossed the Meidan. In half an hour a most pacific answer was received, and we mounted our horses. At the verge of the Meidan lay the dead body of the Druse that we had seen killed. He lay on his back; the countenance showed he had died in pain; his turban was rolled off his head, a long tuft of hair streamed from the crown of his scalp, and more than an hour's exposure to the sun had swelled up his body to an immense size. We now passed through what had been the bazaar. The horses picked a road through a grey mineral dust, like dirty snow; for the action of the heat had completely pulverized the stone. The dust was mixed with charcoal, and my horse, as he occasionally put his foot into this mass, started as if he had trodden on quick-lime. All around was blackness and ruin, where, but a month before, I had seen rows of well-furnished shops, and many groups of buyers and sellers. In the great square, or market-place, not a soul was to be seen. In a narrow street abutting in it, was a barricade of large stones, breast-high; behind which was a picquet of half a dozen men. The gate of the Seraglio being barricaded inside and outside, we effected our entrance by a postern door, and the scene which the court-yard presented baffles all description. Three-fourths of the Christian families had taken refuge here, and in the neighbouring convent; so that three thousand men, women, children, horses, and mules, were all crammed together. We now ascended a long narrow staircase, to the reception room of Emir Beshir, an apartment of noble proportions, but plainly furnished, with a mat and a divan of red cloth running round the walls. The Emir sat at the side. He was dressed in a crimson suit, and the fold of his turban was a cashmere shawl of the finest texture. His *nishan*, or decoration, hung from his neck, and a handsome diamond-hilted dagger was stuck in his girdle. His greeting was cordial, and, far from being dejected, he appeared to possess a degree of equanimity scarcely to be looked for under such melancholy circumstances. After reposing an hour or so, I descended with some of the officers to look about me. I met many of my acquaintances, but scarcely recognized them. This was the fourth day since the first attack, and three dreadful vigils had rendered pale, hollow-eyed, and hollow-cheeked, men whom I had seen a few days before with ruddy mountain complexions. Others I had known had been killed or wounded. Ibrahim, the principal merchant of the town, was one of the first to relate his doleful tale. I, myself, had known this man living in comparative affluence, living in a handsome new-built house, and surrounded with a numerous family and servants. He had lent sums at interest in various parts of Lebanon. Thus his debts have been wiped out with a vengeance. To get him out of the house, the Druse caused some one to say that his son Halil was lying wounded at the bake-house: he proceeded thither, but found this was a pretext. When he returned home, he found his house plundered, his brother lying dead, and in the same evening his house was burnt. At sunset we all dined with the Emir Beshir, in the Arab style; that is to say, we all squatted down to a large circular tray, and eat with our fingers of sundry preparations of mutton, fowl, and vegetables. Next morning, as early as seven o'clock, his highness was taking his walk in the verandah, and chatting with the attendants. This would have been a perilous promenade twenty-four hours sooner. To give an idea of the danger in which the emir had been, I may mention, that eighteen bullet marks were perceptible on the end wall of the Ckaa, or divan of reception. The superior of the Maronites having presented his respects to the consul-general, the latter gentleman proceeded to the convent of this sect, which is a tolerably spacious building adjoining the Seraglio, and, along with another massive keep, formed the stronghold of the Christians. We passed down through a cut-throat sort of staircase, into the passage between these two buildings, protected by the only bazzar in the town left unburnt by the Druses, and on the other by the smoking terraces of the ground, between the town and the bottom of the ravine. Eighty Christian bodies had been buried hurriedly in these terraces, during the three days previous; and I had not emerged two yards from the postern before I was compelled to put my handkerchief to my nose. The olfactory and visual nerves were put to an equally severe test on entering the convent; for here were congregated, or crammed, I should rather say, the poor and the wounded. In the Seraglio it was painful to see families I had known living in comfortable houses, stowed away into little rooms; but here were dozens of families dwelling in the open court-yard and passages of the convent. Women quarrelling about the right to sleep upon a piece of pavement, or to sit on a step, and the screams of the children mingled with the cries of the wounded.

A truce having been effected through Eyoub Pacha and the British consul-general, many of the Christians visited their houses on this evening, and we were also enabled to move about the town. Our first visit was paid to a family that, having barricaded their doors, defended themselves with the greatest bravery during the three days, and killed about forty Druses. The barricades not having been yet removed, we were admitted by one of those secret passages, in the proper construction of which consists the great art of an Oriental architect. Having first scrambled on the top of an outhouse, we entered a hole in the wall, about three feet square, and thus gained, after various ascents, turnings, and windings, the interior of the house: the last door we passed through was, when viewed from the room, in the guise of a cupboard regularly furnished with shelves. The house formed two sides of a court-yard, paved with marble, and adorned with a fountain, which had proved of signal utility in the hour of need; since, but for the water, they must have surrendered at discretion. A pleasing variety of overgreens covered the other two sides of the court-yard, formed by a high wall, pierced by doors which had been broken open; but so vigorously had the family kept up the fire from the windows, which served as embrasures, that the Druses were obliged to give up the attempt after several attacks. The youngest son, a fine intelligent boy, of twelve or thirteen years of age, had been at first exempted from service, and placed among the women, but he slung on a cartridge-box, seized a musket, and kept up a brisk fire to the last. The old lady of the house, who still retained traces of considerable beauty, far from being shaken by such a severe trial, was full of spirits and determination, and far from alluding to the extreme danger in which they had been placed, she only complained of the harassing watches which they had been obliged to keep day and night. But I have said enough. Such was Dair-el-Kamar in October, 1841."—*Modern Syrians, p.* 115.

From such scenes as these may God in his mercy preserve our country! What political improvements could recompense a nation for such a dread and fearful visitation, as that which has been just described, and which took place among our own fellow-christians, at the very time perhaps that we ourselves were whiling away the days of our existence, as if pain, and sorrow, and calamity, were nowhere upon the earth? It is well to talk of the glorious pomp and circumstance of war while it is at a distance from us, and while we see only its dazzling mimicry; but when the dread and horrible calamities which ever follow in its train are displayed before us, and when we contemplate the possibility of these being brought home to our own doors, and bursting upon the heads of those most dear to us, the very contemplation of such a contingency makes our blood run cold. The following extract, describing the customs, religious and social, of the Druses, we have been obliged to abridge from the interesting pages before us:—

"The Druses are divided into two classes—the Akkals and the Djahils. Akkal means wise, and Djahil means ignorant; that is to say, the former are the individuals initiated in the mysteries of the Druse religion, the latter uninitiated. This distinction is altogether irrespective of temporal rank or wealth; for every Druse, whether male or female, may pass from the uninitiated to the initiated state, on making certain declarations, and renouncing the indulgences permitted to the Djahils. It is not uncommon to see a drunken, lying Djahil, become all at once an abstemious and veracious Akkal. The Djahils, as might be expected, form the great majority of the nation. No religious duties are incumbent on the Djahil, but he knows the leading features of the religion, such as the transmigration of souls, &c. The secret signs of recognition are known to the Djahil as well as to the Akkal. He eats, drinks, and dresses as he pleases. The Akkals are the depositories of the mysteries of the religion. They wear a round white untwisted turban, and are not allowed to dress in embroidered or fanciful apparel; but when in Damascus or Beyrout they may do so, that they may not be distinguished from the Moslems. The Akkal neither smokes tobacco, nor drinks wine or spirits, nor does he eat with, nor share in the festivities of, the Djahils. Naman Djonbelat, when he became an Akkal, procured permission to continue to smoke tobacco; but such dispensations are rare. The Akkal never pronounces an obscene word, nor does he swear on any account, or tell a falsehood. Profound respect and precedence is entertained and accorded to them, but if they do not adhere to their vows, they are excommunicated and become outcasts. The hour of meeting for religious purposes is on Friday evening, immediately after dusk. The temples are generally structures without ornament, and invariably built in secluded situations. A wooden railing separates the male from the female Akkals. The proceedings commence with a conversation on politics. All news is communicated with the strictest regard to truth. They signalize such and such an individual, as an enemy to their nation. Another individual, oppressed by government, is recommended to protection and support. A third, being poor, is assisted by the collection of money. They then read extracts from the books of their religion, and sing their warlike hymn. They then eat some food, such as figs, raisins, &c., at the expense of the endowment. The company then disperses, and only the highest Akkals remain, who concert the measures to be taken in consequence of the news that has been communicated. Other news of a still more private nature, may then be communicated without reserve; and when profound secrecy is required, they appoint a committee of three. In every case, certain heads of the six families in hereditary possession of Mokettas, even though Djahils, are parties to political measures. The greatest crime that a Druse can commit, is to reveal a national secret. Besides the bonds of blood and religion—to say nothing of habits of secretiveness acquired from infancy—there is also the fear of punishment, as a traitor would, on discovery, be hacked to pieces. When a Druse, in a strange place, wishes to discover a co-religionist, he says, 'Do the peasants in your country sow the seed of the hleledge?' A stranger says, 'No,' but a Druse answers, 'Sown in the hearts of the faithful.' The Druse women are all taught reading and writing, which is remarkable, when we consider the abasement and ignorance of both Moslem and Christian females in Syria. There can be very little doubt that incest has been, for many years, prevalent among them, though it is said to have become less frequent than it was. No stranger ever sees the face of a Druse female, as they appear to me to be more carefully veiled than even Moslem women. Unlike other Eastern nations, a plurality of wives is forbidden."—*Page* 88.

The truth seems to be, from a comparison of all the accounts we have seen, that though the origin of the Druse relegion may ostensibly date from the apostles of the Caliph Hakem, it really is very little better than a remnant of the old paganism, which even before the Christian era may have been practised in these mountains, and which neither Christian nor Moslem have been able to extirpate. The Moslem himself disdains any connexion, and the Druse is a Christian with the Christians, and a Mahometan with the Mahometans, whenever, and as long soever, as it suits his purposes. Some practices he may have adopted from the people by whom he is surrounded, as convenience or habits of imitation may lead him to; but it is probable that in all his leading social, religious, and political principles, he has continued unaltered, and what he was three thousand years ago, such he is at the present day.

Besides the patriarch of the Maronites, there is also residing in the mountains another prelate, who, under the title of delegate apostolic of the Lebanon, exercises jurisdiction over those who follow the Latin rite, and is the representative of the Holy See for all the oriental Christians who follow the rites of their respective nations and are in communion with Rome. Dr. Fazio filled that office some years since, when the troops of Ibrahim Pacha got possession of Syria. As the Christian population are exempted from military service, many of the Druses affected conversion, and sought baptism at the hands of the Latin missionaries, to share in this immunity. Ibrahim sought to prevent conversion, under any circumstances, under the pretext of this abuse, and commanded the Emir Beshir to use his influence to that effect with the Maronite and the Latin prelates. Dr. Fazio wrote an able and zealous vindication of his conduct to the emir, and while he reprobated the use that had been made of the Christian ordinances, asserted his right to receive into the bosom of the church the repenting or converted sinner, whoever he may chance to be. It was almost the last act of his ministry, for he died in 1838; and the high and important office which he exercised, is now efficiently filled by Dr. Villardel. Besides the Latin population, there are within his vicariate eight houses of the religious orders—two of the Lazarists, two of the Jesuits, two of the Capuchins, one of the Carmelites, and one of the Franciscans. These convents, as well as many more of the Syrian, Melkite, and Armenian rites, have been erected on ground voluntarily ceded by the Maronites for the purpose.

The three rites just now mentioned have each a patriarch residing in the Libanus, who exercises authority over them. Those who follow these rites are not embodied into distinct and separately existing nations, like the Maronites and Druses, but are scattered in the towns and villages of the country. They have been indebted for this establishment to the kind friendship of the Maronites, whose assistance was never denied to their brethren and fellow-christians. Until the occupation of Syria by Mehemet Ali, they were not allowed to fix themselves out of the territory of the Libanus, but under his sway they were released from their painful and degrading servitude. This enlightened and liberal policy of the new government, permitted them to remove and fix themselves where they thought proper, and gave them the most perfect toleration as far as regarded the erection of churches and the celebration of public worship. In those places where they had no house for the performance of divine service, the Maronite church was always at their disposal. The hopes which the Christian churches of the Levant entertained from the liberality of the Egyptian pacha, have unfortunately been nipped in their first blossoming. Blood and rapine have, as we have just now seen, desolated their dwelling-places and shed their ravages over the sanctuaries of religion; and they have been again subjected to the withering influence of a tyranny the most destructive of social prospects that God in his justice or his vengeance has ever permitted to crush a nation's welfare. It was so in its best days; but in these the last stage (if it be the last stage) of its decrepitude and corruption, the effect and worn-out government of the Porte has become a thing utterly contemptible. The secession of France from the other European powers on the Syrian question, was an evil to be deplored, above all others, by the poor Christians of that country. They always looked up to the French nation as their protector, their defender, their trust in the time of need; they had become almost identified in name with the principal foreigners of the west; but in the hour of need, when one stroke of the pen would have secured them peace and prosperity and independence, their protector was found to be as powerless as themselves, and the Christians were abandoned once more to the barbarity of the Turks—the hereditary enemies of their race, their country, and their creed. It was a great mistake, that the European powers who had Syria at their command, instead of making it once more the victim of Turkish misrule, did not make it a Christian nation and a Christian people. It is easy to perceive that the spirit of chivalry has departed, that princes and rulers are animated with but a little of that noble and generous ardour which once stirred the breasts of kings, when the warriors of Christendom started with eagerness to their steeds, to avenge the insulted majesty of this land where the Man-God lived and died. Now, alas! the money-changers have again got possession of the temple. The destinies of nations and peoples have become a mere thing of pounds, shillings, and pence, to be weighed in the scales with as much worldliness and cupidity, as if there was question only of a light sovereign or a counterfeit Napoleon, and to be decided upon by the Jews and capitalists of London and Paris and Vienna. If it were not so, the consecrated land of Syria, and the holy plains of Palestine, would not have been given over to those who have profaned the sanctuary for more than a thousand years, who have erected in the holy place the abomination of desolation; the crescent would not gleam over the towers of Nazareth, nor would the insolent tread of the Turkish soldier pollute the cave of Bethlehem or the hill of Calvary. We fear that the Christian powers of Europe have been criminally and shamefully deficient in the reverence that they owed to the birth-place and sanctuary of their religion. Let us hope that God may yet honour the land he loved, that he may yet smile upon its hills, and look with complacency upon the promised dwelling-places of his people, where oft his voice was heard communing with men. Then shall the desert bloom like the rose, and the glory of Libanus shall not have departed for ever.

Two other short extracts we cannot withhold from our readers, and with them we must conclude a notice which has already extended beyond its intended limits. One contains a description of the author's visit to a Maronite nunnery.

"On entering the court-yard of Dair-el-Niah, which is one of the most considerable nunneries of the Lebanon, we found it to be a substantial edifice, with grated windows. Access to the cloisters was, of course, not permitted; but we found shade in a cool, lofty, well-constructed recess, in the facade of the buildings. The superior informed us, that the establishment consisted of thirty nuns, and that three priests attended to their spiritual wants. Their seclusion partakes of the character impressed upon it by Oriental manners; for they, during their lives, never cross the threshold of the building. On proceeding to the roof of the convent, we found it to be all on one level; and the priest who accompanied us said, that it was the favourite promenade of the ladies of the establishment. A luncheon, with some of their best wine, was served up to us; and as a great favour we were permitted to have an interview with the ladies. When the appointed time arrived, we were ushered into a small, dingy apartment, and seated with our backs to the light. Opposite us was a grating of wood six feet by four feet high. A foot behind this grating was another; beyond this all was darkness. We were told that several of the nuns were behind; and the conversation began and ended without our being able to discover any thing of the form, features, or dress of the fair recluses."—*Page* 136.

The other tells us how the wind blows, if we may employ so homely a phrase, with the Protestant missions, which have for some time been established throughout Syria by the English and American societies. The Baptists of the United States are particularly busy in the Lebanon.

"The Syrians have very extraordinary notions of John Bull. They hear from the European Catholics vague and marvellous accounts of the ignorance and distress of the poorer classes in England; and they see at the same time, that the richer classes in England subscribe large sums for the purpose of giving instruction, medical advice, &c., to the poor of Syria; who, if allowance be made for the difference of climate, are infinitely better fed and clothed; and as far as reading, writing, and cyphering go, better instructed than the poor of any manufacturing town in England. I have nothing to say against the agents of this misdirected benevolence. There are some* Protestant missionaries in Syria, for whom I entertain the highest respect, but the natives cannot comprehend the scheme. I heard many singular anecdotes of a certain Greek Catholic, whom I shall call on this occasion, Mousa. This individual had inherited a small property from his father, which he first dissipated in riotous hospitality; he then became a bankrupt; lived for a while on the proceeds of his wife's jewels; then sold his house to raise the wind; and, at last, was reduced to the necessity of working a few hours a-day, in order to gain his bread; but this being rather irksome to a man of pleasure, he, one morning, paid me a visit, and announced his intention of becoming Protestant! Mousa had the sharp visage, hollow-eye sockets, and nervous manner of a battered roué. His mantle was of finer cloth than usual; but having seen service, was greasy at the neck; and his body-robe of striped silk was faded and shabby.

"'I have resolved,' said Mousa 'to become a Protestant, and place myself under British protection.' 'Ha!' said I, with seeming self-gratulation; 'you must admit that the English are a very wealthy and respectable nation.'

"'Oh yes,' said Mousa, catching at my words, his haggard, desperado countenance, kindling with hope and avidity; 'no nation like the English; their rajahs are like princes, and their nobles like sultans.'

"'Ay, ay, I thought I understood your motive,' said I, drily.

"'You mistake,' said Mousa, evidently bothered at having let the cat out of the bag; 'my abhorrence and contempt of Popery are sincere. I have not gone to confession for months. I despise the goods of the world.'

"'It does not follow, that because you are a bad Catholic you would make a good Protestant.'

---

* And only some.

"'Mousa finding that I gave so little encouragement to his religious projects, tried to negotiate the loan of a few hundred piastres, on his bond; but failing in this, bade me a good morning, with sundry philosophic reflections on the vanity of riches, and the duty of submission to the will of God."—*Page* 162.

This incident, for which we feel grateful to the author of "The Modern Syrians," whoever he be, illustrates the working of the Protestant missions of Syria. We find that the old story of the Pope weeding his garden and throwing the weeds outside the walls, holds true from the island of Achill to the very walls of Damascus.

THE RUSSIAN AND ANGLICAN HIERARCHIES.

[From the Rambler.]

"In the eyes of Rome," says Father Gagarin, "the Russian Bishops are true Bishops, and the Russian priests true priests." This conclusion was not admitted with regard to a considerable portion of the hierarchy without some very sharp disputes, —disputes similar to those which are now with the same breath being both invited and deprecated in England. There are, if we are to believe Mr. Henry Collins, a recent convert, many Anglicans who have been prevented becoming Catholics only by the "bitterness of the tone" of some of us. "The number of conversions that has been impeded, or altogether hindered, can never be fully known." Among "bitternesses of tone," our opinion of the invalidity of English orders holds a foremost place; we ought for the sake of peace either to change it or to conceal it.

"What right has any Catholic to press upon Anglicans, and to insist upon it, that their Bishops are mere laymen? The Church has never decided it, or spoken positively: no man may therefore speak positively of it (!). It is an open question; and in winning over others whose faith is in any way different, all open questions are better avoided, especially if they wound the feelings of those we would gain. To speak disagreeable things is never the way to win men; they should never, then, be spoken except when absolutely necessary. Why take a pleasure in hunting out methods of annoying one whom we would convert? The fact that Anglicans value orders is a point on our side; for if they value them, they value their absolute certainty. But the point being open, Catholics may and some do, hold the opinion that Anglican orders are valid, and that, if they are not certain, yet a very great deal more can be said for their validity than for the contrary part; but it is enough that, upon an open question, it is highly impolitic to exasperate one whom we would win. The belief in orders is one more point upon which the Anglican Church holds the true faith in union with Catholics. It is a very great blessing that one hindrance to unity is taken away, and a greater still it were, if, upon examination, their orders should be pronounced valid by authority. It is an essential point for the Church to have orders, but the having orders does not make any church the Catholic Church, nor part of it either. The Nestorian heretics, the Copts, &c., have orders, but are no part of the Church, though this is a point of union between them and the Church which has providentially been preserved. The Donatists had orders, and held the Catholic faith; their position was not because of this justifiable; on the contrary, holding so much, it was the more unjustifiable that they should have continued separate from the Catholic Church, and strangers to the promises." a

We do not wish to hurt any one's feelings; but we do not see why compassion should take the place of argument, or why we should refrain from urging on people who think themselves safe with their sacraments, that their orders have ever been considered doubtful in the Church, and that converts from their body are ordained afresh under the eyes of Popes, without the smallest consideration for the ordinations of the Anglican Bishops. It is surely a topic that may be discussed without exasperation. Now that the Nag's-Head story is shown to have been a mistake, we should be the last to re-affirm it: but, at the same time, the representatives of those who banished, imprisoned, robbed, and hanged the Catholics; who shut up, as far as might be, all sources of information from them; who burn their books, dispersed their schools, and used every means that an unprincipled ingenuity could suggest to prevent their ever knowing the exact state of affairs, ought to be careful not to call that fable a " foul lie " It was not a foul lie,—it was a natural mistake; and it was natural to mistrust the refutations of it when they were produced by men convicted before of manifold misrepresentations, and were founded on documents which it was supposed might easily have been forged. It was not their fault if the English Catholics, as Bramhall reproaches them, " were great strangers to the true

a *Difficulties of a Convert*, by H. Collins, M. A. (Dolman, 1857), p. 9.

passages of those times, knowing nothing but what they heard at Rome, Rheims, or Douai."

With respect to the ordinations of the Oriental Churches in general, there is no more doubt than there is of the Latin ordinations; that is, there is none at all. The doubts that have arisen concerning the validity of some or the Russian consecrations have their origin in a fact which happened as lately as 1630, and of which we proceed to give an account.

At the Council of Florence, Isodore, metropolitan both of Kief and Moscow, had been one of the most zealous promoters of the union. On his return to his sees, he caused this great act to be accepted at Kief, and its suffragan dioceses, Bransk, Smolensk, Peremyszl, Turow, Wladimir in Volhynia, Polock, Chelm, and Halitz; but he failed entirely in the province of Moscow. Even at Kief the union only lasted till the beginning of the sixteenth century.

Nevertheless the greater part of the Bishops and clergy of Kief again renounced their schism in 1594 and 1595 at the famous councils of Brest. The Bishops of Peremyszl and Lemberg alone, under the influence of Constantine, prince of Ostrog, refused to be re-united. They soon died; and the non-uniates of Poland,—for a portion of the people refused to follow its Bishops,—were left without a head, and even without any hope of obtaining one; for the laws of Poland forbade the consecration of a Bishop without the king's consent. Sigismund III. was firm; neither prayers, nor remonstrances, nor reasons of policy moved him; and in 1620, when the Cossacks, who were called out to fight against the Turk in Wallachia, threatened to desert his flag if he any longer refused them a schismatic metropolitan, he answered them, "I will rather lose my crown and go into exile than consent to the renewal of the schism."

But for the last three years there had been residing in Muscovy an envoy of the Sultan, who assumed the title of Patriarch of Jerusalem. Nobody seems to have had a doubt of his being really Theophilus, patriarch of the Holy City. He was even requested to preside at the installation of Philarete as patriarch of Moscow, and to confirm the re-establishment of the patriarchate of that city, which had been first instituted in 1588 by Jeremias II., the deposed patriarch of Constantinople. But these acts can have no influence on the decision of the question in hand. Philarete, the father of the Tsar Michael Feodorowitch, and the stock of the imperial house of Romanoff, had been metropolitan of Rostoff before he was taken prisoner by the Poles; and after he regained his liberty he became head of the Russian orthodox Church. It is an error, then, to say that Philarete was consecrated by the pretended patriarch of Jerusalem; he received from him no sacramental imposition of hands, but only installation in the patriarchal chair. No objection, then, can be brought against the orders of the Bishops consecrated by the patriarch Philarete.

But Theophilus did not stop with installing the Patriarch of Moscow. The Cossacks, taking advantage of the wars and difficulties into which Sigismund III. was plunged, caused this mysterious personage to come to Kief, where, without the assistance of any other Bishop, he proceeded, August 15, 1630, to consecrate three Bishops: Job Borecki anti-metropolitan of Kief, Meleci Smotricki anti-archbishop of Polock, and Joseph Kuscewicz anti-bishop of Wladimir. Some time after, he consecrated four more Bishops: Isaias Boriskowicz Czerczicki anti-bishop of Luck, Isaias Kopinski anti-bishop of Peremyszl, Païsius Hippolytowicz anti-bishop of Chelm, and Abraham Stragouski anti-bishop of Pinsk. All these sees were then occupied by united Ruthenian Bishops.

One can fancy the troubles that followed the enterprise of Theophilus. The schismatic Bishops soon succeeded in filching from the Catholic prelates a good portion of their flocks; they took forcible possession of the churches, drove away the Catholics, and in a short time destroyed the fruit of twenty years' labours. As all this was done in contempt of the laws of the state, Sigismund, far from recognising these Bishops, issued an edict for their apprehension; but by means of disguises and other precautions they managed to escape pursuit, and even to visit the churches, and to ordain every where priests opposed to the union.

They were soon strong enough to begin persecuting the Catholics. Wladislas IV., who succeeded his father Sigismund in 1632, felt himself obliged to command the Catholics to give up the churches to the anti-unionists; he called the schismatics to the senate, and allowed them to have an episcopate on nearly the same footing as the Catholic Ruthenian hierarchy. This schismatical episcopate has been continued to our day.

It is in relation to these Bishops that the question of the validity of their consecration has place. Of course there is no question about their *legitimacy;* no one can be a legitimate Bishop unless he is in communion with the universal Church built on the authority of St. Peter and his successors: the simple question is, whether the ordinations of Kief are valid; whether, that is, the anti-unionist Bishops of that province really have the episcopal character; for as baptism administered by heretics is valid when there is no essential change in form, matter, or intention,—so orders administered by heretics or schismatics are valid as long as all that is necessary is observed; that is to say, as long as they are conferred with the prescribed forms by a Christian who has the episcopal character.

From the very first there have been Polish Catholics who have maintained the consecrations made by the pretended patriarch of Jerusalem to have been null. They depended on two proofs: first, that the essential forms had not been observed; secondly, that the consecrating Bishop had not the episcopal character.

They pretended that a consecration made without the presence of three Bishops, as prescribed by the canons, is null, except in cases where the Holy See permits the consecrating Bishop to be assisted by two priests.* Now it was publicly notorious that the consecrating Bishop had no assistant whatever. This is the same argument afterwards used against the consecration of the first Jansenist Bishop of Holland, who was consecrated by the archbishop of Babylon

---

* As allowed by St. Thomas Aq., sum. iii. q. lxxii. art. 11, ad 1.

alone. Now, as no one could maintain the validity of these illegitimate orders in Belgium or Holland, without being almost reckoned an adherent of the schism of Utrecht; so in Poland, in the midst of the passions awakened by the events at Kief, a man was obliged to declare that Job Borecki and company were not real Bishops, because three Bishops had not taken part at their consecration.

This argument went too far; for though the canon which prescribes the presence of three Bishops ought to be religiously observed, yet it does not thence follow that it is of divine right, and that its non-observance entails the nullity of the act. Could the Pope ever dispense with it, if it were essential to the Sacrament? What Catholic nowadays calls in question the validity of the schismatical **ordinations** of Utrecht? And how can they be attacked, without attacking the consecration of Pope Pelagius I., who received the imposition of hands from two Bishops only, assisted by one priest? It is certain that the Council of Sardica commands any Bishop who happens to be the sole remaining one in any ecclesiastical province to consecrate Bishops for the towns that require them, without allowing the neighbouring Bishops to have a hand in these consecrations, except when the above-mentioned Bishop refuses to make them. Who would reject the orders of those Bishops who, according to the testimony of the first Council of Arles were often consecrated in France by a single Bishop, or of those who, in conformity with the apostolic canons, were consecrated by two? Who would call the consecration of John of Châlons invalid, given, as St. Sidonius Appolinaris affirms, by Patiens of Lyons alone? Who ever called in question the orders of the Catholic Church in England, where St. Gregory the Great dispensed with the presence of any assistants whatever, and wrote to St. Augustine, "In the English Church, wherein there is no other Bishop but thyself, thou canst not ordain a Bishop otherwise than alone"? Who objects to Bellarmine for allowing that in case of necessity a Bishop and two mitred abbots may consecrate a Bishop? [a] The Council of Riez, in invalidating the ordina-

---

[a] De Eccl. Mil. iv. c. viii.

tion of the Bishop of Embrun, because it was only performed by two Bishops, yet implicitly allows it when it permits the deposed Bishop to confirm, and the new Bishop to continue the priests ordained by the deposed one in their offices. It is clear that the sentence had reference to the irregularity of the proceeding, and not to the validity of the Sacrament.

To put forth, then, the principle, that no consecration which is not performed by three Bishops is valid, is to raise doubts about all ordinations. For what Bishop could ever be sure that among his ancestors in the priesthood there are not some such as those spoken of in the councils above mentioned?

The second argument against the validity of the orders of the non-united Bishops of the province of Kief has the same flaw. Not that we pretend to defend Strahl, who, in his Russian Church History, can only see through the spectacles of the Russian orthodox writers; nor Count Krasinski, who writes solely in the interests of Protestantism in the Sclavonic provinces; nor the Dominican Lequien, in his *Oriens Christianus*, written from the Catholic point of view; who all assure us that it was really Theophilus patriarch of Jerusalem who came into Muscovy and re-established the non-uniate hierarchy of Kief. We will allow that his name was not Theophilus, but Theophanes; with James Susza, the author of the Latin life of the Blessed Josaphat Kuncewicz, we will admit that he was but a pretended patriarch, *uti se nominabat patriarcha Hierosolymitanus*; that he was a *pseudo-patriarch*, as the Jesuits Cordara and Albert Viak call him; that he was only a quack, *circulator*, brought from Greece by the Russian monks and Popes, and that his magnificent title of Patriarch turned to the disgrace of the schism as soon as it was proved that he had no right to it, as Viak again says; lastly, that he was merely a vagabond sycophant, *sycophantes vagabundus*, who usurped the pompous title of Patriarch of Jerusalem, as the theologian John Aloysius Kulista calls him. We admit that all these hard words are deserved; but it by no means follows from thence that Theophilus, or Theophanes, had not the episcopal character. All those who were most directly interested in knowing whether he was truly a Bishop, were convinced that there was no doubt whatever on the matter.

Our proofs are these: Meleci Smotricki, who had been ordained by the pretended patriarch of Jerusalem for the archiepiscopal see of Polock, returned afterwards to the unity of the Church. Whether it was to escape the penalties he had incurred as one of the principal instigators, direct or indirect, of the murder of the Blessed Josaphat, the legitimate Archbishop of the same see, or for any other unknown reason, Smotricki had fled to Greece. There he found the Church in the greatest confusion and disorder: this sad spectacle made a happy impression on his mind; he resolved to abandon the schism, and even set about writing a book in favour of the union. He was betrayed by a false friend, and cited before a schismatic synod of Kief, where he had the weakness to recant, and to tear up his book with his own hands. But grace soon regained its supremacy; he went to Rome, was absolved by the Pope, and returned into Lithuania with the title of a Bishop *in partibus*, because he could not be placed on the see of Polock, which was occupied by the legitimate successor of the Blessed Josaphat. He persevered till the end of his life in the unity of the Church, and at his death there happened prodigies, recorded by Viak.

Now neither the Pope, nor the Catholic Bishops of Lithuania, nor Smotricki himself, ever showed the least doubt about the validity of his consecration. Indeed, a layman wrote to the Bishop *in partibus* to beg him to be re-consecrated; but Smotricki took good care not to comply with the invitation.

Here is another fact. In the beginning of the eighteenth century, Innocent, schismatic Bishop of Vinnitzy, demanded to be received with his whole flock into the communion of the Holy See. Innocent was looked upon at Rome as a relapsed heretic. The papal nuncio in Poland was also against him, and Mgr. Malacoski, the uniate Bishop of Vinnitzy, was his open enemy. The demand of Innocent was generally considered as a trap. People said, when he is sole Bishop of Vinnitzy, he will once more abandon the union, and will take with him, not only his old flock, but a great number of Catholics also. There is nothing to gain, much to lose, by his admission into the Church.

The king of Poland was of a different opinion. He deputed his confessor, the Piedmontese Jesuit Vota, to go to Rome and to treat with the Pope. Innocent XII. referred him to the Congregation of the Propaganda, which was infected with all the prejudices current in Poland against Bishop Innocent. At a meeting of the Congregation, under the presidence of Cardinal Altieri, Cardinal Casanatta spoke with great power against the admission of Bishop Innocent. His chief object was to prove that the Bishop was not in good faith. But when it was Vota's turn to speak, he answered the Cardinal with such success, that the admission of the Bishop of Vinnitzy was unanimously decided upon. In consequence, Malacoski was transferred to the see of Chelm, to make room for Innocent, who afterwards showed so much zeal and devotedness for the union, that by his means the Archbishop of Lemberg and the Bishop of Luck were induced to renounce the schism.

Here, then, are three Bishops whose orders are derived from Theophanes, or Theophilus. They were received, not without difficulty, into the communion of the Roman Church. The cause was discussed, examined on all sides, in the presence of ardent, numerous, and powerful enemies; and the only argument which was not produced was that which, if producible, would have been decisive, but which no one either in Poland or Rome thought of, namely, the invalidity of their ordinations.

After such plain facts, to attack the validity of the Russian orders looks like attacking the Holy See itself; it throws a doubt over the orders of the uniate Bishops of Galicia, and in particular over those of Mgr. Lewicki, Archbishop of Lemberg, Cardinal of the holy Roman Church, and successor of the former schismatical Bishops. There are plenty of good arguments to prove to the Russians that their ecclesiastical position is not regular, without being obliged to use weapons which wound the hand that wields them.

The case of the Anglican orders is very different. In the

first place, the Holy See, which has shown itself so circumspect in its dealings with the orders of Utrecht and Kief, in spite of the prejudices of the Catholics of the Low Countries and of Poland, and has thereby proved that she would never deny the validity of the ordinations of heretics merely from a spite against their persons,—the Holy See has from the first treated the Anglican orders as nullities. The same respect that would teach us to refrain from questioning the episcopal character of Cardinal Lewicki would make us refrain from acknowledging such a character in Archbishop Sumner or Bishop Wilberforce.

But as we may be speaking to some with whom respect for the Holy See is not a decisive argument, we must enter into the particulars of the case, and show that the Anglican orders are historically in the highest degree doubtful; so doubtful, that no one who values his salvation and believes that to obtain it he must have valid sacraments, can be finally satisfied with the security they promise, even though he may be prepared to die in schism. Let us begin with the two old objections discussed by Courayer. "The first regarding Barlow, Parker's consecrator; the other, the form he used in the ceremony of their ordination. It is pretended that Barlow was not consecrated himself, and that the rite of which he made use is entirely insufficient to insure the validity of ordination. Either the one or the other of these facts would be sufficient of itself to annihilate the English hierarchy." [a]

The third point shall be, the intention with which the first Elizabethan Bishops were made, as judged not so much from the known opinions of themselves, as from the meaning attached to the word 'bishop,' and to the functions he was to exercise, by the English Protestants of the period. There are Bishops and Bishops. The Catholic Bishop is the *summus sacerdos*, the centre and fount of sacramental power for his diocese; he is the chief sacrificer, as well as the governor of his flock. The Lutheran Bishop, on the other hand, is a mere superintendent, not the source of the power of the clergy, but

[a] Courayer, Dissertation, chap. iii.

only their governor and head. Is the Anglican Bishop,—or rather, was he in the minds of the Protestants of Elizabeth's days,—more like the Catholic or the Lutheran type? Was he the *summus sacerdos*, or only the minister who was made a royal commissioner, to look after the morals and conduct of the other ministers of his charge? Was his highest function to sacrifice or to preach? Is it not true to say of the Anglican Church and her episcopate, *Nomen callide retinuit; rem ipsam definiendo sustulit*,—she cunningly retained the name; the thing itself she totally detroyed by her definitions?

The fourth point is, to inquire into the probability of the nullity of the baptism of several of the Anglican hierarchy, who, if they were not Christians, evidently could not be Christian Bishops.

Was Barlow, the consecrator of Parker, ever consecrated himself? There are the gravest doubts on the subject. He was elected Bishop of St Asaph, January 16th, 1536. The king's commission for his consecration was dated Feb. 22d, 1536,[a] and directed to Cranmer. Did Cranmer act upon it; or did both he and Barlow consider that the king's commission was to all intents and purposes a valid consecration, nay, that it would please the king to treat it as such, omitting all further ceremonies? In the first place, there is no direct testimony of Cranmer's having proceeded to consecrate Barlow, or directed a commission to other Bishops for his consecration. The Lambeth register, which contains all the other documents relating to Barlow,—his election, confirmation, &c.,— is quite silent about his consecration; and though Godwin [b] positively says, that " William Barlow, prior of the Canons regular of Bisham, was consecrated Feb. 22d, 1535(6)," this is impossible, as we shall afterwards show; and no other author attempts to fix the date of this act. Cranmer acted at once on the royal commission of Feb. 22d,—not, however, to consecrate, but only to confirm,—and this by proxy, for Barlow was in Scotland. The consecration, says Courayer (cap. iii.), cannot have been delayed long after, both because

[a] Rymer, vol. xiv. p. 559.
[b] De Præsul. Ang., p. 663.

the law (25 Hen. VIII. cap. 20, § 7) fixed the limit of twenty days after the king's letters-patent to "consecrate" the Bishop-elect under pain of præmunire, and also because there is proof that Barlow was already consecrated by the following April. He adds, that Strype does not hesitate to place Barlow's consecration in 1535(6). These reasons of Courayer are all ill-founded. Strype's unhesitating decision is a mere assumption of a man who had no more information than we have. As to the proof that Barlow was consecrated by April 1536, the proof is all the other way, as we shall soon have to show. And the law which prescribed to the Archbishop the duty of confirming, investing, and consecrating the prelate-elect was duly fulfilled, so far at least as to avoid the penalty, by one of **the** acts. The pains **were** threatened if the Archbishop " shall refuse, and do not *confirm, invest*,[a] and consecrate, with all due circumstance .... within twenty days." These three acts are portions of one whole and single act; and if this act were commenced within the twenty days, the law was satisfied. Thus Bonner was elected and confirmed Bishop of Hereford in October 1538,[b] but not consecrated; in October 1539, he is translated to London, and in April 1540, and not before, he is consecrated Bishop of London,[c] having remained Bishop of Hereford a year, and Bishop of London half a year, without consecration. Therefore the law 25 Henry VIII. does not even suffice for a presumption that Barlow was consecrated as well as confirmed within twenty days after Feb. 22d, 1536.

Next, with respect to Courayer's assertion, that there is proof of Barlow's being consecrated before April 1536, it is so far from being true, that the direct contrary is demonstrable. We must return to Barlow's history. January 16, 1536, he was elected to the see of St. Asaph. February 18, the same year, Richard Rawlins, Bishop of St. David's, died; before news of this had reached court, the mandate of Fe-

---

[a] These two words are omitted in Courayer's quotation of the act; the insertion of them would have deprived his argument of its whole force.
[b] Cran. Regis. 218.
[c] Ibid. 241.

bruary 22d had been issued, and Barlow had been confirmed by proxy as Bishop of St. Asaph; two months afterwards he was transferred to the see of St. David's, the temporalities of which were restored to him by the king's letters, dated April 26th, 1536.[a] Now we affirm (1), that it is plain, from the public records relating to his successor at St. Asaph, that Barlow was not consecrated as Bishop of that see. And (2) that it is plain, from all the documents relating to his election, confirmation, &c. at St. David's, that he was treated as if he had been a consecrated Bishop *before* his election to that see. And our explanation of this curious fact is, that Cranmer and Barlow, both of whom mocked at the " apostolic succession," conspired to shirk the ceremony of consecration, not without an idea of flattering the king, whose theological acumen had just discovered that he was the sole source and channel of episcopal grace and power.

Barlow was not consecrated before his removal to St. David's, as may be gathered from the *congé-d'élire*, or license to the Dean and Chapter of St. Asaph to elect his successor. These *congés* always specify the cause of the vacancy; if the former Bishop is dead, they run, *vacante per mortem naturalem ultimi Episcopi;* if he is translated to another see, *per translationem ultimi Episcopi;* if deprived, *per deprivationem ultimi Episcopi:* and whenever the Bishop mentioned was only elected and confirmed, and not consecrated, he is always, we believe without exception, in all formal documents called *Bishop-elect* only. Now in the *congé-d'élire* to the Dean and Chapter of St. Asaph to elect Barlow's successor, Barlow is called *Bishop-elect*, and the cause of the vacancy is said to be his *exchange: vacante sede per liberam transmutationem Wilhelmi Barlow ultimi Episcopi electi;* and so he is described in all the formal documents relating to the history of his successor. There is no other instance in which a translation is described by any other word than *translationem*,[b] nor in which a con-

---

[a] Mason de Ministerio Anglicano, lib. iii. cap. x. p. 365.
[b] The invariable form used when the translated Bishop has been consecrated

secrated Bishop is called only *Bishop-elect*. The clear meaning of these expressions is, that in consequence of the bishopric of St. David's falling vacant before Barlow was consecrated to St. Asaph, the "Bishop-elect" was not "translated," but "freely exchanged" to St. David's.

To this argument Courayer replies (chap. iv.) by producing a case which he calls "altogether parallel with that of Barlow," where a consecrated Bishop is called *Bishop-elect*.

"In the year 1633, after the death of Godwin of Hereford, Juxon had been chosen to succeed him in that see. Before he was consecrated and installed, he was translated to London. He was confirmed in this new see, Oct. 23, 1633, and consecrated, Oct. 27, Lyndsell of Peterborough succeeded him in Hereford, March 7, 1634. The king consented to Lyndsell's election, March 21, 1634; and on the 24th he was confirmed by Archbishop Laud. Now, in the acts of election and confirmation of Lyndsell, Juxon, though consecrated and confirmed in the see of London, is all along styled Bishop-elect of Hereford. . . . Cum sedes Herefordiensis tam per mortem naturalem Francisci Godwin nuper episcopi ibidem, ac per promotionem Willmi Juxon in episcopum ibidem electi ad episcopatum Londiniensem, nuper vacaverit, &c. Should we have any right to conclude from these words, that Juxon was not at that time consecrated, when we have the record of his consecration prior by four months?"

We reply, that we have the right to conclude, from the words, "Bishop-elect of Hereford," that Juxon was never consecrated to the see of Hereford; and this conclusion is historically correct. His consecration, after his removal from Hereford to London, could not possibly make him the consecrated Bishop of Hereford. He never had been more than

---

before his translation is, "Vacante per translationem dni A. B. ultimi Episcopi ibidem." In the documents of Barlow's successor at St. Asaph's, the cause of vacancy is several times expressed, but never in this mode. In the letters-patent (Cran. Reg. 194 a, it is "per liberam transmutationem," &c., as in the text; in the petition (ib. 194 b), "per cessionem, dimissionem sive transmutationem reverendi patris dni Willmi Bariowe ultimi Epi copi electi ibidem." In the instrument of assent (ib. 195 b), "per liberam dimissionem, cessionem et transmutationem reverendi patris dni Willmi Barlowe, ultimi Epi ibm electi." In the process of election (ib. 195 b), "per liberam renunciationem, cessionem sive transmutationem reverendi patris dni Willmi Barlow ultimi et immediati Episcopi ibidem in eardem ecclesiam cath. Assaphen. electi." In the same (196 a), "per transmutationem, cessionem sive liberam dimissionem reverendi patris Willmi Barlowe ultimi presulis sive pastoris electi." In the same (196 b), "per liberam renunciationem, cessionem, dimissionem et transmutationem dni Willmi Barlowe ultimi et immediati presulis et pastoris et Epi ejusdem electi." In the final sentence (ib. 197 b), "per liberam transmutationem dni Willmi, Barlowe ultimi Epi ibm electi et confirmati." Not a word about his consecration; but a studious avoidance of the word, and of all other expressions generally used for consecrated prelates.

Bishop-elect of that see; and so he is called in these acts, which, in treating of Hereford, have no occasion to meddle with London. In the same way, we conclude that as Barlow, after his removal to St. David's, is called "late Bishop-elect of St. Asaph's," he was never consecrated while he had possession of the see of St. Asaph's.

But the case does not stand on mere verbal criticism. Barlow *could* not have been consecrated to the see of St. Asaph; because he was absent in Scotland during the whole time of his holding that see. The mandate for his consecration was issued February 22d; it was confirmed by proxy the next day (Cran. Register); therefore he was not present. A letter of his is extant, written from Scotland in March the same year, whither "the Bishop-elect of St. Asaph" had been sent with Lord William Howard, by Henry VIII., to induce James V. to throw off the Pope's authority. This letter is signed "Will'm Barlow," though he was then confirmed in his see. He was elected to the see of St. David's, April 10th; and on the 21st was confirmed in person at Bow church: the record is perfect; but there is no mention of consecration. After this he departed for Scotland again, and was there by May 13, when he signs his letters "Will'mus Menev.," as if he had been consecrated Bishop of St. David's: no mandate for his consecration to this see appears either in the Rolls or in the register at Lambeth, but merely the royal assent, which simply commands the Archbishop, *ut quod vestrum est in hac parte exequamini*. The king, we suppose, was privy to the fraud; and accordingly the record of Barlow's confirmation to the sees, both of St. Asaph and St. David's, is closed with a certificate from the Archbishop to the king of his confirmation only; proving that he was not then consecrated. Further, he was called to Parliament by a writ of summons, April 27, 1536, in which he is named, according to Courayer, not Bishop-elect, but Bishop, as though consecrated; and yet, when he took his seat in the House of Lords, June 30, 1536, he took precedence (according to the Lords' journals) *after* Reppis of Norwich, who was consecrated June 11, 1536. For this reason his consecration is assumed to be *after* that date by the late Anglican editor of Bramhall's works. Yet the man must have sat somewhere. If he was summoned to Parliament without consecration, we cannot see why he may not have sat there without it too.

Barlow, then, was not consecrated to the see of St. Asaph, as Courayer says he must have been. Was he, then, consecrated after his "transmutation" to St. David's? In the register, all the documents about this affair are perfect; but there is no record of his consecration. On the contrary, throughout these documents, even in the royal assent, which commands Cranmer "to do what to him pertaineth," Barlow is described as "late Bishop of St. Asaph," and never called "Bishop-elect;" that is, he is assumed to be a consecrated Bishop; and as such he is elected and confirmed in his new see without any thought of consecration. The register may be searched equally in vain for any record of his consecration on his removal to the see of Bath and Wells, in 1548. Indeed, it would be preposterous to expect **that a** man who had once passed himself off for **a consecrated Bishop,** would ever be likely afterwards to incur the danger of confessing that he had never received the rite.

We **su**ppose, then, to use Courayer's words (chap. iv.), that there was a collusion or conspiracy between Cranmer and Barlow to omit the ceremony of consecration. "As these two prelates were **of very** Presbyterian sentiments, and did not acknowledge **the necessity** of consecration, nor the efficacy of the sacrament **of orders, it is very possible that** Cranmer, —who knew Barlow's sentiments with respect to the inutility and inefficacy of ordination, and his aversion to the ceremonies of the Pontifical, and who, moreover, was of the same opinion himself,—might, in concert with Barlow, have given him letters of institution and installation, **by** means of which **he was** invested with his bishopric."

Courayer owns this **conjecture to be** very ingenious, and to have all the force a conjecture can have. But he objects, that the omission of consecration is not very possible. It was not an affair between Cranmer and Barlow alone; three Bishops at least **were** required at the consecration; and certificates of consecration had to be shown before investiture could be had. In a matter so impossible to be concealed, Cranmer and Barlow would rather have swallowed the whole Pontifical than have subjected themselves to the præmunire, by omitting the consecration. In this part of his answer, Courayer quite forgets the opportunity for collusion and jugglery which the translation of Barlow afforded; and we have produced documentary evidence that seems to show that Cranmer and Barlow profited by the occasion. In records that would come under the eyes of the chapter of St. Asaph, who knew that Barlow was unconsecrated, he was always called "Bishop-elect." But he was palmed off on the chapter of St. David's as consecrated. It was a case in which suspicion might easily fail to be excited; and the chapter, when it received documents signed by the Archbishop, which treated Barlow as consecrated, would be very unlikely to demand proofs of the act, especially in the case of the translation of a Bishop, whom they would naturally presume to have been consecrated to his former see.

There was, then, an opportunity for such a collusion. But, says Courayer, Henry VIII. was very strict, and an enemy to innovators. Was it an easy thing to impose upon him? We answer, that there was no need for concealment or imposition with regard to the king. On the contrary, we believe that the whole affair was intended as a delicate piece of flattery to the head of the Anglican Church. We know, by a document which we shall quote directly, that in 1540 a notable theological idea had taken possession of the monarch's head; namely, that the power of consecrating Bishops was given *provisionally* to the Apostles and their successors, to last only till they had a Christian king among them, to whom the power was eventually to belong. What more acceptable compliment, than to come to a king in this frame of mind, and tell him that Barlow considered himself validly consecrated by his highness's commission, and to beseech him that in this case all superfluous ceremonies might be omitted? And what more likely tool for such an act of sycophancy than the willing pander of all Henry's adulteries; the man who married him to Anne Boleyn before he had pronounced Catherine's divorce; the man who was always ready in marriage or divorce to bend all laws to Henry's will,—Cranmer? Or what more likely conspirator in the fraud than Barlow, the apostate monk, who had "buried the Mass" in 1519, written against the marriage of priests in 1531, recanted his grievous errors of denying the Mass and Purgatory, and slandering the Pope, in 1533; who became a creature of Anne Boleyn the next year, and by her means was made rector of Sundridge, prior of Haverfordwest, and prior of Bisham; who was sent ambassador to Scotland to promote schism, and preach the Gospel, in 1536; who united with Cranmer in opposing the Six Articles in 1539, and in assenting to them when passed; in denying the Sacraments, and recognising the king as the fountain of orders, in 1640; who was employed in composing almost every heretical document of importance during the reigns of Henry and Edward, and in translating part of the Apocrypha for Parker's Bible; who wasted the property of the see of St. David's, and utterly ruined that of Bath and Wells; and who married within a few years of his publishing his dialogue against the marriage of the clergy;—a man, in short, whose whole history shows him to have been an unprincipled scoundrel?

But, urges Courayer, it could not have been concealed from the Church. This is just what we contend it could have been by the opportunity of collusion afforded by the "transmutation" from St. Asaph to St. David's. The rite, though always performed almost privately, was never questioned, never doubted. The occasion of omitting it was convenient; it only remains to prove that Henry VIII., Cranmer, and Barlow were in the mind to take advantage of the opportunity.

In 1540, Henry, who was always inventing new dogmas, put certain questions to the Bishops and other divines, which, with the answers, may be seen in Burnet's *History of the Reformation*, vol. i. p. 201. Amongst them are the following questions, with the answers of Cranmer and Barlow:

Questions. "Whether the Apostles, *lacking a higher power, as is not having a Christian king among them*, made Bishops by that necessity, or by authority given of God?"

Cranmer. "The civil ministers under the king be lord chancellor, lord treasurer, admirals, sheriffs, &c. The ministers of God's word, under his majesty, be Bishops, parsons, vicars, and such other priests as be appointed by his highness to that ministration; as, for example, the Bishop of Canterbury, the Bishop of Durham, the parson of Winwick, &c.; all the said offices be appointed, assigned, and elected in every place by the laws and orders of kings and princes. In the admission of these offices be divers comely ceremonies and solemnities, and which be not of necessity, but only for a good and seemly fashion; for if *such offices and ministrations were committed without such solemnity, they were nevertheless duly committed;* and there is no more promise of God that grace is given in the committing of the ecclesiastical office, than it is in the committing of the civil office."

Barlow. "Because they lacked a Christian prince; by that necessity they ordained other bishops" [*i. e.* to the prince properly belongs the power of ordaining, which was only lent to the Apostles till the lack of a prince was supplied].

Question. "Whether Bishops or priests were first; and if the priest were first, then the priest made the Bishop?"

Cranmer. "The Bishops and the priests were at one time, and were not two things, but both one office at the beginning of Christ's religion."

Barlow. "At the beginning they were all one."

Question. "Whether in the New Testament *be required any consecration* of a Bishop or priest, or only appointing to the office be sufficient?"

Cranmer. "In the New Testament he that is appointed to be a Bishop or a priest *needeth no consecration* by the Scripture; *for election or appointment thereunto is sufficient.*"

Barlow. "Only the appointing."

Besides these answers, we read of articles being exhibited against Barlow in November 1536, seven months after his removal to St. David's for having preached, "If the king's grace, being supreme head of the Church of England, did choose, denominate, and elect any layman, being learned, to be a Bishop, that he so chosen, without mention made of any orders, should be as good a Bishop as he is, or the best in England."[a] Courayer preposterously asks, "Does not this proposition, be it never so heretical, prove evidently that he had been consecrated himself?" Persons reduced to such "evidence" must be very doubtful of their cause.

We have proved the opportunity, and the will of the three

---

[a] Strype's *Memorials*, vol. i. Appendix, p. 287, and Collier's *Eccl. Hist.* vol. ii. p. 135.

parties concerned; this alone furnishes a ground for thinking the omission probable. There is no register whatever of the performance of the act of consecration; on the contrary, the registers speak of Barlow as having left St. Asaph's unconsecrated, and imply that he came to St. David's consecrated. Now, as he could not have been consecrated while he **had** no see,—indeed, as he only left one see to go to the other, as he was called " Bishop of St. David's " at the same moment that he ceased to be " Bishop-elect of St. Asaph," and therefore had no time to be consecrated during his transmutation,—we seem to have the clearest documentary evidence possible under the circumstances that he was never consecrated at all.

To recapitulate : considering the openly expressed opinions of both Cranmer and Barlow, that consecration was not necessary; that as this opinion **was** pleasing to the king, so it would not offend him to act upon it; that there was a most convenient opportunity of acting upon it; that there is no **record** of any consecration of Barlow by Cranmer, or any one commissioned by him, or by any one at all; that the documents relating to Barlow's successor at St. Asaph speak of him as having been " Bishop-elect" only, that is, unconsecrated, and use words to describe the cause of the vacancy, **which are** studiously varied from those which describe the translation of a true Bishop; considering too, that **the** documents relating to his induction to St. David's tacitly assume without asserting that he was already consecrated, though it is notoriously impossible that he could have undergone this rite *in transitu* from St. Asaph's to St. David's; considering also that it was a time of revolution in Church and State, the king grasping at absolute power in both, the Bishops and higher clergy infected with the new heresies, and the people bewildered with constant changes in religion, so that nothing was stable, and no man despaired **of introducing** any novelty, —it becomes utterly improbable **that** Barlow **was** ever consecrated at all; such considerable doubts are thrown on **the** point as **to** be equivalent to an entire denial of it; **and, in** the words **of** Courayer, the English ordinations **are** "ruined past all remedy." For where salvation is at stake, who would put up with such an utter uncertainty when he can have an infallible certainty?

It is utterly irrelevant to object that Barlow was summoned by writs to Parliament, and sat in convocation like a consecrated prelate; or even that, on the 19th of February 1541-42, he, with the Bishop of Gloucester, assisted the Bishop of Salisbury in consecrating Bulkeley. Of course he did; believing himself to be as good a Bishop as any one else, and having succeeded in palming himself off upon the world as a properly consecrated Bishop, we cannot be surprised either at finding him acting as such, or at seeing the world looking on unsurprised. Nor is the negative argument, which Courayer supposes to be "of no less force than the rest," of any weight; for it is not true. "Is there," he says, "one author found who during more than seventy years accused him of usurping the episcopate without consecration?" In those dangerous times, we must not expect to find all the suspicions of Catholics written out at length and published; but in matter of fact misgivings of the power of Barlow, Scory, and Coverdale to consecrate Parker and the rest did exist, as may be seen by the words of the commission by virtue of which the consecration was performed. This commission contained the following clause, quite unheard of before:

"Supplying nevertheless by our supreme authority, if there is or shall be wanting for the performance of the premises any of those things which, by the statutes of this realm, or by the laws of the Church, are required, or are necessary to that effect, either in those persons who are to be consecrated by you according to our command aforesaid, or in you or any of you, *in consequence of your condition, state, or faculties.* This being required by the necessity of the times and the urgency of the matters."

There was a doubt, then, and a public and urgent doubt too, about the *condition, state, and faculties* of the Bishops who were required to consecrate: and this doubt was not discussed according to the canons, but in consequence of the "necessities of the times" stifled by a royal writ; as Sanders says, "being therefore destitute of any legitimate ordination, when they were commonly said, and by the English laws themselves were truly proved not to be Bishops, they were obliged to invoke the secular arm" to confirm them in an office they had usurped "without any episcopal consecration."ᵃ What more natural than that Barlow, conscious of his own want of the episcopal character, but believing that "a Christian prince" had the apostolic power of raising men to that dignity, should seek such a proviso from the queen? especially considering there was a question whether the royal dispensations did not cease with the life of the prince, and require renewal in a new reign. Thus Archbishop Parker, anno 1569, in the case of marriage dispensations, though he would by no means dispute the queen's absolute power or papal juridiction, yet thought dispensations unsafe, because though during the prince's life such grants might be covered from dispute, yet another reign might call for retrospection.ᵇ

This doubt of the consecration of Barlow, Parker's consecrator, is, as Courayer owns, sufficient in itself to annihilate the English hierarchy. But English divines have attempted to find a loophole by affirming that Barlow's assistants at that ceremony, being real Bishops, consecrated him. But this objection comes with a very ill grace from those who altered the old rubric, and forbade the assistants to pronounce the words of consecration. The consecration comes from the consecrator, not from the assistants; they present the consecrand to the Archbishop, or his commissary, saying, "Most Reverend Father in God, we present unto *you* this godly and well learned man to be consecrated Bishop;" and then, as the rubric directs, "the Archbishop and Bishops present shall lay their hands upon the head of the elected Bishop, *the Archbishop saying*, 'Take the Holy Ghost; and remember that thou stir up the grace of God which is in thee by imposition of hands,' &c." Parker's consecration was conducted according to this form; yet we read, Barlow, Scory, Hodgkins, and Coverdale imposed their hands on the Archbishop, and said, "Take the Holy Ghost," &c.—"*Accipe* (*dixerunt Anglice*) *Spiritum Sanctum.*" How is this? The rubric is clear that the con-

---

ᵃ Sanders de Schism. lib. ii. (ed. 1585), fol. 166.
ᵇ Collier, Eccl. Hist. part ii. lib. vi. anno 1569.

secrating prelate alone pronounces the words of consecration, the assistants laying their hands on the Bishop-elect, and saying nothing. Barlow had helped to frame this rubric, which altered the old practice.[a] If there had been an intended and predetermined departure from this innovation, it would have been noticed distinctly, and not in so accidental a manner as this, of which it is impossible to determine whether it is not only a slip of the pen. There is no proof that the writer adverted to the fact that the *dixerunt* was a departure from the rubric, and as such to be noted by some little explanation of the cause, or other emphasis. Such a note being absent, it is much easier to believe that there was some oversight of the reporter than a transgression of the rubrics of the service which was being performed. But as all sacraments consist *in rebus et verbis*, as St. Thomas says,[b] both in symbol and words, he who only uses the symbol without pronouncing the words cannot be said to confer the Sacrament. And this was the case of the assistant Bishops, if they obeyed the prescriptions of the form which they professed to follow,—which we must suppose they did in spite of the plural verb used by the notary.

But even if they did all utter the words when they laid their hands on Parker, they did no more than the assisting Bishops at the consecration of a Catholic Bishop : yet we do not own that these Bishops do in any sense consecrate; but we say that they assist as witnesses, and to signify their assent, in the same way as the priests present impose their hands with the Bishop at the ordination of priests. That this was the intention of the Church in directing the presence of the assistant Bishops, is evident from the fact that they may in special cases be replaced by priests, as in the case of Pope Pelagius I., mentioned above. We have inquired of Bishops who have been assistants, who have told us that they never

---

[a] *Why* this alteration was made we cannot pretend to explain. Possibly they thought that so many pronouncing the same words at once was "mumbling" or "mummery;" at any rate, the alteration proved that they did not intend the assistant Bishops to be in any sense consecrators. The clear intention of the rubric is that the Archbishop *alone* consecrates.
[b] Sum. supp. ix. 35, art. v. sed contra.

intended to confer the Sacrament, but left that to the consecrator. The Catholic Church, therefore, will never recognise English orders, even though it could be proved that all Barlow's assistants at Parker's consecration were real Bishops, and that they all pronounced the words.

But can this be proved? With regard to the consecrations of Scory and Coverdale, they are represented in Cranmer's Register to have been performed on *the same day* (Aug. 30, 1551), and by the same prelates, Cranmer, Ridley, and Hodgkins; but at two places,[a] twelve miles apart—Scory's at Croydon, Coverdale's at Lambeth. Moreover they are attested by the same witnesses (one of the four being absent in Coverdale's case), and a sermon on the same text preached at both. Farther, on examining the certificate of the consecration which occurs in the Register next before those of Scory and Coverdale, namely Hooper's, it appears that Scory's is an exact copy of it down to the parties present, the person reading the mandate, the text of the sermon, and the mistakes in the spelling.

The records of the consecrations of Scory and Coverdale **are so** suspicious, that we may almost pronounce them to be forgeries; at any rate, they either are falsified, or else so carelessly drawn up that there is no reason to trust them; the credit of the notaries who drew them up, and the witnesses who signed them, is irreparably damaged;—and among these are Anthony Huse, the registrar, and John Incent, one of the notaries, both of whom drew up or signed what purports to be the account of Parker's consecration, and on whose authority the **word** *dixerunt* rests.

It is **besi**des very easy to account for the plural verb without any supposition of fraud. These notarial accounts are evidently drawn up after a fixed form. Now when the service of consecration was changed in 1550, the register was made **much more brief; but the** old **diffuse** method was restored in

---

[a] It cannot be said that the difference of places is a mere oversight, for the place at which either Scory or Coverdale's consecration took place (we forget which) is written over an erasure.

the first year of Elizabeth. Huse, the registrar, who had filled the same office in Catholic times, would naturally follow the old form of describing the ceremony as nearly as might be, just introducing the necessary alterations. Now in the Catholic service *all* the Bishops not only lay hands on the head of the consecrand, but also pronounce the words; the form, therefore, would be "*Accipe, dixerunt, Spiritum Sanctum.*"[a] By a mistake, this form might be allowed to remain in the registers, though the service itself had been altered. The Bishops themselves had altered the rubric, and therefore certainly altered the old practice. The registrar did not know, or did not happen to observe, the change, and so recorded the act in the same words as he had always been accustomed to record it; that is to say, the use of the word *dixerunt* in the register proves nothing against the rubric; and neither Scory, Coverdale, nor Hodgkins (who was a true Bishop, consecrated by Bonner in St. Paul's, Dec. 9, 1537), can be shown to have attempted to confer the Sacrament by using the full ceremonies, that is, by pronouncing the words as well as imposing the hands. It is noticeable, that the registrar in the same way make *all* the Bishops also pronounce the long sermon, "Give heed unto thy reading." &c.,—a thing very unlikely. It is also to be noticed, that this form of registration is afterwards changed, and brought into conformity with the rubrics.

Our investigation of the question whether Barlow was ever consecrated has extended to such a length, that we must resume our discussion of the other points on a future occasion. These points are, the validity and legality of the form used; the intention of the reformed Church of England in instituting Bishops—whether, that is, it was intended to make Catholic Bishops, or ministerial overseers; and the probability of the want of baptism in many Bishops through whom these same orders have been handed down.

---

[a] The rubric in the Pontifical is, "Deinde consecrator et assistentes Episcopi ambabus manibus caput consecrandi tangent, dicentes, 'Accipe Spiritum Sanctum.'"

THE ANGLICAN PRIESTHOOD.

[From the Rambler.]

"If Barlow was not consecrated," says Courayer, "the English ordinations are ruined past all remedy." But English divines will not allow this; they say that Barlow was assisted by three Bishops, about the orders of one of whom at least (Hodgkins) not a doubt can be raised. Now all these imposed hands on Parker, and all pronounced the words of consecration; if, therefore, any one was a real Bishop, that one consecrated Parker validly.

To this we answer, first, that it is very uncertain whether all did both **impose hands** and **pronounce the** words. In the Roman Catholic form of consecration all the assistant Bishops do so. In the Anglican form the rubric is altered, and the Archbishop or consecrating prelate alone pronounces the words. Now it is absurd to suppose that Baptism is conferred by pouring water only, **wi**thout using **the form of** words; **or** the Eucharist consecrated **by** one who takes bread into his hands, **but** makes no commemoration of the words of Christ. **So neither** are orders conferred by one who only imposes hands, but says nothing. In the English ordinal, therefore, **the** assisting Bishops are only witnesses, but in no sense consecrators. Barlow, Parker's consecrator, was one of the prelates who drew up the English ordinal, and therefore was very unlikely to have changed it. Moreover Parker, or his secretary John Jocelyn (in the short history of Parker's life in the *Antiquitates Britanniæ*), declares that he used "the very same solemnitie and manner of consecration (that was used towards himself) towards his brethren Bishops upon whom afterward he laid his hand." And there we know by the registers that he alone pronounced the words. Again, Parker's register declares that the consecration was *juxta forman libri* **auctoritate parliamenti** *editi*, according to the form of the book published by authority of parliament, *i. e.* the Prayer-Book of Edward VI., in which the rubric directs the consecrating prelate only to pronounce the words.

Against this we have the testimony of the register, which says that all four Bishops laid hands on Parker, and *dixerunt Anglice* (said in English), "Take the Holy Ghost, and remember that thou stir up the grace of God which is in thee by imposition of hands; for God hath not given us the spirit of fear, but of power and love and soberness." After this, they delivered the Holy Bible into his hands, using to him words to this effect: "Give heed unto thy reading, exhortation, and doctrine; think upon those things contained in this book; be diligent in them, that the increase coming thereby may be manifest unto all men: take heed unto thyself and unto thy teaching, and be diligent in doing them; for by doing this thou shalt save thyself and them that hear thee, through Jesus Christ our Lord."

Now we ask any unprejudiced person, who considers the unsacramental hortatory form of these words, whether it is more likely that they were mumbled out by four persons at once, contrary to the rubric, contrary to every principle and feeling of Protestants, especially contrary to the prejudices of Coverdale, one of the four, who would not even appear in a surplice; or that the registrars, who had been accustomed to to the Catholic form, where the three words, *Accipe Spiritum Sanctum*, are so pronounced, inadvertently used *dixerunt* for *dixit?* These registrars were not infallible, nor were they over-careful people; we have already noticed a blunder they committed about Coverdale, or Scory. To pin our faith, even our hopes of salvation, on their *obiter dicta*, their bysayings,—nay more, on a single word which they may have used only to obviate the trouble of having to reconstruct a Latin sentence,—is frightfully hazardous and presumptuous. And if they did make a mistake, as there is every reason to suspect, then Anglican orders depend on Barlow alone; and what a broken reed he is we sufficiently proved in our last article.

We have now to proceed to the other questions which we promised to discuss. The first of these is, whether the form prescribed by the ordinal of 1552 is valid. Now we concede without difficulty that the **form** considered in itself, if used in a Church where there is a true notion of priesthood, would be valid. But it does not thence follow that it was valid in England, much less that the very adoption of this form can be defended from a charge of temerarious presumption, which by itself proves that the Anglican body at that period cared nothing at all about the security of their succession.

Our grounds for this assertion are two—political and theological. First, the Protestants were in such a hurry to get rid of the old Catholic ordinal, that they risked all kinds of legal difficulties in order to introduce a new one as soon as possible. The new ordinal was first authorised to be drawn up 3 and 4 Edward VI. c. 12. It was composed and published by March 1549-50, and Cranmer immediately began to act upon it; the first Bishop to be consecrated after that date was John Ponet for the see of Rochester, 29th June 1550, when the new rite was used. Yet it was only authorised 5 and 6 Edward VI. c. 1, § 5, in 1552. It was swept away entirely by Mary, in 1553. When Elizabeth came to the throne, her first care was to restore the Common Prayer of Edward VI. An act was passed for that purpose, but by some oversight no mention was made of the ordinal. When, therefore, in 1559, Parker was to be consecrated, it became a question what rite was to be used. They would not use the Catholic rite; therefore the lawyers determined, "the order of King Edward's book is to be observed, for that there is none other special made in this last session of parliament." On this William Cecil, the prime mover of the whole matter, writes a note: "This book is not established by parliament."[a] But in spite of its being unsanctioned, and therefore invalid in law, they determined to go on with it; every body knows the consequence. When Bonner objected to Horne of Winchester that he was no true Bishop, and therefore incompetent to require the oath from him, the judges of the land were unable to affirm the legality of Horne's consecration; and a retrospective act of parliament had to be made (8 Elizabeth, c. 1, § 3), declaring that all ordinations made according to the new rite

---

[a] State-Paper Office, Dom. Eliz. vol. v. no. 25.

were to be considered valid to all intents and purposes. Such was the utter recklessness with which things were done in those days, that they did not wait for legal securities, but risked every thing for the present favour of men in office.

Secondly, though it is true that the more general opinion at the present day is, that the only essential matter and form of orders are imposition of hands and prayer, yet when the Anglican ordinal was framed the great majority of scholastics held that the essential matter was the tradition of the sacred vessels. Dr. Champney tells us that the only schoolman who asserted the present opinion, argued for it on these grounds: three Bishops are essential to consecrate a Bishop; but the only thing which the three do together is to impose hands, and invoke the Holy Ghost; this, therefore, is the only essential matter and form. The argument, besides erroneously assuming that three Bishops are essential, was certainly not applicable to the Anglican ordinal, where the assistants only impose hands without any invocation. The theologian, therefore, who was with them on one point was doubly against them on another. They must therefore have known that their proceedings were against the opinion of Christendom; that none but themselves thought the form sufficient; that it was therefore extremely rash and scandalously reckless to adopt it, when they could not possibly have *known* its sufficiency. It was a random shot, fired by people who did not care whether they hit the mark or not. "The new form of ordination," says Champney,[a] "was not established by parliament on any grounded persuasion that it was conformable to the manner used by the Apostles; but rather as a mean, both to leave the Catholic manner and yet to retain some external semblance of ordination;" the world not being yet ripe for their refined religion in its nakedness. Even still, the general opinion mentioned above is only the most probable: if the tradition of the vessels is accidentally omitted, it must be supplied; and if not supplied, the ordination is considered doubtful, and that though the consecrator was an undoubted Bishop

---

[a] Vocation of Bishops, p. 161.

in full communion with Rome. *A fortiori*, it is doubtful when conferred by Barlow in the Anglican schism. Yet we will not pretend that these things by themselves invalidate the Anglican succession. We only adduce them to show the *animus* of the first reformers; their heedless disregard of consequences, the absence of any anxiety to be right, unscrupulous rashness, and, in fine, the secret intention of abolishing the sacerdotal succession, and every vestige of a sacrificing priesthood.

But what have we to do with secret intentions? asks the Anglican. We deny *in toto* your doctrine about intention, which we say invalidates your Sacraments, so that you can never be sure you have them at all.

What, then, is the Catholic doctrine of intention? First of all, as even Anglicans confess, and bear witness against Wicliffites, Hussites, Albigenses, and the like, "the unworthiness of the ministers hinders not the effect of the Sacrament." "Non nocet," says Innocent III.,[a] "malitia Episcopi vel presbyteri neque ad baptismum infantis, neque ad Eucharistiam conferendam, vel ad cætera ecclesiastica officia,"—" the malice of the officiating Bishop or priest does not hurt the Sacraments they administer." Next, "there are three things necessary for the Sacrament of the Eucharist: a certain person, namely a priest, regularly ordained by a visible tangible Bishop, and properly set apart for this office; next, the solemn words of the canon; and thirdly, the *faithful intention* of the person uttering them." Eugenius IV., in his Bull to the Armenians, repeated this more clearly: "All Sacraments require three things—the things as matter, the words as form, and the person of the minister to confer the Sacrament with *the intention of doing what the Church does.*" This expression was adopted by the Fathers of the Council of Trent, and sanctioned by an anathema:[b] "If any one says that an intention *at least of doing what the Church does* is not required in ministers who consecrate or confer the Sacraments, be he anathema;" so again in the fourth canon *de Baptismo*.

[a] Ep. d. 4 id Maii 1210.
[b] Sess. vii. can. 11.

It had been previously used by the Council of Florence, which said that a woman, a pagan, or a heretic, might, in cases of necessity, be minister of baptism, " provided that the person observed the form of the Church, *and* intended to do what the Church does. Here the observance of the ceremonies seems to be made a distinct thing from intending to do what the Church does, as if the ceremonies might be used without the intention: hence perhaps Alexander VIII. prohibited the proposition, " Baptism is valid when conferred by a minister who observes the whole external rite and form of baptising, but internally resolves in his heart, ' I do not intend what the Church does '" Hence the safer school of Catholics teaches that what the Church does is not the mere external ceremony, but the whole act, external and internal. The Church, they say, does what Christ does, that is, the whole Sacrament; and in what she does she is not to be separated from Christ. The Church and Christ, although distinguishable in reason, are mystically one ; and therefore unless the minister have the intention of really doing what Christ does, he does not confer the Sacrament. But, as Anglicans utterly reject this doctrine of intention, it is futile to insist upon it in arguing with them ; indeed, they turn round upon us and say, that if such intention is requisite for its validity, we can never be sure that we have a valid Sacrament. Stories are told of Jews, still Jews in heart, being Archbishops and Bishops in Spain ; how can we tell what their intention was? With them, therefore, we must take the lower ground, and use the opinion of Catherinus, that external intention only is requisite in the minister; that is to say, it is only when sacramental matter and form are used inadvertently, or in joke, that they do not constitute Sacraments. Even Anglicans must admit that these defects of intention invalidate Sacraments. For example, if a priest at dinner, with a loaf of bread before him, in the course of argument with a Protestant happens to pronounce the words *hoc est corpus meum*, does he consecrate? If a Bishop in earnest talk puts his hands on a man's shoulder and says, " I hope and pray that you may receive the Holy Ghost, and be a good priest or Bishop," does he ordain or consecrate him? Is the grace of God so tied to the form of words, that the effect *must* follow with whatever intention they are uttered, so that if a priest pronounces the words of consecration by accident in a baker's shop he converts all the loaves into the Body of our Lord? The idea is preposterous. Some doctrine of intention is quite necessary; and that of Catherinus is the lowest possible. Luther certainly taught that a priest absolving in jest really absolved: [a] and the Council of Trent denounced all who "trusted so much to faith as to fancy themselves absolved, though they had no contrition, and though the priest had no intention of acting seriously and absolving truly;" and declared that "the man would be most careless of his salvation, who knew that a priest absolved him in joke, and yet did not look for one who would act seriously." [b] The use of the right matter and form inadvertently, or in joke, therefore, does not constitute a Sacrament. Now suppose that the Anglican ordinal preserves the true matter and form for making a priest, we assert that this preservation was inadvertent and unintentional.

Put the case in this way. If a Bishop, called upon to ordain a priest, should object that he believed neither in the apostolic succession, nor in the sacerdotal character of the priesthood; but afterwards, from secular motives, should consent to confer the orders: if he used the matter and form prescribed by the Church, he would certainly confer a valid Sacrament in spite of his disbelief. But suppose that the person to be ordained, and those who demanded his ordination, all chimed in and said, "Neither do we believe in the succession, nor in the sacerdotal power; therefore alter the matter and form of the Sacrament so as to leave out the expression of these doctrines." Suppose hereupon they should leave out the phrase, "Take power to offer sacrifice to God, and to celebrate Mass for the living and the dead," from the ordinal of priests, as expressive of the sacerdotal character, and retain only, "Receive the Holy Ghost: whose sins thou

---

[a] Eleventh prop. condemned by Leo X.
[b] Sess. xiv. cap. vi. and can. 9.

dost forgive, they are forgiven ; and whose sins thou dost retain, they are retained. And be thou a faithful dispenser of the word of God, and of his Holy Sacraments," as being expressive of a certain *ministerial*, not *sacerdotal*, power, which alone they intended to confer. Suppose, at the same time, they abolished the liturgy of the Mass, denounced the doctrine of Transubstantiation, or indeed of any Real Presence at all, except in the heart of the believer, carefully weeding out every mention of oblation, sacrifice, or any other sacerdotal act. It is clear, if, in spite of all these endeavours, the form still retained is in itself sufficient to confer sacerdotal power, it is so only accidentally, and is used in such sense quite inadvertently,—that the officiating prelate who uses it with the intention of conferring *ministerial* powers only, no more confers the sacerdotal powers by it, than the priest who in the course of argument says the words *hoc est corpus meum* while sitting at the breakfast-table consecrates the bread he holds in his hand, because he does not intend to do what the Church does.

Hence, even supposing that the doctrine of intention only guarded against accidental consecrations, without invalidating a single act where the form and matter are used, with whatever *private intention* the minister might use them, it by no means follows that it guards the Sacraments in the same way against a *public and notorious intention*, especially when that intention declares itself by a change in the received form of celebrating the Sacrament, and such a change as is intended to exclude that which is an essential part. The Mass is abolished, and declared blasphemous ; but a new religious service is invented, in which the form and matter of the Sacrament are retained. Yet before he begins, the priest turns to the people and says : " Observe, I have made great changes in the rite, in order to show that there is no Real Presence, no sacrifice ; you all bear me witness that the words I utter, though the same as the *hocus-pocus* of the old massing priests, are intended to operate no essential change in the elements." Does the use of the form and matter under such circumstances operate against the publicly expressed will and intention of the minister and his conventicle, and effect that which he intended it should not effect? In other words, let us ask the ministers of the Establishment, Do you, in spite of articles, homilies, and the concurrent voice of all your doctors, make the bread which you take in your hands into the Body of Christ which was born of the Virgin Mary and crucified on the cross? Have you a power as individuals which your Church repudiates as a body? Can you strain your intentions beyond her meaning? And is not her meaning with regard to the sacrifice of Christ in the Eucharist, and His real presence under the species of the elements, only too distinct, too plain?

But if you doubt what to answer about this Sacrament, take the case of another. In Baptism and the Eucharist there is this peculiarity, that there is but one Baptism, one Eucharist,—that the matter or form of these Sacraments cannot be used for any other ecclesiastical purpose than to confer them, and them alone. But as for the matter of imposition of hands, and the form, " Receive the Holy Ghost," they are applicable to all sorts of intentions. There is one Spirit, but different gifts, says the Apostle, in a text which the reformers were always quoting: " And He gave some apostles, and some prophets, and other some evangelists, and other some pastors and teachers." There were also elders, presbyters, or priests; a word which *need* signify nothing sacerdotal, and which the English reformers, in order to deceive the people, determined to retain. An elder, who is a mere teacher, a preacher of the Word, and a dispenser of Sacraments identical with the Jewish, requires the gift of the Spirit; therefore requires the imposition of hands. Let us therefore retain the word 'priest' in this signification of elder, and ordain him with convenient matter and form for the function of minister. Now as there are different gifts of the Spirit, all given by imposition of hands and prayer, how can you be sure that you get one when you seek another? If there was but one gift given by these means, you might perchance attain it accidentally by the use of the means, though with a wrong intention; but when there are different gifts, and you solemnly repudiate one, and claim another, with what face can you, half a century afterwards, turn round and tell us that you had the one you repudiated? You would not be sacerdos, but chose only to be presbyter. Is it likely that you were surprised into being made sacerdos instead of mere presbyter, when the form used was (to put the case mildly) indifferent for either?*

It was this want of sacrificial authority which furnished the great argument of the English Catholic doctors of the sixteenth century against the new Anglican ministry. Thus Cardinal Allen:

"Among the scoffs there is one chief, that touches not our persons only, but the whole order of priests. We are called 'massing priests' not only in the queen's proclamation, but also by the new preachers in their pulpits (those true 'seats of the scornful') to show their contempt and scorn. Now although this name is used in most unseemly wise in the proclamation (which ought to be a serious document), we interpret it as a confession that we Catholics, who alone make use of true sacerdotal powers, are really distinguished from the new Calvinist ministers, whom the people, because of their sham imitation of our divine worship, usually call priests: though the Protestants themselves avoid the name, and with reason; for their ministers have no right to be called so, because they have no more power to administer the Sacraments of Christ (except Baptism, which a woman may confer) than they have to create a new sun or moon.

The Church of God acknowledges no other priests; Christ himself ordained no other priesthood than those whom our enemies scornfully call 'massing priests.' For to them alone, and not to others, did our Saviour give power to consecrate and offer His Body and Blood: and this is the same as saying Mass, or offering sacrifice."*

But, says Courayer,* the English have always admitted

---

a We have purposely weakened our argument, to adapt it to Anglican scruples about intention; if we had taken the higher ground, it would have run thus: since imposition of hands is in itself an indifferent ceremony, applicable to benedictions, to confirmation, to cures, as well as to orders, its meaning must be determined by some special intention. In the ordination of priests, the Church intends by imposition of hands to convey a sacrificial power. The Anglican reformers, on the contrary, intended *not* to convey a sacrificial power: their use, therefore, of imposition of hands was *toto cœlo* different from that of the Church; and consequently, as they neither did, nor intended to do, what the Church does, their ordination was null and void. If it be objected that they called their ministers priest and Bishops in the ordinal, this does not prove the intention. They hanged all sacrificing priests; therefore their priests were not sacrificing priests. Their Bishops held no more the same office with a Catholic Bishop (that of *summus sacerdos*) than an elector of Westminster with an Elector of Hanover.

b Apology for the Priests of the Society and of the Seminaries against the Proclamation, chap. vi; apud Bridgewater, Concertatio, fol. 163 b.

c Apology, chap. xii.

the Eucharistic sacrifice; they allow "a representative and commemorative sacrifice, *which is no ways different from that of the cross*, and which bears its name because it is the image and memorial of it, and *because the same victim is there offered.*" Courayer was abominably hoaxed by some High-Church Anglican, if he really believed this statement. The English always admitted this, forsooth! However, leaving the fact at present without settlement, Courayer here owns that if, during any single generation of ministers, the Eucharistic sacrifice, identical with that of the cross, and consisting of the same victim, **was** denied, such denial invalidates their orders then, and of course ever after. For that which a man has not, he cannot give. Bramhall admits as much: "They who are ordained priests ought to have power to consecrate the Sacrament of the Body and Blood of Christ, that is, to make them present after such manner as they were present at the first institution."[a] But of course, like all heretics, he appeals to his Bible, and declares that then they were not present as the Church teaches they were, namely, subtantially and really, under the species of the elements. This appeal to Scripture is the dodge of all heretics. The Sabellian or Unitarian believes in Father, Son, and Holy Ghost, "as they are taught in Scripture." The Pelagian believes in original sin, "as found in the Bible." But all refuse alike to believe these doctrines as the Church defines them; they will be their own judges, and will not listen for a moment to the condemnation that the whole Church pronounces against them.

But now as to the *fact*. Do Anglicans even yet believe in the Real Presence? Will they worship It? This is the test. Worship follows faith, says St. Augustine. The rule of both is the same. They use Catholic words; but not in a Catholic sense. Nor did they always use Catholic words; for three-quarters of a century at least it was excommunication, if not death, to believe in the real presence of Christ in the elements. The only Real Presence tolerated was that of

---

[a] Consecration of Protestant Bishops vindicated, chap. xi.

Christ in the soul of the faithful receiver, as taught by the "judicious" Hooker, who in his day was looked upon as a marvel of boldness for daring to teach even this. Poor Cheney, the Bishop of Gloucester, whose faith on this point was sound, refused to attend the Convocation of London in April 1571, where some of the lingering Catholic usages were to be denounced, especially those that seemed to point towards a belief in the Real Presence, or the Eucharistic sacrifice. Those who administered communion were thenceforth to put the bread, not into people's mouths, but into their hands; they were to use no ceremonies or gestures not appointed by the Book of Common Prayer.[a] All altars were to be pulled down, and the altar-stones defaced and put to some common use—generally that of paving-stones in the porch, that all feet might trample on that whereon sacrifice had been offered. Cheney was the *only one* who protested against this; and that not openly, but only by absenting himself: and for this he was excommunicated by Parker and the other Bishops!. But it is of no use to collect testimonies,—that has been done authoritatively by the judge who decided on the stone-altar case; he showed that the Church of England has no real and proper sacrifice, and therefore no altar; therefore, again, no priesthood, and no Real Presence.

It is foolish to pretend that there can be a real presence of the Lamb of God without a sacrifice. He is the everliving Victim; where He is, He is present as the sin-offering for the world. When He comes into the hands of His priests, and is held in their hands, and elevated in the sight of angels and men, as an act of homage to the Eternal Father, it is a sacrifice. To deny it, is to deny that Christ is still the Lamb of God; it is to deny that He has taken His own blood to heaven, and that He ever lives there to be our propitiatory victim. The Real Presence and the sacrifice go together; the Church of England in its origin, and for three-quarters of a century, denied both. In the exigences of controversy, some of the doctors admitted sometimes one, sometimes the other;

---

[a] Collier's Eccl. Hist. in ann. 1571.

but only unreally and deceitfully, as the Arians admitted the eternal Sonship. Sometimes they would admit with Cranmer that He was "present sacramentally; by which, as Dr. Heskyns pointed out, they meant, "much as the wine is present in the bush that hangs at the tavern-door to denote it, or the husband's love in the wedding-ring; which manner of presence is next door to nothing." Or with Hooker, they would deny any real presence in the bread, of which our Lord says, "This is My Body," and would place it hypothetically in the believer's soul. Sometimes they would, with Zuinglius, deny it altogether. So about the sacrifice. Jewell, pressed by Harding, will allow a sacrifice of praise, of thanksgiving, of our own bodies, of a commemoration or representation of the death of Christ; but of Christ himself never. "You will say, Ye offer not up Christ really unto God His Father. No, Mr. Harding, neither we nor you can so offer Him; nor did Christ ever give you commission to make such sacrifice." Nay, if any man pretended to make such a sacrifice, queen, bishops, clergy, and Protestant laity, conspired together to hand him without mercy. "How does a man dare," asks Lawrence Humphrey, Regius Professor of Theology and Vice-Chancellor of Oxford, "to accuse Judge Manhood of cruelty; and defend Maine, the sacrificer, the Masssayer, the Bull-bearer, whom he hanged?" This sentence of the "Jesuitismus" occurs in a passage where Humphrey is striving to prove that our martyrs were not executed for religion. It was not religion to pretend to sacrifice. "You say," he writes in another place, "if they visit our churches, 'they will be deprived of the benefit and privilege of the Catholic religion, the sacrifice of the altar.' Happy loss, to lose the papistical sacrifice, which derogates from the Passion of Christ! No loss, but gain! 'They will not see the angels ascending and descending at the elevation of the Body of Christ.' We are not so mad as to think there are any angels present there, where Christ neither is nor wishes to be present; nor will we profess to see what nobody ever saw or could see."ᵃ Again, "The Jesuits are more sacrilegious than

---

ᵃ p. 134.

the Pharisees: these only sacrificed cattle; the Jesuits offer the Body of Christ to the Father—they elevate it, and devour it."[a] The means which were used to impose this misbelief on the English people may be seen from the speech of Feckenham, Abbot of Westminster, in the Parliament of 1559, against Elizabeth's reforms.

"Dr. Cranmer was so contrary to himself in this matter, that in one year he did set forth a catechism, dedicated to Edward VI., wherein he doth most constantly affirm and defend the real presence of Christ's Body in the holy Eucharist; and very shortly after he did most shamefully deny the same, falsifying both the Scriptures and doctors, to the no small admiration of all learned readers. Dr. Ridley, the notablest learned of that opinion in this realm, did set forth at Paul's Cross the real presence of Christ's Body in the Sacrament, with these words (which I heard, being there present), 'How that the devil did believe that the Son of God was able to make the stones bread; and we English people, that do confess that Jesus Christ was the very Son of God, yet will not believe that He did make a bread His very Body. Therefore we are worse than the devil, seeing that our Saviour ... took bread, and said ... This is My Body, which shall be given for you.' And shortly after, the same Dr. Ridley, notwithstanding this speech at Paul's Cross, did deny the same; and in the last book of Dr. Cranmer and his complices (the very one which the bill under discussion was to restore), the words *Hoc est corpus meum* did so trouble their wits, that they left out the verb substantive *est*, and made Christ's words in English thus, 'Take, eat, this My Body,' and not, 'this is My Body.' This thing being espied by others, and great fault found with it, they were fain to patch up the matter with a little piece of paper clapped over the foresaid words, whereon was written the verb substantive *est*."[b]

In Cranmer's days the English were not quite ripe for his reforms; but in the first year of Elizabeth, before any reforming law was carried, the people began "spoiling the churches, pulling down the altars, treading the Sacrament under their feet, and hanging up the Knave of Clubs in the place thereof;" and the new clergy encouraged them. They taught that there was no "change of the substance of bread and wine;" that the Body is only given, taken, and eaten after a heavenly and spiritual (by which they meant *unreal*) manner; that the Sacrament may not be elevated or worshipped (Art. 28); and that the sacrifice of Christ in the Mass for quick and dead was a blasphemous fable and dangerous

---

[a] p. 174.
[b] Somers Tracts, vol. i. p. 81. Spoken April 16, against the second reading of the bill for the introduction of the Common Prayer.

deceit (Art. 31). The Bishops called those priests who refused to forsake the priesthood and become ministers[a] "wicked impes of Antichrist,"[b] "hedge-priests,"[c] "beasts,"[d] "*Romanenses sacrificuli*," "bloody butchers of Christ," "shamble ministers," "conjurors." If they retained a form of ordination **which in** itself was sufficient to confer a power of which they thought such scorn, was it not simply through inadvertence, and against their will, and therefore no **more** valid than the words *hoc est corpus meum* inadvertently pronounced?

Again, at the time when such notions of the priesthood were rife, what notions of the apostolic succession would there be? There was no miracle in the Eucharist; it was a mere memorial, that any layman might make. What need of the succession of supernatural power or authority where none such was wanted, where there was no supernatural work to perform? What wonder then, if, as in the "Catena Patrum" for the Eucharistic sacrifice, the authors of the *Tracts for the Times* had to leave out all the first and second generations of English reformers, except Jewell, the "irreverent dissenter," whose testimony makes directly against them, and to begin with Bilson, Hooker, Overall, Field, and the divines of the **close of the sixteenth** century, so in **the** Catena on apostolical succession all the earlier "fathers" had to be passed over likewise! If they had but gone back to the spokesmen of the English Church in 1580, to those whom the government and Bishops of England put forward to conduct the controversy with the "Romanists," whom they racked before conference and hanged afterwards,—they would have found a different kind of testimony. "I would not have you think," says Dr. Whitaker, Regius Professor of Divinity at Cambridge, "that we make such reckoning of your orders as to hold our own vocation unlawful without them."[e] After-

---

[a] Archbishop Parker tendered a submission to Sir John Southworth, expressing his contrition for having "relieved certain priests who had refused the ministry." State-Paper Office, Domestic, July 13, 1568.
[b] Dom. Eliz. vol. xviii. no. 21.
[c] vol. xix. no. 18.
[d] vol. xx. no. 5.
[e] Answer to Campion's Ten Reasons, Op. tom. i. p. 225.

wards, when harder pressed by Bellarmine and Stapleton, he said, " Though our Bishops and ministers be not ordained by papistical Bishops, yet they are orderly and lawfully ordained." He maintains that the "ordination" of the French Calvinists by a lay cobbler was lawful ; and taunts his adversaries that they account none lawful pastors but such as are created according to their form or order. Dr. Fulke, another cruel enemy of our martyrs, and Margaret, Professor of Divinity at Cambridge, says, " You are highly deceived if you think we esteem your offices of Bishops, priests, and deacons better than layman ; . . . . and with all our hearts we defy, abhor, detest, and spit at your stinking, greasy, Antichristian orders." [a] Yes, this "greasing" was the mark of the very thing they wished to get rid of, the sacerdotal sacrificial power : " Thou shalt pour the oil of unction upon his head ; and *by this rite shall he be consecrated.* Thou shalt bring also Aaron and his children, and put mitres upon them, and they shall be priests to me by a *perpetual ordinance.*" [b] So they abolished, defied, abhorred, detested, and spat at the holy unction ; if what they retained was in itself sufficient to confer this power they so hated, what was it but an accident, an inadvertence ?

Harding, writing against Jewell,[c] says : .

"Epiphanius writeth of Zaccheus, *Ludenter sancta mysteria contrectabat; et sacrificia, cum laicus esset, impudenter tractabat* ('He illusively handled the sacred mysteries; and whereas he was a layman, impudently took in hand the sacrifices'). What sacrifices, I pray you, hath your religion that a layman may not handle as well as a priest? But because you have abandoned all external sacrifice and priesthood, therefore you judge this example belongeth not unto you."

Jewell had declared that the example touched not the Anglicans, because their Bishops were made " in form and order." Harding answered, that they did touch them in this point, " because priests are not so consecrated with you that they may stand to offer the sacrifice of the altar." Bristow, Sanders, Stapleton, made the same objection : You have no

[a] Fulke's Answer of a true Christian, p. 59; and Retentive against Bristow's Motives, p. 69.
[b] Exord. xxix. 7-9.
[c] Detection of sundry foul Errors, &c. p. 234.

orders, for your ministers have no sacrifice to offer that laymen may not offer as well. This opinion was shared by the Anglicans. In 1582, Dr. Aubrey, Archbishop Grindal's Vicar-General, acknowledged Scotch Presbyterian orders: this had been already done on a much larger scale for ministers ordained abroad. The consecrations of the Bishops were conducted in most slovenly style. Udall, a Protestant writer,[a] complains of the " unreverent beginning and proceeding with the ordaining of Church ministers in a corner." We do not believe the Nag's-head fable; but neither do we believe in the prim decency of Parker's register. Consecrations and ordinations *were* " unreverently" performed by the first Elizabethan Bishops. On the 17th of June 1586, William Johnson, the secretary of Adderton, **Bishop** of St. David's, informs the Privy Council of some particulars of his master's conduct; among the rest we are told that,

"At another time he made **two** ministers in Kent in the house of one Whiskerd, a minister also, and commanded me to make their letters of orders; which I did, and set down these words, *in œdibus* such a one, naming Whiskerk (whose Christian name I cannot remember): whereat my Lord Bishop was angry, and said that I should have set them down *made in the church*. My answer was, that I desired his lordship to pardon me in that, because I might be called to justify the truth upon my oath, which then must be contrary to my **writing, whereunto** I would not consent."[b]

It is not our intention here to *prove* that the priesthood of the new law is a sacrificing priesthood. It would take us too long to do so in the present article; we only say, that *if* it is, if the 200,000,000 of Catholics and 60,000,000 or 70,000,000 of orthodox Orientals,—not to mention the other Eastern heretics, who, however, are orthodox on this point,—happen to be right, while the Protestants are wrong, then the Protestant succession is null, even though the form or ordination is sufficient for a Church which confesses the sacerdotal power. The position of the Church of England is one without precedent; before her no other heresy ever at the same time denied the sacerdotal power and claimed the sacerdotal

---

[a] Demonstration of Discipline, p. 43.
[b] State-Paper Office, Domestic, 1586, June 17.

succession. And yet Anglican divines have settled the whole affair as magisterially and infallibly as if each Bramhall or Taylor had been a Pope, instead of a strenuous denier of any infallible authority whatever in the Church; and this though they had no precedents to appeal to, and though every Church in Christendom that had any pretence to episcopal succession at all was dead against them. Never, perhaps, has the world seen another such example of self-confident, self-appointed pastors, "feeding themselves without fear," as these Anglican divines, pretending to absolute certainty in a matter where no absolute certainty can possible be.

The last argument on which we depend for showing the extreme uncertainty of Anglican ordinations, is the uncertainty of their baptisms. No one can be a Christian priest who is not a Christian. Now in the beginning of this century the English Vicars-Apostolic, after careful inquiries, and a minute personal inspection of the way in which Baptism was then administered, decreed that all Anglican or English dissenting baptisms since 1773 were to be reckoned doubtful unless distinctly proved to be certain. This decree was embodied in a canon by the first synod of Oscott, and was allowed and confirmed by the present Pope, March 13, 1853. The canon runs as follows:

"Since the causes have grown more urgent which in the beginning of this century led the Vicars-Apostolic to decree that all persons born since 1773, and baptised among the Protestants, when converted, were to be baptised under condition, we absolutely renew this rule, and command that all converts from Protestantism are to be conditionally baptised, unless it is most abundantly evident from indubitable proofs that in their baptism all things were properly performed so far as matter and form are concerned."

This must be taken to be the decree of the Catholic Church concerning the uncertainty of Anglican Baptism, and therefore, a *fortiori*, concerning the uncertainty of Anglican orders, even if no other argument of their invalidity could be produced. And the experience of many persons will justify the decision of the Church. Every clergyman who takes care how he baptises has experienced the wrath of the monthly nurse for wetting the child's face, or spoiling its cap, or for insisting on the removal of that covering. The nurses have no patience with the new-fangled scrupulosity of Puseyites. It is quite contrary to what they were always used to. We remember a Catholic, who was present at the baptism of one of the royal family, declaring solemnly that the late Archbishop of Canterbury was in such a fuss about the Jordan water, and the lace that muffled the royal child, that he first poured the water, and then after a considerable lapse of time added the words, as if he had forgotten them. We can call to the remembrance of a certain fellow of Brazenose College, Oxford, that once, when travelling in Cumberland, he undertook to administer Baptism in a village church there, and only some days after adverted to the fact that *he had used no water*. The writer of this article was once present at a Baptism, when the officiating Protestant clergyman dipped his forefinger into the water, then put his finger to his tongue, and then applied it to the child's forehead and repeated the words of baptism; washing the child, if at all, not with water but with spittle. On inquiry afterwards, he was told that this was done to prevent the child taking cold. He has also repeatedly heard from a gentleman who was curate in a populous parish of London, that the practice of his fellow-curates was to range around the font the thirty or forty women who used every Sunday to bring children to be baptised, and then with one form of words to sprinkle the water round, without knowing or caring whether it touched the be-bonneted and be-capped children at all, or whether he only washed the nurses and godmothers. When baptismal regeneration is an open question in the Anglican communion, and when the majority of clergymen deny that doctrine, who can wonder at any amount of carelessness in the administration of the form?

These two last arguments apply as strongly to the Irish as to the English succession. Through whomsoever the clergy of the Irish Establishment first derived their orders, at any rate they have no sacrificing priesthood, and their baptisms are as uncertain as those of their English brethren. Not to mention the other interruptions of the succession by the transfer of English Bishops to Irish sees, and of the ordination by commission or otherwise of Irish Archbishops in England, are we mistaken in supposing that Dr. Whately was himself consecrated in Lambeth? But this is a question of little importance, when we are satisfied that the succession is lost in other ways.

To conclude, we beg our Protestant readers not to confuse the argument by introducing the Caroline divines. Suppose we granted that they were orthodox as regards the succession and sacerdotal powers (which we are far from doing), what influence would that have on persons who lived half a century before? We assert that the succession was lost in 1550; how can a return to right sentiments in 1600 rehabilitate it? "Other foundation can no man lay than that which is laid." You are built on Barlow, Scory, Coverdale, and men of that kidney. You may build what you please on this foundation; but no amount of gold and jewels heaped upon the sand and mud will change such a quagmire into the rock of Peter.

ANTHONY, EARL OF SHAFTESBURY,
A PROTESTANT CHAMPION OF THE SEVENTEENTH CENTURY.

[From the Rambler.]

MANY years ago there was an enormously wicked club, whose members had resolved to evoke the Prince of Darkness; and the question amongst them then arose as to what shape his Satanic majesty should be requested to assume. Some proposed a dog, an ass, or an ape; others voted for some human monster of iniquity—a Nero, a Borgia, or, if we are rightly informed, the Regent Duke of Orleans. Could the query by any possibility have been proposed to ourselves, we should have perhaps suggested Anthony Ashley Cooper, first Earl of Shaftesbury, grandfather of the author of the *Characteristics*, and ancestor of the present coryphæus of Exeter Hall in London. Such a combination of astuteness, cleverness, and wickedness, the world has rarely seen; and it is not a little remarkable, that his inherent animosity to the Church of God has descended, though of course without his moral vices, like an heir-loom in his family. Charles II. once told him, that "he was the most abandoned profligate then alive within the British dominions;" to which accusation Shaftesbury bowed a polite assent, upon condition, as he implied, that the charge should be limited to the king's subjects, and *not extend to royalty*.

About two miles from Cranbourne, in Dorsetshire, stands the magnificent seat of Wimborne St. Giles, with the adjoining park watered by the river Allen; but it was not in the present mansion that the Achitophel of Dryden was born. Its predecessor existed for generations as a residence of humbler dimensions, and was brought into the family by Anne, daughter and heiress of Sir Anthony Ashley, who married the son of Sir John Cooper of Rockburn, in the county of Southampton. The fruit of this alliance was our hero, who first saw the light under the patrimonial roof-tree of his mother, at Wimborne, on the 22d of July 1621. The grandson of two baronets—magnates far less common then than now—was sure to attract some attention in those rural districts, where brains were scarce, and his future possessions were to be large. But as a boy he was precocious, and every way remarkable. At fifteen he went to Oxford, and was admitted at Exeter College, where he studied hard for a couple of years; removing subsequently to Lincoln's Inn, that he might bury himself, as he afterwards said, "in the lumber of legal lore." What he learned from it was an acuteness of cunning, in which no man of his age could match him. Had he been destined for an attorney, he would have combined the faculties of the crocodile and alligator to the perfect satisfaction of the most critical Sir Joseph Jekyll. As it was, however, his ambition developed on a larger scale, and he advanced from a survey of the practice to an analysis of the principles of law; proceeding, moreover, still further, until he had thoroughly mastered the entire theory particularly developed in the constitution of his country. Here, in other words, he laid the foundations of his later career. Into the pleasures of the metropolis he just so far plunged as not to enervate his intellect, although they destroyed his moral principles, or at least materially helped to do so. There was a national crisis at hand, which would be sure to interest a mind like his, even more than sensualism. He got elected for Tewkesbury to that brief Parliament which met at Westminster on the 13th of April 1640, only to be dissolved almost immediately by the infatuated Stuart. Thunder-clouds gathered rapidly over the political horizon. Hampden, Pym, Eliot, and Oliver Cromwell, were already the idols of the hour.

It was an age of suppressed internal agitation and profound hypocrisy. Hollowness seems to have been the order of the day. Patriotism, morals, and religion, moved in one universal masquerade. The court carried on government with no inconsiderable degree of apparent dignity; but with utter unconsciousness that the ground would before long actually yawn beneath its feet, and swallow up the crown of the sovereign, the coronets of the aristocracy, and the gilded croziers of a pretended Protestant episcopacy, in the common earthquake. Puritanism, too, sat dreaming over pious projects of its own,—liberty of a particular kind, Presbyterianism in all the platitude of its dullness, sermons of interminable length, prayers uncircumscribed by forms, ministers with sour faces and no surplices, sabbaths wrapt in sackcloth, a suppression of fairs, wakes, mummers, dancing, dice, cross-buns, hot cakes, and spiced ale; and above and beyond all, the deletion or destruction of every conceivable vestige of Popery. Neither party seemed to have any notion that they were musing or mocking over a mine of moral gunpowder,—the righteous results of an unhallowed spiritual revolt, covering its deeds of darkness beneath the name and pretences of a Reformation. The nation, therefore, having gone wrong for a hundred and twenty years, reeled forward in its judicial blindness; many a sincere conscience feeling inwardly that matters could never be right, yet few or none able to see or know how the awful spell of illusion might be really dissolved. Thus affairs effervesced into the very essence of imposture. The social and political atmosphere swarmed with knaves and pretenders. Maladies enough there evidently were, and on such a colossal scale, that every quack with his notions, texts, or nostrums, could obtain a hearing generally far beyond his deserts. The horrors of what Clarendon so pompously describes as the Great Rebellion, were the natural consequences flowing from the events that had gone before, and could no more have been avoided than any other effect proceeding from its original causes. Mankind had sown the wind, and had for their just punishment to reap the whirlwind.

The wealthy heir of Wimborne St. Giles had closed neither his eyes nor ears to the phenomena amongst which he was thrown. Full of that self-conceit, which too many of his contemporaries called philosophy, he resolved to carve out a course which, come whatever might, should be at least favourable to his private fortunes. Hobbes had already written, although he had not published, his book *De Cive*, which afterwards grew up into the *Leviathan;* but the future Earl of Shaftesbury was one with him in several of his grand axioms, particularly as to its being lawful under any circumstances to make use of evil for our own advantage. "If I were cast," says the sophist of Malmsbury, "into a deep pit, and the devil would lend me his cloven foot, I would gladly lay hold of it to be drawn out." It should never be forgotten that the essence of Protestantism is infidelity, where its genuine principles are carried out into their logical consequences. Both these reasoners held revelation as not being obligatory upon the conscience; that civil laws are the only rules of good and evil; that antecedently to them every action is in its own nature indifferent. The separation of their systems merely began from certain tendencies in Hobbes towards an apparent admiration for absolutism as a form of social government; whereas, even at the commencement of his career, Shaftesbury might be termed a constitutionalist, like the Girondists in France, or their successors the late Doctrinaires. He had profited too well in his midnight lucubrations at Lincoln's Inn not to sympathise with the well-grounded popular grievances of the Star-Chamber and High Commission Courts, martial law instituted by royal proclamations, privy-council warrants, forced loans, purveyance, wardships, embargoes, prohibitions, arbitrary imprisonments, ship-money, and the dispensing powers of the crown. But at the same time, he recoiled from the canting patriotism of the conventicles, and their awful preachers, until selfishness had rendered him case-hardened to it. When Charles I. therefore hoisted his standard, young Cooper avowed his allegiance, and even joined the court at Oxford, where he projected a scheme not for subduing or conquering his country, but for reducing such as had either forsaken or mistaken their duty towards the executive. It may well be imagined how little all such wire-drawings would be relished amongst the needy, boisterous cavaliers, who clung to the pure divine right of kings, as an article of their creeds almost as dear to them as their hounds, their harlots, or their horses. Even decent hypocrites, like Hyde and Colepepper, not to mention the solemn honest Lord Falkland himself, displayed rather a cold shoulder towards the youthful wit, who knew far more than they or their master did of the real limits of prerogative, and where its cruel assumptions chafed the pride and privileges, or annihilated the loyalty of a justly irritated people. Wounded at once with the polished arrogance of such lofty courtiers, and probably foreseeing how certainly their folly would be followed by its own punishment, his mind fell back upon the parliament; and notwithstanding the receipt of a royal autograph from Charles to invite his further attendance at Oxford, he removed to the metropolis, where a cordial welcome awaited him. Clarendon tells us, that he now " gave himself up body and soul" to the popular party. Accepting a commission from that power, whose manners and pretensions he loathed and despised, we find him raising forces, and capturing Wareham by storm in the month of October 1644. Within a short interval he subdued all the adjacent parts of Dorsetshire, and was thenceforward considered an implacable antagonist towards the Stuarts and every one of their adherents.

The next year he became high sheriff for Wiltshire, amidst the most abundant professions of respect for the rights of man. But, as Lingard justly remarks, whether his services were engaged for the king or the roundheads, he remained still the same character, displaying in his conduct a singular fertility of invention, a reckless contempt for principle, and a readiness to sacrifice the welfare of others in the pursuit of his object, " whether it were the acquisition of power, or the gratification of revenge." In 1651 his name appears among the committee of twenty appointed to take into their consideration a reformation of the laws, and he was also a member of the convention that met after Cromwell had dissolved the Long Parliament. It is observable that he seemed one of the very few statesmen able to take the real intellectual measure of the great Protector. Overawed neither by military successes, nor the results of his profound dissimulation, Shaftesbury comprehended him from the first; for on being returned once more to Parliament in 1654, we find him in active opposition, foremost in the ranks of those who signed that famous proposition which charged the usurper with aiming at arbitrary power, and resolute on nearly all occasions in resisting to the uttermost his illegal measures. On the deposition of his successor Richard, when the Rump again rose on the crest of the revolutionary wave, its leaders nominated Sir Anthony Ashley, Cooper as one of their council of state, as well as a commissioner for managing the army, which latter department of his duties he performed to perfection. At that very period a secret correspondence between himself and the friends of Charles II. had commenced, and every nerve of his abilities throbbed and strained in the service of an expected restoration. Although trembling at the sword of Damocles hanging over his head,— for such traitors have rarely any real friends,—he trod with unshaken firmness that narrow bridge of peril on which, had his foot but slipt for a moment, it must have precipitated him into destruction. As it was, he obtained a seat in the healing Parliament for his native county in April 1660, and wormed his tortuous way with the subtlety of a serpent towards the altitudes of political eminence and power. With eleven other members of the House of Commons he embarked for Holland to invite the royal exile back again to the throne of his fathers. Upon the journey, a hired carriage, in which Sir Anthony happened to be seated, broke down; the horses ran away, after having overturned the vehicle; and when the parties thrown out came to be set on their legs again, it was discovered that the representative of Dorsetshire had received a dangerous wound between the ribs, which ulcerated many years after. But meanwhile the conferences at Breda issued in the Restoration, nor was it long before the injured envoy had his name on the list of his majesty's most honourable privy council.

Few among the renegades and traitors of the time more willingly unfurled their sails to the breezes of royal favour. His swallow was as large as his stomach seemed strong. Piles of patriotic plunder lay every where around; so that the vultures had little else to do than to gather and devour. Some persons imagined he would hesitate at being nominated for the trial of the regicides, many of them his former comrades and associates. But the moral digestion of that age surpassed the physical powers of the ostrich, and could dine very comfortably upon iron nails. Cooper therefore, without wincing, assisted at the condemnation of Harrison, Clements, Scroop, Colonel Hacker, Peters the preacher, and Sir Harry Vane, with several others; all and each of the victims devoutly believing that they were the witnesses foretold in the Apocalypse. Their judges, little less guilty than themselves, only appeared anxious to display both the extent of the sovereign's clemency and the sincerity of interested loyalism. By letters patent, dated the 20th April 1661, the member for Dorset was created Baron Ashley of Wimborne St. Giles; being soon also made chancellor and under-treasurer of the Exchequer, as well as finally named one of the lords-commissioners for executing the office and functions of the white staff, among the most lucrative appointments in the realm. Ten years followed of unlimited licentiousness and iniquity. He had married the niece of Lord Southampton, and gained the friendship of the Duke of Albemarle. Wealth poured into his coffers; no woman at court, or in the country, whom he adressed, could long withstand his wiles; in parliament his eloquence, talents, and matchless intrigues, drew around him numerous adherents: the king hated, feared, and laughed at him; patriots, or such as called themselves by that venerated title, fell headlong into the meshes of his cajolery; he foresaw with the eye of an eagle, and the prescience of a prophet, whatever would promote his private advancement; nor had he the shadow of compunction in grasping at power through the ruin of the public welfare. Clarendon, having disgusted his master, cheated the Presbyterians, and disappointed the nation, discovered in his banishment the true characteristics of the cockatrice he had left behind him. The monarch, surrounded by his mistresses, had been long listening to the artifices of Buckingham, supported and prompted by Ashley. As a courtier, the latter turned to good account the taste for buffoonery inherent in his ducal compeer. They both assured his majesty that Hyde was neither more nor less than his schoolmaster. They mimicked his absurd pomposity of manner, by marching up and down in the royal apartments, one carrying the bellows, just as the late chancellor used to bear his official purse, whilst Colonel Titus would shoulder the fire-shovel to represent the mace on state occasions; and thus all old associations of friendship and regard being smothered for the only adviser who preserved the smallest respect for decency, a road was at last opened for the impeachment of Clarendon and the disgraceful culmination of the Cabal.

This too celebrated title in the history of cabinets comprised the initials of five ministers, whose disastrous influence continued, more or less, from the year 1668 to 1674; and, in fact, at intervals, through some of its individual components, to a much later period. Clifford, Arlington, Buckingham, Ashley, and Lauderdale, constituted the atrocious conclave. The last but one, however, proved himself the genuine Asmodeus of the party. His ideas had soared far beyond the vulgar purposes of procuring for the king a new courtesan, or pecuniary supplies from France; although from such projects his name and sanction were never withheld, or veiled under any motives of delicacy or morality. His plans fundamentally involved an overthrow of Catholicity in the country, through working upon the national abhorrence of Popery, inflamed as he alone could inflame it; that soaring upon the wings of the tempest he might annihilate all opposition, and establish himself in irresistible political power for the term of his natural life. In addition to which, he fancied there might be enthroned, perhaps for ever, that system of Whiggery, as it came to be subsequently called,—beneath whose auspices priestcraft would wither and perish, and statecraft flourish in its stead. His measures therefore took their shape and course accordingly. For this purpose his mind reflected with brilliancy every kind of colour, monarchical, aristocratical, or republican, just as might suit the current tide of circumstances. He had got to know that about 1668-9 the Duke of York ceased to be a Protestant; that on his royal highness communicating his situation to the sovereign, the latter avowed his personal sympathy with his brother; and that most others in the higher circles, whenever they thought about the matter at all, had their religion still to choose. It is a well-ascertained fact, that a meeting occurred between Charles and James, in which the former, with tears in his eyes, lamented the hardship of being compelled to profess a faith contrary to the convictions of his understanding; and that he declared his determination to emancipate himself from such a restraint, requesting the opinions of those present as to the most eligible means of doing so with safety and success. They advised him, it is said, to communicate with Louis XIV. on the subject; from which moment there commenced a series of chicanery and false professions, sufficient to corrupt and degrade an entire national mind; but of which Ashley worked the secret springs, at once as active as he contrived to be for the time invisible. Charles might very possibly be, as historians affirm he was, the most accomplished dissembler in his dominions; but whilst he imagined himself to be overreaching both his brother and the Grand Monarque, there stood a Satan at his side more discerning and potent than himself, pushing forward a scheme with such ability, that it must have succeeded, were it not that truth is a talisman identical with the designs of Omnipotence.

The expiration of an act of parliament in 1670 against conventicles had raised the hopes of Dissenters that the prelates of the Establishment would at length remember them in mercy; but the most bitter disappointment awaited them, even from the very measures of Ashley and his adherents. A bill for the suppression of certain places of worship, in which Nonconformists celebrated their services, came up to the House of Lords from the Commons, and met with the strongest opposition from the Duke of York, supported by the Catholics and the Presbyterians. Ashley took care not to lay any overt claim to what was at least the fair progeny of his own principles, as well as the original suggestion of his own wily policy; but, at the same time, he drew pointed attention to the growth of Popery, thus manifested by the votes and speeches of the first prince of the blood, drawing after them, as they did, the influence of Hamilton and others into the same groove. Whilst whispering, wherever it seemed safe to do so, that Protestantism was in danger, he laughed in his sleeve when the act ultimately passed, and subjected many Puritans to a portion of those severities which had been so frequently inflicted on the Catholics. Spies and informers multiplied; sons of Boanerges, whose fanaticism shook the realm, found it convenient to abscond; houses were entered by force, and searched without ceremony, to look for Howes and Baxters and Flavels, as well as pious priests and Jesuits; their inmates were dragged to prison, and condemned to pay fines, or expire of jail-fevers, to the number of many thousands. Meanwhile Lord Ashley assured his gullible countrymen, that by no better means could the Establisment be preserved, which seemed a sort of breakwater, erected through the care of Providence to beat back from these happy shores the advancing billows of Rome. And when the public mind had become sufficiently heated, so as even to tolerate for a time the persecution of Nonconformity for this particular purpose, he threw the energies of his evil genius into another project baser than any that had yet been started.

When Charles II. resided at the Hague as an exile, "keeping the asses of his father," according to the witty epigram of Andrew Marvel, a handsome young Welshwoman, named Lucy Walters, or Barlow (for it is uncertain which was her proper cognomen) ensnared the royal wanderer, and presented him with a boy known at Paris for some years as James Crofts. Even this disgraceful parentage has been disputed, the genuine paternity of the lad being attributable, on strong grounds, to Algernon Sydney, or possibly his brother, Colonel Robert Sydney. The king, however, at all events fancied and adopted the youth, placed him for education at the Oratory, and evidently intended him to be brought up a Catholic. Through some caprice, his majesty afterwards ordered him to England, changed his religion, married him to a wealthy heiress, and created him Baron Tinedale, Earl of Doncaster, and Duke of Monmouth. It was now resolved by Ashley and Buckingham, the leaders of a grand Protestant conspiracy, to set up this pretender as a competitor for the crown against the claims of the Duke of York. The queen having no offspring, nor affording the probability of any, Lord Ashley intimated to Charles, in the presence of the Earl of Carlisle, that if he were willing to acknowledge a private contract of marriage with the mother of Monmouth, it would not be difficult to procure witnesses who would confirm it. The monarch replied that, "much as he loved the child of his former mistress, he would sooner see him hanged at Tyburn than own him for his legitimate son." Nevertheless, most unhappily for the minion himself, as well as for the nation, the royal fondness and folly increased every day. Titles, honours, and preferments were showered upon his empty head. The exterior graces of his person, if we may believe De Grammont, were such, that nature never seemed to have formed any one more accomplished. His countenance was manly and noble, yet made up of features each presenting its own peculiar beauty and delicacy. *Il fit les plus chères délices du roi*, says the enthusiastic memorialist; nor was Dryden supposed to have gone beyond the fair limits of adulation, when, in portraying the modern Absalom, he exclaimed,

> "In him alone 'twas natural to please,
> Whate'er he did was done with so much ease;
> His motions so accompanied with grace,
> That Paradise was open'd in his face."

He was only just of age when pounced upon by Ashley and his partisans to play an important part in their political drama. In smothering the favourite with flatteries, the affections of the doting father came only to be more effectually than ever deceived and secured. James became really alarmed at an attempt being made in 1671 to procure for his rival the lord-lieutenancy of Ireland. When the second Dutch war broke out, the same year in which Louis XIV. had purchased for large pecuniary considerations the alliance of Charles II., Monmouth marched to Charleroi at the head of 6000 British soldiers. In Flandres, at St. Germains, and at Calais, French courtiers paid him such startling tokens of respect, that his reputation expanded into almost imperial dimensions, supported, as it happened just at that period to be, by some military successes. His two children were ostentatiously baptised, as young princes, by the Archbishop of Canterbury, with royal gossips and all imaginable christening formalities. He was chosen Chancellor of the University of Cambridge, in which high office he curtailed the hair and periwigs of the clergy, and commanded them to deliver their sermons without books, either committing them to memory, or preaching them extemporaneously, after the fashion of the Puritans. Public opinion conferred upon him the sobriquet of "the Protestant duke," as an implied insult towards the real presumptive heir of the crown; who married in 1673 the youthful and saintly Maria d'Este of Modena. Charles now pretended to intimate that matters ran forward too fast, and that the Anglican Establishment must be at least treated as though it were in danger. He meanly refused the new Duchess of York a public chapel, although the use of one had been expressly stipulated for in the nuptial pre-arrangements. He forbade all Catholics, or even persons reputed to be such, ever entering his presence, or walking in the parks, or availing themselves of any indulgence from the rigour of the penal laws. With a sanctimoniousness that makes the heart sick to think of, he enjoined a general fast, on the application of parliament, that the entire nation might implore the protection of Almighty God for the preservation of the Church and State from the insidious approaches and practices of Popery. Our readers will be good enough to remember that this very sovereign had no great while before subscribed a solemn engagement with the Grand Monarque, setting forth the following verities: "*The King of Great Britain, being convinced of the truth of the Catholic religion, and resolved to make a declaration of the same, and to reconcile himself with the Roman Church*, so soon as the welfare of his kingdom will permit, has every reason to hope and promise himself the affection and fidelity of his subjects, that none of them, even of those upon whom God shall not have yet sufficiently shed his grace to dispose them by this august example to be converted, will ever fail in the inviolable obedience that all people owe to their sovereigns even of a contrary religion." Millions of livres were paid over by his ally to this royal deceiver, who, in his foul companionship with Mrs. Palmer, Elizabeth Killegrew, Catherine Peg, Nell Gwyn, Louisa de Queronaille, and Mary Davis, could dare to preach up a mockery of mortification to his people, persecute those loyalists to the true faith whom he was more especially bound to protect, and prefer the bastard of Lucy Walters to the conscientious son of his own father and mother. *O tempora, O mores!* and this too in moral England.

For it must never be forgotten that there were considerable intervals during which, from the influence which Lord Ashley and his creatures possessed over the royal mind, a positive alienation of interest and affection supervened between the two brothers. It required masterly astuteness and subtlety of observation and action to effect this on the part of the tempters; for there was a good-nature in the soul of Charles which every now and then returned on itself, and baffled all previous anticipations. In 1670, when he had abruptly refused to acknowledge the shadow of any marriage between himself and Lucy Walters, it was suggested that a divorce from the queen might be possible, so as to afford him an opportunity of taking a second consort. Should such a union prove fortunate, its issue would cut out the Duke of York altogether from the succession; to which idea the king for a time paid the most eager attention. He went so far as to consult both divines and lawyers. The covert criminality of Gilbert Burnet, that godly commentator, who "laid forty stripes upon the Anglican Articles save one," when applied to in this shameful business, is well known; for it cost him his favour at court even in the estimation of its licentious sovereign, and fixed the character of his ulterior politics as well as his polemics. The future Bishop of Salisbury had decided, in an elaborate judgment, that barrenness in a wife furnishes, in particular instances, a lawful cause for polygamy or divorce. As the precedent of Luther, Melancthon, and the Landgrave of Hesse, appeared out of the question, it was recollected that, in cases of separation, no legal marriage had ever been then heard of pending the lives of the parties. Buckingham, who had already proposed to convey Catherine away, if necessary, by a forcible abduction, now undertook to get over the technical difficulty by creating a sufficient precedent for the royal purpose. Lord Ashley assented to and promoted the scheme. Lady Roos had long lived in adultery, separated from her husband by an ecclesiastical sentence; and her children by the paramour had been declared illegitimate by act of parliament. A bill was therefore introduced into the Upper House to enable the Lord Roos to marry again, which passed, amidst immense clamour and the unusual attendance of the king in person, only by a majority of two. The effect of it was, that the permission to marry again has ever since been inserted in all bills of divorce; and had his majesty been disposed to put aside his faithful Catherine, on the ground of her infecundity, he might have availed himself, under the precedent, of a similar liberty. Yet, when it came to the point, his sense of justice assumed some temporary ascendency: the queen remained unmolested, and her profligate persecutors could merely brood over their intrigues whilst waiting for other opportunities of mischief. Monmouth added crime to crime throughout the very period in which the active elements of Protestantism were gathering beneath his banner. His outrage upon Sir John Coventry, and the murder of a beadle with his own hand, occasioned indeed some transitory murmurs; but a pardon from the Crown sheltered him from the dock and the gallows, and a certain military cock of the hat, in which his grace indulged, quite came into fashion as a sign of evangelical orthodoxy. The Cabal, at this crisis, culminated towards its highest infamy; its members extended their itching palms to France, or any one else who could bribe them with gold or power. The best commercial interests of England were under their guidance, just so many commodities for sale or barter: Charles, as well as themselves, had descended to be pensioners upon the bounty of Louis. When more money had to be raised, after the scandalous dissipation of the parliamentary subsidies, Ashley conceived and executed a plan for shutting up the Exchequer, which placed about 1,300,000*l*. at the mercy of ministers. A general shock was thus given to the credit of the whole country and metropolis. Many bankers failed in consequence. Numbers of annuitants, widows, and orphans were reduced to a state of the lowest distress. An attempt on the part of the cabinet to regain some of their popularity, about the commencement of the subsequent spring, by an almost piratical interception of the Dutch fleet before hostilities had been fairly declared, failed as it deserved. They then embarked in projects of indulgences to soothe and cajole the Dissenters; although Ashley took care that "this benefit of public worship according to the dictates of tender consciences" should not be extended to Catholics, " who, if they sought to avoid molestation, must confine their devotional assemblies to private houses." It must not be forgotten, that the entire affair was to emanate from the mere dispensing prerogative of the Crown, as the head of an Established Church,—an unconstitutional procedure from first to last, by none more hotly contested and impugned than by the Nonconformists themselves.

Its opponents, nevertheless, caught at the boon thus thrown to them, and then growled over it. They complained that indirectly it tolerated Popery, and consequently idolatry. The Anglicans also frowned at any freedom being afforded to schismatics, oblivious altogether of their own inherent sectarianism:

"Quis tulerit Gracchos de seditione querentes?
Clodius accusat mœchos, Catilina Cethegum."

Meanwhile the solitary gleam of victory illuminating the iniquities and disasters of the second Dutch war altogether arose from the gallantry of the Catholic heir to the throne. The Duke of York gained his sanguinary triumph over De Ruyter in Southwold Bay, on the 28th of May 1672. Ashley ruled over the cabinet, and seemed to monopolise the royal favour; so delighted was the monarch with the fertility of his invention and the fearlessness of his courage. He created him Baron Cooper of Pawlet in the county of Somerset, Earl of Shaftesbury, and Lord-Lieutenant of Dorsetshire. Charles deemed himself bound in honour to shelter some of the bankers, whose fortunes he had locked up in the Exchequer, from the pursuit of their creditors. They applied for protection to the Court of Chancery, then presided over by Sir Orlando Bridgeman, ancestor to the present Earl of Bradford. The lord-keeper hesitated as to whether it was a case in which he could conscientiously interfere; upon which Shaftesbury, who had no conscience at all, seized upon the occasion to represent him to the king as an old dotard, unequal to his situation. The hint was taken; the Great Seal was transferred from Bridgeman to Shaftesbury; and in November the latter found himself no less a personage than Lord High Chancellor of England. Once seated in the marble chair, his natural vanity and self-sufficiency broke out beyond all tolerable bounds. His abilities were undoubtedly immense, but they failed to preserve him from the effects of intellectual intoxication. Instead of the sober and decent robes worn by his predecessors in office, "he appeared on the bench in an ash-coloured gown silver-laced, and with full-ribboned pantaloons," setting the whole gravity of the bar at defiance. Westminster Hall laughed outright—although, perhaps, with some sediment of malice; for, in coming down to open the term, he had chosen to ride on horseback instead of being drawn in a carriage, one result of which was, that the prothonotaries, counsel, and judges had to accompany him, according to etiquette, in a similar manner. Few of those venerable sages were accustomed to equestrian exercise; and some of them lost their equilibrium amidst the gibes of an unwashed multitude, far too happy to see the ermine and powdered curls of Justice Twisden laid prostrate in the mire. Two very different accounts are given of his administration in equity. Certain barristers, with lungs of leather and brows of brass, occasionally worried him to death; and that he proved a supple instrument for political purposes can scarcely be denied. The wishes of his sovereign as to the recent financial measures were cautiously yet effectually realised. Proceedings against the bankers were stayed in the inferior courts; and the suspension of payment to the public creditors was continued by proclamation for another six months. His official speeches in Parliament appear to have been not less eloquent than successful. During the prorogation from October to February 1672-3, in order to strengthen his interest in the Lower House, he issued writs for new elections out of his own Chancery, instead of waiting until the meeting after the recess, when in regular order they would have been directed from the Hanaper Office of the Commons. A batch of his devoted adherents thus got returned, in addition to those already in the legislature; which so annoyed the cavaliers and churchmen, that they resolved to dispute the seats of the new members. Shaftesbury, moreover, had an attack of illness, through his accident twelve or thirteen years before in Holland: an ulcer formed under the ribs which had then been broken. The operation of tapping having become necessary, and his overweening vanity having given some currency to the notion that he expected to be chosen King of Poland, innumerable squibs circulated throughout town, styling him Count Tapsky, and the Earl of Shiftsbury instead of Shaftesbury; so that he felt his popularity to be somewhat on the wane. His fearful licentiousness also augmented the number of his personal enemies among the aristocratic classes. When the Houses at length met, the opposition carried their point in the Commons, that new writs could only be issued in virtue of a warrant from the Speaker. Charles himself began to suspect that he might have to cast his Chancellor overboard, as a tub to amuse the popular whale; nor was that virtuous minister unaware that no trust was to be placed in princes. It seems to have been the solitary text of Scripture in which he ever believed—if, indeed, he believed any thing; besides which, his ulterior designs were advancing to their maturity.

The country party, as they called themselves, now directed their efforts to procure the revocation of the indulgence for Dissenters, on the ground that it was altogether contrary to the constitution. An address to that effect secured a large majority; but Charles declared that he would dissolve rather than give way. Shaftesbury applauded his spirit with many courtly expressions; yet in reality he was preparing a path for his own open secession to the popular side. The House of Lords roused itself to battle for the prerogative; but the wily Chancellor would not venture to place it, as he said, in the balance against so august a body as the House of Commons. The king finally yielded, as the keeper of his conscience had foreseen he would. Nonconformity, amidst all its harassment from Anglican opponents, became at length bitten to the fullest extent with the mania of anti-Catholic antipathies. Its rivalry towards episcopacy was surrendered with no more resistance than the exhibition of sundry grimaces not particularly agreeable to those making them, and doubtless most hideous to the beholders. Rumours of every description spread like wildfire. It was observed that several officers commanding the small British force engaged in continental service were Catholics; and that Lord Clifford, with some others, had embraced the same faith. Were governmental influences at home, and a standing army from abroad, at the conclusion of the war, it was asked, to be employed for the establishment of Popery and arbitrary power? Then appeared the Test Act, which excluded from the public service every individual who should decline the oaths of allegiance and supremacy, or refuse to receive the sacrament after the rite of the Church of England, besides subscribing an impious protest against the doctrine of transubstantiation. Charles was brought to give his assent by that logic which, being built upon money, had more charms for him than any other sort of reasoning. Large subsidies dangled before his eyes, to be voted by his obsequious Commons so soon as his majesty would promise compliance with their wishes. Here again the

Dissenters were deluded by their new allies through the mirage of an accompanying measure, which professed to draw a distinction between articles of doctrine and those of mere discipline, so that Nonconformists objecting to the later alone might be relieved, to a certain extent, from the Act of Uniformity; but the measure never passed. The Duke of York and Lord Clifford resigned their offices; the former soon afterwards effecting his second marriage, already alluded to. Shaftesbury, no longer caring for royal menaces, pursued his contemplated course, avowing himself an adversary of the court, and the champion of a Protestant people. Charles, having granted him a full pardon for all offences against the crown, gave the Great Seal to Sir Heneage Finch; yet with some ludicrous circumstances, illustrating that intellectual sorcery which the late keeper must have exercised over the mind of the king.

The noble patriot now walked daily on the Exchange, with his hat in his hand, for every discontented partisan or factious fanatic who might think proper to address him. In the estimation of his new associates the acquisition of such a prize atoned for every past transgression; while he feelingly deplored with them the miseries of the nation, the depression of trade, the necessity for peace with Holland, and the dangers threatening religion through the prevalence of Popery. "Doubtful as it was whether he believed or not in revelation," observes an able writer, "Protestant theologians were found to describe him from the pulpit as a martyr to liberty of conscience, and the modern saviour of Christianity: foretelling that his fame, like that of the woman mentioned in the Gospel, would live throughout future generations." How far his genuine mortifications might go, may be more easily guessed than ascertained; yet, most true it is, that his present representative could not have supplicated for a day of penitential abstinence in reference to the Maynooth question, or the Russian war, with greater visible unction than was exhibited by the first Earl of Shaftesbury, in 1674, about analogous subjects. He supported a motion made in the House of Lords, that any prince of the blood should forfeit his right to the succession if he married a Catholic; and although it was not then carried, the exclusion of James from the throne, by fair means or foul, became the prevalent topic of the times. Monmouth rose in favour with all parties. He suffered his flatterers to toast him at their banquets as Prince of Wales. He begged from his reputed father the appointment of commander-in-chief, which was granted by patent; in which document, moreover, attempts were offered for omitting allusions to his illegitimacy when described as a son of his majesty. Charles for once remained firm on the right side; though such seemed his doting fondness for the handsome profligate, that, generally speaking, he would refuse him nothing. Shaftesbury, however, beginning to doubt, from his knowledge of the English nation, whether so base an instrument could be brought permanently to answer the purposes of Protestantism, had already secured another string to his bow in the person of William, the Dutch Stadtholder. Charles becoming partially cognisant of this fresh intrigue, kept his eye more carefully than ever upon the late chancellor; who frequently represented his life to be in danger through his zeal in resolving to rescue his country from the Catholics. To defeat, as he gave out, their indefatigable malice, he procured lodgings in the house of an Anabaptist preacher; announcing to the citizens of London that he confided his safety to their vigilance and fidelity. In consolidating the plans of opposition, there was not a single leader prepared as he was to go all lengths, and incur all hazards. Danby, considered at that time prime minister, had no possible chance of maintaining himself at the helm, except by at least bidding up to the patriots in parliament, or even doing more if necessary. He therefore brought forward another Test Act, more outrageous than its predecessors, involving the important point of non-resistance to the regal authority under any conceivable circumstances whatsoever; upon the plea that only some such abjuration could save the crown from its double range of antagonists,—the Dissenters on one hand, and the adherents to the Church of Rome on the other. Shaftesbury, according to the exigencies of the moment, then just changed his tactics, and gathered fresh laurels of popularity by accusing the premier of aiming at absolutism upon the ruins of private judgment. With the most withering sarcasm he demolished orator after orator. The two houses soon got entangled, through his artifices, in a technical dispute about appeals on writs of error; and his "Letter from a Person of Quality to a Friend in the Country," was voted to be a "lying, scandalous, and seditious libel." After being burnt by the common hangman, there seemed yet one course open to the ministry, which was a prorogation of Parliament. This continued for the unprecedented term of fifteen months; during which the real anti-Catholic agitators were busy in rearranging their combinations.

During the session an adventurer came upon the stage of public affairs, who proved himself the worthy precursor of those who, three years later, figured in the Popish Plot. The child of an actress at Paris, called by his mother, or from his own presumption, Hyppolite du Chastelet de Luzancy, after being usher in a school, servant to a bishop, inmate in a monastery, and companion to an itinerant missionary, professed himself in London, under various feigned names, as a convert from Popery to the Church of England. The crime of forgery, perpetrated in Picardy at Mondidier, had compelled him to fly from justice; but his apostasy to Protestantism made amends, it would seem, for any mere breach of morals. He became what Achilli and Gavazzi have been in our own days,—the petted monster of myriads of pious Evangelicals. A tissue of marvellous lies brought him in triumph before the Privy-Council and a committee of the Commons; where, although an investigation unveiled his real character and history, followed up as it was by a swindling transaction in which he got involved at Oxford, yet such an agitation in consequence shook the composure of the upper and middle classes, that Shaftesbury conjectured how much might be done, were cleverer agents employed upon a better constructed plan. The miscreant received Protestant orders from Dr. Compton, the grand episcopal patron, as Burnet styles him, " of all converts from Catholicism;" and obtained, after an interval, the fair vicarage of Dover Court, in Essex. When the parliament again assembled, in February 1677, Buckingham, under the guidance of Shaftesbury, argued that, from the recess having lasted more than a year, it amounted in law to a dissolution; which proposition the earl so ably supported, that it led to his arbitrary committal, together with the duke who had moved the question, and Lords Salisbury and Wharton, who spoke for it. The four peers, being ordered to beg pardon, declined, and were sent to the Tower. Buckingham, Salisbury, and Wharton subsequently made their submission, and were discharged; but Shaftesbury remained a prisoner for thirteen months, concocting that wonderful conspiracy which has clothed him with so unenviable an infamy in history. Danby, meanwhile, played the game of his incarcerated opponent, by heightening the general terror with a series of anti-Popish bills for limiting the prerogative of James, should he ever inherit the crown; for plundering Catholics of their fortunes and freedom; depriving them of their children when old enough to be educated; still subjecting priests to the penalty of death, and laymen to the forfeiture of two-thirds of their property; and identifying recusancy with treason, according to the wisdom of those Protestant and sagacious legislators, never weary "of raising barriers against the toleration of a false and idolatrous worship." Shaftesbury had also appealed in vain to the King's Bench for enlargement by the writ of *habeas corpus*. It at least kept him before the gaze of the world, dissatisfied as every body felt at the general mismanagement of affairs, the culmination of France, the known corruption of senators, the disjointed state of society, and the indefinable fears of all ranks and classes.

The Earl of Shaftesbury, moreover, had at last discovered an agent perfectly to his mind,—Titus Oates, the unscrupulous son of a ribbon-weaver, as full of the letter of Scripture as any of our vagrant Bible-readers, formerly an Anabaptist preacher, and lately an orthodox, yet rather loose, clergyman of the Establishment. When chaplain on board a man-of-war, his delinquencies seem to have assumed a coarser

and darker character. The result was, that sinking deeper in
the social scale, he felt himself ready for the first employment
that might offer, when Dr. Tonge, rector of St. Michael's in
Wood Street, London, befriended him as an instrument for
obtaining information relative to the imagined designs of
Jesuits and other Papists. This fanatical divine published
quarterly a sort of Record, filled with details of plots and conspiracies carried on, as he believed, by the Roman Church for
the extinction of all faithful followers of the Reformation.
Had he lived now, he would merely have been the bosom-
friend of Dr. Cumming; but existing a century and three-
quarters ago, he became the dupe of Titus Oates and Lord
Shaftesbury. It was arranged that the indigent parson, directed by the more respectable incumbent, should feign himself a convert to Catholicism, and under that cover obtain
access to the most secret councils of his instructors. This
was done, and the artful spy found a temporary home among
the English Jesuits at Valladolid and St. Omer's. So disgraceful was his conduct, that he had to be expelled from both
places; yet, on repairing to his patrons, the solitary fact of
any apparent importance which he could tell was that several
Jesuits had, in the month of April last, held a private meeting
in the British metropolis. Even the locality was not accu-
rately described; but the bold informer declared that it was
neither more nor less than a secret conclave for devising the
king's assassination, and the subversion by force of Protestantism. The fable was further based upon an enormous mass
of pretended confirmatory evidence, detailing the conveyance
of treasonable letters, subscriptions of monies, distributions of
military means, and other attractive falsehoods, written in
Greek characters by Oates, copied into English ones by Tonge,
and, finally, communicated with much mystery to an individual employed in the royal laboratory, named Kirkby.
Such was the diabolical machinery which presently plunged
these realms in guilt, bloodshed, perjury, confusion, and
misery. His majesty received the earliest intimation when
walking in the Park, on the 13th of August 1678. A full
development of the imposture would occupy more volumes

than we have devoted pages to this article; but the simple fact was, that the popular mind was just then like a coal-mine charged with fire-blast, into which, when the conspirators introduced their first candle, the whole atmosphere exploded into the most terrible and fatal conflagration.

The depositions of Titus Oates were made before Sir Edmundbury Godfrey. His subsequent suicide harrowed up the public mind, already more than sufficiently agitated; and was attributed to the Papist, as the first-fruits of their projected assassinations, to get inconvenient testimony out of their way. His funeral attracted thousands upon thousands, anxious as they professed themselves to do honour to the Protestant proto-martyr; whose mangled remains, thus exposed to general view, with a short sword sticking through his heart, stirred up for two whole days the worst passions of an inflamed populace. Councils assembled; sermons were preached; royal personages believed all manner of lies, and were adored; or they hesitated over such gross delusions, and were execrated. Houses were fortified, streets barricaded; magistrates surrounded themselves with guards and weapons; a general massacre was expected, besides the blowing up of Whitehall, and the burning of the City. Parliament, when it met, added thunder and lightning to the political hurricane. Senators conjured their sovereign to be careful of his meals, and to see that they were furnished, or at least prepared, by orthodox cooks abjuring transubstantiation. Committees of inquiry were appointed by both houses; in which Shaftesbury and his creatures contrived to gain so entirely the ascendency, that the earl might be said to have usurped the government. He was always at his post, self-possessed in the consciousness of his power, receiving information, granting warrants for searches and arrests, examining and committing his victims, instructing officers, informers, and jailors; and, in one word, compounding all the ingredients of perjury, persecution, and falsehood into the poison of his magic caldron. Men, otherwise sober, went mad for months together on this particular subject. The seizure of Coleman's papers threw oil of vitriol upon the flames. Not that there was any thing really palpa-

ble or substantial in them; but he had been expensive and
unguarded in his habits, was fond of diffusive correspondence,
had been an Anglican, and had become a not very edifying
Catholic, was secretary to the Duchess of York, had offered
his obtrusive services on behalf of the faith to Father La
Chaise, had tampered with three French ambassadors and got
money from them, and had proposed that Louis XIV. should
provide him with 20,000*l.* to effect important purposes.
"There lay a mighty work," he wrote, "upon the hands of
the children of the Church, no less than the conversion of
three kingdoms; and by that, perhaps, the subduing of a
pestilent heresy, which had so long domineered over a great
part of the northern world." Luzancy had formerly accused
him before the Privy-Council, but he then faced and silenced
the informer. His attempt to do the same by Titus Oates
brought him to the scaffold, with an army of far nobler martyrs.
Meanwhile, document after document, and assertion after
assertion, brought forward by the agents of Shaftesbury, were
proved to be forgeries and fabrications. It mattered little.
Both Houses of Parliament passed a resolution that "there
had been, and still was, a damnable and hellish plot, contrived
and carried on by the Popish recusants, for sacrificing the
king, subverting the government, and rooting out Protestantism."

Amidst the universal frenzy, every vestige of reason, justice,
and equity vanished from the land. Five Catholic peers, Powis,
Stafford, Petre, Arundell, and Balasyse, were committed to
the Tower. For the security of the capital, batteries of field-
pieces, ready loaded, were planted in the principal squares.
The metropolitan prisons alone contained two thousand suspected Papists; nearly thirty thousand more found themselves
compelled to withdraw at least ten miles from Whitehall.
Every Catholic residence was searched for arms; whilst from
London the alarm and confusion extended gradually throughout the entire country. The Test Bill of Lord Danby was
now carried; but his hold on the helm had long passed away,
since another statesman, more wicked than himself, had out-
bid him in perjured zeal and fury against the Church of God.

Titus Oates, blasphemously flattered, together with his patron, as having redeemed these realms from idolatry and destruction, now received further support from the absurd depositions of William Bedloe, a flagitious villain, recently discharged out of Newgate, who had once been employed in the stables and household of Lord Belasyse. Both the vile informers attempted to implicate the queen, yet in vain; for, singular to relate, the only individual of mark whose calmness remained unperturbed was her royal consort and sovereign. Staley, Ireland, Grove, Pickering, Prance, Hill, Green, Berry, with far too many more to enumerate, on the most mendacious evidence, suffered at Tyburn. Their pretended trials constituted so many mockeries of justice. No jury dared to acquit, no judge doubted for a moment to condemn. Even the episcopal clergy hounded on the executioners to their horrible work from Sunday to Sunday. Sancroft, Barlow, Sharp, Burnet, Tillotson, and Stillingfleet, roared as loudly in their churches as the most vulgar Anabaptist or Independent in his conventicle. Nor in the higher ranks of laymen was there any legislator more bitter than the belauded William Lord Russell, even down to the death of the saintly Stafford. The members of the Society of Jesus, Whitbread and Fenwick, together with Harcourt, Gavan, Turner, and Langhorne, an eminent Catholic lawyer, as also three Benedictine monks, Corker, Marshall, and Rumby, went to their bloody martyrdom in 1679; besides Pleasington, who was executed at Chester; Evans and Lloyd at Cardiff; Lewis at Uske; Postgate at York; Mahoney at Ruthin; Johnson at Worcester; and Kemble at Hereford. These latter were several of them priests, of whom two had passed their eightieth year! In Ireland, the persecution raged with almost equal violence, terminating with the tragedies of Archbishops Talbot and Plunkett; the one worn down to a painful death in his dungeon, the other judicially murdered in open daylight.

Danby, about 1678-79, had witnessed the end of his administration; an annihilated politician, in every sense of the word, betrayed by his subordinates, deserted by his master, shipwrecked by circumstances, and irrevocably superseded by

Shaftesbury. That wonderful impostor now appeared at the summit of his ambition. All the Privy-Council were dismissed at once, and an entirely new cabinet formed, with the noble author of the Popish Plot at its head as lord president. This was on the 21st April 1679. Finding the Prince of Orange less manageable than he had expected, the great agitator had concluded a close compact with Monmouth, whose conduct and prospects he had lately considered rather perilous speculations. It was given out upon solemn evidence that the Catholics had endeavoured to set fire to London; that French troops were marching to the coast for making a descent upon England, that James might be substituted for Charles, and Catholicity for Protestantism; so now the single hope for national and religious safety lay in a Bill of Exclusion, which should finally set aside the Duke of York from the succession. Thus began an energetic contest, terminating ten years after in the Revolution of William and Mary; yet at its commencement, their ignoble rival might have been thought by some persons almost nearer to the coveted prize than themselves. Shaftesbury sent him northward in the summer to subdue the Scotch Covenanters; and is supposed to have suggested all his subsequent efforts towards accumulating political capital out of rural progresses, gunpowder-processions, formation of clubs, inflammatory publications, and anticipated suppressions of Bibles in the vulgar tongue. Through an apprehension of this last calamity, the author of *Robinson Crusoe*, with many others, set themselves to copying the Old and New Testament into short-hand, that they might not be destitute of their favourite consolations in the hour of distress. De Foe, then a very young man, declares that he worked at the supererogatory labour like a horse, until he had transcribed the Pentateuch; at which point, however, his fingers grew so tired, that he was willing to risk the remainder, and trust a good Providence even under a Romish monarch. Macaulay justly declares, that if there was a point about which Charles II. really entertained a scruple of conscience or of honour, that point was the descent of the crown. He was willing, nevertheless, to consent to the Exclusion Bill for 600,000$l.$; and the negotiation came to be broken off only because he insisted upon being paid beforehand. Monmouth, after his victory at Bothwell Bridge, returned in triumph to London, to be addressed publicly as his Highness by those who were short-witted or short-sighted. In August, just as his popularity seemed at its zenith, since the Duke of York had been banished to Brussels, the king suddenly fell ill with a fever at Windsor; which awakened some remorseful affection towards his absent brother, not a little augmented by the outrageous presumption of the royal minion, in demanding from his father that James should be ordered not to leave the capital of Flanders. Charles, therefore, secretly sent for his brother, and welcomed him with open arms. When the uncle and nephew thus encountered each other, the former, greatly to his honour, tendered an offer of reconciliation, which Shaftesbury, as an evil genius, persuaded the latter to decline. Gleams of common sense from that instant began to pierce through the selfishness of the royal mind. Monmouth was deplumed of his overgrown preferments, and sent to Holland. James went back to Brussels, but ultimately took up his residence in Scotland. Intrigues multiplied on all sides, amidst which the lord president was dismissed in October 1679. When Parliament was prorogued to the same month of the following year, affairs were only falling into fresh confusions.

Shaftesbury and his associates resolved to keep alive the fears of both the sovereign and his subjects. The first had persuaded Monmouth to withdraw from the kingdom, in obedience to his father; but he now recalled him, and played him off as the grand hope of the nation. He also organised a system of petitions precisely analogous to those of the present Anti-Maynooth Association. Yet, strange to say, instead of achieving his purpose, it merely produced an imitation of his plan on the part of the old cavaliers, by way of reaction. James returned to London. His opponents, maddened by his reception, revived the story of Monmouth's legitimacy. But the conspiracy of the Black Box, as it was termed, proved too gross; while the populace, fickle as it always is, began to tire even of Titus Oates, the Popish Plot itself, and all its concomitants. Every lie carries the worm of its own destruction at the core. Still, however, struggling for his supremacy, Shaftesbury dared to present the Duke of York as a Popish recusant; an impudent scheme twice attempted, and as often defeated. Then followed the Meal-Tub Plot, the affair of Dangerfield involving fresh executions, the negotiations of the patriots with France and the Hague, the factions of Whig and Tory, and a final effort to pass the Exclusion Bill. Had it succeeded, Shaftesbury would have wreaked his vengeance upon the Catholics, and have possibly extirpated their holy religion from these realms as effectually as it has been done from the Scandinavian kingdoms. But Charles obtained his ultimate advantage through getting rid of the Parliament altogether. It was dissolved at Oxford on the 27th of March 1681. Halifax and his companions having now the seals of office swept the cabinet clear from all its recent occupants; and determined to prosecute the late lord president, upon charges of high treason, for having meditated a change of government, as well as of dynasty, to be effected by violence, if other means failed. It was curious to see the tables turned upon the mighty agitator; who was committed to the Tower on the 2d July 1681, and after four months was tried, acquitted, and dismissed. The mob had hooted him as he went into custody; bell-ringings and bonfires attended his return, with shouts for "Monmouth and Shaftesbury." Some of his papers, however, still implicated him; nor could be forbear mixing himself up with men of the most desperate fortunes and character. Meanwhile James had been well received in the metropolis; and even his old enemy once thought of seeking a reconciliation with him. An overture of the sort being but coldly received, the fallen earl, having urged his friends to rise in open insurrection, betook himself in the disguise of a Presbyterian parson to Harwich, and from thence to Holland; where anxiety and vexation undermined his health, until, gout attacking his stomach, he expired shortly after his departure from England, in the fourth week of January 1683. His remains are interred at Wimborne.

Thus perished from the earth a statesman who, had he

lived in the earlier ages of Christianity, would have infallibly found a place in the treatise *De Mortibus Persecutorum*. He had written a history of his own times, and confided it to the care of John Locke the philosopher; but that author, although an immense admirer of the earl, alarmed at the prosecution of Algernon Sydney, and fancying that this Ms. also might exhale an odour of treason, cast it into the flames for the sake of his own safety. Fragments of it are still extant; and its rather pusillanimous destroyer, feeling that a debt remained due to the memory of his noble friend, coalesced with Thomas Stringer, who had been clerk of the presentations to Lord Shaftesbury, in some endeavours towards drawing up a suitable biography of their patron. Their papers not having been printed during their lives, were afterwards used by a poet named Benjamin Martyn, in 1732, as the groundwork of a memoir; but this also never emerged from the press. It was put into the hands of Gregory Sharpe, master of the Temple, who passed it on to Doctor Kippis and the *Biographia Britannica*. The fact was, that, however mortifying it might be to his family, if the truth were to be told at all, the founder of this celebrated earldom could be portrayed as no other than one of the moral monsters of history; a single solitary sunbeam alone falling upon the picture, namely, our being indebted to Shaftesbury for the perfect form in which England now possesses the Habeas Corpus act. He had suffered so much himself in attempting to get out of the Tower in 1677, that he knew from sad experience where the shoe pinched, and therefore took pains against a repetition of the torture. It is sufficiently remarkable, nevertheless, that in thus really conferring a benefit upon future generations, he cautiously excluded from the advantages of this act *all persons imprisoned in consequence of the Popish Plot*. His agent, Titus Oates, had received 1200*l*. per annum for his perjury; yet such were his crimes, that the law at length caught him, in May 1685; when he was fined two thousand marks, degraded from his orders, twice publicly whipped, and sentenced to stand every year of his life five times in the pillory. After the Revolution, William III. granted him a full pardon, settled on him a pension of 400*l.* a year, and always considered him, perhaps with some irony, among the suffering personifications of Whiggery and Protestantism. Towards the close of the century, he was received once more as a repentant sinner by his former friends the Baptists; but they also expelled him within twelve months, " as a disorderly person and a hypocrite; a man of cunning, mere effrontery, and consummate falsehood." He died in **1705,** full of days and iniquities. Verily might it be **said** of him, that *prævaricatus* **est,** '*ut abiret in* **locum** *suum.*

INDEX.

	PAGES.
The Church and the People	1
Schools of the Benedictines	17
St. Ursula and the eleven **thousand Virgins** . . .	30
Hofer and the Tyrolese War of Independence . . .	37
Maitland on the Reformation	68
Ancient Irish Dominican Schools	96
Oliver Cromwell	126
Masters and Workmen in the middle ages . . .	158
King William III	181
A Chapter in **the History** of the Reformation in Ireland .	205
The Chancellors in England	220
The Maronites and Druses	244
The Russian and Anglican Hierarchies	275
The Anglican Priesthood	300
Anthony, Earl of Shaftesbury	319

CARONDELET, DE LA SALLE INSTITUTE PRINT. OFFICE.